A History of Civil Law in Early China

Legal History Library

VOLUME 60

The titles published in this series are listed at *brill.com/lhl*

A History of Civil Law in Early China

Cases, Statutes, Concepts and Beyond

By

Zhaoyang Zhang

BRILL
NIJHOFF

LEIDEN | BOSTON

Cover illustration: The AD 28 Legal Case Excavated from the Juyan site. Photo by Junmin Zhang

The Library of Congress Cataloging-in-Publication Data is available online at https://catalog.loc.gov
LC record available at https://lccn.loc.gov/2022018235

Typeface for the Latin, Greek, and Cyrillic scripts: "Brill". See and download: brill.com/brill-typeface.

ISSN 1874-1793
ISBN 978-90-04-39373-8 (hardback)
ISBN 978-90-04-51390-7 (e-book)

This book is printed on acid-free paper and produced in a sustainable manner.

Contents

Acknowledgments

This work is based on my book in Chinese published eight years ago, *Zhongguo zaoqi minfa de jiangou*, with very important and substantial revisions. I would like to take this opportunity to thank all those people and institutes for their invaluable assistance during this four-year-long process of translation and revision.

I thank my wife Gao Yi and my daughter Elaine for their company during the whole process. I thank my parents for their encouragement. I thank all my former advisers and teachers, both in China and the U.S., for the training I have received. I thank the Shanghai Jiaotong University's School of Humanities for its support. I thank Jiandong Chen and Tony Edwards from Sydney and my student Jenny Chen for their assistance. I would also like to thank the following friends and colleagues: Xing Hang at Brandies University, Ji Li at the University of Hong Kong, Liang Cai at the University of Notre Dame and Junmin Zhang at Gansu Provincial Institute of Artifacts and Archaeology. I thank Professor Tongdong Bai at Fudan University and Professor Zhiping Liang at China Art Research Institute for their inspiring scholarly exchanges with me. In addition, my appreciation goes out to the editorial team of Brill and the anonymous reviewers for taking the time to look over the manuscript and their insightful suggestions.

Zhaoyang Zhang
Shanghai Jiao Tong University

Figures and Tables

Figures

Tables

Introduction

1 Background

China had a very long legal history in her pre-modern times. From the ancient Lüxing 呂刑 (Marquis Lü on Penal Laws) of the Western Zhou period preserved in the *Book of Documents* to the Great Qing Code, Chinese legal tradition had yielded plenty of legal materials, which include statutes, ordinances, case-books, treatises, and so on.[1] Scholars have often characterized traditional Chinese law as penal law, because the law codes of the various dynasties seemed to be dominated with the desire to implement penalties to maintain public order or to secure the functioning of the administrative organs. However, there is an intriguing question exists that we need to explore: how were matters not concerned with public orders handled? Were there civil laws as well?

"Civil law" is a concept that contrasts with criminal law; criminal law is concerned with the maintenance of public order and aims to punish criminal deeds that endanger society, whereas civil law is used to adjust the economic or personal relationships among individuals. The term "civil law" was derived from *juries civilie* in Roman law and was nonexistent in classical Chinese literature. However, during the late Qing and the Republican era, when China imitated the Western legal systems to reform the Chinese law code and legal institutions, the terms such as "civil statute" (*minlu* 民律) and "civil law" (*minfa* 民法) started to emerge and gain currency in China. Even though "civil law" is undoubtedly a borrowed term in Chinese, did pre-modern China have de facto civil law, that is to say, a civil law without being called Civil Law? This is an important question that scholars have argued about for more than a century, given the complexity of traditional Chinese law and the implication of the issue, that is, our fundamental understanding of the function and nature of traditional Chinese law. Due to the limitations of extant sources and academic perspectives and different understandings of the term, there have been huge controversies among scholars, which could be roughly divided into three major camps:

Camp 1: No civil laws existed in pre-modern China (No-Civil-Law). This group of scholars utterly deny the existence of civil laws in pre-modern China. They

1 For the details of these extremely rich materials, see the very extensive annotated bibliography of Chinese legal history complied by Chang Wei-Ren 張偉仁, *Zhongguo fazhi shi shumu* 中國法制史書目 (Taipei: Academia Sinica Press, 1975).

 | DOI:10.1163/9789004513907_002

believe that traditional Chinese laws were only concerned with crimes and social order, having no concerns over civil disputes and the protection of individual interests. The preeminent scholar Liang Qichao 梁啟超 (1873–1929) in the late Qing period was perhaps the initiator. He stated the following:

> The most deplorable fact in our legal system is the total absence of private law.[2]
>
> 我國法律界最不幸者，私法部分全付闕如之一事.

This opinion and its variations are spread internationally and are also echoed by Chinese scholars. For instance, A.F.P. Hulsewé stated the following in 1986:

> It is characteristic for the whole of traditional Chinese law as embodied in the codes that it is solely concerned with public matters, being administrative and penal. Private law, pertaining to the family and to trade and commerce other than the state monopolies, remained outside the field of regimentation by public authorities and continued to be ruled by custom and usage.[3]

In 1988, Shiga Shuzo 滋賀秀三 stated that although China had a long history of developed civilization, it never formed a private law system from its own tradition. Law in [pre-modern] China was penal law on the one hand, and administrative law to organize the bureaucracy on the other.[4]

Similarly, as recently as 2006, Michael Loewe wrote:

> The statutes and ordinances of Qin and Han did not set out to protect men and women from the oppression of officials, though such intentions are sometimes visible in their provisions. Their purpose was to maintain law and order and to control the people and their work on the land.

---

2 Liang Qichao 梁啟超, "Lun Zhongguo chengwen fa bianzhi zhi yange deshi" 論中國成文法編制之沿革得失, in *Yinbingshi heji* 飲冰室合集 (Beijing: Zhonghua shuju, 1989), vol. 16, 52. This point is first raised by Yu Jiang 俞江, "Guanyu gudai Zhongguo you wu minfa wenti de zai sikao" 關於古代中國有無民法問題的再思考, *Xiandai faxue* 現代法學 no. 1 (2001): 35–45.

3 *The Cambridge History of China, Vol. 1: The Ch'in and Han Empires, 221 BC–AD 220*, eds., Michael Loewe and Denis Twitchett (Cambridge: Cambridge University Press, 1986) [hereafter, *CHC*], 525.

4 Shiga Shuzo 滋賀秀三, "Zhongguo fa wenhua de kaocha: yi susong de xingtai wei sucai" 中國法文化的考察: 以诉讼的形态为素材, *Bijiaofa yanjiu* 比較法研究 3 (1988): 18–26.

> Carefully regulated sanctions and punishments instructed officials how to eliminate crime.[5]

These examples are only the tip of the iceberg, but are strong enough to demonstrate how deeply rooted this view of No-Civil-Law is in the field.

Camp 2: China had civil laws since ancient times (Having-Civil-Law). This view also emerged very early. Japanese scholar Torao Asai 淺虎武夫 (1877–1928) in his book *Shina hoseshi* 支那法制史 (History of Chinese Law, 1904) claimed that pre-modern Chinese law was the hybrid of civil law and criminal law.[6] His claim indicated the existence of civil law in pre-modern China, even though this civil law was mixed with criminal law. Influenced by Torao Asai, Chinese scholar Yang Honglie 楊鴻烈 (1903–1977) classified traditional Chinese law into two parts: criminal law and civil law in his book *Zhongguo falü fada shi* 中國法律發達史 (History of the Development of Chinese Law), and he narrated all laws in pre-modern China according to this civil vs. criminal framework. This view had been overlooked for many years until the recent discoveries of legal materials and the shift of perspective in the field.

In 1996, Philip Huang challenged the mainstream view by pointing out that the Qing dynasty had very rich civil laws, which were reflected in legal practices.[7] In 2003, the comprehensive work *Zhongguo minfa tongshi* 中國民法通史 (A General History of Chinese Civil Law) was published. This work organized a group of outstanding legal historians to depict the development of civil law tradition in China from the ancient period through modern times.[8] This work compelled many scholars to reevaluate civil law in pre-modern China.[9] Since then, civil law has become a popular topic in the field.

Camp 3: Neither civil law, nor criminal law existed in pre-modern China because traditional Chinese law had its distinctive internal logic (Internal-Logic). This view is mainly advocated by Liang Zhiping 梁治平 in his book *Xunqiu ziran zhixu zhong de hexie* 尋求自然秩序中的和諧 (Searching for Harmony in Natural Order, 2002). He argued that previous scholars mostly

---

5 Michael Loewe, *The Government of the Qin and Han Empires* (Cambridge: Hackett Publishing Company, 2006), 120.

6 Torao Asai 淺虎武夫, *Shina hoseshi* 支那法制史 (Tokyo: Hirobumi Kan, 1904), 202–203.

7 Philip Huang, *Civil Justice in China: Representation and Practice in the Qing* (Stanford: Stanford University Press, 1996).

8 *Zhongguo minfa tongshi* 中國民法通史, ed., Zhang Jinfan 張晉藩 (Fuzhou: Fujian renmin chubanshe, 2003).

9 Wei Sen 韋森, "Zai Hafo du Zhang Jinfan jiaoshou zhubian de *Zhongguo minfa tongshi*" 在哈佛讀張晉蕃教授主編的中國民法通史, in *Shichang, faü yu minzhu: yige jingji xuejia de richang sikao* 市場、法律與民主: 一個經濟學家的日常思考 (Shanghai: Shanghai renmin chubanshe, 2008).

focused on the surface level, such as that pre-modern China had no civil code, or that the law codes of China had little civil regulations. They either asserted that civil laws of pre-modern China were under-developed or the traditional law was a hybrid of civil laws and criminal laws. Liang believed that those scholars unconsciously perceived pre-modern Chinese law from a modern-Western perspective, which obstructed the significance of the self-autonomy of its object and resulted in the loss of its integrity. Then Liang proposed a new perspective as such: pre-modern Chinese law was material in its own form. According to its internal logic, the distinction between civil and criminal was groundless, and the assertion of private law is self-contradicting.[10] Liang further observed that there was a tendency to criminalize "civil matters" in pre-modern China. For instance, according to Tang law, criminal punishments were applied to the indebted; therefore, the distinction between civil and criminal law did not matter.[11]

What caused these conflicting views among scholars? With regard to the No-Civil-Law camp, three scenarios exist. First, the false impression was created by the loss and dispersion of evidence. This is especially the case in the study of pre-Tang laws. Because most of the statutes and regulations prior to the Tang Code were lost, we could only examine a tiny fraction of the laws from the pre-Tang period. This situation allows us to infer what the laws were concerned with, but not what they overlooked and disregarded. When we are over confident of what we have not seen, we may fall into the trap of overstatement. It is deplorable to see many great scholars claim that civil laws never existed because of the lack of evidence, but they are rebuffed by the discovery of new evidence.

Second, sometimes the evidence exists but scholars fail to see it due to oversight or lack of access. For instance, William Jones initially studied the Qing Code in 1974 based on a selected translation made by George Thomas Staunton (1781–1859).[12] From this translation, Jones saw no civil regulations. Thus he believed that civil law did not exist during the Qing period. He claimed that no civil laws could exist in the entire history of pre-modern China because the concept of citizenship was absent there, and the notion of citizenship was crucial to civil law. However, twenty years later, Jones changed his opinion and provided a different view of the Qing law after he translated the Qing Code and

10 Liang Zhiping 梁治平, *Xunqiu ziran zhixu zhong de hexie* 尋求自然秩序中的和諧 (Beijing: Zhongguo zhengfa daxue chubanshe, 2002), IX–X.

11 Ibid., 237–241.

12 William Jones, "Studying the Ch'ing Code-The Ta Ch'ing Lü li," *The American Journal of Comparative Law* 22, no. 2 (1974): 356–357.

saw much more evidence than what he had in his 1974 article. His later view cautioned against seeing the code as wholly punitive, he mentioned that it dealt with private matters on occasion.[13]

Third, scholars sometimes hold a somewhat dogmatic understanding of civil law that disqualifies its "non-Western" counterparts. Professor Xu Zhongming 徐忠明 once summarized that in the eyes of certain scholars, because traditional China lacked notions that are viewed as fundamental to the society and ideas in Western civil law such as individualism, rights-based law, and the autonomy of private law, traditional China had no civil law to talk about.[14] Aside from its Western-centric bias, this line of argument is perhaps also ahistorical. For instance, a recent study argued that ancient Roman law did not have the notion of "rights" in the modern sense; it was projected back to the Roman law by latter scholars who interpreted *ius* as "rights" according to a particular context.[15] Therefore, if we apply the dogmatic understanding of civil law to Roman law, we would arrive at a paradox: *ius civile* is not civil law. In any case, would it not be possible for traditional China to have a civil law that handles civil matters based on traditional Chinese notions?[16]

Compared to No-Civil-Law scholars, Having-Civil-Law scholars are interested in finding new evidence to challenge the stereotypical view of traditional Chinese law as merely criminal. To a certain degree, they succeeded in propelling scholars to deepen their understandings of traditional Chinese

---

13 William Jones, "Introduction," *The Great Qing Code* (Oxford: Oxford University Press, 1994), 1–12. Jones's change of attitude was a prelude to an emerging new trend in the field when scholars started to turn their attention from the law codes to the legal practices reflected in local archives. Philip Huang (*Civil Justice in China*, 1996) revealed an intellectual trap that hampered scholars from seeing the whole picture: scholars were often misled by the official representation of the Qing law, which presented itself as a carefree approach in handling civil matters. Furthermore, the officials used moral teachings to solve civil disputes. From the cases recorded in local archives, Huang discovered that it was the opposite in practice. As civil disputes were very common, the officials often adjudicated the cases by applying the law. Moreover, Huang argued that more than 80 statutes and 300 regulations could be considered as "civil" in nature. For further details, see Huang, *Civil Justice*.

14 Xu Zhongming 徐忠明, "Zhongguo falüshi yanjiu de keneng qian jing: Chaoyue xifang, huigui bentu" 中國法律史研究的可能前景: 超越西方回歸本土, *Zhengfa luntan* 政法論壇 no. 1 (2006): 8.3–15.

15 Fang Xinjun 方新軍, "Quanli gainian de lishi" 權利概念的歷史, *Faxue yanjiu* 法學研究 no. 4 (2007): 69–95.

16 For example, Paolo Santangelo argues that the concept of "individual importance" existed in traditional China, but its reason differed from Western individualism. See Santangelo, *Individual Autonomy and responsibility in Late Imperial China* (Amherst: Cambria Press, 2021).

legal culture. Nevertheless, many of them still presuppose modern civil law as the model to understand China's past. They tend to apply modern notions and frameworks to analyze and reshape traditional Chinese materials, and this approach leads to an unintended problem, as Xu Zhongming determined:

> In summary, the well-defined order of the knowledge of traditional Chinese law is broken down due to interpretation and reconfiguration through Western legal notions and theories, which were the products of foreign culture. This also obstructs our recognition of the order of the traditional Chinese legal knowledge. Furthermore, this twists our recognition of the order of traditional Chinese society and life reflected in the traditional legal knowledge system.[17]

> 概括地說，原本"井然有序"的傳統中國法律的知識秩序，經由作為"異質"文化類型的西方法律概念和法學理論的解讀以及重構，終於割裂了傳統中國法律的知識秩序，也遮蔽了我們對傳統中國法律知識秩序的認知；進一步來講，這種研究範式還扭曲了我們對通過固有法律知識體系反映出來的傳統中國的社會生活秩序的認知.

For instance, the pioneering work, *Zhongguo minfa tongshi*, attempts to systematically reconstruct the civil law of pre-modern China, but the project adopted modern civil law notions and the structure to analyze and reshape the materials. This approach results in a problem: the characteristics and internal logic of traditional Chinese law cannot be captured.

Regarding the Internal-Logic camp, although their approach is very innovative, their conclusion is questionable. For instance, professor Liang believes that pre-modern Chinese legal tradition tended to criminalize civil matters by studying the regulations concerning debt in the Tang code, where criminal punishments were used to solve debt disputes. Regardless, if this view does justice to the whole of Tang law, then the Tang code itself is not the whole of traditional Chinese law, especially pre-Tang law.

Through multiple studies, which are based on concrete evidence, especially legal cases that demonstrated the real operation of the law, free of dogmatic understandings that are biased against traditional non-Western notions and reflections upon the internal logic of pre-modern legal institutes are needed to answer if there were civil laws in pre-modern China. Focusing on the Warring States (475–221 BC) and Qin-Han (221 BC–AD 220) periods, this research will demonstrate that in early China, matters of debt, compensation and many

17 Xu Zhongming, "Zhongguo falüshi yanjiu de keneng qian jing," 9.

others were not criminalized. Following the internal logic of early Chinese law, we can see clear distinctions between civil justice and criminal justice. Therefore, civil law existed in early China.

2 Definition of Terms and a Survey on Important Sources

This work tackles civil law in early China in order to solve the debate regarding the existence of civil law. In addition, this work draws the framework of the early civil law system and analyzes its distinctive characteristics. "Early" in this context mostly refers to the Warring States and Qin-Han periods. During this crucial era, the Chinese legal tradition took its form and laid down the foundation for laws in latter dynasties; the regulations, notions, and practices that emerged in this period deeply influenced traditional China. The term "civil law" as defined by this study requires clarification. To reflect the early Chinese milieu, the term, which is derived from Western legal tradition, is detached from its modern/Western connotations, such as individual property rights. It refers to laws and practices that dealt with "civil" matters in a "civil manner" based on distinctive Chinese notions and ideas. It comprises three dimensions: (1) The "civil" matters refer to the economic and personal relations among individuals, including compensation, debt, inheritance, and household divisions. Evidence shows that these matters were regarded as of a different nature from crimes in early China and were under a different category, (2) the relevant laws and practices include rules authorized by the state to solve what one would be called civil matters and legal practices, demonstrating features that are not penal-like. That is to say, the authorities do not apprehend the parties, do not apply tortures to try the disputes, and do not inflict penal punishments to the liable party, and (3) what behind the rules and practices were a set of distinctive Chinese legal notions, such as *zhi* 直, *mingfen* 名分, and *min-si* 民-私.[18] Admittedly, this working definition is not perfect but it has two merits that made it preferable: on the one hand, it is consistent with the common understanding of the basic functional features of civil law among international scholars, but on the other hand, it does not suppose a set of quasi "Western" notions as the underlying principles by re-interpreting and re-configuring Chinese ideas. The "civil law" in this book is defined as civil law with ancient Chinese characteristics and values, which protected one's due interests, but did not pivot on the idea of individual property rights.

---

18 For a detailed study on these notions, see Chapter 5.

Although from a broader sense, customs concerning civil matters could also be regarded as civil law, they are nonetheless excluded from the inquiry of this work due to two reasons: (1) Strictly speaking, customs were not "law" in the classical Chinese sense. For instance, the Qin legal text excavated from Shuihudi 睡虎地, *Yushu* 語書 (Admonitions), states that its mission is to eradicate the local customs by employing laws promulgated by the state. It openly states that:

> Therefore, the sage king made laws to adjust the hearts of the people, to eradicate their evilness and eliminate their bad customs.[19]
>
> 是以聖王作為法度，以矯端民心，去其邪避（僻），除其惡俗.

(2) My predecessors have noticed that customs were often applied to handle civil matters in early China (actually, the entire pre-modern China). When they argued that there were no civil law in early China, they really meant that no civil law was promulgated and enacted by the state. For instance, Hulsewé stated that "Private law, pertaining to the family and to trade and commerce other than the state monopolies, remained outside the field of regimentation by public authorities and continued to be ruled by custom and usage."[20]

Given the magnitude and prevalence of previous scholarship, how could such a study on early Chinese law that challenges the traditional account be possible? It is largely due to the discovery of new materials. Understandably, these scholars, prior to the most recent excavations, drew their conclusions from the fact that the transmitted laws of pre-modern China, and even the excavated Qin laws from Shuihudi in 1975,[21] were apparently preoccupied with public matters. A cursory look at the excavated Qin laws or the better-known transmitted *Tang Code* illustrates their preoccupation with penal laws.[22]

---

19 "Yushu" 語書 in *Shuihudi Qinmu zhujian* 睡虎地秦墓竹簡, ed., Shuihudi Qinmu zhujian Zhengli xiaozu 睡虎地秦墓竹簡整理小組 (Beijing: Wenwu chubanshe, 1990) [hereafter, *SHD*], 13.

20 *CHC*, 525.

21 The *SHD* documents are diverse, rich and detailed in content, and they are the first excavated early laws. Their focus is predominantly penal, but a number of civil provisions are scattered among the penal statutes. Scholars have by and large overlooked those civil provisions.

22 The *Tang Code* is preserved in the famous *Tanglü shuyi* 唐律疏議 (The Tang Code with Commentaries, 635). For the complete translation, see Wallace Johnson, *The T'ang Code: Vol. I, General Principles* (Princeton: Princeton University Press, 1979) and *The T'ang Code: Vol. II, Specific Articles* (Princeton: Princeton University Press, 1997).

However, evidence excavated from Zhangjiashan 張家山, first published in 2001, offers an opportunity to reassess and revise this view.[23] The Zhangjiashan strips were excavated from Tomb 247 at Jiangling 江陵, Hubei 湖北 by archaeologists from the Jingzhou 荊州 Museum in 1983. There are 1,236 strips in total, dated from 202 to 186 BC[24] These discoveries were first reported in the *Wenwu* 文物 in 1985, with the full set of strips published in 2001 in the *Zhangjiashan Hanmu zhujian* 張家山漢墓竹簡 (Strips from a Han Tomb at Zhangjiashan), with a revised edition in 2006.[25] The editors classified the strips into eight texts, mostly under their original titles, of which the *Zouyan shu* 奏讞書 (Reports of Cases to Be Reviewed, 228 strips in total) and *Ernian lüling* 二年律令 (The Statutes and Ordinances of the Second Year, 526 strips in total) are extremely important legal documents. The *Zouyan shu* is a collection of twenty-two legal cases presumed to mostly have taken place from 202 to 186 BC *Zou* 奏 means "to report," and *Yan* 讞 refers to the discussion of sentences. The collection reflects the appeal procedure and details of court debates, vastly expanding the amount of historical information about the legal system as it actually functioned beyond what had hitherto been available to scholars. The *Ernian lüling* consists of twenty-seven statutes and one set of ordinances that had been previously unknown to scholars. Among these statutes, Statutes on Households (Hulü 戶律), Statutes on Establishing Heirs (Zhihoulü 置後律), and Statutes on Registration (Fulü 傅律) are clearly concerned with civil matters such as land ownership, division and inheritance of households, and females' due share over property.[26] Furthermore, there are also guidelines for compensation, commercial transactions, and debts as defined by other statutes.

While these examples hardly constitute a systematic or codified approach to civil laws, they are sufficient to challenge the earlier view that traditional Chinese laws were exclusively criminal and administrative. They compelled

---

23 See *Zhangjiashan Hanmu zhujian* (*ersiqi hao mu*) 張家山漢墓竹簡 (二四七號墓), ed., Zhangjiashan ersiqi hao Hanmu zhujian zhengli xiaozu 張家山二四七號漢墓竹簡整理小組 (Beijing: Wenwu chubanshe, 2001) [rev. 2006] [hereafter, *ZJS*].

24 A.F.P. Hulsewé, "Fragments of Han Law," *T'oung Pao* 76, nos. 4–5 (1990), 208–233; cf. Ōba Osamu, "The Ordinances on Fords and Passes Excavated from Han Tomb Number 247, Zhangjiashan," *Asia Major* 14 (2001): 119–141, trans., David Spafford et al. See also Cao Lüning 曹旅寧, *Zhangjiashan Hanlü Yanjiu* 張家山漢律研究 (Beijing: Zhonghua shuju, 2005).

25 Zhangjiashan ersiqi hao Hanmu zhujian zhengli xiaozu 張家山二四七號漢墓竹簡整理小組, "Jiangling Zhangjiashan Hanjian gaishu" 江陵張家山漢簡概述, *Wenwu* 文物 no. 1 (1985): 9–15. See also *ZJS*.

26 The notion of due share is related to *mingfen* 名分 (title and portion). This term will be discussed in Chapter 5.

us to reexamine both transmitted and excavated materials thoroughly for evidence that may have been overlooked. We found that prior to Zhangjiashan, relevant evidence was excavated, including: (1) case reports regarding debt and compensation disputes, contracts, and statutes scattered in the records excavated from the Gobi Desert of northwestern China; (2) the Han legal contract among business partners, namely "Zhongfu gongshi yue" 中服共侍約 (Agreement on Joint Business Partnership) excavated from Fenghuangshan 鳳凰山, Jiangling, Hubei in 1973; (3) the last will concerning inheritance excavated from Xupu 胥浦, Jiangsu 江蘇 in 1984. These materials were published prior to the Zhangjiashan strips and drew research interest, but they were not strong or rich enough to compel scholars to claim and reconstruct early civil law.

After the excavation of Zhangjiashan, new evidence kept emerging, including: (1) records of the Warring States period Chu 楚 State excavated from Baoshan 包山; (2) records of the Qin excavated from Liye 里耶, Hunan 湖南; (3) the looted Qin legal materials bought by the Yuelu 岳麓 Academy; (4) Eastern Han records excavated from Changsha 長沙, Hunan; (5) looted Qin and Han records purchased by Peking University; (6) records excavated from Marquis Haihun's 海昏 tomb, Nanchang 南昌, Jiangxi 江西. Except for a few selected portions, the majority of these materials have not been published yet. However, from the published portions, we found that there is rich evidence regarding early civil law.

In addition to the excavated materials, we can find evidence in the received literature as well. The land disputes criticized by official histories and the stories concerning inheritance, debt, and disputes over ownership in various anecdotal written sources reflect civil disputes to various degrees when viewed from the perspective of civil law. Moreover, the early classicists, such as Zheng Xuan 鄭玄 (AD 127–200) and Wei Zhao 韋昭 (AD 201–273), often unintentionally left us with evidence regarding civil law in their annotations to the classics. This evidence from received literature proves how the regulations we know from the excavated materials were practiced.

With these discoveries and a renewed burst of scholarship, we have begun to see that civil suits were far more common in early China than previously assumed, and that the legal system included a body of civil statutes and some sort of orderly civil procedure.

CHAPTER 1

Early Cases concerning "Civil" Matters

The present chapter will systematically analyze the known cases concerning "civil" matters,[1] including debts, compensation, transaction, inheritance, and so on. from the earliest periods and summarize the characteristics of litigation concerning "civil" matters taken from within these cases. On account of the limited materials available, the present chapter will concentrate on the relevant cases preserved in the Juyan strips which were dated to the Han period.[2] Paying particular attention to the procedures, this chapter will argue that litigation concerning "civil" matters had already taken shape as a mature system no later than the Han period. Specifically:

During the Han period, the method of handling economic disputes over debts and compensation had five obvious differences from that of criminal cases:

1. Individuals were able to bring complaints against one or more persons in matters such as compensation and property disbursement and distribution.
2. The authorities sought to assess appropriate compensation or determine the proper disbursement or distribution of property for the successful plaintiff.

---

1 See the Introduction of this book for the definition of "civil matters."

2 Juyan strips were excavated from the deserts and Gobi in Edsen-gol, Inner Mongolia in two separate excavations. The first excavation was conducted in the 1930's by a Sino-Sweden joint archaeological team that yielded 10, 272 strips. The first major publication, which included 2,555 strips, was the *Juyan Hanjian jia bian* 居延漢簡甲編 (Beijing: Kexue chubanshe, 1959). The complete collection of strips was published in *Juyan Hanjian yibian* 居延漢簡甲乙編 (Beijing: Kexue chubanshe, 1980). Meanwhile, Lao Gan 勞榦 published about 10,000 strips in *Juyan Hanjian* 居延漢簡 (Taipei: The Institute of History and Philology Special Publication, 1960). The second excavation was conducted in 1972–1974 by a Gansu archaeological team that yielded 19, 400 strips. The strips were published in *Juyan xinjian:Jiaqu houguan yu disi sui* 居延新簡: 甲渠候官與第四燧, eds., Gansu sheng wenwu kaogu yanjiusuo 甘肅省文物考古研究所 et al. (Beijing: Wenwu chubanshe, 1990) [hereafter, *JYX*]. In addition, from 1990 to 1992, the Gansu Institute of Archaeology excavated 23,000 strips from Xuanquan 懸泉, Dunhuang 敦煌, which is very close to Juyan. These Xuanquan strips dated from 111 BC to AD 107. A selection of 300 strips is presented in *Dunhuang Xuanquan Hanjian shicui* 敦煌懸泉漢簡釋粹, eds., Hu Pingsheng 胡平生 and Zhang Defang 張德芳 (Shanghai: Shanghai guji, 2001). It is very striking that even this small sample of Xuanquan strips include legal documents, such as wanted circulars, edicts of amnesty, and statutes.

 | DOI:10.1163/9789004513907_003

3. In cases of debt or compensation that resulted in a judgment assigning liability, the authorities could be asked to help the successful plaintiff collect compensation from a recalcitrant defendant, but it remained up to the plaintiff to decide if he or she would pursue the judgments.
4. Punishments were rarely imposed by the state on liable parties. In the cases in which a punishment was imposed, the punishment was limited to fines and excluded such punishments as forced labor service, exile, beating, confinement, mutilation, or execution.
5. Social status was not a factor in assessing liability. The parties involved in disputes over property were treated as equals by the authorities: a person with a higher rank had no legal privileges beyond those of a person with lower rank. Those with high social status had no privilege granted by law.

These characteristics suggest that the state did not consider economic disputes over debts and compensation as threats to social stability or public order and thus handled them in a "civil" manner. Furthermore, this chapter will reveal that civil stipulations were already promulgated and were referred to during the trials, which indicated the maturity of the civil litigation.

1 The Initial Stages as Reflected in the Western Zhou Bronze Inscriptions down to the Chu and Qin Strips

The initial stages of litigation concerning "civil" matters seem to be traceable back to the Western Zhou period. In the *Xi Zhou fazhi shi* 西周法制史 (History of the Western Zhou Legal System, 1988), Hu Liuyuan 胡留元 and Feng Zhuohui 馮卓慧 noticed that records from the bronze inscriptions contain materials related to litigation concerning "civil" matters.[3] In 2009, Feng again analyzed in detail the Western Zhou bronze inscriptions from the Hu *ding* 曶鼎 (ca. late 10th or early 9th century BC) which records a slave trade dispute, the Chousheng *gui* 琱生簋 (823–822 BC) which records agricultural land disputes, and the Liyoucong *ding* 鬲攸從鼎 (795 BC), which records land leasing disputes. Feng believed that these inscriptions proved the existence of civil litigation systems during the Western Zhou. Furthermore, Feng mainly used records taken from the *Zhouli* 周禮 (Rites of Zhou) to summarize the characteristics of the Western Zhou civil litigation system. She maintained that the Western

3 Hu Liuyuan 胡留元 and Feng Zhuohui 馮卓慧, *Xizhou fazhi shi*西周法制史 (Xi'an: Shaanxi renmin chubanshe, 1988). Skosey accepted and developed the argument of Hu and Feng. See Laura A. Skosey, *The Legal System and Legal Tradition of the Western Zhou CA 1045–771 B.C.* (Chicago: University of Chicago Press, 1996), 272–281.

Zhou civil litigation system at that time was comparatively more advanced than that of the *Hammurabi Code* or the Roman *Laws of the Twelve Tables*.[4]

The line of argument and conclusions of this research require further discussion. First, philological research made it clear that the *Zhouli* was not completed as far back as the Western Zhou. Scholars Qian Mu 錢穆, Yang Xiangkui 楊向奎, Gu Jiegang 顧頡剛 and others all consider it to have been completed during the Warring States period.[5] The content is colored by an intensely idealized Confucianism, which was further refined by later Confucian scholars. There are significant issues in using these types of texts to corroborate the systems of the Western Zhou. Within the text, many elements were imagined and inferred by later generations and cannot be viewed as reliable history. However, it is difficult to place trust in the commentaries on the *Zhouli* to analyze the systems of the Western Zhou, as the commentators always projected the affairs and theoretical ideas of their own time into the past.

Moreover, by using only three cases, we can prove that civil cases do exist during the Western Zhou period. However, it is difficult to elevate such cases to an institutional level. At this level, we must know whether there were corresponding laws or regulations and whether or not there were formal and conventional procedures and channels to accept these types of cases. According to my calculation, of the known cases of Western Zhou inscriptions, six of these can be regarded as "civil" litigation or "civil" matter.[6]Apart from the three cases

---

4 Feng Zhuohui 馮卓慧, "Cong Chuanshi de he xin chutu de Shaanxi jinwen ji xian Qin wenxian kan Xizhou de minshi susong zhidu" 從傳世的和新出土的陝西金文及先秦文獻看西周的民事訴訟制度, *Xibei zhengfa daxue xuebao* 西北政法大學學報 no. 4 (2009): 159–168; Yang Yifan 楊一凡 holds a similar view, as shown in "Zhonghua faxi yanjiu zhong de yige zhongda wuqu: 'zhufa heti minxing bufen' shuo zhiyi 中華法系研究中的一個重大誤區:'諸法合體、民刑不分'說質疑," *Zhongguo shehui kexue* 中國社會科學 no. 6 (2002): 78–94, 206.

5 The date of the *Zhouli* is controversial, and opinions varied from the authentic work of the Duke of Zhou to the forgery of Liu Xin in the Han period. The mainstream view is that the work was very possibly compiled in the Warring States period. Refer to the following publications: Qian Mu 錢穆, "Zhouguan zhizuo shidai kao" 周官制作時代考, *Yanjing xuebao* 燕京學報 no. 11 (1932): 1–109; Yang Xiangkui 楊向奎, "Zhouli de neirong fenxi jiqi chengshu niandai" 周禮的內容分析及其成書年代, in Yang Xiangkui, *Yishi zhai wenji* 繹史齋文集 (Shanghai: Shanghai renmin chubanshe, 1980); Gu Jiegang 顧頡剛, "Zhougong zhili de chuanshuo he zhouguan yi shu de chuxian" 周公制禮的傳說和周官一書的出現, *Wenshi* 文史 6 (1979): 172–242.

6 The following works were consulted in my research: *Jiagu jinwen jiandu falü wenxian* 甲骨金文簡牘法律文獻, eds., Liu Hainian 劉海年 et al. (Beijing: Kexue chubanshe, 1994); Li Xueqin 李學勤, "Xizhou jinwen zhongde tudi zhuanrang" 西周金文中的土地轉讓, *Li Xueqin wenji* 李學勤文集 (Shanghai: Shanghai guji chubanshe, 2005), 225; Wang Pei 王沛, "Xizhou jinwen falü ziliao jikao" 西周金文法律資料輯考, *Zhongguo gudai falü wenxian yanjiu* 中國古代法律文獻研究 7 (2012): 16–65.

already listed, there are records of transactions of agricultural land from the Wusi Qiuwei *ding* 五祀裘衛鼎 (913 BC) and Liyou *xu* 鬲攸盨 (801 BC), along with a record of an exchange of land for horses in the Pengsheng *gui* 倗生簋 (917–900 BC, which is also called Gebo *gui* 格伯簋). These cases are all fundamentally concerned with land property, except for the Hu *ding* which involves the buying and selling of slaves.[7]

For instance, the inscription of the Pengsheng *gui*[8] states that:

> 唯正月初吉癸巳, 王在成周. 格伯受良馬乘於倗生. 厥賈卅田, 則析. 格伯履, 殴妊彶佗厥從. 格伯安彶甸, 殷厥糿, 零穀杜木, 邊穀旅桑. 涉東門, 厥書史戠武立, 盥成. 壘鑄保簋, 用典格伯田. 其萬年, 子子孫孫永保用.
>
> During the 1st day of the 1st month, which is *kuisi*, the king was in Chengzhou (Luoyang). Gebo gave four good horses to Pengsheng. The worth of the horses was 30 fields,[9] and the contract was split [into halves]. Gebo fulfilled [the contract]. Yiren and Tuo followed Gebo walked to the field to inspect the land: from the birch-pear trees in the Yin stream to the mulberry trees in the Yu stream, crossing the eastern gate. His Scribes, Shi and Wu, shoveled earth to build up a mound, and cast the treasured vessel, in order to document the transfer of the fields to Gebo. Ten thousand years! The subsequent generations shall preserve and use the vessel for ever.[10]

In this case, Gebo (Duke Ge?) gave Pengsheng 4 horses, and in exchange, Pengsheng provided Gebo with 30 fields. Gebo inspected the land and ordered his scribe to document the boundaries, and a bronze vessel was cast to

---

7 These characteristics reflect the extremely weak state of the commodity economy during the Western Zhou period, as the disputes created by such transactions were quite rare.

8 Preserved in Shanghai Museum.

9 The unit of area is not specified by the inscription. Perhaps, the default unit was obvious to the parties involved.

10 Zhongguo shehui kexueyuan kaogu yanjiusuo 中國社會科學院考古研究所: *Yinzhou jinwen jicheng shiwen* 殷周金文集成釋文 (Hong Kong: Xianggang zhongwen daxue zhongguo wenhua yanjiusuo, 2014) , vol. 2, 402. Here, I adopted Li Xueqin's interpretation of the case from "Xizhou jinwen zhongde tudi zhuanrang." This document, which has inspired various interpretations, focused on the nature of the transaction and initial owner of the land. For instance, see Li Feng, *Bureaucracy and the State in Early China: Governing the Western Zhou* (Cambridge: Cambridge University Press, 2008), 16–20. Li Feng believed that the initial owner was Gebo. Thus, he summarized the case as follows: Gebo purchased horses from Pengsheng in exchange for thirty fields. My translation consulted the work of Li Feng, with important modifications.

commemorate the deal. Thus, this is a record of a land transaction through a system of barter. The function of the inscription was to authorize the transaction, to entitle the new owner of the land, and to be used as evidence when disputes arose.

In another example, the Wusi Qiuwei *ding* records a lawsuit regarding land between two nobles: Qiu Wei 裘衛 against Bangjun Li 邦君历, and the judges involved were Duke Xing 刑伯 and four other officials. The case went as follows: Qiu Wei complained that when Bangjun Li conducted an irrigation-work, he promised to give Qiu Wei five fields to compensate for his loss (supposedly, the irrigation-work affected Qiu Wei's field and caused damage) but failed to fulfill the promise. The judges summoned Bangjun Li to investigate and ordered him to provide the land that he had promised to Qiu Wei. The judges also sent officials to demarcate the boundaries, and a formal ceremony was held to cement the transfer of land.[11] As we can tell that the lawsuit was concerned with the fulfillment of an agreement concerning land, the judges were high nobles, and the disputants were also nobles. These features were consistent with our previous observation from the Pengsheng *gui*.

These lawsuits regarding land seem to contradict the rules of the land tenure system of the Western Zhou, the Well-Field system.[12] Supposedly, all the land was owned by the king and was not allowed to be bought and sold. It is said that 'Under the wide heaven, all is the king's land'.[13] However, those cases above studied indicated that land could be bought and sold and the authorities even heard cases regarding the transactions. Thus, we wondered: what happened? Because all known cases involved quite high ranking nobles,[14] one plausible explanation is that lawsuits regarding land in China initially arose from within the greater nobility because they had the power to override the

11 Discovered from Qishan, Shaanxi in 1975 and presently preserved in Shaanxi History Museum. It was first reported in the *Wenwu* no. 5 (1976). See also *Yinzhou jinwen jicheng shiwen* (2014), vol. 3, 375.

12 Regarding the Well-field system reflected in the bronze vessel inscriptions, see Li Ling 李零, "Xizhou jinwen zhong de tudi zhidu" 西周金文中的土地制度, *Xueren* 學人 2 (1992): 224–256. Li Xueqin 李學勤 also discussed this issue in "Xizhou jinwen zhong de tudi zhuanrang." According to Li Xueqin, these records suggest that land could be sold and pursued under the Well-field system. However, I believe these land transactions were unusual cases and did not reflect the norm; rather, they were the privileges of nobles and were practiced beyond the norm.

13 *The Book of Songs*, Mao no. 211. Translation follows James Legge, *The Chinese Classics* (Hong Kong: Hong Kong University Press, 1960), vol. 4, 360.

14 It needs to be cautioned that this phenomenon could be a false impression created by our biased evidence. We rely on bronze vessel inscriptions to study the lawsuits of the Western Zhou period. However, only resourceful nobles could afford to cast bronze to commemorate their legal victories or land purchases.

Well-Field system. Blood relationships and political status empowered them with actual control of the land, a situation that the Son of Heaven during the Zhou period tacitly accepted. The greater nobility could buy, sell, and exchange land at will, and any disputes that emerged could be resolved by recourse to quasi-judicial channels. However, in terms of these types of disputes, it was impossible to have formal legislation and clearly defined systems because this would have been tantamount to denying the existence of the Well-Field system. Therefore, of the known cases that were heard, we can observe none whatsoever that cite the law and rules as the basis for judgment. The entire process closely resembles "Khadi Justice", that is, to judge a matter as it stands and to depend upon ethical considerations and common sense to decide what right from wrong. Such practices cannot be thought of as institutionalizing or systematizing the system of "civil" litigation.[15]

Although there are several points that can still be argued, the research of Feng Zhuohui illustrates that lawsuits regarding land already existed during the Western Zhou. Moreover, there was no adoption of criminalized means when dealing with these lawsuits. For example, in the cases from the Hu *ding* and Liyoucong *ding*, both parties came to court to defend themselves. Fundamentally, the outcome of handling these cases did not involve criminal punishment (The Liyoucong *ding* did however involve moderate punishment – that of exile). They went as such:

> 償曶禾十秭, 為廿秭. ☒來歲弗償, 則付卌秭 (Hu *ding*).[16]
>
> [The judge ordered the defendant] to compensate Hu grain of ten *zi*[17] and make it 20 *zi* in total. If [the defendant] fails to compensate [Hu] until next year, then he shall pay [Hu] 40 *zi*.
>
> 虢旅乃使攸衛牧誓: 我弗具付鬲比其祖射分田邑, 則放 (Liyoucong *ding*).[18]
>
> Therefore, Gulü ordered Youweimu to swear: If I do not give Libi his due of field and settlements, I shall be exiled.

15 Khadi Justice was a concept initiated by Max Webber to characterize the traditional legal practices in the Arab world. Lin Duan seriously criticized its usage in the field of Sinology. See Lin Duan 林端, *Weibo lun Zhongguo falü chuantong*: *Weibo bijiao shehuixue de pipan* 韋伯論中國法律傳統: 韋伯比較社會學的批判 (Taipei: San min shuju, 2003).

16 *Yinzhou jinwen jicheng shiwen*, vol. 2, 414.

17 This unit of measure was used in ancient China, in which 1 *zi* was equal to 200 bundles.

18 *Yinzhou jinwen jicheng shiwen*, vol.2, 348.

Therefore, from these cases we can glimpse at the earliest stages of litigation concerning "civil" matters. These early stages were preliminary as the relevant laws and rules had not yet appeared, and the disputes concerning "civil" matters we are aware of were the result of activities that overrode the privileges of the system. We are incapable of speculating on whether or not the numerous lower classes and lower strata of the nobility had similar "civil" disputes, or if they had such issues, and how they were resolved.

"Civil" disputes during the Spring and Autumn period generally continued in a similar manner to that of the Western Zhou in that they were characterized by only involving the nobility.[19] However, pertinent disputes from the common populace appeared in Baoshan 包山 strips from the middle of the Warring States period.[20] The Baoshan strips preserve many legal documents which clearly illustrate the judicial system of the Chu State during the Warring States period.[21]

For example, in 1992, Li Xueqin 李學勤 elaborated in his research a case involving land inheritance and trade. The case verified that land could be traded in addition to being annexed during the middle of the Warring States period.[22] In 2001, Liu Jinhua 劉金華 carried out further research on this basis. He considered that during the time when the Baoshan strips were composed, the Chu State was experiencing a process of intensive land privatization, and that therefore "the disputes caused by activities such as land mortgages, exchanges, compensation, renting and grants etc. became even more complex."[23]

19 Ning Quanhong 寧全紅, *Chunqiu fazhi shi yanjiu* 春秋法制史研究 (Chengdu: Sichuan daxue chubanshe, 2009), 170–80.

20 *Baoshan Chu jian* 包山楚簡, ed., Hubei sheng Jingsha tielu kaogu dui 湖北省荊沙鐵路考古隊 (Beijing: Wenwu chubanshe 1991). The Baoshan strips were excavated from Tomb No. 2 at Jingmen 荊門, Hubei 湖北 in 1987, comprising 278 strips from the Chu State dating no later than 316 BC. These findings were first reported in 1988 in Hubei Jingsha tielu kaogu dui 湖北荊沙鐵路考古隊, "Baoshan er hao mu zhujian gaishu" 包山二號墓竹簡概述 *Wenwu* no. 1 (1988): 25–29. The entire set of strips was published in *Baoshan Chujian* 包山楚簡, ed., Hubei Jingsha tielu kaogu dui (Beijing: Wenwu chubanshe, 1991). The best transcription was from Chen Wei's 陳偉 team. See *Chudi chutu Zhanguo jiance (shisizhong)* 楚地出土戰國簡冊［十四種］, eds., Chen Wei et al. (Beijing: Jingji kexue chubanshe, 2009).

21 Chen Wei, *Baoshan Chu jian chu tan* 包山楚簡初探 (Wuhan: Wuhan daxue chubanshe, 1996), 132–49; Susan Weld, "Chu Law in Action: Legal Documents from Tomb 2 at Baoshan," in *Defining Chu: Image and Reality in Ancient China*, eds., Constance A. Cook and John S. Major (Honolulu: University of Hawaii Press, 1999), 77–97.

22 Li Xueqin 李學勤, "Baoshan Chu jian zhong de tudi maimai" 包山楚簡中的土地買賣, *Zhongguo wenwu bao* 中國文物報, March 22, 1992.

23 Liu Jinhua 劉金華, "Cong Baoshan Chu jian kan Chu guo de minshi falü guanxi" 從包山楚簡看楚國的民事法律關係, *Jianghan kaogu* 江漢考古 no. 2 (2001): 46–50.

There were issues related to the private ownership of land along with issues that arose from land transfers. There were also issues with land trade, inheritance, credit, and liability. Liu arrived at the conclusion that "the people of Chu not only had a considerable large amount of legal practices in aspects related to property ownership and personal relationships, but also had a certain degree of involvement in aspects of legal relationships related to the rights of creditors."[24]

Indeed, there are many cases from the Baoshan strips which involve property disputes. According to Chen Wei's 陳偉 study, there are a total of twenty-nine cases from the "Shuyu" 疋獄 section (Documents Regarding Crimes) that had clear causes. These can be divided into five types: "human trafficking", "personal injury", "inappropriate handling by officials", "transgressing status and household registration system", and "disputes related to property debt". There were seven items included in the "disputes related to property debt": "burial", "the aftereffects of theft", "bribery for land", "debt" and so on. These seven cases account for more than twenty-four percent of the cases.[25] If we view these seven records of disputes related to property debts as a whole, we can find nothing to show that they were dealt with by criminal means. If we look at the outcomes of how they were handled, there were no criminal forms of punishment involved. We can therefore refer to all of these as cases concerning "civil" matters.

What is most deserving of our attention however, is that compared with the bronze inscriptions which only contain disputes among the nobility, the Baoshan strips mainly involve the lower strata of the populace. For example:

> On the *wushen* day of the ninth month, Gaodaliu ordered Zhou Yan, who is the bond-servant of Zhou Sha, to launch a lawsuit against Zhou Yao and Zhou Dui who are residents of the Fuyu locality, saying the defendant buried their relatives in his land. Eventually [Zhou] Yao, [Zhou] Dui and [Zhou] Yan settled the problem. Only Zhou Xi's wife could be buried in the land. The scribe Xin recorded it, and the judge was Yicong.[26]
>
> 九月戊申之日，佫大六令周殺之人周雁訟付輿之關人周瑤、周敚，謂葬於其土，瑤、敚與雁成．唯周鼠奚之妻葬焉．疋忻識之，從為李．

This document recorded the litigation of Zhou Yan against Zhou Yao and Zhou Dui, because the latter two people buried their relatives on Zhou Yan's land.

24 Ibid.

25 Chen Wei, *Baoshan Chu jian chutan*, 133–34.

26 Chen Wei, *Chudi chutu Zhanguo jian ce*, 37.

After negotiation with local officials, both sides reached an agreement. It is obvious that such a case shows "civil" characteristics. In the document, the complainant was designated as "the bond-servant of Magistrate Zhou Sha" (*gao da liu ling Zhou Sha zhi ren* 俈大六令周殺之人). This designation illustrates that he was the noble official Zhou Sha's bond-servant, and the defendant was designated as a resident from a certain locality, which is the equivalent of a registered householder during later periods.[27] Taking into consideration that the two names do not contain any indication of nobility or rank, we can be certain that both parties were commoners. Therefore, this is a "civil" dispute among commoners. This fact illustrates that during this time, commoners already had some control and interest in relation to land.

Compared with the materials from the bronze inscriptions from the Western Zhou, we find that there were not only many cases concerning "civil" matters in the Baoshan strips with diverse causes, but also that the parties involved were mainly commoners. Although, the outcomes of such comparisons may illustrate regional differences; the cases from the Western Zhou inscriptions were concentrated in the northern regions, and the Chu State as represented in the Baoshan strips was in the southern region, or the differences may be due to the different nature of the sources: bronze vessels were exclusively used by nobles, so the cases reflected in the bronze inscription were all related to nobles, but bamboo documents were widely used by the state to administrate its subjects, thus disputes among commoners were recorded by Baoshao strips. However, if we take into consideration the broader historical background, this type of contrast more likely reflects changes between different eras. From the Western Zhou to the Warring States period, each feudal state transformed dramatically. The commodity economy developed from insignificant levels to extreme importance, and the land went from being "state owned" to "privately owned".[28] As a result, the common populace obtained the freedom to participate in economic activities as well as own land. On account of this, economic disputes also increased daily. This caused the development of "civil" litigation, meaning that the section of society this could be applied to was greatly enlarged to include the lowest strata of society, and that related legislation was perhaps also enacted.

---

27 Chen Wei emphasizes that the word "ren" 人 is equivalent to "*bianhu qi min*" 編戶齊民 in the phrase "the *ren* of x place," while the word "*ren*" in the phrase "the *ren* of x person" refers to the bonded servant of someone. See Chen Wei in *Baoshan jian chu tan*, 110–112. As for the ranks of the Chu State, see Gu Jiuxing 顧久幸, "'Zhigui' za kao: jianlun Chuguo juezhi" '執圭'雜考: 兼論楚國爵制, *Jianghan lun tan* 江漢論壇 no. 5 (1992): 79–81.

28 For these economic changes, see Li Jiannong 李劍農, *Xian Qin liang Han jingji shi gao* 先秦兩漢經濟史稿 (Beijing: Sanlian shudian, 1957), 68–95.

It is a pity, however, that there are no laws and rules found among the legal documents in the Chu strips, only cases. Fortunately, the Qin strips from Shuihudi and Longang 龍崗 in Yunmeng 雲夢 county in Hubei make up for the deficiencies in the Chu strips. Even though these two caches of Qin strips are basically concerned with criminal law, they are mixed with several cases concerned with inheritance and compensation laws and rules. They are the earliest examples of "civil" laws and rules.

There is a case excavated from the Shuihudi strips known as the 'Fight over a Cow' (*Zheng niu* 爭牛) which is rather interesting.

> A *gongshi* [named] Jia from a certain village and a commoner [named] Yi went [to court in relation to] cattle [which was] a black female with horns. [They] testified saying that the cow was theirs and that it was lost. They both found it and came to court to dispute [ownership] of it. The judge ordered the clerk of the magistrate to examine the cow's teeth and discovered the cow was six years old.[29]

> 某里公士甲、士伍乙詣牛一, 黑牝縻有角, 告曰: "此甲、乙牛也, 而亡, 各識, 共詣來爭之." 即令令史某齒牛, 牛六歲矣.

Of the two parties involved in the dispute, one belonged to the *gongshi* 公士, which was the lowest rank of orders of honor, and the other was a soldier without any orders of honor, so both can be categorized as commoners. The two parties took their dispute to the authorities on account of the ownership of a cow. The authorities investigated the cow's age in order to arrive at a judgment as to the verity of the party's claims. These are obviously not the characteristics of a criminal case and can be considered as "civil".

Based on a comprehensive analysis of the above, we discover the following pattern: From the bronze inscriptions down to the Chu and Qin strips, the cases concerning "civil" matters gradually diversified, and the lower strata of the populace gradually became more involved. Most of the content of these cases are economic disputes and were not handled in a manner involving criminal punishment. It is especially noteworthy that Chen Wei paid attention to the following issues: First, litigation from the Baoshan strips, which involved official business on account of them being put forward by the official administrators in charge, and second, litigation which involved private matters that

---

29 *SHD* strip (*Fengzhenshi*) nos. 23–24, p. 152.

were put forward by the victim himself or the victim's relatives. This touches upon differences in the process of litigation.[30]

However, even during the Qin dynasty, related cases and laws and rules which can be analyzed are of such rarity that we are incapable of differentiating between criminal and cases concerning "civil" matters. When we come to the Han dynasty, however, a large number of "civil" laws and rules and related disputes come into view. The differences between "civil" and criminal litigation can be clearly illustrated on account of the complexities of the various parties and the widespread nature of the regions involved.

2 Distinctions between Litigation concerning "Civil" Matters and Criminal Matters Reflected in the Cases of the Han Dynasty[31]

2.1 *Kou En* 寇恩 *vs. Su Jun* 粟君

Cases concerning "civil" matters in early China have generally been overlooked by scholars. However, they did exist. With the advancements in our understanding made possible by the Zhangjiashan and other recent excavations, we can now more fruitfully revisit the famous case of "Hou Su Jun suo zhai Kou En shi" 候粟君所責寇恩事, which prompted Hulsewé to speculate in 1979 on the possible existence of civil suits in early China.[32] The thirty-six-strip text that describes the "Hou Su Jun suo zhai Kou En shi" case was excavated from the Juyan site, Inner Mongolia in 1974, and first published in the journal *Wenwu* 文物 in 1978. The text describes a suit brought by a military officer Su against a civilian commoner Kou En. Su hired Kou En to sell goods for him at a specified price. When Kou En proved unable to sell the goods at the agreed upon price, Su demanded that Kou En compensate him for the shortfall. Not satisfied by the amount of compensation made by Kou En, Su brought a suit against Kou En for full satisfaction. Despite the document's length, the record is sadly incomplete, leaving the final disposition of the suit unclear.[33] We do know,

30 Chen Wei, *Baoshan Chu jian chutan*, p. 134.

31 Part of this section has been published in the article "Revisiting the A.D. 28 Case from Juyan: How Was Civil Justice Different from Criminal Justice in Han China?", *Journal of Asian History* 47, No.1 (2013): 51–79.

32 A.F.P. Hulsewé, "A Lawsuit of A.D. 28," in *Studia Sino-Mongolica*, ed., Herausgegeben Von Wolfgang Bauer (Wiesbanden: Franz Steiner Verlag, 1979), 29.

33 Professor Hsing I-tien 邢義田 argues that the 36 strips included only a small part of the complete case concerning the dispute between Su and Kou En. See Hsing I-tien, "Handai shuzuo wenshu yongyu 'ta ru mou mou' ji 'Jianwu san nian Hou Su Jun zhai Kou En shi' jiance dang'an de goucheng" 漢代書佐文書用語'它如某某'及'建武三年候粟君責

however, that hearings were conducted by a local bailiff in order to determine the facts in the case and to assess the claims and liabilities of the parties.

The following is a summary of the case (See Hulsewé's article for the complete translation):

On January 30, AD 28, bailiff Gong 宮, upon receiving the complaint of Su, transmitted to him by the county court of Juyan, summoned Kou En to the district office. Before questioning him, the bailiff explained the statutes governing the issues in the case. The relevant statutes covered the following:

1. Incidents in which the accused party is unable to provide evidence of his innocence.
2. Incidents involving money and goods in which the accused is charged with being intentionally untruthful.
3. Incidents in which the amount in dispute is 500 cash or more.
4. Incidents when statements of the accused party are not altered or challenged for three full days.
5. Incidents in which false accusations can be punished by "reversal", (i.e., the accuser risks the same punishment that the falsely accused party stood to suffer had he been found guilty or liable).[34]

After setting forth the relevant laws, the bailiff questioned Kou En.

According to Kou En, one year earlier, His Honor Su, who was a military officer, enlisted two subordinates to sell fish for him. When these subordinates were unable to perform the service, they gave Su the money to hire Kou En, a civilian, to transport and sell 5,000 fish at the market in the nearby county of Lude. Kou En agreed to bring Su 400,000 cash after selling the fish. In return, Su agreed to pay Kou En one ox and twenty-seven bushels of grain, in advance, for the service. Su paid Kou En the full amount in advance, after which Kou En went to the market and sold the fish. When Kou En failed to get the full anticipated price for the fish, he sold the ox as a way of making up the difference. But even after selling the ox, Kou En only managed to bring back a total of 320,000 cash, which he delivered to Su's wife. Kou En subsequently purchased various goods whose combined value was 24,600 cash. Kou gave these to Su's wife, which still left him 55,400 cash short. Kou En ordered his son to catch fish for Su for a hundred days without wages in lieu of the outstanding debt

寇恩事'簡冊檔案的構成, *Lishi yuyan yanjiusuo jikan* 歷史語言研究所集刊 70, no. 3 (1999): 559–588.

34 In the report, the five statutes were referred to by their conventional abbreviations. Therefore, the details of the statutes are unknown. My translation of these abbreviations follows Hulsewé, "A Lawsuit of A.D. 28," 24–25 (slightly modified).

of 55,400 cash. In response to Su's charges, Kou En claimed that he had in fact delivered to Su the full amount of his obligation.

On February 12, AD 28, bailiff Gong summoned and questioned Kou En for a second time. The same procedures were followed, and Kou En gave the same statement.

On February 15 AD 28, the bailiff reported the result of his inquiry to the county court. The bailiff believed that Kou En had no liability.

On February 24, AD 28, the county court of Juyan forwarded Su's testimony to the company commander of Jiaqu, where Su served. [It is worth noting that the text is corrupt here.]

Unexpectedly, Su was condemned by the county court for violating laws prohibiting "dishonesty in the administration." Since the remainder of the text is lost, we do not know what punishment, if any, Su received.

In his commentary on the text, which he faithfully translated, Hulsewé raised the core question being examined in this book when he asked:

> Was it a civil suit or a criminal one? Or were cases, which in our society would be considered civil suits, inevitably drawn into the criminal sphere? Hence, was a claim automatically transformed into an accusation?[35]

While this was a rare occasion that a great scholar pondered the possibility of there being an apparatus of civil laws in early China, the distinction between civil and criminal jurisprudence and procedures was as yet impossible to make due to the lack of relevant evidence in 1979. Even so, certain aspects of the case stand out. Especially noteworthy is the seemingly well-defined procedure followed by all parties involved, including all the officials with jurisdiction over the case. The plaintiff Su submitted his complaint to the county court, but it was appropriately handed over to the lower-ranking bailiff. This was because suits of this nature were supposed to go to the bailiff first. The bailiff held hearings for Kou En at intervals of thirteen days in order to test the consistency of Kou En's statements, all of which suggests the prudence and refined methods for establishing the reliability of testimony. Each time, before questioning Kou En, the bailiff explained the relevant statutes, a practice that very closely echoes modern notions of due process. This practice of enumerating and explaining pertinent statutes to the parties in contention is mentioned frequently in Juyan strips. For example, Juyan new strip no. E.P.T. 52.417 states:

35 Hulsewé, "A Lawsuit of A.D. 28," 29.

> [The judge] informs [the defendant] of statutes concerning false testimony in advance, then questions the defendant.[36]
>
> 先以證不請律辨告, 乃驗問.

From *ZJS* strip (*Statutes*) no.110, we know that this procedural step was mandated by Han laws:

> The official must carefully inform the accused party or the witness [of pertinent statutes] in advance [of his giving testimony].[37]
>
> 吏謹先以辨. 告證.

These procedural safeguards, seemingly designed to both elicit truthful testimony and protect all parties from the consequences of giving false statements and making false accusations, point to the sophistication of the Han legal system. The fact that the procedure included detailed written reports, signed and dated by lower officials and forwarded to higher authorities, only underscores the point. One of the more surprising aspects of this case is that Kou En, a civilian commoner, and Su, a military officer, were treated as equal parties; Su was granted no special privileges in deference to his rank and status. The other striking feature of the case is its efficiency: from the first hearing to sentencing, only twenty-six days passed.

Upon a closer reading of the text, two intriguing questions arise. First, how is it that Su, as a plaintiff, ended up being the one convicted?[38] Kou En was found not liable, but Su was condemned on the basis of "dishonesty in administration" (*zheng bu zhi* 政不直). Second, was the nature of the case criminal or "civil"? Because the document is corrupt, we cannot be sure of the specific offense with which the county court charged Su. We might suspect it was a matter of Su making a false claim of debt. However, since the statute referred

36 *JYX* strip no. E.P.T. 52.417, p. 256. In this context, *Qing* 請 should be taken as a loan word for *qing* 情. This aspect occurs quite often in Qin and Han strips. *Buqing* 不請 (情) literally means "not the real situation"; hence I translate the phrase as "false testimony."

37 This is in the context of offering testimony.

38 In modern Western courts, a failed complaint will typically leave the complaining party with empty hands, or subject to court costs at most. False accusations would be adjudicated separately or in a counter-suit. There is no indication in the text that Kou En officially complained against Su. The charges against Su were leveled by an official at the county level.

to is titled "dishonesty in the administration," which implies some sort of institutionalized power in performing official duties, Su's false claim of debt should not have been the basis for the charge. Kou En, as a civilian, was not under the military administration of Su. We can reasonably assume that Su and Kou En's relationship was based on a contract,[39] and we know that no institutionalized administrative power was involved. Moreover, if the basis for the charge against Su was a false accusation, then the statute referred to should be "if he makes a false accusation he will be punished by reversal," rather than "dishonesty in the administration."[40]

The most likely explanation derives from the way the statutes were abbreviated. The underlying cause of Su's offense was an abuse of administrative power. We can therefore speculate that there may have been three reasons for Su's conviction: (1) as a military officer, Su inappropriately engaged in large-scale commercial activities; (2) before hiring Kou En, Su attempted to get two of his subordinates to sell fish for him at the market; and (3) even though Su's subordinates did not perform the task, they did provide the funds to hire a substitute. We can justly infer that using subordinates for commercial purposes was against the rules for military officers. A comparable case from Juyan throws some light on this question. The following depicts a military officer who prevailed upon soldiers in his command to sell goats or sheep on his behalf:

> [1 BC] Xian, who is the deputy commandant of the Juyan, Zhangye commandery, informs the *zhanghou* (commander) of Jiaqu company, saying: Officer in command of a platoon Yang Bao had his soldiers sell goats (or sheep) for his private gain for one day. *Buli* (officer?) Gu Gui[41] was absent for forty-five whole days. And Zhang Tan, who is an officer in command of a section, is not capable. Please [missing one character] remove them from their posts.

---

39 Whether the contract was oral or written is not clear in the text.

40 We can further argue that, if that was indeed the case, paying Kou En the claimed debt would constitute punishment. It would be very odd to base that punishment on "dishonesty in administration."

41 I am not confident about how to render the phrase *buli gugui* 部吏故貴. However, as two other people (Zhang Tan and Yang Bao) are both initially identified by their official titles followed by their full names, I assume *buli* here is also an official title, and Gu Gui is a full name.

> [元壽二年] 張掖居延都尉博庫守丞賢兼行丞事謂甲渠鄣候言：候長楊褒私使卒並積一日賣羊，部吏故貴（四十）五不日跡一日以上，隧長張譚毋狀,[42] 請□免.

To understand this case, we first need to briefly review the organization of the military on the northwestern frontier at that time. According to Professor Michael Loewe, there were four levels of military organization: commandant headquarters (*duweifu*); companies (*houguan*); platoons (*hou*); and sections (*sui*).[43] A commandant controlled perhaps four companies. Each company consisted of several platoons. Each platoon consisted of several sections. See Table 1 and Figure 1 for the details.

TABLE 1 Officers[a]

Level of organization	*Duweifu* 都尉府	*Houguan* 候官	*Hou* 候	*Sui* 隧
Commanding officer	*Duwei* 都尉	*Hou* 候	*Houzhang* 候長	*Suizhang* 隧長
Deputy commanders	*Cheng* 丞 *Wei* 尉 (*Chengwei* 丞尉)	*Wei* 尉 (*Saiwei* 塞尉)		
Other military officers	*Sima* 司馬 *Qianren* 千人 *Bairen* 百人	*Shili* 士吏		
Civil officials	*Yuan* 掾 *Caoshi* 曹史 *Zushi* 卒史 *Shu* 屬 *Shuzuo* 書佐	*Lingshi* 令史 *Weishi* 尉史	*Houshi* 候史	

a Ibid., 387.

42 According to Xu Shihong 徐世虹, "*wuzhuang*" 毋狀 is a generic term, meaning "not capable" or "without achievements." See Xu Shihong, "Juyan Hanjian zhong de 'wuzhuang' yu 'zhuangci' 居延漢簡中的 '毋狀' 與 '狀辭,'" *Chutu wenxian yanjiu* 出土文獻研究 4 (1998): 52–56.

43 Michael Loewe, *Records of Han Administration* (Cambridge: Cambridge University Press, 1967) [hereafter, *RHA*], vol. 1, 384.

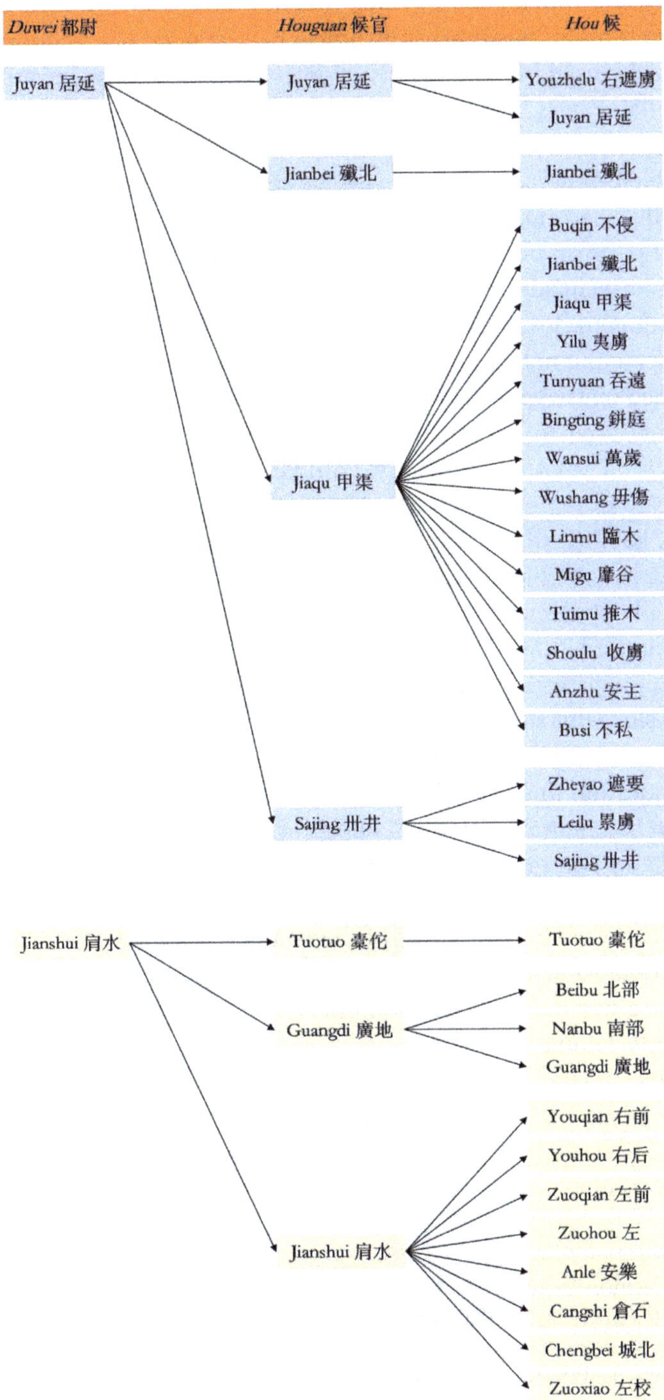

FIGURE 1
Major units in the northwestern frontier
Note: Ibid., 385–386.

With this military structure in mind, we find that in the 1 BC case above, the removal of Yang Bao from his position as the officer in command of a platoon was sought because he used his soldiers to sell livestock for his own private gain. Su's case parallels Yang's in that it involved a military officer attempting to use subordinates for private profit. However, Su's case differs from Yang's in two marked ways. First, Yang's case did not involve claims for debt or matters involving debt liability. Second, Yang's case did not involve payments of subordinates to a third party. In both cases, the military officers were criminally charged with "dishonesty in administration".

Having clarified the puzzle concerning Su's military status and obligations, we can now investigate the nature of the case brought by Su against Kou En. There were really two matters involved: Kou En's liability for a debt, and Su's misconduct in attempting to use his subordinates for private profits and accepting their money. The latter was clearly criminal, and Su was charged for his crime, "dishonesty in the administration", by the county court. However, regarding Kou En's liability, the nature of this matter is not very clear. It is worth noting that it was the bailiff Gong, not the county court, who decided that Kou En was not liable for any debt owed to Su. Gong merely reported the disposition of the matter to the county court. This contrasts with how Su was sentenced, suggesting a distinction in jurisdiction that we will discuss in detail in Part 2. Moreover, since this suit was about debt, and since Kou En was found not liable, we can assume the case was not criminal.[44]

We can further question this "civil" hypothesis by asking what would have happened if Kou En had in fact been found liable for the debt claimed by Su. If he was punished as a criminal, then the matter was clearly dealt with as a criminal case by the authorities. The information in the document provides us with no solid proof to determine the nature of the matter concerning Kou En's liability. If he was found liable for the debt, and if criminal punishments were applied, then the case was indeed a criminal one, despite being lodged for a "civil" cause – an unpaid debt.

Therefore, to determine the nature of the matter concerning Kou En's liability, we need to compare what happened under other similar circumstances. If under similar situations the defendant was found liable and compensation was ordered but no criminal punishments were imposed, then we know that

44 We should not be hasty in deciding if this is a civil case, because the existence of civil laws is the main issue to be demonstrated in this chapter. By contrast, we can readily identify a case as criminal, because criminal cases are well-studied. Thus, if the case was different from what we know about criminal cases, then the case should be considered to be "civil" at the minimum, leaving the matter of what specific kind of a "civil" case for later.

the defendant who lost was not treated as a criminal. In addition, we need to be aware that Han laws might have changed over time. To make a fruitful comparison, the cases ideally should have taken place roughly in the same time period as that of Kou En's case to reduce the risk of overlooking potential changes in the legal system. To that end, let us examine another case, also from Juyan, concerning debt: that of Zhang Zong 張宗 vs. Zhao Xuan 趙宣.

2.2 *Zhang Zong* 張宗 *vs. Zhao Xuan* 趙宣

In this case, unlike Kou En, the defendant Zhao Xuan was found liable for the debt claimed by Zhang Zong. Zhao Xuan was required to repay the debt, but no criminal charges were brought, and no other punishments were imposed. The report says:

> Zhang Zong, a male from Dachang ward, demands debt for a horse from Zhao Xuan, who serves as an officer in command at the Shoulu section, Jiaqu company, Juyan. The total debt is 4,920 cash. Summon Xuan to the office [missing one character] and inform [missing one character] [him] of the statutes [concerning]: first, being intentionally untruthful in matters of money and goods; second, [cases in which] the illegally obtained profit is 250 cash or more [missing six characters]. Mr. Zhao was once a section head at the Shoulu section. Officer Zhang Yu was in the same camp. During the first month of the second year in the Yongshi period (15 BC), Zhang Yu was ill, and his younger brother Zhang Zong rode a mare (*yi pin hu ma*) to visit Yu. [Soon] Zhang Yu died.[45] On a certain day in the same month, Zhang Zong discovered wild camels outside the pass ... [Zhao Xuan] rode Zhang Zong's horse to go out of the pass to chase the camel. He went about thirty *li*, captured a camel, and then returned. Before Zhao Xuan came back to the section, the horse suddenly died.
>
> Zhao Xuan gave the dead horse and camel to Zhang Zong, but Zhang Zong refused to accept them. Zhao Xuan told Zhang Zong: "You forced me to ride your horse and it unfortunately died, so I will not compensate you for the horse" ... *gongping* [the meaning of the phrase is unclear]. The value of the horse of Zhang Zong was 7,000 cash. [The authority] ordered Zhao Xuan to compensate Zhang Zong. Zhao Xuan paid Zhang Zong 1,600 cash right away. In the fourth month, the third year of the

45 The phrase "*Yi pin hu ma*" 驛牝胡馬 is hard to render. *Yi* means post, *pin* means female, and *huma* means horses from the northern steppe. It seems that this particular horse was a female horse that originated from the northern steppe and was put into service at a specific post.

Yongshi period [16 BC], Zhang Zong asked Shou Ziyuan, who was an officer (*gongcao*) in the Jianshu commandant headquarters (*duweifu*), to demand the debt from Zhao Xuan. Shou Ziyuan obtained money from His Honor Yang, who was the commander of Jiaqu company at that time [i.e., Yang was the immediate supervisor of Zhao Xuan]. In the second month of the third year (corrupted and lost here).[46]

▨書曰: 大昌里男子張宗責居延甲渠收虜隧長趙宣馬錢凡四千九百二十, 將告宣詣官, □以□財物故不實臧二百五十以上□已□□□□□□辟▨. 趙氏故為收虜隧長, 屬士吏張禹宣與禹同治. 迺永始二年正月中, 禹病, 禹弟宗自將驛牝胡馬一匹來視禹. □死. 其月不害日, 宗見塞外有野橐佗□□□□▨宗馬出塞逐橐佗, 行可卅餘里, 得橐佗一匹. 還未到□. 宗馬萃僵死. 宣以死馬更所得橐佗歸宗, □不肯受. 宣謂宗曰: 強使宣行馬, 幸萃死, 不以償宗馬也. ▨□共平宗馬, 直七千, 令宣償宗. 宣立以□錢千六百付宗. 其三年四月中, 宗使肩水府功曹受子淵[47]責宣. 子淵從故甲渠候楊君取直, 三年二月盡六

We know that the plaintiff Zhang Zong was a civilian commoner, because the account simply identifies him as a "male" (*nanzi* 男子). By contrast, the defendant was identified by his military rank as "the officer in command of a section" (*suizhang* 遂長). Civilian Zhang claimed that military officer Zhao Xuan owed him 4,920 cash. The suit cited above was actually the third action that Zhang Zong brought against Zhao Xuan over compensation for the death of his horse, whose value was estimated at 7,000 cash. Even though the document we possess contains no clear information regarding how this dispute was first brought to the attention of the authorities, we do know that a judge estimated the horse's value at 7,000 cash and ordered Zhao Xuan to compensate Zhang Zong in full for its loss. Thus, we can tell that the case was, at least initially, strictly about compensation.

46 Juyan strip nos. 229.1–229.2, p. 371. See *Juyan Hanjian shiwen hejiao* 居延漢簡釋文合校, eds., Xie Guihua 謝桂華, Li Junming 李均明 and Zhu Guozhao 朱國炤 (Beijing: Wenwu chubanshe, 1987) [hereafter, *JY*].

47 "Shou Ziyuan" 受子淵 is somewhat difficult to render. I think "Shou" is Ziyuan's surname. We know that Ziyuan is a name because the following sentence says that Ziyuan received money from His Honor Yang. I tend to take Shou as his surname because it follows a pattern, i.e., the way this file addresses Zhang Yu, Zhang Zong, and Zhao Xuan. When a figure first occurs, he is identified by his full name and only then is an individual identified by the given name. Thus, I believe that Shou Ziyuan is the full name of Ziyuan, and hence, Shou is his surname.

Certain facts in the case stand out. Zhao Xuan paid 1,600 cash immediately but failed to pay the rest. Zhang Zong waited a year and three months before making his complaint to the authorities. For some unknown reason, Zhang Zong complained to the Jianshui commandant headquarters, not the Juyan commandant headquarters where Zhao Xuan served. Nevertheless, officer Shou Ziyuan at Jianshui forwarded Zhang Zong's complaint to Zhao Xuan's immediate supervisor, the company commander of Jiaqu, His Honor Yang. His Honor Yang garnished Zhao's salary for several months,[48] which perhaps amounted to 480 cash, and delivered it to Zhang Zong through Shou Ziyuan. Indeed, garnishing salaries to settle debts was a common practice, as evidenced by many other similar cases from Juyan. One report states:

> The official [*houguan*, company commander][49] notifies the officer in command of the no. 4 platoon Xu Qing: garrison soldier Zhou Li claims he is owned a debt of [missing characters] hundred by Ji You, who serves as the officer in command of the no. 7 section. The notification arrives. [Xu Qing] should go meet the official, bringing Ji You's salary of three months.[50]
>
> ☒官告第四候長徐卿，鄣卒周利自言：當責第七隧長季由☒百. 記[51]到，持由三月奉錢詣官.

Here, Zhou Li, a garrison soldier, seeks repayment of a debt owed to him by Ji You, the officer in command of the no. 7 section. Zhou first approaches the official in charge of the case, who then enlists the debtor's immediate supervisor to garnish three months of Ji You's salary to pay off the claim.[52]

In the case of Zhang Zong vs. Zhao Xuan, after Zhao's salary was garnished, there was still a shortfall of 4,920 cash. Hence, Zhang Zong took this third action to demand repayment of the rest of the debt. Because the document

48 The text is not clear on how many months' worth of salary was garnished.

49 According to Li Junming, "*guan*" here refers to "*houguan*" 侯官. See Li Junming 李均明, *Qin Han jiandu wenshu fenlei jijie* 秦漢簡牘文書分類輯解 (Beijing: Wenwu chubanshe, 2009), 111; cf. Shen Gang 沈剛, *Juyan Han jian ciyu huishi* 居延漢簡語詞彙釋 (Beijing: Kexue chubanshe, 2008), 155.

50 *JY* strip no. 285.12, pp. 480–481.

51 Based on the context, *ji* 記 is likely a type of official notification. As our evidence shows, in the Juyan strips, there are *zhaji* 劄記 (letters), *shiji* 市記 (market records), and *fuji* 府記 (a type of document from the commandant headquarters). See Shen Gang, *Juyan Han jian ciyu huishi*, 54, 68, 147.

52 In addition, we can find the same practice in the following: *JY* strip nos. 282.9a–b, p. 472; *JY* strip nos. 213.41a–b, p. 333; *JYX* strip nos. E.P.T. 51.225a–b, p. 192; and *JYX* strip nos. E.P.T. 52.88a–b, p. 233.

is corrupt, we do not know the result of this third suit. However, that does not prevent us from noticing three important phenomena:

First, the case discussed above employed basically the same procedure followed in the case of Kou En vs. Su Jun: the defendant was first informed of the pertinent statutes[53] and only then was a hearing held to establish the facts. In the first two actions taken by the plaintiff, the defendant was never convicted as a criminal for debt; he was simply ordered to compensate the plaintiff.

Second, the defendant somewhat successfully delayed payment, forcing the plaintiff to repeatedly complain to the authorities to request repayment of the debt. It is also important that the defendant did not go to jail.

Third, the defendant's service at the military post was not affected by the judgment. He still served in Jiaqu company as a section head, which explains why the defendant's immediate supervisor could garnish the defendant's salary to compensate the plaintiff in the second suit.

These features illustrate the ways in which, in suits of this nature, the authorities might help a plaintiff extract compensation from an unwilling defendant. They also show that it was up to the plaintiff to decide if he or she would pursue legal action. Thus, even if the plaintiff won the initial case, if the defendant proved reluctant to pay, he had to repeatedly ask the authorities to help him collect the debt. By contrast, we know of no cases in which the victim of a crime needed to ask the authorities to carry out the sentence imposed by the court against the convicted. The victim had no "right" to request the execution of the case, even though he had the "right" to bring the case to the authorities. The state would punish the convicted person as it saw fit.

One element of the case is still unclear: who actually "owned" the horse? Did Zhang privately own the horse, or did he borrow the horse from a post (*yi* 驛). We know that not all horses in the posts belonged to the state. It was not uncommon for a post to rent horses from Han subjects. For example, we have the record: "on the right column, a private horse is registered" (*you sima yipi* 右私馬一匹).[54] Thus, without the modifier *gong* 公 (official) vs. *si* 私 (private), we cannot determine the ownership of "Zhang's" horse. If the horse indeed belonged to the post, then Zhang would have to compensate the post for the death of the horse. According to ZJS strip (*Statutes*) nos. 433–434, if someone damaged official property, that person was required to compensate at fair value for the damage, but the person faced no criminal punishments

53 Coincidentally or not, these are very similar to the five statutes in the case of Kou En vs. Su Jun.

54 JY strip no. 19.1, p. 29.

or even fines.[55] Therefore if the horse indeed belonged to the state, this case then actually involved a chain of compensation: Zhang Zong compensated the post while Zhao Xuan compensated Zhang Zong. Our evidence does not mention if Zhang Zong compensated the state or not. Given the lack of evidence, we still do not know if the horse indeed belonged to Zhang Zong. However, the ultimate ownership of the horse was irrelevant to the nature of the case, because Zhang was responsible for the horse at the time and he was not on official duties. Thus, the dispute was between Zhang and Zhao Xuan, not the state vs. an individual. Moreover, even if the horse belonged to the state, as just mentioned, damaging official property was not treated as a crime, only compensation was required, and no criminal punishments or fines were to be imposed. In short, we find that the authorities held no public interest in the case of Zhang Zong vs. Zhao Xuan on the basis of its outcome and process. Only compensation was ordered, no criminal punishments were imposed on the losing party, and it was up to the successful plaintiff to pursue the accrued compensation.

With what we have learned from this case, we now can determine the nature of Kou En's case concerning debt. Since Kou En's case was very similar to the case of Zhang Zong vs. Zhao Xuan, it is reasonable to believe that even if Kou En was found liable, he would have just been ordered to repay his debt, and no criminal punishments would be imposed. Therefore, Kou En's case concerning debt was "civil". What makes this conclusion more likely is that the two cases took place roughly during the same time period; 15 BC for the case of Zhang Zong vs. Zhao Xuan, AD 28 for Kou En's case, reducing the risk of overlooking potential changes in legal practice over time. Thus, we have resolved Hulsewé's puzzle. The case he studied in 1979 was a combined case. The plaintiff Su's debt dispute with Kou En itself was "civil". However, Su committed a crime prior to hiring Kou En: Su abused his power in asking his subordinates to make profits for him and took their money when they could not do so. This crime was coincidentally discovered when the judge investigated the debt dispute.

2.3 *A Compensation Case regarding a Dead Horse*

Almost simultaneous with Kou En's case, a lawsuit regarding the compensation of a dead horse took place in Juyan (hereafter, Dead Horse Case). This case interestingly combined the features of the Kou En case and Zhao Xuan case studied above. This case report consists of 16 strips. The first strip contains two lines on the upper column whereas the lower column is left in blank. It states:

55 I will discuss the statutes in detail later.

> [The officer of the] Jiaqu platoon states: Yong was performing his official duty to send an alarm announcement. The foal was kept in the platoon and died. Yong was not liable for the dead foal.[56]
>
> 甲渠言,永以縣官事行警檄,牢駒隧內中.駒死,永不當負駒.

These words must be the abstract of the investigation and verdict, and were attached to the report to close the case file. The remaining 15 strips are the main content of the file, which could be divided into four parts:

The first part indicates the date and the identity of the official who conducted the investigation. It says:

> In the *dingsi* day, the 12th month, which was *guichou*, the 3rd year of Jianwu period, the officer of the Jiaqu platoon bowed his head as if deserved the death penalty and dared to state.[57]
>
> 建武三年十二月癸丑丁巳, 甲渠鄣候獲叩頭死罪敢言之.

The second part recounts the content of the complaint forwarded by the headquarters: deputy head Fang 放 sued Jiao Yong 焦永 who was the head of the Zhihai 止害 section for the liability of a dead horse, which Fang borrowed from another person. Fang provided the information of two witnesses – Xian 憲 and Gong 恭. The headquarters forwarded the case down to the Jiaqu platoon to investigate.

The third part is the investigation conducted by the Jiaqu platoon. The officer interrogated Fang and the two witnesses. The three people were consistent in their statements. They all claimed that Jiao Yong was on an official errand to the Shouxiang 收降 pavilion of Juyan, and the deputy head Fang borrowed the horse of Jiao Yong. In exchange, Fang lent the horse that he borrowed from a friend and its foal to Jiao Yong. Then they traveled to the Tunbei 吞北 section together. There, Fang kept the horse he borrowed from Jiao Yong at the stable and rode a horse that belonged to the Tunbei section to travel to other places. Meanwhile, Jiao Yong needed to conduct his official duty but was not able to find his horse. So, he rode the horse which Fang lent to him together with the foal for the errand, and the foal died later on.

The last part is the conclusion of the investigation, saying:

---

56 *JYX* strip no. E.P.F. 22: 186, p. 489.

57 *JYX* strip no. E.P.F. 22: 187, p. 490.

Investigation: Yong was performing his official duty of sending an alarm announcement. He was afraid of being late, so he rode the horse of Fang to send the announcement. The foal was fatigued and died. Fang never gave the corpse of the foal to Yong, and Yong was not liable for the death of the foal. Fang borrowed the official horse without authorization. This offence shall be punished according to the law concerning the illegal profit of theft. Please apply the law to punish him. Huo failed to teach Fang and shall be burdened with collective responsibility. I dare to report this, bowing my head as if deserving of the death penalty.[58]

案：永以縣官事行警檄，恐負時，騎放馬行檄，駒素疲勞，病死；放又不以死駒付永，永不當負駒．放以縣官馬擅自假借，坐贓為盜．請行法；獲教敕要領放毋狀，當並坐．叩頭死罪死罪，敢言之．

The conclusion of the case deserves our attention. Professor Xu Shihong believed that the conclusion contains two judgments: one is about the civil liability of Jiao Yong – Jiao Yong was not liable for the dead foal. The other one is about the crime of Fang, who shall be punished according to the law concerning the illegal profit of theft.[59] However, why doesn't the first strip, which serves as an abstract, mention the judgment for the crime of Fang? It only mentions the judgment regarding Jiao Yong's liability. The strip contains a large blank, so obviously, the omission was not due to a lack of space, but lack of significance. The criminal matter was not the major point of the conclusion. Moreover, the language used, "please apply the law to punish him" (*qing xing fa* 請行法), sounds like a suggestion instead of a decision. Thus, I believe the conclusion does not contain two judgments. Instead, it contains a judgment regarding civil liability and a suggestion regarding criminal matters.[60] The judge perhaps only had the authority to pass judgment of civil matters such as

58 *JYX* strip nos. E.P.F. 22:199–201, pp. 490–491.

59 Xu Shihong 徐世虹, "Handai minshi susong chengxu kaoshu" 漢代民事訴訟程式考述, *Zhengfa luntan* 政法論壇 no. 6 (2001): 122–130.

60 This case file only contains the statement of the complainant and two witnesses but does not have the statement of the defendant. It appears that the judge decided without even inquiring the defendant. Momiyama suspects that the excavated material about the statement only represents half of the original case file, with the other half being lost. I disagree. I believe that, in the eyes of the judge, the statements of the complainant and the two witnesses were ironically sufficient to prove the innocence of the defendant. Hence, the defendant need not be investigated. Obviously, the grievant was not aware that the problem regarding his complaint was due to his own misconduct, and he was not aware that he committed a crime when he rode an official horse without authorization. This development of the case is quite similar to the Kou En case.

liability but had no authority to judge criminal matters. The main point of the lawsuit here is a civil matter concerning compensation.

This case shares three features in common with the Kou En case: (1) They both are civil and criminal combined cases, while civil matter was the main focus. When the authorities investigated the civil liability, the criminal deeds of the disputants were coincidentally discovered. (2) They both demonstrate that the authorities treated civil matters differently from criminal matters: to the former, the authorities only passed judgment on liability without applying penalties, but to the latter, the authorities applied penalties to deal with. (3) In both cases, the party that initiated the lawsuit had higher social status but lost the case. This shows that the law treated the parties involved as equal parties, and the party with higher social status did not enjoy privileges. In addition, this case also has similarities with the Zhao Xuan case: They both were about the liability over a dead horse. This finding shows that this type of dispute was quite common in the area and was often solved by legal means. Therefore, this case confirms the patterns we discovered from the Kou En case and the Zhao Xuan case.

2.4 *Expanded Investigation*

Departing from the above study, we can further argue that in general, all cases that only involved debt and compensation were deemed "civil". By my count, the Juyan strips alone identify fifty-three cases involving debt.[61] Among them is a concise report from Juyan:[62]

> [A certain plaintiff] complained to the authorities to demand a debt of 120 cash from a *shili* (officer) named Sun Meng for oil. [A certain official] carefully questioned *shili* Sun Meng. He admitted the debt. Now [the plaintiff] has already received 120 cash from Sun Meng.[63]
>
> ☑自言:責士吏孫猛脂錢百廿.謹驗問,士吏孫猛辭服負.已收得猛錢百廿.

The report seems not to be a case document, but merely a summary intended to illustrate the unidentified judge's performance.[64] Despite the document's lack of detail, the development of the case is clearly outlined. A plaintiff sued

61 See Appendix 1 for the survey.

62 Alternatively, the fragmentary report is simply a summary of a case document.

63 *JYX* strip no. E.P.T. 52.21, pp. 228–229.

64 This aspect is perhaps related to the Han merit system. For a review of the system, see Gao Heng 高恆, "Handai shangji zhidu kao" 漢代上計制度考, in *Qin Han jiandu zhong fazhi wenshu jikao* 秦漢簡牘中法制文書輯考 (Beijing: Shehui kexue wenxian chubanshe,

the defendant Sun Meng over a debt. During the hearing, the defendant admitted his debt and the authority ordered him to make compensation; no criminal punishment was indicated.

Due to the fragmentary nature of our sources, we are not certain about the final dispositions of many cases, but in cases that do note final dispositions, no criminal punishments for liability of debt have been found to date. Thus, we can tentatively conclude that cases concerning debt were treated as "civil" matters by the authorities.

At this point, we should have noticed one striking feature of these cases concerning "civil" matters concerning debt: the parties, regardless of their social status, were treated as equals. In the case of Kou En vs. Su Jun, in which a military officer sued a commoner over debt, we saw that the officer enjoyed no special privileges. In the case of Zhang Zong vs. Zhao Xuan, we saw that a commoner could, without prejudice, successfully sue a military officer. In fact, even a convict could sue a military officer for debt as the case of Wang Jin vs. Dongmen Fu from Juyan illustrates:

> A claim was lodged by convict Wang Jin for money due from Dongmen Fu, the officer in command of the Chengbei platoon; the claim was not admitted. [We] forward the despatch of his personally formal statement for the meeting on the tenth day of the month; one item, one sealed document. Sealed by *weishi* Tong Zou, on *guihai*, the fourth month.[65]
>
> 徒王禁責誠北侯長東門輔錢. 不服. 移自証爰書, 會月十日. 一事一封. 四月癸亥尉史同奏封.

In this matter, a convict named Wang Jin sued a military officer Dongmen Fu to demand repayment of a debt. The officer was required to respond to the suit and attend the hearing, even though he contested the claim. This sharply contrasts with what happened in criminal cases. For example, ZJS strip (*Statutes*) no. 134 states that those who were in jail or convicted and serving their sentences as male well-builders (*chengdan* 城旦), female grain-pounders (*chong* 舂), male gatherers of firewood for spirits (*guixin* 鬼薪), or female sifters of white rice (*baicui* 白粲) had no "rights" to accuse people of crimes.

2003), 320–340; cf. Michael Loewe, *The Men Who Governed Han China* (Leiden and Boston: E.J. Brill, 2004), 71–74.

65 JY strip no. 259.1, p. 249; cf. RHA, vol. 2, 11. My translation follows Loewe (slightly modified).

> Never take cases brought forward by these people. Those who are less than ten years old, those who are in the jails, or those who are convicted as male wall-builders, female grain-pounders, male gatherers of firewood for spirits or female sifters of white rice.[66]
>
> 年未盈十歲及毄（繫）者，城旦舂、鬼薪白粲告人，皆勿聽.

From the cases thus far examined, we know that one's status did not pose an obstacle for seeking redress from authorities in claims of debt, and that the outcome of these cases did not depend on the status of either party.[67] This feature contrasts sharply with criminal cases in which certain categories of convicts, due to their criminal status, were prohibited from making criminal accusations. We also see that the social status of the convicts in the system of orders of honor[68] was an important factor in criminal laws in determining the punishment for the convicted in two senses.

---

66 ZJS strip (*Statutes*) no. 134, p. 27. This aspect also represents a contrast between civil and criminal procedures. The criteria used to determine whether to take on a civil case differed from those concerning criminal cases. I will discuss this issue in the next section.

67 In addition, gender was not a problem. Women could also initiate suits concerning debts against military officers. For instance, *JYX* strip no. E.P.T. 52.201 records a group of women collectively suing two officers over debts (Wang En and others vs. Xu Guang and Wang Gen): "Female Wang En and others (females?) demanded debts of 440 cash and 5 *shi* of millet from *houshi* [assistant officer to the company head] Xu Guang and section head Wang Gen ..." (女子王恩等責候史徐光, 隧長王根, 錢四百四十, 粟五石 ...). Gender was also not an issue in criminal cases because women could make criminal accusations. While this is not a point of contrast, it is still worth noting.

68 There were 20 degrees of ranks in Qin and Han: from *chehou* 徹侯 (marquis, the highest) to *gongshi* 公士 (the lowest). These 20 degrees of ranks have been well-studied. For the classic work on the subject, see Nishijima Sadao's 西嶋定生, *Chūgoku kodai teikoku no keisei to kōzō: Nijittō shakusei no kenkyū* 中國古代帝國の形成と構造: 二十等爵制の研究 (Tōkyō: Tōkyō daigaku shuppankai, 1961). Nishijima argued that the orders of honor during the Han dynasty were not ranks of nobility because the ranks were not only granted to the nobles, but also generally extended to the commoners. Nishijima classified the ranks into two categories: (1) ranks for ordinary people (ranks below *wudafu* 五大夫) and (2) ranks for officials with salaries above 600 *shi* (ranks above *wudafu*). Nishijima also emphasized that having orders of honor was fairly common to people in the Han dynasty, as there were many channels for them to acquire and increase their orders of honor. For instance, people who had military honors or who donated grain to the state could be rewarded with orders of honor. Furthermore, people who were forced to emigrate from their native place to other places could be compensated with orders of honor. The emperor also often granted orders of honor to all his adult male subjects to celebrate certain ceremonials of the royal family, such as the accession of an emperor, heir, or empress.

First, for most crimes, one could use their rank to redeem or reduce the punishment.[69] As Hulsewé points out:

> The practice of redemption is closely connected with the practice of taking away noble rank (orders of honor) from a holder of such rank, either partly or wholly, in lieu of other punishment, and also with the practice of affording commoners the opportunity to buy noble rank with the express purpose of using the rank to redeem punishment.[70]

Second, for punishments of mutilation or hard labor service, people of rank two and above, their wives, and a certain group of relatives of the imperial clan enjoyed the privilege of having their punishments automatically reduced by one degree. In this situation, without losing their ranks, their punishments could be less severe than those inflicted on people of lower ranks convicted of the same crime. As ZJS strip (*Statutes*) no. 82 makes clear:

> When a person who has the rank of *shangzao* (rank 2) or above, the wife of a person at that rank, or a grandson or grand-grandson of the imperial clan, commits a crime, if he or she needs to be punished with mutilation and condemned to male wall-builders or female grain-pounders, lessen the punishment [of one degree] to *nai* (shaving off the beard and hair on the temples)[71] and make him or her a male gatherer of firewood for spirits or female sifter of white rice.[72]

---

69 See RHL, 214–224.

70 Ibid., 205. For detailed discussions on this matter, see Ibid., 214–222.

71 *Nai* 耐 penalty, according to Hulsewé, means to "shave off the beard," indicating that this penalty only applied to males (RHL, 130). For counter-reference, see Cao Lüning, *Qinlü qintan* 秦律新探 (Beijing: Zhongguo shehui kexu chubanshe, 2002), 222. In my research, I found that females were also subject to this penalty. Therefore, I think Cao Lüning's interpretation is better. He argues that *nai* means "to shave off the beard and hair on the temples." According to this interpretation, for females, the *nai* penalty was to shave off their hair on the temples. I adopted Cao's interpretation. Hence, I consequently render *nai* as "shaving off the beard and hair on the temples."

72 ZJS strip (*Statutes*) no. 82, p. 20. According to Zhu Honglin 朱紅林, *neigongsun* 内公孫 refers to the grandsons of the emperor's clan, whereas *waigongsun* 外公孫 refers to the grandsons of the empress's clan. The word *xing* 刑 has a specific meaning: mutilation. See Zhu Honglin, *Zhangjiashan Han jian Ernian lüling jishi* 張家山漢簡二年律令集釋 (Beijing: Shehui kexue wenxian chubanshe, 2005), 73–74.

However, a puzzling aspect is that the imperial relatives and people who had relatively low ranks were grouped together. Perhaps these so-called grandsons or great-grandsons of the imperial clan refer to very remote relatives of the imperial family. The terms might have meanings that differ from the literal translations of Zhu Honglin.

上造、上造妻以上、及內公孫、外公孫、內公耳玄孫有罪，其當刑及當為城旦舂者，耐以爲鬼薪白粲.

In this examination of cases involving parties of different rank or status, the question arises: why did creditors in positions of power bother to take their claims to court at all? Why, for instance, didn't the powerful military officer Su simply send his soldiers to seize Kou En and demand payment? One reason may be that, according to *ZJS* strip (*Statutes*) no. 187, creditors were prohibited from demanding repayment of debts by force.

> Those who have claims of debts and venture to forcefully extort pledges are to be fined with four *liang* of gold.[73]
>
> 諸有責（債）而敢強質者，罰金四兩.

This statute implies that in disputes over debt, creditors were required to lodge their complaints with the appropriate authorities, in essence, filing a suit. Even before the Zhangjiashan Han statutes became available, we find similar regulations in the Shuihudi Qin strips. *SHD* strip (*Falü wenda*) no. 148 says:

> When the common people have debts, one should not venture unauthorizedly to extort pledges.[74] The unauthorized extortion of pledges, as well as accepting pledges with mutual consent, are both fined with two suits of armor. It is the practice of the court that he who extorts a pledge from another person is sentenced; he who gives the pledge is not sentenced. In the case of accepting a pledge with mutual consent, the person who gives the pledge is [also] sentenced.[75]

According to Hulsewé, male wall-builders (*chengdan* 城旦) and female grain-pounders (*chong* 舂) were the most onerous of the hard labor punishments, whereas male gatherers of firewood for spirits (*guixin* 鬼薪) and female sifters of white rice (*baican* 白粲) were considered less severe. See *RCL*, 14–15.

73 *ZJS* strip (*Statutes*) no. 187, p. 33. This aspect partly blurs the distinction between criminal and civil matters. I have only found one other instance in which a fine is stipulated for a civil matter. In particular, *ZJS* strip (*Statutes*) no. 253 states that if A's livestock eats B's crops, then A will be fined a certain amount of gold in addition to the compensation he/she must make to B. The statute does not mention who receives the payment of the fine; I suspect that the state receives it.

74 *Qianzhi* 強質 (extorting pledges) specifically means to "detain the debtors by force," according to the editors of *SHD*.

75 *SHD* strip (*Falü dawen*) no. 148, pp. 127–128; cf. *RCL*, 162.

百姓有責（債），勿敢擅強質，擅強質及和受質者，皆貲二甲．廷行事強質人者論，鼠（予）者不論；和受質者，鼠（予）者□論．

This prohibition against extorting pledges was deeply rooted in early China, and this prohibition reminds us that the approved method for settling disputed matters of indebtedness was to appeal to a legal system represented by designated authorities.[76]

Since all debts imply an agreement of some sort between parties, these agreements constitute some form of binding contract. This fact raises the necessary question of what form these agreements took in early China. Were these "contracts" written or oral, and did they require witnesses or notaries? In other words, on what basis could a person claim that another person owned him a debt? Hulsewé was aware of the use of contracts in early China when he discussed the use of evidence in trials:

> Written evidence is repeatedly referred to and we hear of the existence of written contracts. In the latter case we have one of the rare exceptions where we are allowed to learn something of the field of civil law; fortunately, some actual contracts have come down to us, due to archaeological finds.[77]

While Hulsewé was aware that Han laws touched upon civil matters, he believed that such legal proceedings were exceptional and limited solely to contracts. Lacking solid evidence to discuss contracts in any detail, Hulsewé simply sidesteps the subject in his *Remnants of Han Law*, despite the fact that the Classics make repeated references to contracts.

The "Qiuguan" 秋官 chapter of *Zhouli* says:

> Whenever there is a debt [dispute], if [the plaintiff] has documentation to prove [the debt], then [the authorities] hear the case.[78]

凡有債者，有判書以治，則聽．

Quoting Zheng Zhong 鄭眾 (d. AD 83), Zheng Xuan comments in this way:

---

76 Of course, creditors could behave irrationally, but this aspect is a different matter.

77 *RHL*, 11.

78 *Zhouli zhushu* 周禮注疏, in *Shi san jing zhu shu* 十三經注疏 (Ruan Yuan 阮元 1815 edition, rpt., Taipei: Yiwen chubanshe, 1976), 35.533.

> Nowadays, when buying something in the market, the parties involved make a contract [make several copies of the contract], and each party keeps one copy. When disputes arise, each of the parties then uses his respective copy to prove his claims.[79]
>
> 今時市買，爲券書以別之，各得其一，訟則按券以正之.

The "Tianguan" 天官 chapter of *Zhouli* says:

> On the basis of the *fubie* [a type of contract], [the authorities] would hear cases concerning *chengzhai* [loans].[80]
>
> 聽稱債以傅別.

In Zheng Xuan's comment on the line, he writes:

> *Chengzhai* refers to loans, and *fubie* refers to contracts. When [the authorities] hear cases concerning debt, they make judgments based on contracts.[81]
>
> 稱債謂貸予，傅別謂券書也．聽訟債者，以券書決之.

Recently excavated materials verify this use of contracts in early China. In the case of Kou En vs. Su Jun, we know that there was a previously agreed upon value of the fish that Kou En took to market. This agreement implies some form of contract, either oral or written. Judging from the subsequent dispute over Kou En's payments to Li, that contract must not have been sufficiently detailed since Kou En apparently believed that he could repay the debt in either cash or goods. Another report from Juyan states:

> One market contract. In advance [inform the defendant of] the statutes concerning intentionally and untruthfully making false testimony in matters of money and goods.[82]
>
> ☒市券一. 先以證財物故不以實.

79 Ibid. Zheng Xuan was a famous legal expert. We will discuss about him in detail in the next chapter.

80 *Zhouli zhushu*, 3.44.

81 Ibid.

82 *JYX* strip no. E.P.T. 51.509, p. 213.

This fragment is obviously part of a judicial document concerning a dispute over a commercial contract. Once more, we observe the legal procedure in operation with the judge informing the defendant of the pertinent statutes. The market contract mentioned in the report was perhaps the proof provided by the plaintiff to defend himself against the charge of making false testimony.

Examples of written contracts from excavated materials are by no means rare. In 1987, archaeologist Lian Shaoming 連邵名 conducted a survey of documents concerning debts and other commercial transactions in Han strips.[83] Eleven of the documents he studied are contractual in nature. According to the account by Li Junming 李均明, seventeen contracts involving the sale of goods have been excavated from Juyan and Dunhuang.[84] For example:

> On the tenth day of the seventh month, Zhang Zhonggong, who is a garrison soldier, purchases a blue singlet made of cotton at the price of 353 cash. Zhang Junzhang, who is a *houshi* [officer], receives the money [of the first installment] and agrees that the rest will be paid by the twelfth month of the year. The witness of the contract is Xie Zifang who is a scribe from Lintong.[85]
>
> 七月十日鄣卒張中功貰買皁布章單衣一領， 直三百五十三. 堠史張君長所錢，約至十二月盡畢已. 旁人臨桐史解子房知券.

In this concise contract, the date and month of the transaction, the items, price, scheduled deadline of payment, and the name of the witness are all noted. Interestingly, the year of the transaction is not indicated, which suggests that the parties assumed that the transaction would be completed within the year. Then again, not designating the year may have simply been an omission.

JY strip no. 262.29 shows a similar example:

83 Lian Shaoming 連邵名, "Hanjian zhong de zhaiwu wenshu ji shimai mingji" 漢簡中的債務文書及貰賣名籍, *Kaogu yu wenwu* 考古與文物 no. 3 (1987): 77–83; cf. Huge T. Scogin, "Between Heaven and Man: Contract and the State in Han Dynasty China," *Southern California Law Review* 63 (1990): 1326–1401.

84 Li Junming 李均明, *Qin Han jiandu wenshu fenlei jijie* 秦漢簡牘文書分類輯解 (Beijing: Wenwu chubanshe, 2009), 436–437. The 17 contracts are as follows: *JY* strip nos. 26.1, 91.1, 163.3, 163.16, 184.3, 262.16, 262.29, 273.12, 557.4, 564.7; *JYX* strip nos. E.P.T. 52.323, E.P.T. 52.460, E.P.T. 57.71, E.P.T. 59.555, E.P.T. 222.419a–b; *DH* strip nos. 1449a–b, strip nos. 1708a–b. "*DH*" stands for *Dunhuang Hanjian shiwen* 敦煌漢簡釋文, eds., Wu Rengxiang 吳礽驤, Li Yongliang 李永良, and Ma Jianhua 馬建華 (Lanzhou: Gansu renmin chubanshe, 1991).

85 *JY* strip no. 262.29, p. 436.

> On *bingwu*, the leap month, in the second year of the Jianzhao period (37 BC), Dong Zifang, who serves as a civil officer at Jiaqu, purchases a fur robe from garrison soldier [missing one character] Wei. The price of the clothing is 750 cash and they agree to make the full payment by spring.[86] The witness is Du Junjuan.[87]
>
> 建昭二年閏月丙戌，甲渠令史董子芳買鄣卒□威裘一領，直七百五十，約至春錢畢已．旁人杜君雋．

While the contract is precisely dated, the spring due-date remains vague, unless the parties and the witness understood this to mean a specific date, either the Start of Spring (February 4th or 5th) or the Spring Equinox (March 21 or 22).[88]

The following contract is much more precise in terms of dates and stipulated responsibilities, as it even stipulates fines for failure to meet the payment deadline.

> On *gengzi* day, seventh month, the first year of the Yuanping period (74 BC), Feng Shi, who is a *qinkouzu*, sold six *tuoluo* to Yang Qing at his place. The parties agree that Yang gives Feng seasonal wheat seven bushels and six pints by the tenth day in the eighth month. If the payment is made after the fifth day of the eight month, [the fine is] one pint of wheat per day.[89]
>
> 元平元年， 七月庚子， 禽寇卒馮時賣橐絡六枚楊卿所， 約至八月十日與時小麥七石六斗．過月十五日，以日斗計．

These three examples suggest that contracts were known to the common people, because the parties to these contracts were definitely not elites. They were ordinary soldiers and very low-ranking officers. The basic formats of these

86 The meaning of *zhichun* 至春 is unclear. Is it one word, which is a synonym of *lichu* 立春 (Start of Spring) that is one of the twenty-four climatic seasons? Or does *zhichun* represent two words, *zhi* (until) and *chun* (Spring)? In the other two contracts, the word *zhi* clearly means "until"; thus, I believe that *zhi* in this contract also means "until". However, there is another possibility: *zhichun* may read *zhi zhichun*, whereas the second *zhi* is dropped either for convenience or by transmission error. In addition, there is one more possibility: *zhichun* may read *zhi chunfen* 至春分 (until the Spring Equinox), with the last word *fen* dropped by mistake. In summary, *chun* may refer to either the Start of Spring (February 4th or 5th) or the Spring Equinox (March 21st or 22nd).

87 *JY* strip no. 26.1, p. 38.

88 Ibid.

89 *DH* strip nos. 1449a, p. 150.

contracts are very similar to contracts in modern societies, another indication of the sophistication of these Han contracts. It is likely that there were statutes concerning commercial contracts, based on a strip from Juyan that contains the following fragmentary information:

> Doing business but not admitting [agreements] in buying or selling, intentionally untruthfully making false testimony in matters of money and goods, having illicit profit over 250 cash[90]
>
> ☒賈而買賣而不言，證財物故不以實，臧二百五☒

As we know from cases previously studied, especially the case of Kou En vs. Su Jun, the phrases "intentionally untruthfully making false testimony in matters of money and goods" and "having illicit profit over 250 cash" were both conventional abbreviations for certain statutes of which the defendant was informed of prior to a hearing; therefore the phrase at the beginning of the strip, "do business but not admitting [agreements] in buying or selling," must also be an abbreviation for a statute dealing with commercial contracts. We unfortunately cannot know the details of the statute.

Despite all the evidence, our understanding of cases concerning "civil" matters is still limited. For example, even though the case of Kou En vs. Su Jun was "civil" and is very valuable in studying "civil" procedures, there is a problem. The statute referred to near the end of the file was not concerned with civil matters, because by then, the case had become a criminal case with Su as the defendant.[91] This hybrid quality reduces the value of the case in defining the nature and form of "civil" suits. Additionally, in the other fragmentary cases discussed above, specific statutes were not cited as the basis for judicial decisions; either there were no pertinent statutes or the references to pertinent statutes were not preserved in the fragments. This phenomenon makes us wonder if these cases were tried by following customs or by relying on written laws. Were there any statutes concerning compensation? Even though customary laws were still laws, as long as they were recognized and enforced by the authorities, the existence of written laws would indicate a much greater sophistication and systematization of the legal regime in terms of dealing with cases concerning "civil" matters. Fortunately, we have a case from Dunhuang

---

90 *JYX* strip no. E.P.T. 54.9, p. 301.

91 Just to remind my readers, this case consists of two separate sub-cases: the liabilities of Kou En and the crimes of Su.

(Shao Zhong's case), in which a statute concerning compensation is clearly referred to.

> Yanlü says: "When livestock [of different owners] kill each other, [the owner of the animal that killed another person's animal] should compensate [the other person] one third of the value of the animal killed." Thus, He (和) ordered Shaozhong to pay 3,000 cash and give back the skeleton of the dead horse to Xun to settle the case.[92]
>
> 言律曰: "畜產相賊殺, 參分償". 和令少仲出錢三千及死馬骨肉付循請平.

We cannot reconstruct the complete case or the procedure used in the trial, because we only have this one strip, which appears out of context. No other relevant strips were found. The strip seems to be a paragraph in the middle of a report. Despite its incomplete nature, we can tell that this is a case about compensation and the judge referred to a specific statute in making his judgment.

We have a technical issue here: how to render the two consecutive words "*yan-lü*"? Is it a title for certain statutes or does the word *yan* simply mean "to state"? If "*yanlü*" is a title, then what does that title mean? That is impossible to tell. Also, "*yanlü*" is never mentioned in any sources regarding Han statutes. I think it is more likely that "*yan*" means "to state." Who is the subject? We can speculate that the subject is He 和 (the judge). Thus, we can reconstruct the case as follows:

1. The two parties involved were Shaozhong 少仲 and Xun 循.
2. The cause for the suit was that Shaozhong's animal killed Xun's horse.
3. The judge was He 和.
4. When making his judgment, the judge referred to a certain statute that says, "When livestock [of different owners] kill each other, [the owner of the animal that killed another person's animal] should compensate [the other person] one third of the value of the animal killed."[93]
5. The judgment is that Shaozhong should pay 3,000 cash and return the skeleton of the dead horse to Xun.

We can tell that in this case, when a person's animal is killed by another person's animal, the restitution is set at one third of the value of the dead animal (plus, apparently, the carcass). Because of the incomplete nature of the document (only one strip is preserved), we cannot determine the details of how the facts

92 *DH* strip no. 2011, p. 215.

93 The statute referred to demonstrates that there were indeed statutes that dealt with civil matters. We will discuss again this point later.

were established or how the judgment was reached. We can reasonably assume, considering the cases studied, that hearings were held, statements were taken, and other details of the trial were carefully documented as well. What is most significant about this case, is that in making his judgment, the judge referred explicitly to the statute "Yanlü." With some confidence, we can therefore assume that judges based their judgments on statutes whenever available.

The case also draws attention to statutes concerning compensation. We notice that sister statutes are found from Zhangjiashan.

ZJS strip (*Statutes*) no.50 says:

> If a dog kills or wounds livestock belonging to another person, the owner of the dog must compensate that person.[94]
>
> 犬殺傷人畜產, 犬主賞 (償) 之.

ZJS strip (*Statutes*) no. 253 says:

> If A's horses, oxen, sheep or pigs eat B's crops, then A will be fined one *liang* of gold per horse or ox. Four female pigs are equivalent to ten sheep, and a male pig is equivalent to an ox. Then order A to compensate B, the owner of the crops.[95]
>
> 馬、牛、羊、　豰彘、彘食人稼穡, 罰主金馬、牛各一兩, 四豰彘若十羊、彘當一牛, 而令撟 (?) 稼償主.

Indeed, prior to the Zhangjiashan excavation, the Qin legal documents from Shuihudi already contained discussions concerning liability under similar situations.

> "A" is small and not fully six feet (tall). He has one horse, which he personally takes to graze. Now the horse is *bai* (frightened)[96] by another person and eats one bushel of another's grain. Question: is he warranted to be sentenced or is he not warranted? He is not warranted to be sentenced nor to repay the grain.[97]

---

94 ZJS strip (*Statutes*) no. 50, p. 15.

95 ZJS strip (*Statutes*) no. 253, p. 43.

96 The word *bai* 敗 usually means "defeat" or "spoil," but the editors suggest that the word means "frighten" in this context.

97 SHD strip (*Falü dawen*) no. 158, p. 130; cf. RCL, 165. Here, 6 *chi* =1.57 meters is used to determine one's "legal" age, i.e., the qualification for enrollment as adults. See Hulsewé's explanation for this practice in RCL, 122, 138,165. My translation follows Hulsewé.

> 甲小未盈六尺，有馬一匹自牧之，今馬為人敗，食人稼一石，問當論不當？不當論及賞（償）稼.

In this case, the defendant would not be held liable and no compensation is required since the owner of the horse is too young, and the damage is ultimately caused by another person, not the defendant.

The statutes mentioned above concern themselves with compensation for damages caused by one's livestock to the property of others. We find that compensation was clearly identified as a "civil" matter; no punishments, such as forced labor service, confinement, mutilation, execution, or even fines were attached.

Even compensation for damages to official property was also deemed a "civil" matter. ZJS strip (*Statutes*) nos. 433–434 state:

> [If someone] loses, kills, or injures official livestock, or if these livestock cannot be recovered … Under all these circumstances, let [the responsible person] compensate for the loss with its fair value. Compensate for [*rusi* and *rushang*][98] with a reduced value. [If someone] ruins or damages official property, order him or her to compensate for the loss with its fair value. Compensate for [*ruhui*] with a reduced value.[99]

> 亡、殺、傷縣官畜產，不可復以爲畜產 … 皆令以平賈（價）償. 入死、傷縣官，賈（價）以減償. 亡、毀、傷縣官器財物，令以平賈（價）償. 入毀[100] 傷縣官，賈（價）以減償.

Here we find that if someone damages official property, that person must compensate the state for the damage at fair value, or even reduced value depending on the circumstances, and the person faces no other punishment. Thus we may conclude that compensation was carefully regulated and recognized as a "civil" matter.

In sum, the available evidence suggests that there were cases concerning "civil" matters and statutes concerning debt, compensation, and possibly

---

98 These two terms, *rusi* 入死and *rushang* 入傷, are difficult to translate. The problem is the modifier *ru*, and I do not know what it precisely means in this context. It appears that *rusi* and *rushang* may refer to actions that caused the death or injury of official livestock under circumstances that were partially forgivable. Thus, I surmise that they refer to the situation that the corpse of the livestock was recovered by officials.

99 ZJS strip (*Statutes*) nos. 433–434, p. 68.

100 *Ruhui* 入毀 also refers to actions that result in the ruin of official property under circumstances partially forgivable. Perhaps, the remains of the property is recovered by officials.

contracts in early China. These cases concerning "civil" matters, accompanied by pertinent statutes, demonstrate the following features, none of which are found in criminal cases:

1. Individuals, not operating on behalf of the state, may bring complaints against one or more persons in such limited matters as compensation and property disbursements.
2. The authorities seek to assess appropriate compensation or the proper disbursement of property for the plaintiff.
3. A case of debt or compensation results in a judgment assigning liability. The authorities may be asked to help the successful plaintiff extract compensation from a recalcitrant defendant, but it is up to the plaintiff to decide if he or she will pursue it.
4. Punishments are seldom applied by the state to the party that is liable. Even if there are punishments, they are limited to fines. They do not entail forced labor service, exile, beating, confinement, mutilation, or execution.
5. Social status is not a factor in assessing liability. The two parties involved in disputes over property are treated as equals by the authorities: a person with a higher rank has no legal privileges beyond those of a person with lower rank. The losing defendant, regardless of his/her rank, is ordered to pay the debt due to the successful plaintiff. In addition, government agencies have no special privileges over individuals in matters of compensation. If someone damages official property, that person is only required to compensate for the damage at fair value.

By contrast, criminal cases have five characteristics that are not found in cases concerning "civil" matters:

1. Individuals may report certain harmful acts to the authorities, acts which the authorities perceive not only as harming the individual, but also as damaging to the public order.
2. According to Hulsewé, the primary goal of the authorities is to preserve public order and protect the innocent by punishing the person who commits the crime in order to deter others from committing the same crime.[101] Beyond that, their larger concern is to maintain cosmic harmony.[102]
3. A criminal case can only result in a conviction or an acquittal. If the defendant is convicted, he must suffer some kind of punishment, such as forced labor service, confinement, mutilation, or execution. It is not up

101 *RHL*, 339, 341.
102 Ibid., 102–109.

to the victim of a crime to decide whether or not the sentence imposed by the court should be carried out. The state prosecutes and punishes the convicted as it sees fit.

4. Punishments are to be systematically applied. There are at least nine categories of punishments as Hulsewé points out in his *Remnants of Han Law*: death penalty, extermination of relatives, boiling and burning, mutilation, castration, hard labor, exile, fines, and exclusion from office.[103]
5. The social status of the convicted in the system of twenty ranks is an important factor for the authorities to consider when determining the punishment for the convicted in two senses: (1) People of certain high ranks could receive less severe punishments than those inflicted on those of lower ranks sentenced for the same crimes. (2) For certain crimes, one can use their rank to redeem or reduce the punishment.

These sharp contrasts show that cases concerning "civil" matters clearly differed from criminal cases. Of course, the few cases concerning "civil" matters concerning compensation and debt studied are not sufficient to establish any sweeping claims. We need to know how frequently cases concerning "civil" matters occurred. The Juyan strips represent a good source for such a study at the level of a local jurisprudence, because more than 30,000 strips were excavated over the course of two excavations (1930's and 1970's).[104] These strips were not explicitly pre-selected and compiled by a single hand for a particular agenda. They were raw archives in nature. Thus, even if there were some selective processes involved, they were relatively free of selective bias.

Before we get into the details, I must admit the shortcomings of my survey and explain the criteria I use to classify the cases collected. Our cases are mostly fragmentary. In most cases, we have only one strip, and no context whatsoever in which to assess the contents. Thus, we often must rely on key words from the fragments to infer the causes and nature of the cases. For instance, the word *ziyan* 自言 means to sue in person. So, if a strip contains this keyword, we can assume that the strip somehow involves a legal case. The word *yuanshu* 爰書 means formal statement, so if a strip contains that word, we can also assume that the strip is connected with a legal case.[105] The word *zhai* 責 means to demand debts, so if the word appears in a strip, we can assume that that strip concerns a debt and that the nature of the case is "civil". We are not sure how most of the cases were tried, and my classification of them is, with only two

103 Ibid., 102–155.

104 See Note 2 in this chapter.

105 For a detailed analysis of these terms, see *RHL*, 73–80; cf. Gao Heng, "Handai susong zhidu lunkao," 409–467.

exceptions, based on their identified causes, not outcomes. As for classifying criminal cases, given that their causes are very straightforward, such as murder and battery, no extra explanation for the classification is needed.

However, it is worth pausing to clarify my classification of "civil" causes for civil actions involving debt, compensation, commercial transaction, salary, and testamentary wills. Since we have seen that disputes over debt or compensation were tried by the authorities as cases concerning "civil" matters, it is reasonable to categorize cases caused by debt or compensation to fall in the category of cases concerning "civil" matters. Disputes concerning commercial transactions or salaries are very similar to disputes of debts and are often related; thus, I attribute these two types of disputes to "civil" causes as well. Last wills and testaments are also a "civil" matter to be discussed later in this book. When using my classification, we need to be aware that it is also possible for "civil" disputes to become criminal (or "mixed") cases if: (1) crimes are uncovered in the course of an investigation; and (2) someone is found to be testifying falsely (see the chart in Appendix 1).

Due to the fragmentary nature of the sources, this survey must be tentative in nature and necessarily limited in precision and comprehensiveness. Nevertheless, such a survey invites us to see the larger picture of civil laws in early China. In total, I have identified 128 judicial cases from about 30,000 Juyan strips. There are thirty-seven criminal cases, seventy-two cases concerning "civil" matters, and nineteen cases whose cause and nature cannot be determined. Clearly, the frequency of cases concerning "civil" matters is much higher than that of criminal cases: almost twice the latter. The exact time span of most of these cases cannot be determined because only twenty cases, "civil" and criminal, can be specifically dated. The rest give us no clue concerning their dates.[106]

The overall distribution of the causes of the 104 cases whose causes are known is: Criminal causes (37 occasions): battery (9 occasions), misconduct (8 occasions), murder (6 occasions), armed fight (3 occasions), unspecified (3 occasions), crossing the pass (2 occasions), arson (1 occasion), stealing (1 occasion), robbery (1 occasion), lost one's tally (1 occasion), illicit profit (1 occasion), and upheaval (1 occasion). For three additional occasions, the cause is unclear, but the sentences comport with criminal proceedings or the judicial action taken had the characteristics of a criminal investigation. "Civil" causes (74 occasions): debts (63 occasions), commercial transactions (5 occasions), compensation

106 This statement does not mean that the rest of the materials were not originally dated. What I mean is that the surviving material provides no clue.

(3 occasions), a real estate dispute (1 occasion), a last will (1 occasion), and a salary dispute (1 occasion).

The three major causes for criminal cases are battery, misconduct, and murder, while the top three causes for cases concerning "civil" matters are debt, commercial transactions, and compensation. However, debt stands out as predominant among all the causes.

From the analysis above, we know that in Juyan, cases concerning "civil" matters occurred much more frequently than criminal cases, and among all the cases, disputes over debt were the predominant cause. Was this phenomenon typical for the Han as a whole? While we cannot answer this with certainty, we can speculate that the extremely high frequency of debt disputes and the high frequency of transaction disputes may have been peculiar to this region. Considering that Juyan was the communication hub of the Silk Road, we can imagine that its residents by and large had some direct or tangential involvement in commercial activities. Records of many cases involving inheritance and land disputes are found in transmitted Han texts that relate to regions other than Juyan.[107] For example, according to the *Hanshu*, the Yingchuan 穎川 commandery, which is in the middle of Han China, was notorious for frequent disputes over household divisions among its residents.[108] A long last will was excavated from Yizheng 儀征, Jiangsu 江蘇, in southeast China.[109] Moreover, as I mentioned in the introduction of this book, the Zhangjiashan strips (Hubei) yield at least three sets of statutes concerning "civil" matters. Therefore, it is reasonable to believe that throughout the Han, that cases concerning "civil" matters were quite common, and "civil" statutes were quite abundant, even though there were probably regional differences in the type and frequency of "civil" matters that occupied the courts.

Now the question is: How do we understand the nature of these cases concerning "civil" matters such as debt, compensation, salary, inheritance, land disputes? How do we understand the nature of the pertinent procedures and statutes? They resemble modern civil litigation in that they were designed – or evolved – as an orderly way for individuals to resolve disputes by providing official remedies for private complaints. However, can we call them civil laws? Are we projecting modern notions derived from the Roman law tradition on

107 In her study of Han civil procedure, Professor Xu Shihong identified 12 civil disputes from the standard histories. See Xu Shihong, "Handai minshi sushong chengxu kaoshu," 122–123. Of course, there are more cases in the transmitted texts than those cited by Xu.

108 *Hanshu* 漢書 (Beijing: Zhonghua shuju, 1982), 28.1654.

109 Chen Ping 陳平 and Wang Qinjin 王勤金, "Yizheng Xupu 101 hao Xihan mu Xianling quanshu chu kao" 儀征胥浦101號西漢墓先令券書初考, *Wenwu* no. 1 (1987): 20–23. I will discuss this document in detail later.

early China? I believe we can, because (1) Zheng Xuan already made a distinction that *song* 訟, when used as a legal term, referred to what we would now call civil cases, in contrast to *yu* 獄, which are criminal cases; and (2) there were institutional differences between *song* and criminal litigation.

3 Concluding Remarks

Our analysis shows that perhaps the root of "civil" litigation could be traced back to the Western Zhou period. Bronze vessel inscriptions document lawsuits over land between high nobles, and the way these disputes were handled seems to be different from the criminal litigation that we know. In the Warring States, we could discern "civil" disputes between commoners from the Baoshan strips for the first time. Nevertheless, until the Qin dynasty, relevant cases were rare and we cannot see a clear picture of it. In the Han dynasty, the situation changed. From the Juyan cases, we can clearly see how cases concerning "civil" matters differed from criminal litigation as we analyzed above. Now, a further question deserves our inquiry: Do the features we observed from cases from Juyan reflect the overall situation of "civil" lawsuits in the Han dynasty?

Kong Qingming 孔慶明 believed that the Juyan cases were exceptional. He argued that scholars never saw civil lawsuits in materials produced in the center of the Han empire, thus pure civil litigation perhaps only existed in the northwestern frontier.[110] However, Zhang Jianguo 張建國 strongly refuted Kong, saying that we cannot assert that a unique legal system was implemented in the remote frontier region based on the lack of evidence from other regions, since the Han was a unified great empire. He asked: if the Juyan records were not excavated, who would have known the existence of civil litigation in the northwestern frontier of the Han dynasty?[111]

In fact, if we pay attention to received literature, we can find traces of civil litigation in the heartland of the Han empire. For instance, in *Fengsu tongyi* 風俗通義 (A General Account of Customs), Han scholar Ying Shao 應劭 (153–196) recounts two cases of disputes over inheritance, one taking place in 60 BC in the Chenliu commandery and the other one taking place in 8 BC in the Pei commandery. This book also recounts a dispute over the ownership of a cloth

110 Kong Qingming 孔慶明, *Qin Han falü shi* 秦漢法律史 (Xi'an: Shaanxi renmin chubanshe, 1992), 319, 383.

111 Zhang Jianguo 張建國, "Juyan xin Hanjian 'Su Jun zhai Kou En' minshi susong ge'an yanjiu" 居延新漢簡粟君債寇恩民事訴訟個案研究, *Zhongwai faxue* 中外法學 no. 5 (1996): 15–21.

taking place in 33 BC in the Linhuai commandery.[112] In addition, a recent excavation in Changsha, Hunan yielded evidence for civil cases in the Eastern Han Changsha commandery. For instance, a case report dated to AD 183 accounts a lawsuit over inheritance, and the two parties reached a compromise.[113] The *Fengsu tongyi* cases and Changsha cases occurred outside of Juyan and the northwestern frontier, but all shared similar features with the Juyan cases regarding the "civil" manner of litigation.

More importantly, we see a more general pattern from our evidence: the cases of debts and compensation we studied were not randomly judged by the judges, but in accordance with the relevant statutes in the *Ernian lüling*. This pattern suggests that features we observed from the Juyan cases were perhaps not a local practice, but were directed by the law of the Han empire. Therefore, they very possibly reflected a more general practice across the Han empire.

How do we understand the nature of the lawsuits and statutes over debt, compensation, salary, inheritance, and real estate? They appear to be analogous to civil justice and served as a formal means for individuals to solve their disputes. Can we actually call them civil law, which was derived from a completely different legal traditional Roman law? I believe we could do so due to two reasons: (1) Zheng Xuan, one of the most influential Han scholars, articulated the conceptual distinction between *song* (disputes over property) and *yu* (disputes over crimes) multiple times, which was analogous to the distinction between civil litigation and criminal litigation we understand today; (2) My study shows that litigation regarding *song* and litigation regarding *yu* were differentiated in institution and procedure in the Han dynasty.

112 Wang Liqi 王利器, *Fengsu tongyi jiaozhu* 風俗通義校注 (Beijing: Zhonghua shuju, 1981), 589.

113 Refer to the following materials: Wang Su 王素, "Changsha Dongpailou Donghan jiandu xuanshi" 長沙東牌樓東漢簡牘選釋, *Wenwu* no. 12 (2005): 69–75, 40; *Changsha Dongpailou Donghan jiandu* 長沙東牌樓東漢簡牘, ed., Changsha shi wenwu kaogu yanjiusuo 長沙市文物考古研究所 (Beijing: Wenwu chubanshe, 2006), 73–74; Ye Yuying 葉玉英, "Donghan Jiandu hecong shu suojian Donghan ruogan zhidu tansuo" 東漢簡牘和從書所見若干制度探索, *Xiamen daxue xuebao* 廈門大學學報 (social sciences version) no. 6 (2009): 100–105, 112.

CHAPTER 2

The Differences between *Yu* and *Song*

While it is true that there was no exact term equivalent to "civil case" in the classical Chinese language, it does not mean that there was no such concept. In fact, in the second century AD, Zheng Xuan's commentaries to the *Zhouli* 周禮 (ca. 400–10 BC) state that *song* 訟, when used as a legal term, referred to what we would now call civil cases, in contrast to *yu* 獄, criminal cases. Specifically, the "Dasitu" 大司徒 section of the "Diguan" 地官 chapter says: "For all the people who do not follow the moral teachings, there are *yu* and *song*. [The officials] hear the *yu* and *song* together with local overseers to decide these cases" (*Fan wan min zhi bu fu jiao, er you yu song zhe, yu you di zhi zhe ting, er duan zhi* 凡萬民之不服教而有獄訟者, 與有地治者聽而斷之).[1] Zheng Xuan comments: "Disputes over crimes are called *yu* while disputes over property are called *song*" (*zheng zui yue yu, zheng cai yue song* 爭罪曰獄, 爭財曰訟).[2] In the "Dasikou" 大司寇 section of the "Qiuguan" 秋官 chapter, Zheng's commentary on the lines about "using two visits to court to prevent *song* among the people" (*yi liang zao jin min song* 以兩造禁民訟) and "using the submission of two plaints to prevent *yu* among the people" (*yi liangji jin min yu* 以兩劑禁民獄),[3] observes that "*Song* means to sue each other over property" (*Song wei yi cai huo xiang gao zhe* 訟謂以財貨相告者), and that "*yu* means to charge another with crimes" (*yu wei xiang gao yi zui ming zhe* 獄謂相告以罪名者).[4] According to Zheng Xuan, there was thus a clear distinction in the legal system between cases involving property and those involving crimes, respectively designated by the categories of *song* and *yu*. In addition, Zheng emphasizes that *song* pertained to civil cases, as seen in his annotation to a line in the "Xiaguan" 夏官 chapter of *Zhouli*, which says, "If there are *song* over horses, [the official] will hear them" (*ruo you ma song ze ting zhi* 若有馬訟則聽之).[5] Zheng then explains, "*Song* [here] refers to people breaking their words in buying and selling [horses]" (*song wei mai mai zhi yan xiang fu* 訟謂賣買之言相負).[6]

1 *Zhouli zhushu*, 10.27.
2 Ibid.
3 Ibid., 10.162.
4 Ibid., 34. 232.
5 Ibid., 30.456.
6 Ibid., 30.204.

 | DOI:10.1163/9789004513907_004

1 Scholarly Debates[7]

Zheng Xuan's interpretations did not win unanimous acceptance. Some scholars supported his view, while others disagreed. Gao You 高誘 (active 205–212) reiterated Zheng Xuan's interpretation in his annotation to the *Lüshi chunqiu* 呂氏春秋 (The Annals of Lü Buwei, comp. 239 BC), when interpreting the line "*jue yu song, bi zheng ping*" 決獄頌, 必正平.[8] Wei Zhao in the 3rd century also followed Zheng Xuan in his annotations to the *Guoyu* 國語 (Accounts of Various States, comp. 4th century BC).[9] However, Qing philologists often disagreed with Zheng. The philologist Huang Sheng 黃生 (b. 1622) bluntly rebuffed Zheng: "The Classics include no clear language saying that cases over property are *song* and cases over crimes *yu*. Zheng is head-strong here when he makes such a claim" (*zheng cai wei song, zheng zui wei yu, jing wu ming wen, Zheng te yi wei zhi shuo* 爭財為訟, 爭罪為獄、經無明文, 鄭特臆為之說).[10] Sun Yirang 孫詒讓 (1848–1908) also disagreed with Zheng in his edition of *Zhouli zhengyi* 周禮正義 (Commentaries to the Rites of Zhou), citing Huang Du 黃度 (1138–1213): "Minor cases are called *song*, while major cases are called *yu*" (*xiao yue song, da yue yu* 小曰訟, 大曰獄).[11] *Yu* and *song* in Huang's view differ only in their degree of severity.

Modern scholars' opinions also diverged. Legal historian Zhang Jianguo 張建國 argued: "What was called *tingsong* 聽訟? If it was not used in a generic sense, *song* was in contrast with *yu* in the Han dynasty." He believed that *song* in the Han era was comparable with civil litigation in modern times.[12] Xu Shihong 徐世虹 also agreed that the annotation of Zheng Xuan regarding *yu* and *song* reflected that the Han people inherited the terms to distinguish *yu* and *song* since Western Zhou.[13] In Xu's survey of the term *song* in transmitted texts, including the *Shiji* (comp. 87 BC) and *Hanshu* (comp. AD 76), she found that *song* were mostly associated with cases concerning land, rent, debts, and

---

7 Parts of Sections 1 and 3 of this chapter have been published in the article "A Note on Civil Cases in Early China," *Journal of the American Oriental Society* 128, no. 1 (2008): 121–131.

8 *Lüshi chunqiu* [Gao You zhu] 呂氏春秋 [高誘注] (Shanghai: Shanghai shudian, 1985 rpt.), 7.66.

9 *Xu Yuangao* 徐元誥, *Guoyu jiie* 國語集解 (Beijing: Zhonghua shuju, 2002), 230.

10 Huang Sheng 黃生, *Zigu yifu he'an* 字詁義府合按 (Beijing: Zhonghua shuju, 1984), 161–162. Huang Sheng lived in the 17th century. The *Zigu* and *Yifu*, originally two separate works, were combined during the Daoguang 道光 period (1821–1850).

11 *Zhouli zhengyi* 周禮正義, ed., Sun Yirang 孫詒讓 (Shanghai: Shangwu yinshuguan, 1934), vol. 4, 66.28. Huang Du 黃度 was a historian and high-ranking official in the Song dynasty (960–1279). His biography can be found in Chapter 393 of the *Songshi*.

12 Zhang Jianguo, "Juyan xin Hanjian Su Jun zhai Kou En minshi susong ge'an yanjiu," 20–21.

13 Xu Shihong , "Handai minshi susong chengxu kaoshu," 122–130.

goods. Xu found such consistency in the received texts that she argued that *song* always meant "civil litigation" during the Zhou (1122–256 BC) and Han times.

However, many scholars questioned Zheng Xuan. In 1996, the historian Ge Yinghui 葛英會 challenged Zheng Xuan on the basis of archaeological materials. By analyzing the uses of *song* and *yu* in the legal documents in the "Shuyu" section of the Baoshan strips, Ge argued that the distinction between the two terms was not over the source of the dispute, property or social crimes, since this section includes both criminal cases (e.g., murder) and civil cases (e.g., disputes over land). It also appears that the terms *yu* and *song* were used indiscriminately. Ge noted another pattern in the Baoshan materials: the term *song* is used when the documents point to the litigants, while the term *yu* is used when the documents refer to the authority's procedures in investigating and pronouncing judgments. On this basis, Ge argued that the difference between *song* and *yu* did not correspond to civil versus criminal cases. Rather, the two words functioned like two sides of the same coin, depending on the viewer's perspective. According to Ge, a case was called *song* by the disputing parties, but *yu* by the authorities.[14]

Momiyama Akira 籾山明 focused on the Qin and Han periods and proposed a compromising view. He argued that distinctions between *yu* and *song* do exist in Qin and Han materials, but these distinctions do not necessarily correspond to that of civil and criminal litigation.[15] He derived his view by studying the case of Kou En vs. Su Jun and a case regarding a dead horse by saying that even though these two cases were both initially disputes over property, both ended up in turning to criminal matters. That suggested that the boundaries between *song* and *yu* were not clearly defined, but they constituted a continuous and organic process. He believed that the Su Jun case shows that the authorities regarded ill-grounded claims over property as a crime.

These debates reveal an interesting pattern: neither the pre-Han Classics nor the excavated documents from Baoshan provide firm evidence supporting Zheng Xuan's distinction between *yu* and *song*. On the contrary: some counter-evidence can be found in the Baoshan strips as Ge Yinghui has pointed out. However, in the Han texts, evidence supporting Zheng Xuan's distinction can be found, as acknowledged by both Xu Shihong and Momiyama Akira. In fact, we can gain a deeper understanding of *song* by analyzing the usages in the *Shiji*, the *Hanshu*, and excavated Han documents. We will see that *song* was not a legal term in early Western Han, and its connection with disputes

14 Ge Yinghui 葛英會, "Baoshan Chu jian zhi yu wenshu yanjiu" 包山楚簡治獄文書研究, *Nanfang wenwu* 南方文物 no. 2 (1996): 85–91.

15 Momiyama Akira 籾山明, *Chūgoku kodai soshō seido no kenkyū* 中國古代訴訟制度の研究 (Kyōto: Kyōto daigaku gakujutsu shuppankai, 2006).

over property was quite loose, but in the Eastern Han period, *song* was closely related to disputes over property and its usage was relatively stabilized. The distinction made by Zheng Xuan probably reflects the situation of his own time, during the Eastern Han.

2 Examples of the Use of *Yu* and *Song* in the *Shiji*, *Hanshu* and Excavated Official Documents from the Han Period

In the documents from the Han period, *yu* 獄 "criminal cases" and *song* 訟 "civil disputes" were employed under two types of circumstances: simultaneously or individually. We will first analyze the circumstances where *yu* and *song* were used simultaneously. The *Shiji* has two examples, and the *Hanshu* has twelve. Overall, these instances of simultaneous *yu* and *song* usage refer generally to lawsuits, and we have no means to determine whether or not they are examples of financial or criminal disputes. For example, the *Book of Music* (*Yueshu* 樂書) from the *Shiji* states:

> (The feast on) grain-fed animals, with the adjunct of drinking, was not intended to produce evil, and yet cases of litigation are more numerous in consequence of it – it is the excessive drinking that produces the evil.[16]
>
> 夫豢豕為酒，非以為禍也；而獄訟益煩，則酒之流生禍.

This is a description of drinking wine, and because of this, instances of litigation (*yu* and *song*) increased.

Even though we are unable to know what differences there were between *yu* and *song*, disturbances under the influence of alcohol led to disputes. Generally, there seems to be little relationship between disputes resulting from the influence of alcohol and disputes regarding property.

The *Biographies of Upright Officials* (*Xun li zhuan* 循吏傳) from the *Hanshu* says:

> There were none who did not plow crops and work the fields, and the common people returned to the fields. Population increased by double, and thieves, ruffians, and *yu* and *song* declined and ceased.[17]
>
> 莫不耕稼力田, 百姓歸之, 戶口增倍, 盜賊獄訟衰止.

16 *Shiji* 史記 (Beijing: Zhonghua shuju, 1959), 25.1199.
17 *Hanshu*, 89.3642.

Again, this example is a general description, and we are unable to deduce the differences between *yu* and *song*. The following section will analyze the circumstances under which *yu* and *song* were employed individually.

2.1 *The Use of* Yu

The uses of *yu* in the *Shiji* and *Hanshu* are extremely similar and all focus on aspects of "prison" and "criminal cases". These two aspects can be regarded as two sides of the same coin. For example:

> *Shiji* 96.2688: Ba, the Governor of Yingchuan, employed the imperial decrees to bring order to the people, lost property was not taken from the street, men and women took different paths, and within the jails (*yu*) there were no prisoners of a serious [kind].
>
> 潁川太守霸，以宣布詔令治民，道不拾遺，男女異路，獄中無重囚.
>
> *Shiji* 87.2562: Li Si came out of the jail, being arrested together with his second son. Li Si looked at his son and said ...
>
> 斯出獄，與其中子俱執，顧謂其中子曰 …
>
> *Hanshu* 8.253: Nowadays, there were cases in which those who were under arrest died in the jail due to torture, starvation or cold.
>
> 今繫者或以掠辜若飢寒瘐死獄中.
>
> *Hanshu* 60.2679: [when] the Marquis of Dingling went out of the pass, [his] concealed crime was discovered once more and was sent to Loyang prison (*yu*).
>
> 定陵侯既出關，伏罪復發，下雒陽獄.

These four cases all relate to the use of the term *yu* as "prison".

> *Shiji* 87.2561: ... then the second [emperor of the Qin] ordered [Zhao] Gao to investigate the criminal case (*yu*) of the Prime Minister, [Zhao Gao] prosecuted [the Prime Minister with] the crime [according to the law], accusing [Li] Si and his son You with the crime of subversion ...
>
> 於是二世乃使高案丞相獄，治罪，責斯與子由謀反狀 …

> *Shiji* 121.3129: Bu Shu was promoted to Chief Clerk and held the credentials to decide upon the criminal cases (*yu*) of Huainan. With regard to the feudal lords, [he] was able to make decisions independently without reporting [back] …
>
> 步舒至長史，持節使決淮南獄，於諸侯擅專斷，不報 …
>
> *Hanshu* 59.2638: [Zhang Tang] was in charge of the criminal case of [the use of] witchcraft by Empress Chen and [launched a] deep investigation into [her] clique. The emperor considered [him] to be capable and promoted him to Grand Counsellor of the Palace.
>
> 治陳皇后巫蠱獄，深竟黨與，上以為能，遷太中大夫.
>
> *Hanshu* 8.255: Criminal cases are the life of the myriad populations. [They] are that by which violence is prohibited and evil is stopped, and [that by which] the crowds are cultivated and nurtured.
>
> 獄者萬民之命，所以禁暴止邪，養育群生也.

These four cases listed above all relate to the use of the term *yu* as criminal case.

Sometimes the term *yu* has uncertain characteristics. For example, the *Hanshu* says:

> If the ritual of the township wine drinking [festival] is abandoned, there will be confusion in the order of the old and young, and the *yu* of fighting will proliferate.[18]
>
> 鄉飲之禮廢，則長幼之序亂，而爭鬭之獄蕃.

It is unclear whether the "*yu* of fighting" mentioned here refers to property disputes or criminal disputes.

The use of *yu* in the *Shiji* and *Hanshu* is confirmed by evidence taken from Qin and Han excavated legal documents.

18 *Hanshu*, 22.1028.

> In handling criminal cases (*yu*), it is possible to use the recollection [of the respondent] to trace their testimony ...[19]
>
> 治獄，能以書從迹其言 …
>
> [A certain] *shangzao* stole a sheep. The criminal case (*yu*) had not yet been decided, and [he] falsely accused another of stealing a pig.[20]
>
> 上造甲盜一羊，獄未斷，誣人曰盜一猪 …
>
> ... [when] presiding over criminal cases (*yu*), each [case] employs their accusations to verify and decide upon it. [If one] dares to carelessly interrogate, fabricate evidence, implicate [them] in another crime, or make a final judgement without basis on those without accusation, then all of these accusations in regard to criminal cases (*yu*) are not [performed] in an upright [manner]...[21]
>
> 治獄者，各以其告劾治之．敢放訊杜雅，求其它罪，及人毋告劾而擅覆治之，皆以鞫獄故不直論．
>
> The criminal's criminal case (*yu*) was already decided. He took his sentence to be inappropriate and wished to seek an appeal. [The official] approved it.[22]
>
> 罪人獄已決，自以罪不當，欲气（乞）鞫者，許之．

These four cases listed above all relate to the use of the term *yu* as criminal cases and the relationship between criminal case and jail should be obvious.

2.2 *The Use of* Song

The use of the term *song* is extremely diverse and completely different to that of *yu*, and can be divided into five types. One example is listed for each of these five types. (See Appendix 2 for a comprehensive survey.)

---

19 *SHD* strip (*Feng zhenshi*) no. 1, p. 147.

20 *SHD* strip (*Falü dawen*) no. 50, p. 105.

21 *ZJS* strip (*Statutes*) no. 113, p. 24.

22 *ZJS* strip (*Statutes*) no. 114, p. 24.

1. ***Disputes over Property***. The *Shiji* contains four examples, whereas the *Hanshu* contains fifteen. For instance,

> *Shiji* 104.2777: When the Prime Minister of Lu first arrived, the people themselves spoke uninvited to the Prime Minister and argued (*song*) that the king took their property. These people [amounted] to more than one hundred.
>
> 魯相初到, 民自言相, 訟王取其財物百餘人.
>
> *Hanshu* 76.3213: [Han Yanshou] inspected the counties and arrived in Gaoling. Among the people, there were brothers who spoke uninvited to [Han Yanshou] to dispute (*song*) over land ...
>
> 行縣至高陵, 民有昆弟相與訟田自言 ...

2. ***General Litigation***. The *Shiji* contains three examples, whereas the *Hanshu* contains four. For instance,

> *Shiji* 112.2963: If frugality [is employed] to educate the common people, then the arrangement of high and low will be obtained, the kindness [between] one's flesh and blood will be intimate, and the source of disputes and litigation (*song*) will be extinguished.
>
> 儉化俗民, 則尊卑之序得, 而骨肉之恩親, 爭訟之原息.
>
> *Hanshu* 72.3086: The Rectifier to the Prime Minister, Guo Qin, presented a memorial saying, "Xuan's initiatives were confusing and convoluted. When he replaced a Petty Official [working under an administrator with an income of] two thousand bushels to hear 'litigations' (*song*), what [he] was investigating exceeded the clause of the imperial order ..."
>
> 丞相司直郭欽奏 "宣舉錯煩苛, 代二千石署吏聽訟, 所察過詔條 ..."

3. ***Appeals/ Self-defense***. The *Shiji* contains three examples, whereas the *Hanshu* contains twenty-seven. For instance,

> *Shiji* 122.3142: The State of Zhao had a smelting and casting industry. The King [of Zhao] appealed (*song*) several times regarding the affairs

of the Iron Officials [from the central court]. [Zhang] Tang often dismissed the King of Zhao's [complaints].

趙國以冶鑄為業, 王數訟鐵官事, 湯常排趙王.

Hanshu 45.2179: The emperor was of an advanced age and suspected his close assistants of placing a curse [on him] and there were some who fled. There were none who dared to defend themselves (*song*) with regard to this grievance.

上春秋高, 疑左右皆為蠱祝詛, 有與亡, 莫敢訟其冤者.

4. ***To Argue***. The *Shiji contains* one example, whereas the *Hanshu* also contains one example.

Shiji 127.3222: The Calendrical School declared it slightly in-auspicious. The School of Heaven and Man declared it slightly auspicious. The School of Supreme Unity declared it greatly auspicious. [They] debated and argued (*song* did not esteem ritual and propriety) and could not come to an agreement, and so [they] informed the [emperor of the divinitory] markings.

曆家曰小凶, 天人家曰小吉, 太一家曰大吉. 辯訟不決, 以狀聞.

Hanshu 72.3082: [They] did not esteem ritual and propriety, yet remained in the public sphere reproaching and despising each other. [They] spoke irresponsibly, debated, argued (*song*), and were indolent. [Full of] slander, they lost [all proper] composure [as officials].

不崇禮義, 而居公門下相非恨, 疾言辯訟, 媠謾亡狀.

5. ***Public Declaration***. The *Shiji* only contains one example, whereas the *Hanshu* has no examples at all. Specifically,

Shiji 106.2823: [Liu Bi] expressed regards and concerns over talented people and granted awards to the residents and villagers in all seasons. He openly declared (*song*) that he forbade his subjects from handing over the fugitives from other kingdoms and commanderies to their officials who wanted to come to [Wu] to arrest them.

歲時存問茂材, 賞賜閭里. 佗郡國吏欲來捕亡人者, 訟共禁弗予.

6. ***Yu* and *Song* Combined.** This compound word is used as a generic term to refer to all kinds of legal cases. In the *Shiji*, it only occurs once, whereas it occurs ten times in the *Hanshu*.

> *Shiji* 24.1199: To raise pigs and make wine is not meant to incur disasters. However, when criminal and civil disputes (*yusong*) grow day by day, disasters related to wine occur.
>
> 夫豢豕為酒, 非以為禍也, 而獄訟益煩, 則酒之流生禍也.
>
> *Hanshu* 23.1030: The state should set up institutions and rules, and promote rites and music so that the lords would follow the right path, the commoners become simple minded, and criminal and civil disputes (*yusong*) diminish and cease.
>
> 宜定制度, 興禮樂, 然後諸侯軌道, 百姓素樸, 獄訟衰息.

We have tabulated the use of *song* from the *Shiji* and *Hanshu* in Figure 2. The figure clearly illustrates the differences in the use of *song* between the *Shiji* and *Hanshu*. In the *Shiji*, the use of *song* is distributed comparatively evenly, and relatively speaking, it generally refers to litigation. However, in the *Hanshu*, the term primarily refers to appeals and defense with many particular references to disputes over property. At the same time, the combined use of *yu* and *song*

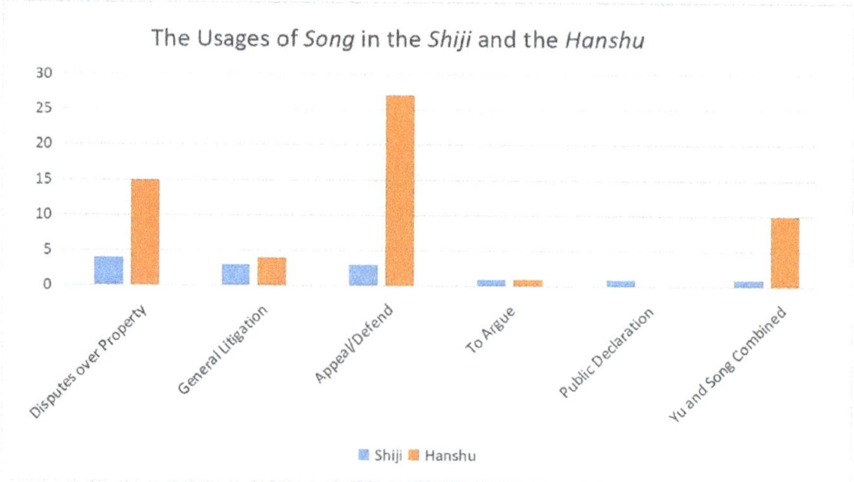

FIGURE 2 The usages of *song* in the *Shiji* and the *Hanshu*

(*yusong*) continues to increase, yet these generally refer to litigation, and we see very few instances of other uses.

This comparison illustrates how the connotation of the term *song* changed dramatically from the time of the *Shiji* to that of the *Hanshu*; the term began to focus on the two meanings of "appeal/self-defense" and "property disputes", and other meanings gradually disappeared over time. This evolution gives us a clue that the term *song* developed from a more general term into a technical legal one. It first refers to instigating litigation or defense. When the term *song* was distinguished from criminal disputes it refers in particular to disputes over property.

The observations above taken from the received historical documents can also be verified by excavated documents. In the early Han text *Ernian lüling*, the term *song* occurs only once, while in the *Zou yan shu* 奏讞書, the term *song* is entirely absent.[23]

The *Gaolü* 告律 section from the *Ernian lüling* contains the following example:

> Slaves and slave-girls defended themselves, [and this] was not investigated. [Therefore], the left foot of the slave was amputated, and the cheekbone of the slave-girl was tattooed and they were given [back] to their master.[24]
>
> 奴婢自訟不審, 斬奴左止 (趾), 黥婢顏頯, 畀其主.

This is the only appearance of the term *song* which clearly has no relation to disputes over property, and should be referred to generally as an instance of litigation.

However, in the *Ernian lüling*, disputes over property are explained as "*zheng*" 爭 (disputes). The Statutes on Households states that when regulating the division of inherited property by means of the dead person's last testament,

23 One phenomenon deserves our attention: the phrase *zhan yu song* 占獄訟 often appears in the Qin documents of divination and fortune-telling (excavated from Zhoujiatai 周家臺), but it never appears in the Shuihudi legal documents of the Qin. Perhaps, Wang Jie's opinion is plausible. He argued that *song* was a legal term in the pre-Qin bronze vessel documents, referring to the action of bringing up a lawsuit or the case itself. However, this term was replaced by *gao* 告 in the legal language during the Qin dynasty. See Wang Jie 王捷, "Jiuti xinzheng: Xianqin yu song de falu yuyong yanbian" 舊題新證: 先秦'獄' 訟'的法律語用演變, *Beifang faxue* 北方法學 no. 4 (2013): 133–138.

24 ZJS strip (*Statutes*) no. 135, p. 27.

> If there is a *zheng* (dispute), use the contractual documents to handle the matter; if there are no contractual documents, then do not hear [the case].[25]
>
> 有爭者，以券書從事；毋券書，毋聽.

The use of "*zheng*" here refers contextually to a dispute over property. However, the "*zheng*" does not exclusively refer to a dispute over property. The Statutes on Robberies (*zeilü* 賊律) has the following example:

> If someone pregnant with child dares *zheng* (dispute) with another, even if the [other] person hits [her] changing her [pregnant state (i.e., she miscarries)], then fine the miscarried woman four *liang* of gold.[26]
>
> 懷子而敢與人爭鬬，人雖毆變之，罰為人變者金四兩.

Here the "*zheng*" is not necessarily related to property.

The *Ernian lüling* is a legal document dating from the early Han and contains a large proportion of content related to civil law, in particular its specific use to regulate relationships regarding property. However, *yu* as a term specifically related to property disputes, has completely disappeared. What does this mean?

It explains that the formula of "disputes over property are called *song*" (*zheng cai yue song* 爭財曰訟) was not established during the early Han, and that the term *song* may not even be a technical legal term during this period. However, in the Juyan Han strips dating from a little later in the period, the term *song* begins to be directly related to disputes over property.

> The *song* (dispute) over the field and house. The female is afraid of the guest. Gong was on his way to collect belongings and run across ...[27]
>
> ☐□訟田宅女子恐客也及功收財物事道逢

25 *ZJS* strip (*Statutes*) no. 335, p. 54.

26 *ZJS* strip (*Statutes*) no. 31, p. 13.

27 *JYX* strip no. E.P.T 40:47, p. 88.

> [someone] states: the officials forwarded the complaint from Juyan to *song* (dispute) over Tawei Qing [one character missing] regarding 2350 *shi* of grain of the Tunyuan platoon.[28]
>
> ☑言之官移居延訟遝尉卿□主呑遠穀二千三百五十石

Although these two strips lack a definite date, the Juyan strips date from sometime between the middle period of the Western up to the Eastern Han.

An instance of similar usage with a verifiable date can be found in the *Zhendao zhongdi bei* 真道塚地碑, which first appeared in the fifth year of the Yanxi era (AD 163):

> Descendants should obtain a dwelling in the mountains to reside [in], and not engage in *song* (disputes) over residential areas, [and not engage] in in disputes [with others] …[29]
>
> 子孫但得宿山居留, 不得爭舍地, 爭訟 …

This is possibly the earliest example of the use of *song* from within the excavated materials, and dates to a time when Zheng Xuan was age thirty-five.

In summarizing the above analysis of examples of the use of *yu* and *song*, we can see that the meaning of *yu* was defined as criminal cases and was commonly used during the Qin and Han. However, compared with *yu*, the term *song* had different regulations. During the Western Han, the relationship between *song* and disputes over property is unclear, but by the time of the Eastern Han, this relationship became comparatively clear. The present work therefore believes that the term *song*, as a similar concept to the contemporary notion of "litigation" gradually arose during the Western Han and began to form fixed patterns in the Eastern Han. After which, Zheng Xuan could conclude that "disputes over property are called *song*".

---

28 *JYX* strip no. E.P.T 54:8, p. 301.

29 On Ikeda 池田溫, "Chugoku rekidai boken ryakko" 中國歷代墓券略考, *Tokyo bunka kenkyujo kiyo* 東洋文化研究所紀要 86 (1982): 193–278. Tomb documents are not official documents, but their language often imitates that of official documents. Thus, the phrasing can be used to study the expressions of official documents.

3 Institutional Differences between *Yu* and *Song*

Even though the conceptual difference between *yu* (disputes over crimes) and *song* (disputes over property) perhaps was not articulated until the Eastern Han, authorities had long distinguished disputes over property and disputes over crimes in legal practice, as our study in Chapter One shows. Built upon that study, this section will further argue that there also existed institutional differences between *yu* and *song* since as late as early Western Han, which were: Civil complaints typically go first to the district bailiff, not the county court. The bailiff summons the conflicted parties to hearings in order to assess liability.[30] However, for criminal cases, the report is typically submitted to the county court for preliminary investigation. Only the county court and superior courts have the authority to try criminal cases.

Indeed, the role of the district bailiff (*xiang sefu*)[31] is crucial to an understanding of civil cases in early China, insofar as his absence from criminal cases itself indicates an institutional difference between civil and criminal procedures. In trying a criminal case, the case in theory should be sent upwards to the magistrate for a trial, even when the case was first taken by district officials. A statute from Zhangjiashan states:

> For those people who want to accuse someone, or who want to confess their own crimes, if they are far from the magistrate's court, then they can make the accusation to the district officials. The district officials should take down the accusations and submit them to the county or march court. Officers of the county or march court could also take accusations.[32]

> 諸欲告罪人，及有罪先自告而遠其縣廷者，皆得告所在鄉，鄉官謹聽，書其告，上縣道官．廷士吏亦得聽告．

This regulation makes it clear that a criminal case could typically be reported directly to the magistrate's court with no involvement of district officials. Under

30 See my previous study in this chapter; cf. Momiyama, *Chūgoku kodai soshō*, 153.

31 Hulsewé, assuming that the county magistrate was the lowest level of judicial authority, failed to note the role of district bailiff in the justice system. He wrote: "As in many other societies, the function of the judge was exercised in China by the local administrative official, and this was also the case during the two Han dynasties. For the vast majority of commoners, the only judge they came into contact with was the *hsien ling* or *hsien chang*: the prefect" (*RHL*, 81). Hulsewé's observation is correct for criminal cases, in which the county magistrate was the lowest level of judicial authority; however, in civil cases, the authority was the district bailiff.

32 *ZJS* strip (*Statutes*) no. 101, pp. 22–23.

extreme situations, such as those living a long distance from the magistrate's court, a case could be first reported to the district officials, who would only carefully note down the accusations before sending the case upwards to the magistrate's court for trial. By contrast, district officials, with bailiffs as their superior, played a central role in *song*. The famous thinker Wang Chong 王充 (AD 27–97) made that contrast very clear:

> The district [officials] judge is concerned with *song* [disputes], while the *yu* [jailors] determine suspected crimes. If right and wrong cannot be determined, and the *qu* and *zhi* [distorted account of the facts and straight account of the facts] cannot be established, people of the time will definitely say that the abilities of the district officials and the abilities of the jail officials are not adequate to perform their duties.[33]
>
> 鄉決疑訟，獄定嫌罪．是非不決，曲直不立，世人必謂鄉獄之吏，才不任職．

The claim that "the *yu* (jailors) determine suspected crimes" is a little bit puzzling, since we know jails were a place to confine criminals, having no authority to determine facts or pass sentences. Perhaps Wang Chong's distinction indicates that only county officials and above had roles in criminal trials. According to a recent study by Song Jie 宋傑, the lowest level of jail was at the county level.[34] Despite the apparent discrepancies in opinions, we find a clear division of judicial duties between the cases assigned to the district (*song*) and county jailor (*yu*) – crime, confirming Zheng Xuan's claim regarding *yu* and *song*. This points to the institutional difference between civil litigation and criminal litigation. According to Wang Chong, district officials were concerned with *song*, but not with crimes.

Wang Chong's claim regarding this institutional difference can be tested by looking at cases in the *Zouyan shu* from Zhangjiashan.[35] The twenty-two cases there are all criminal cases, and the preliminary trials are all conducted by

33 *Lunheng jijie* 論衡集解, ed., Liu Pansui 劉盼遂 (Shanghai: Shanghai guji chubanshe, 1957), 29.571. The word "*xiang*" 鄉 was originally misprinted as "*qing*" 卿 in the received versions. See also Qiu Xigui 裘錫圭, "Lunheng zhaji" 論衡劄記, *Wenshi* 文史 5 (1978): 229. Professor Qiu Xigui corrected that mistake in 1978.

34 Song Jie 宋傑, "Handai jianyu jianzhi sheshi cong kao" 漢代監獄建置設施叢考, *Shoudu shifan daxue xuebao* (*Shehui kexue ban*) 首都師範大學學報 (社會科學版) no. 3 (2009): 6.

35 The *Zouyan shu* is a collection of twenty-two legal cases. According to the Han legal system, when a county judge would encounter difficulty in judging a case, he should first report the case to the commandery judges, then to the superintendent of trials in the central government, and finally to the emperor. The collection of these reports regarding

county courts except in Case 17, in which the case is first taken by the pavilion head (*tingzhang* 亭長), who is a district official,[36] perhaps because he initially assumes that the case involves a dispute over the ownership of an ox. Once the official realizes that the case probably involves the stealing of the ox, a crime, he immediately reports the case to the county court, which immediately takes over the case and begins its investigation.[37]

To understand civil litigation, we must fully understand the role of the district bailiff, who served as the chief officer of a district. We need to first examine the title *sefu*. According to Lao Gan 勞榦 (1907–2003) and Ōba Osamu, *sefu* was a generic title for officials during the Han dynasty; as they point out, there were many kinds of *sefu* working in different offices at different administrative levels. For instance, there was a *sefu* for treasure houses (*ku sefu* 庫嗇夫) and a *sefu* for passes (*guan sefu* 関嗇夫).[38] The district bailiff (*xiang sefu*), as Yan Gengwang 嚴耕望 (1916–1996) observed, was an officer dispatched by the county magistrate to a particular district to represent the state's authority.[39] According to the *Hanshu*'s "Table of the Hundred Officials" (Baiguan gongqing biao 百官公卿表), "The [*xiang*] *sefu*'s duties are to hear cases (*tingsong* 聽訟) and to collect taxes (*shou fushui* 收賦稅)."[40] If *song* means "civil litigation," as Xu and Momiyama argue, the phrase *tingsong*, as used in the case of Kou En vs. Su Jun from Juyan, must mean "to hear civil cases."[41]

---

the discussions of those legal cases formed the *Zouyan shu*, which was likely a reference book for officials in the Han dynasty. See the introduction of this book for more details.

36 The district bailiff was the immediate supervisor of the pavilion head (*ting zhang* 亭長). The administrative structure of a district was defined along the following lines: ten hamlets (*li* 里) formed a pavilion, and ten pavilions formed a district. See Loewe, *The Government of the Qin and Han Empires*, 47.

37 For Case 17, see ZJS strip (*Zouyan shu*) nos. 99–123, pp. 100–102.

38 Lao Gan 勞榦, "Cong Hanjian zhong de sefu lingshi houshi he shili lun Handai junxiang li de zhiwu he diwei" 從漢簡中的嗇夫令史侯史和史吏論漢代郡縣吏的職務和地位, *Zhongyang yan jiuyuan lishi yuyan yanjiusuo jikan* 中央研究院歷史語言研究所集刊 55, no.1 (1983): 9–22; cf. Ōba, *Shin Kan hōsei shi*, 479–519. Neither Ōba nor Lao realized that *tingsong* means "to hear civil cases." Both of them believed that the *xiang sefu* was in charge of criminal cases.

39 Yan Gengwang 嚴耕望, *Zhongguo gudai difang xingzheng zhidushi shangbian* 中國古代地方行政制度史上編 (Nangang: Zhongyang yanjiuyuan lishi yu yanyanjiusuo, 1961), 237–238.

40 *Hanshu*, 19.742.

41 However, there are exceptions in the usage of the word *song* in the Han texts. Wang Fu 王符 (ca. AD 85–162), who was from the generation preceding Zheng Xuan, seemed to disregard the distinction between *yu* and *song*, and the two terms were used interchangeably in the "Duan song" 斷訟 section of his *Qianfu lun* 潛夫論 (Discourse of a Hermit). According to Wang Fu, "Nowadays, even though the *yu* (criminal cases) to be decided number in the tens of thousands, the legal disputes, the occurrences of fighting, the trials

Two other passages from transmitted texts show that the district bailiff indeed heard civil cases. Yu Yu 虞預 (ca. 285–340), in his *Kuaiji dianlu* 會稽典錄 (Records of Kuaiji, comp. ca. 300), tells us:

> Zheng Hong was the bailiff of the Lingwen district. Among the villagers, there was a younger brother who borrowed money from his elder brother and never returned the money. So, the sister-in-law accused the younger brother of acting falsely to Hong [in the name of the elder brother].[42]
>
> 鄭宏為霊文鄉嗇夫, 民有弟用兄錢者, 未還之, 嫂詐訴之宏.

The sister-in-law presented her accusation to the district bailiff, the same bailiff who ultimately heard the case.

Second, the biography of Diwu Lun 第五倫 in the *Hou Hanshu* 後漢書 (comp. 445) states that:

> Lun later on became a district bailiff. He fairly administered the taxes and labor services [among the people] and he resolved their grievances. Thus, he secured their approbation.[43]
>
> 倫後為鄉嗇夫, 平徭賦, 理怨結, 得人歡心.

As a district bailiff, Diwu Lun seems to have had two basic duties: apportioning taxes and labor services, and resolving grievances. The text does not specify the kind of grievances Diwu Lun resolved, but if we compare this expression

handled by district officials, and the trials handled by officials in charge of jails are of the same situation. They are all caused by the lack of honesty within the people who frequently deceived others" (今一歲斷獄, 雖以萬計, 然辭訟之辯, 鬥賊之發, 鄉部之治, 獄官之治者, 其狀一也. 本皆起民不誠信, 而數相紿也). See *Qianfulun Jian jiaozheng* 潛夫論箋校正, ed., Peng Duo 彭鐸 (Beijing: Zhonghua shuju, 1985), 5. 226. It appears that Wang did distinguish the cases resolved by district officials from those resolved by the officials of the jails (*yuguan* 獄官). Perhaps Wang was not very familiar with legal terms and was thus unaware of the subtle difference between *song* and *yu*; however, he did note their difference in legal practice.

42 This passage of the *Kuaiji dianlu* is preseved in *Taiping yulan* 太平御覽 (*Sibu congkan xubian* 四部叢刊續編 edition), ed., Li Fang 李昉 (Shanghai: Shangwu yinshuguan, 1934), 403.11. The final clause is somewhat difficult to translate. From the given context, I infer that the sister-in-law brought a lawsuit against her brother-in-law in the name of her husband, as the latter might have been reluctant to sue his brother. An alternate translation would be "the sister-in-law pretended to act on behalf of her husband and sued the brother-in-law."

43 *Hou Hanshu* 後漢書 (Beijing: Zhonghua shuju, 1965), 41.1396.

from Diwu Lun's biography with that recorded in the "Table of the Hundred Officials," as noted above (*tingsong shou fushui*, "hear civil cases and collect taxes"), it seems very likely that the phrase "to resolve grievances" corresponds with the phrase "to hear cases".

The district bailiff was not the only authority in a district who could handle civil disputes. The *sanlao* 三老 (Thrice Venerable) also seems to have had a role in resolving civil disputes. The stele erected to commemorate Zhao Kuan 趙寬 (dated to AD 180) states:

> The tabooed personal name of the *sanlao* (Thrice Venerable) was Kuan … [The governor] who honored him with the post of *sanlao* treated him as a teacher rather than as a subordinate. Thereupon he started to hear cases and resolve grievances, as well as instruct younger generations in morality.[44]
>
> 三老諱寬 … 優號三老，師而不臣．於是乃聽訟理怨，教誨後生．

According to the stele, Zhao Kuan heard cases when he was a *sanlao*. Derk Bodde (1909–2003) translated *sanlao* as "Thrice Venerable," arguing that it was an honorific title conferred on persons deemed to have had a considerable number of achievements, either scholarly or political.[45] Yan Gengwang believed that the *sanlao* were neither clerks nor officials of the state, but men chosen by the state or elected by the local people to act as intermediaries between the state and its subjects.[46]

Regardless of how the *sanlao* came to office, their role in civil cases has been overlooked by scholars, perhaps, in part, because the *Hanshu* monograph on the bureaucracy observes only that "the *sanlao* were in charge of educating and transforming the people" (*sanlao zhang jiaohua* 三老掌教化).[47] The *Hanshu* reference does not invest the *sanlao* with judicial or quasi-judicial status, nor does it acknowledge any strictly judicial function attached to the title. The term *jiaohua* indicates the moral authority of the *sanlao*, the moral authority that presumably qualified them to arbitrate disputes. The following case shows

---

44 *Han bei ji shi* 漢碑集釋, ed., Gao Wen 高文 (Kaifeng: Henan daxue chubanshe, 1997), 434.

45 Derk Bodde, *Festivals in Classical China: New Year and Other Annual Observances during the Han Dynasty 206 B.C.–A.D. 220* (Princeton: Princeton University Press, 1975), 373–380.

46 Yan Gengwang, *Zhongguo gudai difang*, 246–251.

47 *Hanshu*, 19.743.

that moral arbitration was sometimes adopted as a first step in resolving civil cases[48] before more formal actions were taken by the authorities:

> Wu You was promoted to the Chancellor of the Jiaodong kingdom. When there were cases among the people, he would first order the *sanlao* to instruct those concerned in the precepts of filial piety and fraternal love. He then personally went to their neighborhood to reconcile the disputants. None of the clerks and people dared to cheat him.[49]
>
> 吳祐遷膠東相，民有詞訟，先令三老以孝悌喻解，祐身至閭里和之，吏民不忍欺.

Notably, there is no mention of the district bailiff. In the cases referred to in this passage, we see the *sanlao* playing the crucial role of conciliator by instructing the people in moral conduct and personally arbitrating disputes. Only if the *sanlao* failed to resolve a dispute, would the chancellor, as the kingdom's chief official, personally intervene.[50] The direct intervention of the chancellor was clearly so unusual that it merited notice in the passage cited above. Typically, civil cases would be resolved at the much lower level of the district court presided over by the district bailiff.

The following story from the *Hanshu* captures some sense of the moral, ethical, and arguably ritual elements involved in the administration of justice:

> [Han Yanshou] inspected the counties and arrived in Gaoling. Among the people, there were brothers who spoke uninvited to [Han Yanshou] to dispute (*song*) over land. Han Yanshou was very upset and said: "I am fortunate to hold a position where I am to be the role model for the commandery. I have failed to exemplify moral teachings and transform the people, and so blood relatives have disputes [over land] in civil litigation. This not only damages customary morality, but also humiliates the worthy senior officers, the *sefu*, the *sanlao*, and the Filially Pious and Fraternal (*xiaodi*). This is my mistake, as I am the leader of Pingyi.[51]

48 This aspect is associated with the legal ideal of reforming people's morals to reduce lawsuits.

49 See the biography of Wu You 吳祐 in Xie Cheng's 謝承 *Hou Hanshu*, collected in *Bajia Hou Hanshu jizhu* 八家後漢書輯注, ed., Zhou Tianyou 周天遊 (Tianjin: Tianjin guji chubanshe, 1987), 4.113.

50 The chancellor was a kingdom-level post comparable to that of a governor in a commandery.

51 Pingyi 馮翊 was one of the three metropolitan areas of the capital Chang'an.

> I should withdraw first." That day, Han Yanshou refused to hear any court cases, pleading illness. Then, he went to the shelter belonging to the post and shut himself up, so that he might reflect upon his errors. In the whole county, no one knew what to do. The magistrate (*ling*), deputy magistrates (*cheng*), district bailiff (*sefu*) and *sanlao* all had themselves bound, awaiting punishment.[52]

> 行縣至高陵, 民有昆弟相與訟田自言, 延壽大傷之, 曰: "幸得備位, 為郡表率, 不能宣明教化, 至令民有骨肉爭訟, 既傷風化, 重使賢長吏、嗇夫、三老、孝弟受其恥, 咎在馮翊, 當先退." 是日移病不聽事, 因入臥傳舍, 閉閤思過. 一縣莫知所為, 令丞、嗇夫、三老亦皆自繫待罪.

By explicit admission, the chancellor regarded the brothers' dispute as his personal failure to educate his people. In his failure, he felt that he shamed the county bureaucracy. What happened next is quite interesting: the county magistrate (*ling*), the assistant magistrates (*cheng*), the *sanlao* and *sefu*[53] all took the ritual action of binding themselves as if they were criminals. This suggests that they all considered themselves directly responsible for the resolution of civil cases while the governor and magistrates took ultimate responsibility for the proper handling and disposition of all civil cases in their jurisdictions.[54]

Since at the district level both the bailiff and the *sanlao* could handle civil cases, one may ask if there was any difference between the two. It seems that the *sanlao* may have acted as an arbitrator who tried to reconcile cases, while the district bailiff acted as a judicial officer with an obligation to question the parties, record their statements, draw up preliminary reports, and submit those reports to the county officials. The authority of the *sanlao* in civil cases may have depended on his position as a moral leader in the district. Presumably, then his decisions would have been enforced mainly by custom and public opinion. However, the authority of the district bailiff was based on his official position as a legal officer, presumably giving his judgments the force of law. An account in the bureaucratic monograph of the *Hanshu* explicitly states that the district bailiff had a duty to hear civil cases. Moreover, as the Liye Qin strip no. J1.984 indicates, "The district bailiff performs his duty according

---

52 *Hanshu*, 76. 3213.

53 It is clear in this context that *sefu* refers to the *xiang sefu*, because he is mentioned alongside the district *sanlao*.

54 See *CHC*, 507–508. Each commandery was under a governor (*taishou* 太守). His counterpart in a kingdom had the courtesy title of chancellor (*xiang* 相), but both titles had comparable duties. These officials were responsible for all civil and military affairs within their territories, including the administration of civil and criminal laws.

to the statutes and ordinances" (*Xiang sefu yi lü ling cong shi* 鄉嗇夫以律令從事),[55] suggesting that district bailiffs had comparable legal authority in the Qin dynasty, a likely predecessor to the district bailiffs of the Han.

Clearly, a district bailiff could not adjudicate every dispute in his district without having his administration crippled by an overwhelming caseload. The district bailiff, we should recall, also had other non-judicial duties, including the administration of local taxes and managing labor service. Understandably, there was a screening process to manage the bailiff's caseload. Plaintiffs had to present solid proof of the merits of their complaint (i.e., a credible, substantive basis for legal action) before the bailiff would take their cases. According to Zheng Xuan, in disputes over sales agreements, the parties needed to present their contract to the authorities.[56] Zheng Xuan's observation is consistent with the directive found in ZJS strip (*Statutes*) no. 335:

> If there is a dispute [over inheritance], the authorities should handle the matter based on the document. If there is no document, the case will not be heard.[57]

Similarly, when a dispute over inheritance erupted, the party making the complaint was required to present a will before the case could be accepted for adjudication. This emphasis on providing preliminary proof in order to weed out trivial or frivolous cases contrasts sharply to the corresponding criminal procedure in which officials were required to take all cases involving criminal conduct.

While one of the distinctive features of civil litigation in Han was the generally equal access to the courts accorded to litigants regardless of their status, this principle apparently was not absolute. Another potential barrier to having a case heard by a judicial officer was the relative status of the litigants. ZJS strip (*Statutes*) nos. 133–134 show that the social status of the accuser and the relationship between the accuser and the accused could serve as criteria for deciding whether or not to take a case.

---

55 Hunan sheng wenwu kaogu yanjiusuo 湖南省文物考古研究所, "Xiangxi Liye Qindai jiandu xuanshi" 湘西里耶秦代簡牘選釋, *Zhongguo lishi wenwu* 中國歷史文物 no. 1 (2003): 10; cf. Bu Xianqun 卜憲群, "Qin Han zhiji xiangli liyuan zakao: Yi Liye Qinjian wei zhongxin de taolun" 秦漢之際鄉里吏員雜考—以里耶秦簡為中心的探討, *Nandu xuetan* (*Renwen shehui hexue ban*) 南都學壇 (人文社會科學版) no. 1 (2006): 2. The Liye 里耶 strips were excavated in 2002 by the Hunan Provincial Archaeological Institute. Thirty-six thousand strips were excavated.

56 See footnote 79 of Chapter 1.

57 ZJS strip (*Statutes*) no. 335, p. 54.

When a son accuses his parents, a daughter-in-law accuses her parents-in-law, a slave accuses his or her master or the parents, wife, or son of the master, do not take these cases. Instead, execute the accusers in the marketplace.

Never take cases brought forward by these people: those who are less than ten years old, those who are in the jail, or those who have been serving a sentence as male wall-builders, female grain-pounders, male gatherers of firewood for spirits, or female sifters of white rice.[58]

子告父母, 婦告威公,[59] 奴婢告主、主父母妻子，勿聽而棄告者市.
年未盈十歲及毄（繫）者、城旦舂、鬼薪白粲告人，皆勿聽.

Not all disputes were easily resolved. Equally convincing claims and counterclaims could stymie a bailiff, the case might involve issues not covered by the statutes, or frustrated litigants might refuse to accept the court's judgment. When a bailiff found it impossible to resolve a dispute, he could, and typically did, forward the case to a higher authority. To accommodate such events, there was a hierarchy of appeals in civil litigation, from the district level all the way up to commandery.

The following report of an (AD 24 case) appeal from Juyan describes what happens when lower officials are unable to resolve a dispute over debt:

On the *xinchou* day of the fourth month beginning with the day *yihai*, in the second year of the Gengshi period (AD 24), two officials, who are the *zhangshouhou* (deputy garrison commander?) and the deputy commander of the Jiaqu company forwarded [a testimony?] to Chi. According to the statute, [missing several characters] a certain official questioned [the defendant] and decided to collect the claimed debt from the defendant. The defendant was not willing to accept the judgment. Thus, the certain official reported the problem. [We] forward the testimony of the defendant according to the statutes and ordinances.[60]

更始二年四月乙亥朔辛丑，甲渠鄣守候，塞尉二人移垦池律曰□□□⧄
□□□史驗問收, 責, 報不服. 移自証爰書, 如律令.

58 *ZJS* strip (*Statutes*) nos. 133–134, p. 27.

59 According to Zhu Honglin, *wei* 威 refers to "mother-in-law," whereas *gong* 公 refers to "father-in-law." See Zhu Honglin, *Zhangjiashan*, 100.

60 *JYX* strip no. E.P.C. 39, p. 548.

The dispute was initially investigated by an official who subsequently ruled in favor of the plaintiff. When the defendant refused to admit the debt, the clerk reported the problem to the two officers at Jiaqu. These officers, facing a defiant defendant, followed the procedures set forth in the statutes and ordinances, forwarding their report on the problematic case to their superiors, including the testimony they had gathered. Even if this case involved a disputed debt among military men, and would therefore have been handled by military officials, the appeal process followed the same pattern of appeal it would have followed had the dispute involved civilians.

With what we have learned about the role of the district bailiff in civil litigation, we may now more fruitfully revisit Zheng Xuan's assertion that *song* meant "to dispute property." The *Hou Hanshu* tells us that Zheng Xuan was once himself a district bailiff, and that the post of district bailiff may have been his first official position:

> Xuan was a district bailiff when he was young. When he was on leave, he returned home, where he often visited the local academies. He was not happy to be a local officer. His father was angry with him many times, but he could not stop him [from going to the academies].[61]
>
> 玄少為鄉嗇夫，得休歸，常詣學官，不樂為吏，父數怒之，不能禁.

Zheng Xuan's remark on the word *song* in his *Zhouli* commentary was presumably based on his personal experiences of drawing up reports regarding property cases when he served as a local bailiff. Apparently, he found such tasks irksome.

Given the power of a district bailiff over the lives of district residents, Zheng Xuan's youth raises questions about the qualifications for the position of district bailiff. In Zheng Xuan's case, we have an inexperienced teenager being asked to resolve potentially complex issues involving property, inheritance, commercial transactions, disputed debts, and damages. If an inexperienced, albeit precocious, teenager could serve as district bailiff, was the authority invested in the post or the person when handling civil disputes? According to Wang Liqi 王利器, Zheng was probably eighteen to twenty-one years old when he served as a district bailiff.[62] Despite Zheng's youth, there is little question of the authority of the district bailiff in his district. Exemplary judges of course, acquired additional moral and ethical authority depending on how judiciously

61 *Hou Hanshu*, 35.1207.

62 Wang Liqi 王利器, *Zheng Kangcheng nianpu* 鄭康成年譜 (Jinan: Qi Lu shushe, 1983), 33.

they performed their duties, but it appears that the position itself was the basis of the official authority. In some instances, a district bailiff could overshadow the magistrate and governor in terms of his power over district residents, and in some instances, a district bailiff's opinion could significantly affect a person's career. For example, we read in the *Hou Hanshu*:

> Yuan Yan, whose styled name was Jiping, was a native of Waihuang county, Chenliu commandery. He was poor but studious. He could completely understand the Classics and teach others. His personality was sincere, and he did not speak much … Later, he was enrolled as a district bailiff by the clerk of the magistrate, and benevolent morality was greatly extended. People [in the district] only knew the bailiff without knowing the magistrate and governor.[63]
>
> 爰延字季平，陳留外黃人也．清苦好學，能通經教授．性質慤，少言辭 … 後令史昭以為鄉嗇夫，仁化大行，人但聞嗇夫，不知郡縣．

Yuan Yan, as a district bailiff, was such an authoritative and eminent figure in the district that the local folks held him in high esteem so that his authority eclipsed respect for the magistrate and governor. The telling point is that the post of district bailiff was clearly one with significant responsibilities. Since it was the bottom rung of the official hierarchy, the position was typically a first posting for elite youth and their introduction to a career in officialdom.

Recalling the career of Zheng Xuan in light of the preceding passage, we see that even a young bailiff could earn great respect in his district, the degree of that respect reflecting his ability. Zheng Xuan's personal experience as a district bailiff, even though he disliked the job, unquestionably gave him early and valuable insights into the legal world, especially into the nature of civil cases. He eventually became one of the leading legal authorities in early China. As the *Jinshu* 晉書 (comp. 644) reports:

> The Han dynasty inherited the Qin system. Xiao He fixed the statutes … Later generations had their own understandings, and all annotated the law code differently. There were more than ten experts who wrote "chapters and verses" (*zhangju*) commentaries, including Shusun Xuan, Guo Lingqing, Ma Rong, Zheng Xuan, and other classicists. Each master's commentary was about a hundred thousand phrases long … The more complicated the phrases evolved over time, the more difficult the readers

63 *Hou Hanshu*, 48.1618.

> found them. Therefore, the Son of Heaven (Wendi of the Wei) issued an edict, which said that only Zheng Xuan's *zhangju* (chapters and verses) annotations were to be adopted, and that one need not incorporate all the other experts' [opinions].[64]
>
> 漢承秦制，蕭何定律 … 後人生意，各為章句．叔孫宣、郭令卿、馬融、鄭玄諸儒章句十有餘家，家數十萬言 … 言數益繁，覽者益難．天子於是下詔，但用鄭氏章句，不得雜用餘家．

According to this account, during the Han dynasty, there were many different interpretive traditions, which introduced great confusion into legal practice. To mitigate this confusion, Wendi of the Wei (r. 220–226) decreed that Zheng Xuan's interpretations would become the official interpretation.

Zheng's legal works have been lost for centuries, but recently Long Daxuan 龍大軒 has identified 193 fragments of Zheng's legal works in Zheng's commentaries to the Classics, the *Shiji*, and the *Hanshu*. These fragments of Zheng's work are the most numerous of the 543 fragments of legal commentaries of fifteen early scholars that have been discovered by Long.[65] The empire-wide establishment of Zheng's legal authority in the early third century gives us yet another reason to trust Zheng's claims about the difference between *yu* (dispute over crime) and *song* (dispute over property).

In summary, we find that significant institutional differences between civil and criminal litigation existed in the Han dynasty, which supports Zheng Xuan's claims of the nature of civil litigation. Specifically, civil complaints typically go first to the district bailiff, not the county court. Even when a complaint is mistakenly first submitted to the county court, the county court sends the complaint down to the district bailiff. But for criminal cases, the report, regardless of where it is first received, is typically submitted to the county court for preliminary investigation. Upon receiving the report, the county court sends law-enforcement officers to arrest and detain the suspect for interrogation. District bailiffs and other officials at the district level play no role in the interrogation. Only the county court and superior courts have the authority to try cases of criminal nature.

64 *Jinshu* 晉書 (Beijing: Zhonghua shuju, 1974), 30.922–923.

65 Long Daxuan 龍大軒, "Handai lü zhang ju xue kao lun" 漢代律章句學考論 (Ph.D. diss., Xinan zhengfa daxue 西南政法大學, 2006), 17–46.

4 Military Cases concerning "Civil" Matters

Finally, this chapter will discuss whether or not there were any differences between military or civil, cases concerning "civil" matters. The existing material suggests that while there were subtle differences between the two, they were reasonably consistent overall.

The military had its own particular characteristics. The department which heard the case varied according to the rank of the defendant. This was different to the civil administrative system which was fixed in the districts.

On the one hand, the upper and lower ranks among military personnel were directly subordinate. Military personnel were required to guard their posts and were unable to leave their posts in response to a charge against them. Therefore, if the defendant was a military officer, a case was only able to be heard by their superior officer. Otherwise, it was very difficult to commence proceedings.

For instance, if a reconnaissance scout was pressed for payment on an outstanding debt, the case would have to be brought to his commanding officer, and if a case was brought against a commanding officer, it was required to be filed with the military bureau.

On the other hand, when a dispute was between military personnel, the military system handled it by following the normal procedures of the state, which were the same as those among the civil population. The following case provides an example:

> On the *yiwei* day, the 4th month with Jiawu, the first day of the month, the first year of the Jianshi era, Xian, the head of the Linmu platoon, dared to say: I and Fu, who is the platoon scribe, interrogated section head Zhong and six other people. Prior to the interrogation, we informed them of the statutes concerning purchasing from the soldiers of one's major division or others' divisions without changing words for three days. Both Section Head Zhong and soldier Shang stated information of their household registration in their commandery, county, and district in accordance with their document. Zhong and others did not purchase from the soldiers of their major division or others' divisions.[66]

> 建始元年四月甲午朔乙未臨木候長憲敢言之，爰書雜與候史輔驗問隧長忠等七人，先以從所主及它部官卒買□三日而不更言請書律辨告乃

66 *JYX* strip no. E.P.T. 51.228, p. 192.

> 驗問. 隧長忠卒賞等辭, 皆曰名郡縣爵里年姓官除各如牒. 忠等毋從所主卒及它☐

In the above-mentioned case, which occurred in 32 BC, the defendant was a low-ranking officer (along with six others), meaning that the case was heard by his direct superior officer. When the platoon head heard the case, the platoon scribe assisted. Before the interrogation, the defendant was informed of the law and regulations, and the results were recorded by the scribe and presented to the superior officer. We can note here that there were no differences between the investigation of this case and the case concerning Kou En.

The example below illustrates the system of providing a difficult legal case to superiors:

> On the *xinchou* day of the fourth month, beginning with the day *yihai*, in the second year of the Gengshi period (AD 24), two officials, who are the *zhangshouhou* (deputy garrison commander?) and the deputy commander of the Jiaqu company forwarded [a testimony?] to Chi. According to the statute, [missing seven characters] a certain official questioned [the defendant] and decided to collect the claimed debt from the defendant. The defendant was not willing to accept the judgment. Thus, the certain official reported the problem. [We] forward the testimony of the defendant, according to the statutes and ordinances.[67]

This debt dispute occurred in 24 AD. A low-ranking officer (a certain scribe) was initially responsible for handling it, but the defendant did not admit to the debt. As a result, the scribe reported the matter to the deputy garrison commander and the deputy commander of the Jiaqu company, and again gave this case and the record of confession and related documents to an officer of the next level (perhaps the headquarters). This is also similar to the three-level (district, county, and commandery) civil system.

Finally, how was litigation handled when it occurred between civilians and those in the military? The evidence we have shows that the "principle of the defendant's side" was employed during this period: if the defendant was in the military, then litigation was resolved in the military system. If the defendant was a civilian, then it was resolved in the civil system. For instance, the case of Kou En, which we analyzed earlier and involved a military officer litigating against civilians, was handled by the bailiff.

67 *JYX* strip no. E.P.C. 39, p. 548.

In the *yimao* day, the 12th month with *guichou* the first day, the 3rd year of the Jianwu period, upon receiving the complaint of Jiaqu company forwarded by the county court, the district bailiff Gong summoned En to come to the district office.[68]

建武三年十二月癸丑朔乙卯，都鄉嗇夫宮以廷所移甲渠候書召恩詣鄉.

However, in the case below we are faced with the exact opposite: A civilian brought a case against a person in the military, which was handled by the military system.

Female Shi Junyi from Juli and Wang Ziyu demanded debt of 293 cash from the platoon head officer Li Shengzhi. I carefully interrogated him. Shengzhi stated: I used to serve as the head of the Tianbei platoon together with the husband of Junyi, Peng Zu. In December, the fifth year, I butchered an ox together with four others including Peng Zu. [The cost] had been calculated and paid. I do not owe Peng Zu any money. Peng Zu was transferred to the Baishi division. The complaint was forwarded to Ziyu to demand the repayment of 293 cash.

The statement of self-defense: I do not owe Peng Zu money. The case has been resolved and closed. Four years have passed since Peng Zu finished his service and returned to Chi. Now, Junyi reopened the case and demanded the repayment of debt. The self-defense statement was preserved in the Tianbei company. I would not visit the company. The wife of Peng Zu ...[69]

□居里女子石君佚、王子羽責候長李勝之錢二百九十三. 謹驗問. 勝之辭: 故與君佚夫彭祖為殄北塞外候□五年十二月中, 與彭祖等四人供殺牛, 已校計, 不負彭祖錢. 彭祖徙署白石部, 移書責厶羽錢二百九十三.

厶爰書自證, 不當償彭祖錢. 已決絕. 彭祖免, 歸䲶池, 至今積四歲. 君佚今復責厶錢. 厶自證爰書在殄北候官, 毋詣官. 彭□□妻 ...

We can know that the accuser here was a civilian, as she is described as a female in a local area, and that the defendant was in the military – a platoon head. On the grounds of the final section of the document which states "the self-defense statement was preserved in the Tianbei company. I would not visit the company", we can know that this debt liability case was thrown out by

68 *JYX* strip no. E.P.F. 22:1, p. 475.

69 *JYX* strip nos. E.P.S4.T 2: 52–53a, p. 558.

the Tianbei company, and that the case was somewhat complicated. In the above-mentioned case, the woman's husband, who served together with Li Shangzhi, had a dispute over the killing of some livestock. At that time, it was ruled that Li Shengzhi did not incur any liability for the debts. Four years later, the woman sought recompensation for the debt.

In summary, despite the fact that the military system had its own distinctive features, it was fundamentally the same as the civil system when handling "civil" disputes. Thus, we can safely utilize cases taken from the military system (the many cases from the *Juyan* for instance) to study the overall characteristics of "civil" litigation.

5 Concluding Remarks

Overall, the analysis reveals that as late as the Western Han, the legal practice of China exhibited clear distinctions between how the authorities handled disputes over property and disputes over crimes. These distinctions in practice gradually were translated into legal terms. Zheng Xuan 鄭玄 (127–200) in Eastern Han articulated that disputes over property were called *song*, whereas disputes over crimes were identified as *yu*. The ideas of Zheng Xuan became authoritative with the edict of Mingdi of Wei, and were accepted by and circulated among the contemporary scholars. Given these differences in terminology, institutions, procedures, and outcomes, which were analogous to the distinctions between civil litigation and criminal litigation, we are compelled to conclude that civil law did exist in early China and that it was different and separate from criminal law.

CHAPTER 3

Early Civil Statutes

In this chapter, we turn our attention to the civil statutes excavated, especially those from Zhangjiashan.[1] These statutes are concerned with such significant domestic matters as inheritance, household division, and the property interests of women. This chapter will further demonstrate the existence of civil laws in early China, especially the Han, by focusing on the statutes regulating domestic issues. The sheer existence of these statutes reinforces our conclusion that civil laws existed in early China.

Indeed, the earliest civil statutes could be found from the Qin law excavated from Shuihudi and Longgang; five civil regulations regarding debt and compensation were embedded in the Qin statutes that are predominantly penal in nature.

A. When the common people have debts, one should not venture without authorization to extort pledges. The unauthorized extortion of pledges, as well as accepting pledges with mutual consent, are both fined with

---

1 As a counter-proposition, civil and criminal cases shared certain procedures and institutions. First, except for the use of torture, the trial techniques and process were identical in civil and criminal trials. According to Professor Michael Loewe's research, a criminal trial entailed the following four stages: A) the accused gives his or her statement of what happened, B) the officials question the accused for an explanation of his/her actions, C) the officials question other parties to cross-check the statements, and D) the officials discuss statutes or ordinances among themselves (*The Government of Qin and Han*, 61). The review process for both civil and criminal cases was very possibly identical. If the county court had problems trying a case, it reported the case to higher authorities for review. This hierarchical system of review – from county court to commandery court to the central authority as the superintendent of trials (廷尉 *tingwei*) – is called *yan* 讞, as described in the *Zouyan shu* 奏讞書 (Documents Presented to Higher Authorities, ca. 187 BC) from Zhangjiashan. The common characteristic of this system shared by both civil and criminal cases, is that legal decisions could be appealed to higher courts.

Indeed, civil laws and criminal laws are sometimes blurred in practice, even in modern societies. For instance, English criminal courts can include a "compensation order" in the sentence that they impose, thus bringing elements of civil law into the criminal process. For the details of this practice, see Martin Wasik, "Compensation Orders and Civil Liability," *The Modern Law Review* 48, no. 6 (1985): 707–711. Furthermore, some civil systems also allow for the imposition of "punitive damages," which are intended to punish the defendant. For the details, see *Black's Law Dictionary*, 448.

Overall, even beyond Zheng Xuan's distinction between *yu* and *song*, we find that the differences between criminal cases and civil cases, at least among those we have found, are substantial and far surpass the similarities.

 | DOI:10.1163/9789004513907_005

two suits of armor. It is the practice of the court that he who extorts a pledge from another person is sentenced; he who gives the pledge is not sentenced. In the case of accepting a pledge with mutual consent, the person who gives the pledge is sentenced.[2]

B. "A" is small and not fully six feet (tall). He has one horse, which he personally takes to graze. Now the horse is *bai* (frightened)[3] by another person and eats one bushel of others' grain. Question: is he warranted to be sentenced or is he not warranted? He is not warranted to be sentenced nor to repay the grain.[4]

C. When government horses and cattle are taken out to graze, and horses and cattle die, the county where they have died is to be speedily informed. The county quickly inspects this and collects it. In case this is not done quickly and it becomes spoiled, the responsible officer compensates it with the value it had before it was spoiled.[5]

將牧公馬牛, 馬 [牛] 死者, 亟謁死所縣, 縣亟診而入之, 其入之其弗亟而令敗者, 令以其未敗直 (值) 賞 (償) 之.

D. If one loses or kills horses, cattle or sheep, one shall compensate and be criticized.[6]

馬牛羊殺之及亡之, 當償而誶.

E. Shall compensate the owner grain[7]

稼償主

A, B, and C are legal materials in the form of question and answer, apparently explaining the relevant regulations, while D and E are directly regulations. As a whole, the statutes mentioned above concern themselves with debt or compensation for damages to the property of others. We find that debt or compensation was clearly identified as a civil matter; no punishments such

2 *SHD* strip (*Falü dawen*) no. 148, pp. 127–128; cf. *RCL*, 162. Translation follows Hulsewé.

3 The word *bai* 敗 usually means "defeat" or "spoil," but the editors suggest that the word means "frighten" in this context.

4 *SHD* strip (*Falü dawen*) no. 158, p. 130; cf. *RCL*, 165. Translation follows Hulsewé.

5 *SHD* strip (*Qinlü shibazhong*) no. 16, p. 24; *RCL* 27. Translation follows Hulsewé (slightly modified).

6 Longgang strip no. 101, in *Longgang Qin jian* 龍崗秦簡, eds., Zhongguo wenwu yanjiusuo 中國文物研究所, Hubei sheng wenwu kaogu yanjiusuo 湖北省文物考古研究所 (Beijing: Zhonghua shuju, 2001), 106.

7 Longgang strip no. 162, in *Longgang Qin jian*, 126.

as confinement, mutilation, or execution were imposed. Hence, they arguably could be viewed as civil regulations.

These Qin regulations have sister statutes in early Western Han, that is, legal documents excavated from Zhangjiashan.

ZJS strip (*Statutes*) no. 50 says:

> If a dog kills or wounds livestock belonging to another person, the owner of the dog must compensate that person.[8]

ZJS strip (*Statutes*) no. 253 says:

> If A's horses, oxen, sheep or pigs eat B's crops, then A will be fined one *liang* of gold per horse or ox. Four female pigs are equivalent to ten sheep, and a male pig is equivalent to an ox. Then order A to compensate B, the owner of the crops.[9]

Even compensation for damages to official property was also deemed a civil matter. ZJS strip (*Statutes*) nos. 433–434 state:

> [If someone] loses, kills, or injures official livestock, or if these livestock cannot be recovered ... Under all these circumstances, let [the responsible person] compensate for the loss with its fair value. [If] the corpse of the livestock is recovered by the official, the compensation price can be reduced ...[If someone] ruins or damages official property, order him or her to compensate for the loss with its fair value. [If] the remains of the property is recovered by the official, the compensation price can be reduced.[10]

Here we find that if someone damages official property, that person must compensate the state for the damage at a fair value, or even reduced value depending on the circumstances, and person faces no other punishment.[11] Thus we

8 ZJS strip (*Statutes*) no. 50, p. 15.

9 ZJS strip (*Statutes*) no. 253, p. 43.

10 ZJS strip (*Statutes*) nos. 433–434, p. 68.

11 In modern societies, when a governmental agency sues an individual to demand repayment of a debt, even though the public interest is clearly involved, the case will be treated as if it involves two individuals (a legal person vs. a natural person) instead of state vs. individual. Therefore, it is still treated as a civil matter. This theoretical articulation did not exist in early China, but ZJS strip (*Statutes*) nos. 433–434 show that a similar practice

may conclude that compensation was carefully regulated and recognized as a civil matter in the Qin and Han periods.

If the statutes regarding debt and compensation were scarce, statutes concerning domestic property in early China were very substantial. They constitute the core of early Chinese civil law, including Statutes on Households, Statutes on Establishing Heirs, and Statutes on Registration.

1 Background and Scholarship

The Statutes on Households, the Statutes on Establishing Heirs, and the Statutes on Registration were all excavated from Zhangjiashan. Their excavation prompted a new wave of scholarly interest in the Han domestic justice system. Prior to their excavation and publication in 2001, scholars were almost entirely unaware of the existence of statutes dealing with domestic matters beyond the Statutes on Households, which had been cited by name only for many centuries.

Ban Gu's 班固 (AD 32–92) well-known "Xingfa zhi 刑法志" (Treatise on Penal Laws) from the *Hanshu* neglects to mention any specific statutes. Ban Gu merely states that chancellor Xiao He 蕭何 (257–193 BC) compiled the *Jiuzhanglü* 九章律 (Statutes in Nine Chapters), without offering further details:

> The laws of Three Sections proved insufficient to restrain villainy, so the chancellor Xiao He gathered together the laws of Qin. He chose those that were most suitable for those times, and he made the *Statutes in Nine Chapters*.[12]
>
> 三章之法不足以禦姦，於是相國蕭何攈摭秦法，取其宜於時者，作律九章.

Perhaps Ban Gu, having risen to prominence after the successful restoration of the Han by Emperor Guangwu 光武 (r. AD 25–57), took the efficacy and existence of Han laws for granted and presumed his peers' familiarity with those laws, never imagining that the details of those laws would one day become obscure. Or perhaps, intending his treatise as a critique of mutilating

existed. One question we cannot answer is: can a slave (or indentured servant) demand repayment of debt? We currently do not know of such cases.

12 *Hanshu*, 23.1096; cf., *RHL*, 333. Translation follows Hulsewé (slightly modified).

punishments, Ban Gu never set out to describe the whole legal system in detail. As Hulsewé speculated:

> It might be preferable to say that Ban Gu never attempted to describe the system at all, as it must have been familiar to his readers, but rather that he stresses a few aspects only ... Actually we are forced to conclude that Ban Gu in writing this treatise never set out to give a complete description of the legal system, but that he used this historical treatment of the punishments as a long and complicated introduction to defend a personal standpoint in the ever recurring dispute about the question whether the mutilating punishments should be maintained or abolished.[13]

In any case, prior to the Zhangjiashan excavation, the lacunae in Ban Gu's description of the laws frustrated historians eager to understand the details of Han laws in general, particularly the domestic statutes.

The first mention of the Han Statutes on Households appears in the received texts about four centuries after the fall of the Han dynasty in 220. The *Tanglü shuyi* 唐律疏議 (Tang Code with Commentaries, comp. 635) states:

> During the Han dynasty, Chancellor Xiao He received six chapters (*pian* 篇) of Qin Statutes. He added three new chapters to it: the Statutes on Stables, the Statutes on Levies, and the Statutes on Households. Until the Later Zhou period (Northern Zhou, 557–581), the Statutes on Households had been always named "Statutes on Households." The Northern Qi (550–577) attached statutes concerning marriage matters to the Statutes on Households and named it "Statutes on Marriages and Households." During the Kaihuang period of the Sui (581–600), [entries on] households were placed before those dealing with marriages, and the statutes were renamed the "Statutes on Households and Marriages."[14]
>
> 漢相蕭何承秦六篇律，加廄興戶三篇，迄於後周，皆名戶律．北齊以婚事附之，名為婚戶律．隋開皇以戶在婚前，改爲戶婚律．

Based on this text, we can assume that some form of the Han Statutes on Households was still available in the Tang dynasty (618–907). The Tang Statutes on

13 *RHL*, 313.

14 *Tanglü shuyi* 唐律疏議, ed., Liu Junming 劉俊明 (Beijing: Zhonghua shuju, 1983), 12.211. In addition, the "Xingfazhi" of the *Jinshu* echoes the *Tanglü shuyi*, saying that Chancellor Xiao added three new chapters, including the Statutes on Households, Levies, and Stables, to the transmitted Qin law to create the *Statutes of Nine Chapters*. See *Jinshu*, 30.992.

Households and Marriages incorporated the Han Statutes on Households after a long process of transmission, with major reshaping during the Northern Qi period, when Statutes on Marriage were added to the Statutes on Households to create the precedents for Tang Statutes on Marriages and Households.

We do not know when or the extent to which the Han Statutes on Households were lost.[15] However, when Shen Jiaben 沈家本 (1840–1913) first started to reconstruct Han statutes in his voluminous *Hanlü zhiyi* 漢律摭遺 (Miscellanea of Han Laws), he lamented the absence of evidence relating to the Statutes on Households.

> There are no regulations from the Statutes on Households to be examined. Given that taxes and labor services were considered important business, I put [the reconstructed] provisions regarding taxes and labor services first. [In addition], among the forty-four provisions in the Tang Statutes on Households and Marriages, twenty-five provisions are about household matters. I compiled them in the reconstructed statutes approximately according to their original sequence.[16]
>
> 按戶律目無可靠，其事以賦役為重，故以賦役居先，唐戶婚律四十四條，前廿五條並戶事，餘條略依其次序編入.

While admitting the absence of early extant materials relating to the Statutes on Households, Shen nevertheless attempted to "reconstruct" the statutes, basing his reconstruction on two assumptions. First, he assumed that taxes and labor services were the primary concerns of the Han Statutes on Households. Second, he believed that the Tang Statutes on Households and Marriages preserved the Han Statutes on Households. To reconstruct the lost Han statutes, Shen collected provisions regarding taxes and labor services scattered throughout the *Shiji*, the *Hanshu*, and the *Hou Hanshu*, then combined these historical references with twenty-five stipulations on households from Tang law. Unfortunately, Shen's first assumption is not supported by the Statutes of Households from Zhangjiashan, and his second assumption ignores the

15 Hulsewé noticed that the "Jingjizhi" of *Suishu* does not mention the Han code. Thus, he believed that the loss of the Han law was due to its revision in the Jin dynasty (*RHL*, 26). This speculation, which is unsupported by evidence, is not very convincing.

16 Shen Jiaben 沈家本, *Hanlü zhiyi* 漢律摭遺 (Taipei: Shangwu yinshu, 1976), 14.1. This book has 22 *juan* in total and contains many pieces of fragments of various Han statutes preserved in the *Shiji*, the *Hanshu*, the *Hou Hanshu*, classicists' commentaries on the Classics, and medieval encyclopedias.

likelihood of changes in the household statutes in the centuries from the Han to the Tang.[17]

A few decades after Shen, another great scholar Cheng Shude 程樹德 (1877–1944) shared Shen's frustrations when attempting to reconstruct Han laws in his "Hanlü kao" 漢律考 (A Study on Han Statutes), a part of his monumental project entitled *Jiu chao lü kao* 九朝律考 (A Study of the Statutes of Nine Dynasties).[18] However, Cheng did not follow Shen's speculative approach to reconstructing the Statutes on Households. Cheng simply reiterated the *Tanglü shuyi*'s limited account of the transmission of the Han Statutes on Households.[19]

In the 1950's, Hulsewé noticed the following provision attributed to the Han Statutes on Households compiled by Ying Shao in the *Fengsu tongyi*:

> The commanderies of Hanzhong, Ba and Shu, and Guanghan were allowed autonomously to select the period for the Dog Days.[20]

If this provision was indeed included in the Statutes on Households, it must have been some special emendation addressing the peculiar circumstances of Hanzhong 漢中, Ba 巴 and Shu 蜀, and Guanghan 廣漢. It does not seem to fit within the scope of topics typically covered by the household statutes.

In 1975, two decades after Hulsewé's work, a fragment of the Statutes on Households belonging to the pre-unification Wei state (403–225 BC) was found at Shuihudi along with a valuable trove of Qin laws. This find provided the first piece of hard evidence for the existence of these types of statutes in early China. The Wei fragment shows that the Han Statutes on Households had precursors in the Warring States period. Despite its importance, the fragment unfortunately supplied few details regarding statutes on households, and thus failed to stimulate significant research. Ōba Osamu, in his *Shi Kan hōseshi no kenkyū* (1982), only briefly mentioned the fragmented statutes, confining his discussion to dating.[21] Hulsewé, in his *Remnants of Ch'in Law* (1985), merely translated the fragment without elaboration or commentary.[22]

---

17 For a detailed comparison between Cheng's reconstruction and the excavated statutes, see Zhang Boyuan 張伯元, "Hanlü zhiyi yu Ernian lüling bikan ji" 漢律摭遺與二年律令比勘記, in *Chutu falü wenxian yanjiu* 出土法律文獻研究 (Beijing: Shangwu yinshuguan, 2005), 1–38.

18 Cheng Shude 程樹德, "Hanlü kao" 漢律考, in *Jiuchao lü kao* 九朝律考 (Beijing: Zhonghua shuju, 1963).

19 Ibid., 15.

20 *RHL*, 36.

21 Ōba, *Shin Kan hōseishi*, 69–71. Ōba argued that the date of the fragment should be the 25th year of the Marquis Wu of the Wei instead of the 25th year of the King Anli of the Wei, as the editors believed.

22 *RHL*, 208.

Before the Zhangjiashan excavation, our knowledge regarding the Statutes on Establishing Heirs and the Statutes on Registration was even more limited than our knowledge of the Statutes on Households. No previously transmitted or excavated texts mentioned them, nor were any fragments preserved.[23] The situation changed dramatically in 2001 with the publication of the Zhangjiashan strips, which provided scholars with authentic materials on Han laws. Among them, *ZJS* strip (*Statutes*) nos. 305–346 identify themselves as Statutes on Households, *ZJS* strip (*Statutes*) nos. 367–390 identify themselves as Statutes on Establishing Heirs, and *ZJS* strip (*Statutes*) nos. 354–365 identify themselves as Statutes on Registration. These three sets of statutes govern the creation, division, and perpetuation (inheritance) of households (*hu* 戶). Specifically, the Statutes on Households covers issues involving the administration of five household units, the practice of *mingtianzhai* 名田宅 (see below), rules for household registration, and rules for household division. The Statutes on Establishing Heirs regulates the lines of inheritance for both households and orders of honor (*jue* 爵). The Statutes on Registration regulate the establishment and registration of independent households by non-heirs.[24] Even though we do not know if the statutes unearthed at Zhangjiashan were complete or if they had been altered since Han times, we can be confident that these statutes address many important issues related to domestic activities. With the Zhangjiashan finds shedding light on cases preserved in received texts, it is now possible for scholars to study the domestic justice system of the Qin/Han with far greater sophistication and accuracy than ever before.

In fact, since the publication of the materials from Zhangjiashan, the domestic statutes have attracted scholarly attention. To date, four important works have appeared: (1) Li Junming 李均明, "Zhangjiashan Hanjian suojian guifan jicheng guanxi de falü" 張家山漢簡所見規範繼承關係的法律 (The

23 The Han Statutes on Registration was unknown prior to the Zhangjiashan excavation. An abstract of the Qin Statutes on Registration (Fulü 傅律) was found from Shuihudi, in the *Qinlü zachao* 秦律雜抄 (Miscellaneous Abstracts of Qin Statutes) in the 1975. Based on the abstract, the Qin Statutes on Registration mainly prescribed fines and hard labor for mistakes in registering people for their labor services. However, the content is completely absent from the Han Statutes on Registration that was excavated from Zhangjiashan. This phenomenon is puzzling; it perhaps shows that the Qin Statutes on Registration and the Han Statutes on Registration are two different collections of statutes, even though they have the same title. As an alternative, because both the Qin materials and the Han materials on these statutes we currently possess are incomplete, we simply cannot make an accurate assessment. See *SHD*, 87; cf. *RCL*, 115.

24 Besides the provisions on household registration for non-heirs, these statutes have other provisions, such as the welfare that the elders enjoyed from the state.

Laws Regulating Inheritance as Seen from Zhangjiashan Han Strips, 2002);[25] (2) Yun Jae-seug 尹在碩; "Shuihudi Qinjian he Zhangjiashan Hanjian fanying de Qin Han shiqi houzi zhi he jiaxi jicheng" 睡虎地秦簡和張家山漢簡反映的秦漢時期後子制和家系繼承 (The Heir System and Household Inheritance in the Qin and Han Periods Reflected in Shuihudi Qin Strips and Zhangjiashan Han Strips, 2003);[26] (3) Ochiai Hiroki 落合悠紀, "Kan 'Ninen ritsu ryō' ni okeru shaku to ko no keishō: Keishō yoteisha ni tsuite no ichi kōsatsu" 漢'二年律令'における爵と戸の継承-継承予定者についての一考察 (The Inheritance of Households and Orders of Honor Based on the Statutes of the Second Year: An Investigation of the Candidates for Heirs, 2007);[27] and (4) Liu Xinning 劉欣寧, *You Zhangjiashan Hanjian Ernian lüling lun Han chu de jicheng zhidu* 由張家山漢簡二年律令論漢初的繼承制度 (Discussing the Inheritance System in the Early Period of the Han Based on the *Ernian lüling* from Zhangjiashan, 2007).[28]

Li Junming was the first to use the domestic statutes to study the issue of inheritance during the Han dynasty. In his article, he points out that the Zhangjiashan strips contain more than twenty relevant provisions. He classifies those statutes in two major categories: statutory inheritance (laws that govern inheritance by statute) and testamentary inheritance (laws that govern inheritance based on the last will and testament of the deceased). He further subdivides the former into three subjects: inheritance of status, inheritance of household property, and determination of the order of succession for rightful heirs. He argues that "inheritance of status" meant to inherit the orders of honor and the privileges of the deceased household head, after which inheritance of the household property could take place. He finds the line of inheritance, however, differed depending on whether one inherited the household or inherited the order of honor of the deceased. Regarding testamentary inheritance, Li argues that it was also regulated by the Statutes on Households, supporting his argument by citing an excavated document entitled "Xianling quanshu" 先令券書 which he identifies as a last will and testament.[29]

---

25 Li Junming 李均明, "Zhangjiashan Hanjian suojian guifan jicheng guanxi de falü" 張家山漢簡所見規範繼承關係的法律, *Zhongguo lishi wenwu* no. 2 (2002): 26–32.

26 Yun Jae-seug 尹在碩, "Shuihudi Qinjian he Zhangjiashan Hanjian fanying de Qin Han shiqi houzi zhi he jiaxi jicheng" 睡虎地秦簡和張家山漢簡反映的秦漢時期後子制和家系繼承, *Zhongguo lishi wenwu* no. 1 (2003): 31–43.

27 Ochiai Hiroki 落合悠紀, "Kan 'Ninen ritsu ryō' ni okeru shaku to ko no keishō: Keishō yoteisha ni tsuite no ichi kōsatsu" 漢 "二年律令" における爵と戸の継承-継承予定者についての一考察, *Hō shigaku kenkyūkai kaihō* 漢史學研究會會報 12 (2007): 81–87.

28 Liu Xinning 劉欣寧, *You Zhangjiashan Hanjian Ernian lüling lun Han chu de jicheng zhidu* 由張家山漢簡二年律令論漢初的繼承制度 (Taipei: Guoli Taiwan daxue chuban weiyuanhui, 2007).

29 For the document, see my later discussion in this chapter, especially pp. 104–108.

Li's research was only preliminary. Its major contribution lay in the reconstruction of two parallel but logically separable lines of inheritance: the inheritance of order of honor and the inheritance of household property. In making this observation, Li provided a valuable framework for further work on the statutes.

Yun Jae-seug's scholarship built on Li's initial study, giving Li's insights much greater substance and coherence. In his article, Yun first argues that the Han Statutes on Establishing Heirs had precursors in Qin laws that defined the notion of *houzi* 後子 (heir). He then focuses on the Han Statutes on Establishing Heirs and relevant provisions from other domestic statutes. He demonstrates that Han laws defined the following sequence for establishing an heir for a deceased head of household: sons, daughters, father, mother, brothers, sisters, widow, grandfather, and grandmother. The sons who were candidates for the role of heirs were called *zinan* 子男 (sons) with the principal heir designated as *houzi*.[30] The principal heir enjoyed such privileges as representing the household in ancestor worship, adopting the designation as head of household with its appropriate order of honor, and had the first choice of portion when the household property was divided. Yun then analyzes household transmissions (*daihu* 代戶), household establishments (*lihu* 立戶), and household divisions.

Yun notices that the line of the inheritance for households was quite different from that of establishing heirs, except that the *houzi* in both cases had the first position in the sequence. According to Yun, the most visible difference between the two lines appears in the status of widows: in establishing heirs, the widow was seventh in line, but in household transmission, the widow was third. Yun argues that this disparity reflects the significant influence that widows in general had over household management during the Han dynasty. Regarding household divisions, Yun argues that the statutes "direct" the sons to divide the household property equally,[31] unless this equal division is expressly countermanded by the ultimate authority of the parents, as expressed in a will.

Yun's article greatly contributes to our understanding of these domestic statutes, yet Yun made a serious mistake. Yun believes that when daughters inherited the position of head of households, they could only inherit the household

30 *Houzi* 後子 is ideally the eldest son born by the principal wife. If she had no sons while the husband had concubines, the *houzi* should be the eldest son born by a concubine. If there was a divorce and then remarriage, the *houzi* should be the eldest son of the new wife. Among brothers, those who lived under the same roof with that of the deceased were prioritized over those who lived apart, and the eldest brother was prioritized over the younger ones. The same rule was applied to sisters. See Yun Jae-seug, "Shuihudi Qinjian he Zhangjiashan Hanjian," 33–35.

31 Yun is not cautious enough in this respect. The statutes that we possess are not clear on this matter, even though I tend to believe that equal inheritance might be the case.

property (land and houses) but could not inherit the orders of honor of the deceased head of household. Yun based his conclusion on the mistaken notion that females could not hold any order of honor in Han society.[32] However, as I will elaborate below, women could, and did, hold orders of honor.

Ochiai Hiroki's article focused on the line of inheritance as regulated by the provisions found in *ZJS* strip (*Statutes*) nos. 369–371, 379, and 380. After reviewing the research of two experts, Ikeda Yuichi 池田雄一 and Tomiya Itaru 富谷至, and taking up questions they did not fully address, Ochiai advanced three major points: (1) differences in the lines of succession with regards to the inheritance of order of honor and the inheritance of households indicate that kinship was the crucial factor in determining the former, while the dictates of maintaining the communal life of the household was a more critical factor in determining the latter; (2) the fact that *nu* 奴 (traditionally render as "slave") could succeed as heads of households means that the state put a high value on maintaining household continuity; and (3) when siblings inherited from siblings, they needed to register in the same household. As an afterthought, Ochiai wondered why there was no place for adopted sons in the line of inheritance.[33]

Liu Xinning's book is the most systematic and least problematic treatment of the topic to date. It synthesizes previous studies and raises many interesting new questions. After carefully analyzing the domestic statutes and offering her own interpretations of doubtful passages and phrases, Liu argues that there were two major characteristics of inheritance during the Han dynasty. First, in contrast to the equal-share principle that prevailed in medieval and late imperial China, by which all sons were entitled to be full heirs, the Han laws established a single heir for each household. That heir inherited the order of honor and the status of household head along with all privileges that went with those designations, and commanded a major share in the household property.[34] However, Liu is wrong on the latter point. We know that sons quite likely divided the household property equally, a subject that I will address later. Second, Liu argues that in contrast to medieval and late imperial Chinese laws which held that inheriting the responsibility of maintaining ancestral sacrifices was central and prior to the inheritance of household and any orders of honor, the Han statutes did not touch upon the issue of ancestral worship. Liu concludes that inheritance laws only governed secular privileges.[35]

32 Ibid., 36.

33 This is a good question. In my opinion, perhaps adopted sons, once they were adopted, were treated exactly the same as natural sons.

34 Liu Xinning, *You Zhangjiashan Hanjian*, 143–148.

35 Ibid., 163–168.

I agree with Liu on this conclusion, but her reasoning was partially wrong. She said that since women and elders could be designated heirs and they had no responsibility of performing ancestral worship, inheritance laws only governed secular privileges. However, two problems arise. First, why can elders not perform ancestral worship? Second, women did have a role in ancestral worship as we know from ritual canons. Nevertheless, Liu clarifies many issues. For instance, she points out that the term *xianguan* 縣官, which occurs frequently in the Zhangjiashan strips, did not refer to county officials, but was rather a generic term referring to the state, and sometimes even the Son of Heaven.[36] She also found that the term *sishi* 死事 also had a particular meaning: "died in the battlefield or while performing official duties." Regarding the establishment of heirs, she noted that those who had received the *nai* penalty (shaving off the beard and hair on the temples) could not become heirs, and that those who committed suicide were prohibited from designating heirs.[37] The problem with Liu's research is that her conclusion claims certain distinctive characteristics for the Han laws on inheritance, in contrast to later laws on inheritance, but fails to provide a sufficient description of the laws on inheritance in the post-Han period. Thus, these presumed distinctive characteristics of Han laws are insufficiently demonstrated.

The four scholarly works described above set the stage for this study and provided a valuable initial agenda for examining the questions surrounding the nature and function of domestic statutes in the context of civil laws in general. Inspired by these works, I will provide a synopsis of the domestic statutes.

2 A Synopsis of the Domestic Statutes

In the following synopsis, I will not attempt to reconcile the differences in opinions among various scholars. Rather, I will simply review two areas of agreement regarding the inheritance of orders of honor and the inheritance

36 Liu, *You Zhangjiashan Hanjian*, 31. Michael Loewe also discussed this term. See Loewe, "The Organs of Han Imperial Government: *Zhongdu guan*, *duguan*, *xianguan* and *xiandao guan*," *Bulletin of the School of Oriental & African Studies* 71, no. 3 (2008): 510. According to him, "In the majority of cases, *xianguan* 縣官 refers indiscriminately to organs of government, whether central or provincial, without any specification."

37 Liu Xinning, *You Zhangjiashan Hanjian*, 38–39, 53–67; cf. ZJS strip (*Statutes*) nos. 390, 375, pp. 61, 60. This provision indicates that those who committed suicide were prohibited from having an heir, even if they had suitable candidates, which is very severe as a punishment for committing suicide.

of households,[38] deferring discussion of scholarly differences to a later section of this chapter.

Han laws distinguished between inheriting orders of honor (rank or title) and inheriting households (property and status within the household). The circumstances of one's death sometimes affected how the deceased's order of honor would be passed on to an heir, as Han laws distinguished between those who died in the course of carrying out official duties and those who died otherwise. The laws governing the inheritance of households established a two-step process: only after the head of household was determined was the household property divided among the heirs.

2.1 *The Inheritance of Orders of Honor*

ZJS strip (*Statutes*) nos. 369–371 deal with those who died while carrying out their official duties.

> A person is counted as "dying on duty," if he dies while performing an official duty, or if he is wounded while performing an official duty and then dies within twenty days. Let his son inherit his order of honor [intact].[39] If the person had no order of honor, his heir will be made a *gongshi*. If there is no son, let the daughter inherit the order of honor, and if there is no daughter, let the father inherit the order of honor, and if there is no father, let the mother inherit the order of honor, and if there is no mother, let the brother inherit the order of honor, and if there is no brother, let the sister inherit the order of honor, and if there is no sister, let the wife inherit the order of honor. For those who die on duty and should establish heirs, if they have no parents, no wives or children, and no siblings, let their grandfathers become their heirs. If they have no grandfathers, let their grandmothers who reside in and are registered in the same households with them become their heirs.[40]

> □□□□為縣官有爲也, 以其故死若傷二旬中死, 皆為死事者, 令子男襲其爵. 毋爵者, 其後為公士. 毋子男以女, 毋女以父, 毋父以母, 毋母以男同產, 毋男同產以女同產, 毋女同產以妻. 諸死事當置後, 毋父母、妻子、同產者, 以大父, 毋大父以大母與同居數者.

38 They both belonged to the category of statutory inheritance, which was delineated by the Statutes on Establishing Heirs and the Statutes on Households. The inheritance of household includes the status of the household head and household property.

39 We know that, in this situation, the orders of honor were passed down intact because there are no indications of them being reduced in the provisions.

40 ZJS strip (*Statutes*) nos. 369–371, p. 59.

In brief, the ranking of heirs is sons (*zinan*), daughters, father, mother, brothers, sisters, widows, grandfather, and grandmother. Notably, in the special circumstances of someone dying while performing official duties, the orders of honor are not diminished when passed down. In the more typical circumstances of someone dying while not performing official duties, the order of honor would be diminished by steps. Moreover, if the deceased, at the time when he was performing an official duty, had no order of honor, his heir would be granted one level of honor, upgrading that person to the rank of *gongshi* 公士 (the lowest order of honor in twenty orders).

ZJS strip (*Statutes*) nos. 367–368 concern those who died while not performing official duties.

> To establish heirs for those who died of illness, the heir-child (*houzi*)[41] of a marquis (*chehou*) becomes a marquis (*chehou*). If there are no children born by the wife, let the children born by *ruzi* (a type of concubine) or *liangren* (a type of concubine) become heirs. The heir-child of a lesser marquis (*guanneihou*) becomes a lesser marquis (*guanneihou*); the heir-child of a *qing* becomes a *gongcheng*; the heir-child of a *wudafu* becomes a *gongdafu*; the heir-child of a *gongcheng* becomes a *guandafu*; the heir-child of a *gongdafu* becomes a *dafu*; the heir-child of a *guandafu* becomes a *bugeng*; the heir-child of a *dafu* becomes a *zanniao*; the heir-child of a *bugeng* becomes a *shangzao*; the heir-child of a *zanniao* becomes a *gongshi*. If there are no children born by the principal wife, let the children born by the *xiaqi* (a type of concubine) and *pianqi* (a type of concubine) become the heirs.[42]
>
> 疾死置後者，徹侯後子為徹侯，其毋適（嫡）子，以孺子［子、良人］子．關内侯後子為關内侯，卿侯後子為公乘，［五大夫］後子為公大夫．公乘後子為官大夫，公大夫後子為大夫，官大夫後子為不更，大夫後子為簪裹，不更後子為上造，簪裹後子為公士．其毋適（嫡）子，以下妻子、偏妻子．

With an exception made for the two highest orders of honor, marquis and lesser marquis, the remaining orders are decreased two steps when they are passed down to heirs. When sons inherit their father's order of honor, sons of the principal wife took precedence over sons born of concubines. Elder brothers took

41 I will discuss this term later in this chapter, especially pp. 123–124.

42 ZJS strip (*Statutes*) nos. 367–368, p. 59. According to Wang Zijin 王子今, the words *ruzi*, *liangren*, *xiaqi*, and *pianqi* in the quotation all belong to the category of concubines. See Wang Zijin, "Pianqi xiaqi kao" 偏妻下妻考, *Huaxue* 華學 6 (2003): 151–152.

precedence over their younger brothers, but only after the mother's status is considered. Only after the inheritance of the order of honor was settled was the question of who was to inherit the household resolved.

2.2 *The Inheritance of Household*

As previously mentioned, disposition of the household required two steps: resolving who was to acquire the title status of head of household and distributing the household's property among the heirs. Unlike the laws governing inheritance of an order of honor, the laws for the inheritance of the status of household head made no distinction between the circumstances on the deceased's end, meaning, it was irrelevant whether the deceased was performing official duties at the time of his death or not.

ZJS strip (*Statutes*) nos. 379–381 state:

> After the death [of a head of household], if there is no heir-son to inherit the household, let the father or mother inherit the household. If there is no father or mother, let the widow inherit it. If there is no widow, let the daughters inherit it. If there are no daughters, let the grandchildren inherit it. If there are no grandchildren, let the great-grandchildren inherit it. If there are no great-grandchildren, let the grandparents inherit it. If there are no grandparents, let the nephews inherit the household. When nephews inherit the household, they must have co-habited in the household [with the deceased household head]. The sons of divorced wives are not allowed to compete with the sons of the later legal wife. If the later legal wife does not have sons, let the sons of divorced wives inherit it.[43]
>
> 死毋子男代戶，令父若母．毋父母令寡，毋寡令女，毋女令孫，毋孫令耳孫，毋耳孫令大父母，毋大父母令同產子代戶．同產子代戶，必同居數．棄妻子不得與後妻子爭後．後妻毋子男為後，乃以棄妻子男．

ZJS strip (*Statutes*) no. 383 continues:

> After one's death, if there are no possible heirs except for slaves, let them become commoners, and grant them the land, house and other household property, according to the Statutes (missing one character). If there are many household slaves, only one of them can inherit the household.[44]

43 ZJS strip (*Statutes*) nos. 379–381, pp. 60–61.

44 ZJS strip (*Statutes*) no. 383, p. 61.

死毋後而有奴婢者，免奴婢以為庶人，以庶人律□之其主田宅及餘財. 奴婢多，代戶者毋過一人，先用勞久、有□□子若主所言吏者.

It appears that in ordinary circumstances the siblings of the dead household head were excluded from inheritance, but nephews were not. This somewhat puzzling arrangement is made even more troubling by the inclusion of slaves in the line of succession. I suspect that there might be some sort of textual corruption. *Tongchanzi* 同產子 should be rendered as *tongchan* 同產 and [*tongchan*] *zi* [同產] 子.[45] With this adjustment, the line of succession becomes: *zinan*, parents, widow, daughters, grandchildren, grandparents, siblings, nephews, and finally household slaves.

Once the new head of household was designated, distribution or division of the household property among heirs followed. *ZJS* strip (*Statutes*) nos. 312–313 state:

> For those who have unfortunately died, let their heirs[46] choose the lands first, then distribute the rest [among the other siblings of the heirs]. Other sons who want to establish their households, let [missing one character] be given to them. Those who have established their households but have no lands and dwellings, or those whose amount of land and dwelling does not fulfill the quota, let them inherit land and a dwelling to meet the quota. If their houses are not adjoined with [that of the deceased], they are not allowed to inherit the house.[47]

不幸死者，令其後先擇田，乃行其餘. 它子男欲為戶，以為其□田予之. 其已前為戶而毋田宅，田宅不盈，得以盈. 宅不比，不得.

How was property divided? Was it divided equally? *ZJS* strip (*Statutes*) no. 385 suggests an answer:

> [missing four characters] the eldest son, younger sons, [give?] them their property. Equally let them have a fair share of what they produced together and the interest on it.[48]

□□□□長 (?) 次子, 畀之其財, 與中分其共為也及息.

45 Liu Xinning and Ochiai Hiroki also engaged in a similar speculation. See Liu, *You Zhangjiashan Hanjian*, 95–96; Ochi, "Kan 'Ninen ritsu ryō'," 85–86.

46 From my previous discussion, we know that the heir also inherits the status of the household head.

47 *ZJS* strip (*Statutes*) nos. 312–313, p. 52.

48 *ZJS* strip (*Statutes*) no. 385, p. 61.

The strip is corrupt and very difficult to understand. Despite these uncertainties, since only sons are mentioned here, and since the word *zhongfen* 中分 suggests an equal-share practice,[49] we can be relatively confident in concluding that household property was divided more or less equally among the surviving sons. This conclusion is supported by cases in the received texts, which, according to Liu Xinning, include five cases of dividing household property equally among sons.[50] For instance, the *Taiping yulan* 太平御覽 (Imperial Observation for the Grand Peace, comp. 984) quotes an earlier text, *Xu qi xie ji* 續齊諧記 (Additional Records of Extraordinary Events, comp. ca. 500), which describes an incident during the reign of Emperor Cheng 成 (33–37 BC). Tian Zhen's 田真 joint household consisted of three brothers. Unable to get along with one another, they decided to divide the household, splitting the property into three equal portions.[51]

If our understanding of ZJS strip (*Statutes*) no. 385 is correct, and if we view ZJS strip (*Statutes*) nos. 312, 313, and 385 as a group, we have solid reason to believe that after the death of a father, his household property would be divided equally among his sons. The only privilege enjoyed by the primary heir (typically the eldest son of the principal wife), who by his place in the line of succession inherited the status of household head, was being allowed to choose his portion of the property first, with the remaining property distributed (presumably by the new head of household) equally among the other sons. The amount of land inherited by these other sons seems to be limited by a quota based on their order of honor. A second provision required that the houses of these other sons had to be adjacent to the original household.[52] The role of daughters in this process is unclear. It is worth noting that ZJS strip (*Statutes*) nos. 312, 313, and 385, all of which deal with household division, make no mention of daughters. If we accept that no significant information is missing from these statutes, it appears that daughters were not guaranteed a share in the division of household property, presumably because they had already received their portions in the form of dowries. However, nothing in these statutes explicitly prohibits daughters from participating in divisions of household property. We know of at least two circumstances in which daughters would routinely participate. First, if there were no sons or widows, daughters would become the designated heirs and their inheritances would be regulated according to the provisions stated in ZJS strip (*Statutes*) nos. 312, 313, and 385. Second, as we will

49 Liu Xinning, Cao Lüning, and Li Junming are all in agreement on this line of interpretation.
50 Liu Xinning, *You Zhangjiashan Hanjian*, 146–148.
51 *Taiping yulan*, 421.9.
52 Liu Xinning, *You Zhangjiashan Hanjian*, 122–123.

discuss in a later section devoted to testamentary inheritance, if the deceased head of household decided to pass property to a daughter by composing a will or testament, the will or testament would take precedence. Another way of stating this is that the statutes served as a kind of probate, regulating inheritances when the head of household died intestate.

For convenient reference, Figure 3 summarizes the line of succession in matters of inheritance. This chart illustrates the areas in which inheritance of orders of honor and inheritance of household status and property overlap and where they diverge. Both types of inheritance follow the same simple line of succession when the principal heirs are sons. The complexities begin with household inheritance.

<table>
<tr><td colspan="2"></td><td colspan="3">Household inheritance</td><td colspan="2">Rank inheritance</td></tr>
<tr><td rowspan="5">1st</td><td rowspan="5">Sons</td><td>1st</td><td colspan="2">Eldest son born by the principal wife</td><td colspan="2" rowspan="5">Same as left</td></tr>
<tr><td>2nd</td><td colspan="2">Younger sons born by the principal wife</td></tr>
<tr><td rowspan="2">3rd</td><td>1st</td><td>Sons born by a later wife</td></tr>
<tr><td>2nd</td><td>Sons born by a divorced wife</td></tr>
<tr><td>4th</td><td colspan="2">Sons born by concubines</td></tr>
<tr><td>2nd</td><td colspan="4">Daughters</td><td colspan="2">Father</td></tr>
<tr><td>3rd</td><td colspan="4">Father</td><td colspan="2">Mother</td></tr>
<tr><td rowspan="2">4th</td><td colspan="4" rowspan="2">Mother</td><td rowspan="2">Widows</td><td>Principal wife</td></tr>
<tr><td>Concubines</td></tr>
<tr><td>5th</td><td colspan="4">Brothers</td><td colspan="2">Daughters</td></tr>
<tr><td>6th</td><td colspan="4">Sisters</td><td colspan="2">Grandsons</td></tr>
<tr><td>7th</td><td colspan="4">Widow (principal wife)</td><td colspan="2">Great-grandsons</td></tr>
<tr><td>8th</td><td colspan="4">Grandfather (male lineage)</td><td colspan="2">Grandfather (male lineage)</td></tr>
<tr><td>9th</td><td colspan="4">Grandmother (male lineage)</td><td colspan="2">Grandmother (male lineage)</td></tr>
<tr><td>10th</td><td colspan="4"></td><td colspan="2">Siblings</td></tr>
<tr><td>11th</td><td colspan="4"></td><td colspan="2">Nephews</td></tr>
<tr><td>12th</td><td colspan="4"></td><td colspan="2">Slaves</td></tr>
</table>

FIGURE 3 The order of inheritance
FIGURE BASED ON YUN JAE-SEUG'S CHART WITH REVISIONS. SEE YUN, "SHUIHUDI QINJIAN HE ZHANGJIASHAN HANJIAN," 35

The inheritance of orders of honor was much more restricted and involved a much smaller pool of candidates than the inheritance of households (property and household head status). Most likely, this was because orders of honor were "gifts" granted to subjects by the throne, while households were productive units. The continuity of households was crucial to maintaining good social order, and so the state was predisposed to seek the preservation of households. The distribution of orders of honor, however, entailed legal privileges, whose value was illustrated by the observation that "the practice of redemption is closely connected with the practice of taking away orders of honor from a holder of such rank."[53] If the state was too generous in granting orders of honor, those orders would be devalued, thus defeating the very purpose of granting them. Consequently, the state adopted strict rules governing who was eligible to inherit a given order of honor. The special exemptions made for the holders of the two highest orders of honor, the marquis and lesser marquis, and for those who died in the course of fulfilling their official duties, demonstrates the state's interest in keeping its orders of honor restricted. The fact that for all heirs outside the exempted groups, the statutes required the demotion of inherited orders of honor by two grade levels, underscores the state's interest in maintaining the value of its bestowed honors.

2.2.1 Issues Being Debated

The preceding review of scholarly works shows that there are outstanding questions that deserve further exploration and clarification:

2.2.1.1 *The Possible Qin Precursor to the Han Statutes on Establishing Heirs.*

The scholar Yun Jae-seug proposed such a relationship. Yun found three pieces of evidence to support his claim:

> When somebody without authorization kills or mutilates or shaves his heir-son, this is to be reported. What is the meaning of the term "heir-son"? His son, making him heir to the aristocratic rank order of honor, as well as the heirs-apparent established by the princes or chiefs of states that are subjects [of Qin] are all heir-sons.[54]
>
> 擅殺、刑、髡其後子，讞之. 可（何）謂 “後子”？ 官其男為爵後，及臣邦君長所置為後大（太）子，皆為後子.

53 *RHL*, 205.

54 *SHD* strip (*Falü dawen*) no. 72, p. 110; cf. *RCL*, 139. My translation follows Hulsewé (slightly modified).

> When someone has died in battle for service without surrendering, a decision is taken [to reward] his heir. When again later it is shown that he did not die, the heir is divested of the order of honor. The men of his group of five are freed [of punishment]. The man who had not died is made a bond-servant on his return.[55]
>
> 戰死事不出，論其後．有（又）後察不死，奪後爵，除伍人．不死者歸，以爲隸臣．
>
> For someone who dies before he can be awarded an order of honor based on his merit in battle, the order of honor can be transferred to his heir, except when the heir has committed crimes subject to the *nai* punishment (shaving off the beard and hair on the temples).[56]
>
> 從軍當以勞論及賜，未拜而死，有罪法耐遷其後．

Yun believed that these provisions defined who could become the heir-son, the privileges that the heir-son enjoyed, and the legal status of the heir-son. He argues that the Qin already had such laws concerning the establishment of heirs.[57] Yet, a closer look at Yun's evidence reveals that the texts he cites are less concerned with inheritance in general than with special, one might even say, extreme circumstances. While Yun demonstrates that the notion of heirs did exist under the Qin and that those notions were reflected in Qin laws that dealt with the privileges available to certain heirs, Yun fails to demonstrate that Qin laws regulated the broader issue of how one established heirs. It is quite possible that the reason these statutes were not concerned with how one established heirs in general was because inheritance was typically subject to either

---

55 *SHD* strip (*Qinlü zachao*) no. 37, p. 88; cf. *RCL*, 117. My translation follows Hulsewé (slightly modified).

56 *SHD* strip (*Qinlü shibazhong*) no. 154, p. 55; cf. *RLC*, 82–83. This line is difficult to understand. Hulsewé admitted that he could not understand the statement. I did not adopt his translation for this particular fragment because he did not translate the word *hou*. Of course, my translation is also tentative. Its focus is on the word *hou*, which should be rendered as "heir." In addition, this reference to the *nai* (shaving off the beard and hair on the temples) punishment is very interesting. We find the same reference in the *ZJS* strip (*Statutes*) no. 390, p. 61. A person who was punished with *nai* was not qualified to inherit any orders of honor. This partially explains why *nai* (shaving off the beard and hair on the temples) was a severe punishment. Those who received this penalty were disqualified from enjoying many privileges.

57 Yun Jae-seug, "Shuihudi Qinjian he Zhangjiashan Hanjian," 31–33.

local custom or the testamentary will of heads of households.[58] The statutes cited by Yun appear to deal only with the privileges granted to the heirs already established. Yun sidesteps the distinction between granting privileges to established heirs and establishing heirs, two very different issues that should not be conflated.

There is, however, one piece of evidence from the Qin period that may suggest the existence of statutes governing the establishment of heirs. This evidence comes from the Zhangjiashan strips. Early in an account of a case of illicit sex (Case 21) of the *Zouyan shu*, we find the following citation of an old statute:

> An old statute says, "At the death of a husband, one takes the son as the heir. If there is no son, the man's father or mother is taken as the heir. If there are no parents, then the wife is taken. If there is no wife, then one takes a daughter as the heir."[59]
>
> 故律曰："死夫（?）以男為後. 毋男以父母，毋父母以妻，毋妻以子女為後."

The statute cited clearly addresses the issue of establishing an heir. It regulates a line of inheritance: sons, parents, wife, and daughters. The greater question is what is meant by the binomen "old statute." Just how old was this "old statute?" Since the *Zouyan shu* collection was compiled no later than 189 BC, only seventy years after the fall of the Qin dynasty, the illicit sex case must have taken place earlier. In particular, how much earlier? Very possibly, the old statute referred to in the *Zouyan shu* was indeed a Qin statute.[60] If so, this reference is the single piece of evidence that we have found for the existence of Qin Statutes on Establishing Heirs. Therefore, it is very likely that not only was the notion of heir expressed in Qin laws, but that statutes regulating the establishment of heirs also existed in the Qin period.

2.2.1.2 *Will and Testimonial Inheritance*[61]

Following the 1984 discovery of a document entitled "Xiangling quanshu" 先令券書, from Tomb 101 at Xupu 胥浦, Yizheng 儀征, Jiangsu 江蘇 province,

58 It is also possible that we no longer have the relevant statutes.

59 ZJS strip (*Zouyang shu*) no. 180, p. 108. My translation follows Michael Nylan, "Notes on A Case of Illicit Sex from Zhangjiashan: A Translation and Commentary," 27.

60 As the Zhangjiashan strips date back to 196–189 BC, the case must have occurred no later than 189 BC.

61 According to the *Black's Law Dictionary*, p. 329, the word "will" means "a document by which a person directs his or her estate to be distributed upon death."

scholarly attention shifted to issues involving wills and testamentary inheritance. A complete transcript of the document quoted below was published in the *Wenwu* in 1987 by Chen Ping 陳平 and Wang Qinjin 王勤金.

> On the tenth day of the ninth month of the fifth year of the Yuanshi reign period [AD 5], Zhu Ling of Gaodu village, who lived in Xin'an village, was extremely close to death. Therefore, he requested the Thrice Venerables of the county and district, the large district bailiff (*youzhi*), the *zuo*, the *lishi*, Tian Tan, and others to draw up his will.
>
> [Zhu] Ling himself spoke of there being three fathers, as well as six sons and daughters by different fathers. "I want to let each of them to be [made] aware of his or her father and his or her place within the household. The sons and daughters Yijun, Zizhen, Zifang, and Xianjun have Zhu Sun as their father. My younger brother Gongwen had Shuai Jinjun of Wu as his father. My younger sister Ruojun had Bing Changbin of Qu'a as her father.
>
> The aged widow says, "At age fifteen, Gongwen left home to go out to establish a household under his own surname, and he never sent back any cash to support us. I personally gave land to Zizhen and Zifang. The aforesaid daughters Xianjun and Ruojun are poor and they lack property. On the tenth day of the fourth month of the fifth year [of the Yuanshi reign period], I gave one field of rice and two fields of mulberry to Ruojun, and I gave one field of paddy to Xianjun until the twelfth month. Gongwen injured a person and was sentenced to penal servitude, so he is poor and lacks property too.
>
> On the eleventh day of the twelfth month Xianjun and Ruojun are each to return these fields to me, and I will cede them to Gongwen. When I receive the fields, I will give the two fields of rice and two fields of mulberry and field of paddy to Gongwen. The boundaries of the fields are to remain as they were before, and Gongwen may not transfer the fields in sale to anyone else."
>
> The officials in office now and the witnesses are: the *lishi*, people of the same five household unit, [Tian] Tan, etc., and the relatives Kong Ju, Tian Wen, and Man Zhen. The will is clear. Its provisions can be followed.[62]

元始五年九月壬辰朔辛丑，□高都里朱淩，淩廬居新安里，甚疾其死，故請縣鄉三老、都鄉有秩、佐、里師田譚等為先令券書. 淩自言有三

62 Chen Ping and Wang Qinjin, "Yizheng Xupu 101 hao Xihan mu Xianling quanshu chu kao," 20. My translation follows Bret Hinsch, "Women, Kinship, and Property as Seen in a Han Dynasty Will," *T'oung Pao* 84 (1998): 3–4.

父，子男女六人皆不同父．欲令子各知其父家次子女：以君、子真、子方、仙君父為朱孫；弟公文父□衰近君；女弟弱君父曲阿病長賓．

嫗言公文年十五去家自出為姓，遂居外，未嘗持一錢來歸．嫗予子真、子方自為產業．子女仙君、弱君等貧毋產業．五年四月十日嫗以稻田一處、桑田二處分予弱君．波田一處分予仙君．於至十二月公文傷人為徒，貧無產業．於至十二月十一日仙君、弱君各歸田於嫗，讓予公文．嫗即受田，以田分予公文，稻田二處、桑田二處，田界易如故，公文不得移賣田予他人．

時任知者里師、伍人譚等及親屬孔聚、田文、滿真，先令券書，明白可以從事．

This document was dated AD 5, during the reign of Emperor Ping 平 (9 BC–AD 5). Chen Ping and Wang Qinjin point out that this was the first time this sort of document, a *xianling* 先令, had been found. They render "*xianling*" as "pre-mortem will," based on the annotation of Yan Shigu 嚴師古 (581–645) in the biography of "Jing shisan wang" 景十三王 (Thirteen kings during the Reign of Emperor Jing) in the *Hanshu*, which says: "The term *xianling* refers to the last will made prior to the death [of the testator]" (*Xianling zhe, yu wei yiling ye* 先令者預為遺令也).[63] Chen and Wang analyze the document "Xianling quanshu" as follows: an old widow who married three husbands had six children by them. In AD 5, her eldest son Zhu Ling, who was dying, invited local officials to witness his will.[64] The will stipulated that Xianjun and Ruojun, who were siblings of Zhu Ling, would have to return land to their mother, the aged widow, by the 12th month of the year. The aged widow then intended to grant the lands to her son, Tian Fen, who was due to be released from jail sometime before the 12th month of the year. Chen and Wang further speculated that this excavated text, when viewed in the context of other information about *xianling* in received texts, shows that during the Han dynasty, wills were widely used.[65] Publication of the "Xianling quanshu" by Chen and Wang immediately attracted scholarly attention, in particular, Bret Hinsch's 1998 study of the document, "Women, Kinship, and Property as Seen in a Han Dynasty Will."[66] Hinsch has no doubt that this document is a will, and that it serves as eloquent evidence of the place of testimonial inheritance in Han.

63 Wang Ping and Chen Qinjin, "Yizheng Xupu 101 hao Xihan mu," 21–22.

64 This part is a misreading of the document. The testator was the old widow, not her son. I will discuss this point in detail later.

65 Wang Ping and Chen Qinjin, "Yizheng Xupu 101 hao Xihan mu," 22.

66 Hinsch, "Women, Kinship, and Property," 1–20.

> The highly developed form of the Xupu will attests to legal precedents for employing this sort of device. The handling of wills seems to have been a routine part of Han dynasty local government administration. By addressing a wide range of local functionaries, this document shows the enforcement of wills to have been a duty shared by various minor officials in the local bureaucracy. The recourse to official administrative apparatus shows the division of household property to have been of interest to more than just household members. Upon the death of a head of household, a will placed the distribution of property under state jurisdiction. The document thus helps correct the stereotype that early Chinese law was concerned almost exclusively with criminal rather than civil cases.[67]

In 2000, however, Wei Daoming 魏道明 questioned the view that testimonial inheritance existed in pre-modern China.[68] Wei defines testimonial inheritance as "a person disposing of personal property based on his or her own free will, which is unrestrained by, and takes precedence over any statutory inheritance." Given his definition, Wei argues that the "Xianling quanshu" was not a will because the testator was the elder brother, Zhu Ling, who did not own the property to be disposed. His mother owned it. However, Wei's argument collapses for the simple reason that he erroneously identifies the testator as Zhu Ling, the elder brother. If we read the document closely, we will find that in the narrative, Zhu Ling called the officials together to witness the will. It is Zhu Ling's voice that dominates the first part of the narration, clarifying the issues of kinship, specifically, which sibling was born to which father. Zhu Ling then completely disappears from the remainder of the document. The central figure of the narrative is the aged widow since she is the one dispersing the household property among her children. Thus, it is the aged widow, not the elder brother, who is the actual testator. In other words, the *xianling* was the will of the aged widow, not her son Zhu Ling. Having corrected this misunderstanding of the text, we can now more accurately interpret what is meant by *xianling* and how wills functioned in Han society.

In AD 5, Zhu Ling, who was the eldest brother, lay dying. He felt that the household property needed to be clearly dispersed among his siblings and certain other kinship matters needed to be clarified. Therefore, he suggested that his mother, already quite elderly, make a will, which she did. The major issue to be addressed in the will was the division of the household property. Had

67 Ibid., 15.

68 Wei Daoming 魏道明, "Zhongguo gudai yizhu jicheng zhidu zhiyi" 中國古代遺囑繼承制度質疑, *Lishi yanjiu* 歷史研究 no. 6 (2000): 156–165.

the document been drawn up simply to let siblings know who their respective fathers were, there would have been no need to call upon the local officials as witnesses. In the will, the aged widow disposed of her household property among her remaining children. Thus, contrary to Wei's interpretation, we find that Zhu Ling's role in the process is minor. Perhaps Wei was misled by Chen and Wang's original archaeological report that asserts that Zhu Ling was the head of the joint household, leading Wei to misidentify him as the testator.[69] But even the identification of Zhu Ling as the head of household is wrong. If Zhu Ling were the head of the joint household, he could have disposed of the household property on his own. Clearly, Zhu Ling's aged mother was in charge of the household property, and as such, would be considered the head of the joint household. This context raises the question of why the aged widow was the head of household.

Hinsch's hypothesis is revealing. He argued that after the widow's first husband died, she returned to her natal family along with her son Zhu Ling. He bases his assumption on the fact that the document indicates that Zhu Ling's original village was Gaodu village but that he lived in Xin'an village. Hinsch further speculated that the widow's natal family lacked a son and that "they brought in a son-in-law to oversee the household's assets."[70] The widow remarried twice, bringing two new husbands to her natal household, both of whom died. Thus, the power exercised by the widow as described in the document was "possibly explicable through the uxorilocal nature of her two final marriages. She was simply controlling the property of a natal household that she never left."[71]

One year after Wei's article, the publication of Zhangjiashan strips in 2001 added new fuel to the debate. Discussions focused mainly on the following provisions in the Statutes on Households:

ZJS strip (*Statutes*) nos. 334–336:

> If an ordinary person wants to make a *xianling* (pre-mortem will) to dispose of real estate, slaves, and property, the district bailiff should listen to his or her will in person. Everything needs to be written in three copies and submitted by following the same procedure for household registers. When a dispute occurs, carry out matters according to the written contract. If there is no written contract, do not listen to the dispute. As for the

69 See Chen Ping and Wang Qinjin, "Yizheng Xupu 101 Hao Xihan mu," 24–25. Indeed, not only Wei but also Bret Hinsch mistakenly treated Zhu Ling as the subject of the will.

70 Hinsch, "Women, Kinship, and Property," 5.

71 Ibid., 20.

> farming land and houses that are divided, the recipient can hold them without establishing a household until the 8th month comes to register the household. If the officials obstruct the *xianling* or do not make a written document for it, the fine is one *liang* of gold.[72]
>
> 民欲先令相分田宅、奴婢、財物，鄉部嗇夫身聽其令，皆參辨券書之，輒上如戶籍．有爭者，以券書從事；毋券書，毋聽．所分田宅，不爲戶，得有之，至八月書戶．留難先令，弗爲券書，罰金一兩．

Given these provisions, many scholars were convinced that "*xianling*" meant "will" and that testamentary inheritance was acknowledged and protected by the law. However, following Wei, Cao Lüning 曹旅寧 insisted that neither will nor testamentary inheritance existed during the Han dynasty. In 2005, Cao argued that the provisions quoted above did not refer to testamentary inheritance, but referred to how a head of household divided household property during his or her lifetime among his or her children.[73] In 2008, Cao elaborated his argument into a theory that he called an "inheritance system centered on household division," basically reiterating his belief that the provisions stated in the text were solely concerned with household division.[74] Cao's problem lies in his understanding of what constitutes a will. As we know, the function of a will is to dispose of property freely, which makes a will the means to an end, namely, a clearly defined, ideally uncontestable division of household property. Such prescience on the part of a head of household was not only proper, but also demonstrated a laudatory concern for the future equanimity of his or her descendants. The provisions from the Zhangjiashan document clearly use the term *xianling* to describe the disposition of property based on a will, and implies that such wills were officially witnessed and documented.

Reinforcing this interpretation is a long-overlooked case from Juyan, which received a brief mention in the survey of Juyan cases described in Chapter 1. The *JY* strip nos. 202.8–15 reports:

> [missing one character] *zunyan* [missing one character], the thirtieth day, the first month, the first year of the Shenjue period (61 BC) and the thirtieth day, the second month, [the first year of the Shenjue period].

72 *ZJS* strip (*Statutes*) nos. 334–336, p. 54.

73 Cao lüning, *Qinlü xintan*, 313–317.

74 Cao Lüning, "Ernian lüling yu Qin Han jicheng fa" 二年律令與秦漢繼承法, *Shaanxi shifan daxue xuebao* (*Zhexue shehui kexue ban*) 陝西師範大學學報 (哲學社會科學版) no. 1 (2008): 62–68.

> [Someone] knew that one should follow the *xianling* (pre-mortem will) of the father, and the Statutes on Households. When the father was ill, he went to the Nanxiang district of the county to see the district bailiff Pohu [missing three characters] carefully noted it. Shenhou [the son's name?] served food and wine and observed the situation ... made ... a will concerning family property and cash ... until the *guichou*, the third month, the second year of Shenjue period (60 BC).[75]
>
> ⧄□尊延⧄神爵元年正月卅日．二月卅日⧄⧄知之當以父先令、戶律從⧄⧄父病臨之縣南鄉見嗇⧄⧄[76]□□破胡[77]□□□⧄⧄于□勝不⧄謹之．慎侯⧄⧄強奉酒食察事⧄⧄□□□為□□券書家財物一錢⧄⧄□□□到二年三月癸丑⧄

This fragment seems to come from the middle of a case report. The initial phrase of the fragment "[missing one character] *Zunyan* [missing one character]" □尊延□ is incomprehensible, but the word *zun* 尊 in classical Chinese often refers to one's parents. In context, it seems that this *zun* indicates the father. Thus, *yan* may be part of his name. There is no confusion about the two dates: the thirtieth day, the first month, the first year of the Shenjue period (61 BC) and the thirtieth day, the second month, and presumably also the first year of the Shenjue period. The end of the fragment also includes a date, *guichou*, the third month, the second year of [Shenjue?] period (60 BC?). Thus, we know that the case refers to an incident that occurred no later than 60 BC. Even though we cannot reconstruct the whole story in detail, the case clearly involved a *xianling* made by a father to dispose of his household property. It is striking that the Statutes on Households were invoked to justify the validity of the *xianling*. We know the father went to the Nanxiang district to see the district bailiff, in compliance with the provision in ZJS strip (*Statutes*) no. 334:

> If a person wants to dispose of real estate, bond-servants, and property with a *xianling* (will), the bailiff of the district should listen to his or her will in person.[78]

---

75 *JY* strip nos. 202.8–15, p. 314.

76 From the context, we know that "*se* ..." 嗇□ should be *sefu* 嗇夫, the district bailiff.

77 "... Pohu" □破胡 is not easy to translate. There are two possibilities. Pohu 破胡 is a given name, and the missing character in front of Pohu is the last name of Pohu; alternatively, it is a place name.

78 *ZJS* strip (*Statutes*) no. 334, p. 54.

This evidence from Juyan contradicts Cao Lüning's narrow understanding of *xianling* as a household division document produced during the lifetime of the head of household. This text clearly demonstrates that a *xianling* was in fact a will, incorporating the intentions of the household head concerning the disposition of the household property upon his or her death.

2.2.1.3 *The Status of Women in the Household*

Due to the limitations of our sources, I will only focus on two female roles: daughter and widow. I will discuss the status of daughters and widows in the context of inheritance and household management.

As we have already seen, inheritance in early China distinguished between the inheritance of orders of honor and the inheritance of households. The *Baihutong* 白虎通 (comp. AD 79) provides a purported answer to the question of why women could not inherit an order of honor.

> Why can't females have orders of honor [of their own]? They are *yin* and humble, and have no business outside the household. Therefore, they adhere to the principle of the Three Follows.
>
> 婦人無爵何? 陰卑無外事, 是以有三從之義.

However, this line has been often misread by scholars to mean that women could not have any orders of honor. Perhaps that prompted Yun Jae-seug in 2003 to infer that since women could not hold orders of honor, they could never inherit them.[79] But women in the Han could, and did, have and inherit orders of honor. There are many examples in the *Shiji* and the *Hanshu* of orders of honor being conferred upon women by emperors. For example, the emperor made the sister-in-law of Emperor Gaozu 高祖 (r. 206–195 BC) the Marquise of Yin'an 陰安.[80] The wife of Xiao He was made the Marquis of Zan 酇, and the wife of Fan Kuai 樊噲 was made the Marquise of Linguang 臨光 by Empress Dowager Lü 呂 (r. 187–180 BC).[81] Similar examples from the Eastern

---

79 I need to note that Yun has changed his opinion on this issue in his later article "Qin Han funü de jichan chenghu" 秦漢婦女的繼產承戶, *Shixue yuekan* 史學月刊 no. 12 (2009): 115–125. Yun now also holds that women could inherit ranks. In addition, in his 2009 article, Yun also notices the two pieces of excavated evidence that I am studying here (the lesser marquise widow from Xin'an and the land dispute document from Dongpailou), but readers will be able to tell that his analysis is quite different from mine.

80 *Shiji*, 10. 416. See Ru Chun's 如淳 annotation.

81 Ibid.

Han period (AD 25–220) can also be found. For example, three daughters of the King of Donghai 東海, Liu Jiang 劉疆, were made marquises by Emperor Ming 明 (r. 58–75).[82] These women were from elite families with high rank, making their experiences atypical for society as a whole. Nevertheless, these examples all show that women could have orders of honor.

Moreover, there were at least two formal channels by which ordinary women, i.e., women from non-elite families, could inherit orders of honor. ZJS strip (*Statutes*) nos. 369–370 regulate the inheriting of orders of honor when the original honor holder died while on duty. Those statutes listed a line of succession that begins with the son, followed by daughter, father, mother, brother, sister, and wife. We see that women (daughter, mother, sister, and wife) could inherit orders of honor, even though they fell far behind their male counterparts in the line of succession. A story from the *Shiji* adds authority to the observation that women could inherit orders of honor. During the sixth year of Gaozu's reign (201 BC), the Duke of Lu 魯 died in a battle. Since he had no children, his mother Ci 疵 inherited his order of honor as the Duke of Lu.[83] The event occurred approximately a decade before the compilation of the Zhangjiashan Han statutes, and thus does not directly corroborate ZJS strip (*Statutes*) nos. 369–370. However, even if we assume that there were no laws on the issue of inheritance prior to the composition of the Zhangjiashan Han statutes, the story from the *Shiji* chronicles a widow becoming the head of household after her husband's death, and also inheriting his order of honor. This event is consistent with ZJS strip (*Statutes*) no. 386:

> When a widow becomes heir to her husband, grant her the land and houses. [Also] she inherits her husband's order of honor, just as an heir-son who inherits it from his father.[84]
>
> 寡為戶後，予田宅，比子為後者爵.

A document excavated from a tomb dated to the reign of Emperor Wen (r. 180–157 BC) demonstrates that this provision was obeyed. The document contains the line:

---

82 *Hou Hanshu*, 42.1424.

83 *Shiji*, 18.917.

84 ZJS strip (*Statutes*) no. 386, p. 61.

> Adult female Yan, a lesser marquise widow, who serves as the head of her household in Xin'an.[85]
>
> 新安戶人，大女燕關內侯寡.

Xin'an 新安 must be a place name. *Huren* 戶人 could mean "household members," but if we follow the reading of Professor Hsing I-tien 邢義田, *huren* is a specific term referring to the head of household in Qin and Han documents.[86] Opinions differ on the meaning of the phrase *guanneihou gua* 關內侯寡. In 1994, the archaeologist Huang Shengzhang 黃盛璋 studied the line quoted above and argued that since women could not have orders of honor, when the widow of a noble became head of the household, she was addressed by the title of her [deceased] husband's order of honor.[87] Huang rendered the *guanneihou* (lesser marquis) as the order of honor of the deceased husband, not as the order of honor of the widow, rendering the phrase *guanneihou gua* 關內侯寡 as "the widow of the lesser marquis." Liu Xinning agrees with Huang.[88] However, if we apply *ZJS* strip (*Statutes*) no. 386 to the phrase in question, and if we recall that *ZJS* strip (*Statutes*) no. 367 states without qualification that the heir to a lesser marquis was, in fact, made a lesser marquis, it is very clear that if there were no sons, then the order of honor in question would be passed down to, and hence belonged to, the marquis's widow.[89] Therefore, the fragment is clear evidence that the provisions of the statutes governing the inheritance of orders of honor also applied to women and were duly implemented.[90]

ZJS strip (*Statutes*) nos. 379–380 show that women could inherit household property. A document excavated in 2005 from Dongpailou 東牌楼, Changsha 長沙, self-titled "Guanghe liunian jian Linxiang Li Yong, lidu daozei Yin He

85 *Jinzhou Gaotai Qin Han mu* 荊州高臺秦漢墓, ed., Jingzhou bowuguan 荊州博物館 (Beijing: Kexue chubanshe, 2000), 223.

86 Hsing I-tien 邢義田, "Longshan Liye Qin Qianling xiancheng yizhi chutu mouxiang Nanyang li shi tan" 龍山里耶秦遷陵縣城遺址出土某鄉南陽里試探, http://www.bsm.org.cn/show_article.php?id=744.

87 Huang Shengzhang 黃盛璋, "Jiangling Gaotai Han mu xin chutu gaodice, qiance yu xiangguan zhidu fafu" 江陵高臺漢墓新出土告地策, 遣冊與相關制度發復, *Jianghan kaogu* no. 2 (1994): 41–44.

88 Liu Xinning, *You Zhangjiashan Hanjian*, 158.

89 See my previous study. Those orders of honor below the top two orders of honor, marquis (*chehou* 徹侯) and lesser marquis (*guanneihou* 關內侯), were reduced by two levels before they were passed down to the heirs.

90 The material is also a piece of evidence showing that a widow could inherit the household.

shangyan Li Jian yu Jing Zhang zheng tian xiang hecong shu" 光和六年監臨湘李永、例督盜賊殷何上言李建與精張诤田自相和從書 (Agreement regarding the land dispute between Li Jian and Jing Zhang, submitted by *Jian Linxiang* [Inspector of Linxiang] Li Yong and *Lidu daozei* [Routinely Inspecting Robbers and Thieves] Yin He in the sixth year of the Guanghe period) provides an example of a daughter automatically becoming her father's heiress, the only extraordinary element being that the daughter was his only child.[91]

Turning from the inheritance of orders of honor and inheritance of households to daily household management, we can see from the "Xianling quanshu" that a widow could become a head of household with full control of the household property. She also had the "right" to dispose of that property with a will. The legal basis for that practice can be found in the ZJS strip (*Statutes*) no. 386 which stipulated that when a widow became heir to her husband, she inherited her husband's land and houses.

Based on his reading of the Statutes on Establishing Heirs and the Statutes on Households, the historian Gao Kai 高凱 in his recent article in 2008, identifies six situations in which women could become heads of household:[92]

1. If a grandson dies, his mother could inherit his household, with the restriction that she should not drive out her parents-in-law, invite a new husband into the household, or steal her son's property (ZJS strip [*Statutes*] nos. 337–338).
2. When a father dies without sons or a father to succeed him, his mother could inherit his position as head of household (ZJS strip [*Statutes*] no. 379).
3. If a husband dies with no sons or parents, his widow could succeed him as head of household (ZJS strip [*Statutes*] no. 379).
4. If a father dies with no sons, parents, or wives to succeed him, his daughter could succeed him (ZJS strip [*Statutes*] no. 379).

91 Jia Liying 賈麗英, "Cong Changsha Dongpailou jiandu kan Handai chujia nü de caichan jicheng" 從長沙東牌樓簡牘看漢代出嫁女的財產繼承, *Guangming ribao* 光明日報, July 13th, 2007; Wang Su, "Changsha Dongpailou Donghan jiandu xueshi"; *Changsha dongpailou Donghan jiandu*, eds., Changsha shi wenwu kaogu yanjiusuo and Zhongguo wenwu yanjiusuo, 73–74; Wu Wenling 鄔文玲, "Changsha Dongpailou Donghan jiandu Guanghe liunian zi xiang hecongshu yanjiu" 長沙東牌樓東漢簡牘光和六年自相和從書研究, *Nandu xuetan* 南都學壇 no. 3 (2010): 10–18. In addition, Miranda Brown and Rafe de Crespigny presented a summary of the document in their article, "Adoption in Han China," *Journal of the Economic and Social History of the Orient* 52 (2009): 239–242. I will analyze this case in detail latter.

92 Gao Kai 高凱, "Cong Juyan Hanjian kan Handai de nühu wenti" 從居延漢簡看漢代的女戶問題, *Shixue yuekan* no. 9 (2008): 82–92.

5. A grandmother could succeed if the grandsons have all died and the grandson had no sons, parents, wives, daughters, grandsons, or grandfather to succeed him (*ZJS* strip [*Statutes*] no. 380).
6. When a husband divorces his wife, his wife could retrieve the property she has received as a dowry from her natal family and set up her own household (*ZJS* strip [*Statutes*] no. 384).

Given the range of situations covered by these six possibilities, it seems likely that female heads of household were quite common in the Han dynasty. This speculation is confirmed by the standard histories of the Han. They record more than twenty occasions between 180 BC–AD 85 when the emperor granted cattle and wine to female heads of household.[93] In addition, a strip from Xuanquan 懸泉 also refers to female heads of household.

> The adult female Gao Zhenjun, who is a household head at Wudu, Lihan, registers her household property and transportation facilities.[94]
>
> 驪軒武都里戶人,[95] 大女高者君, 自實占家當, 乘物.

According to Gao Kai, the excavated document collection, "*Limin tianjiabo*" 吏民田家莂 (Documents concerning Government Land Rented Officials and Commoners), dating to 235, fifteen years after the fall of the Han dynasty, in the Wu 吳 kingdom, mentions eighty-six female heads of household.[96]

One may ask if female heads of household enjoyed the same privileges as their male counterparts. Liu Xinning believed that when widows or daughters became household heads, they could only manage or use the household property on behalf of their deceased husbands, but could not dispose of it freely.[97] Liu's assumption, however, is not supported by any evidence. On the contrary, we have already seen a case in which an elderly woman in AD 5 used a will to dispose of her household property.[98]

93 Ibid.
94 *Dunhuang xuanquan*, 96.
95 *Huren* 戶人 means "household head."
96 Gao Kai, "Cong Juyan Hanjian kan Handai," 89. This collection was excavated from Zoumalou, Changsha, Hunan in October 1996 by local archaeologists. This collection is basically a compilation of farming land leases between the households and the Wu state during the Three Kingdoms period. The entire collection was published in *Changsha Zoumalou Sanguo Wujian* 長沙走馬樓三國吳簡 (Wenwu Publishing House, 1999).
97 Liu Xinning, *You Zhangjiashan Hanjian*, 156–161.
98 See my previous study on the "Xianling Quanshu" 先令券書.

Additional evidence is found in the "Treatises on Food and Money" (Shihuozhi 食貨志) of the *Hanshu*:

> The ancestors of Widow Qing from Ba commandery acquired a cinnabar mine. They benefited from it for several generations and their family properties were too many to count. Widow Qing was able to preserve the family business and use the family wealth to protect herself, and thus no one dared to offend her. The First Emperor regarded her as a formidable woman of principle, honored her as a guest, and built a high platform named as "Lady Incorrupt" [to honor her].[99]
>
> 巴寡婦清，其先得丹穴，而擅其利數世，家亦不訾．清寡婦能守其業，用財自衛，人不敢犯．始皇以為貞婦而客之，為築女懷清臺．

While this incident occurred during the reign of the First Emperor of the Qin (r. 247–210 BC), prior to the promulgation of the Han statutes that we are studying, it illustrates the fact that even in the pre-Han period, widows enjoyed a great degree of autonomy, not only in managing their households, but also in managing their family businesses. Even though our scanty evidence does not allow us to establish the principle that all widows who became heads of household enjoyed the privilege of disposing of their household property, no counter-evidence has been found that shows that they were forbidden to do so. In all likelihood, widows enjoyed such privileges.

3 Differentiating and Defining Core Terminology

After analyzing and reconstructing Han dynasty domestic statutes, it is necessary to clarify four types of easily confused terms. There is currently some divergence of understanding in the academic sphere with regard to the understanding of this terminology.

3.1 Hou *Category* (hou, juehou, huhou)

3.1.1 *Hou* 後

Hou is regarded as a legal term in early China and is a general term for an heir. The entirety of the *Zhihou lü* from the *Ernian lüling* revolves around this concept. In terms of its general usage, *hou* indicates "descendants". For example, the *Mencius* includes the phrase, "There are three types of unfilial behavior.

99 *Hanshu*, 91.3686.

Not having descendants is the greatest of these."[100] In terms of legal usage however, the term encompasses a broad range of relatives, including not only direct descendants and descendants from a collateral line, but also relatives of the same generation, and even relatives of an older generation. In a broad sense, great-grandchildren, grandchildren, nephews, widows, younger and elder brothers, younger and elder sisters, parents, and grandparents all qualify as the *hou* of a deceased person.[101] For example, the following section from the *Zouyan shu* states:

> An old statute says, "At the death of a husband, one takes the son as the *hou*. If there is no son, the man's father or mother is taken as the *hou*. If there are no parents, then the wife is taken. If there is no wife, then one takes a daughter as the *hou*."[102]
>
> 故律曰："死夫（?）以男為後. 毋男以父母，毋父母以妻，毋妻以子女為後."

Owing to the fact that there were two forms of inheritance in early China, one being the inheritance of orders of honor (*juewei* 爵位) and the other being the inheritance of household (*hu* 戶), accordingly, *hou* was also divided into the "inheritor of orders of honor" (*juehou* 爵後) and the "inheritor of the household register" (*huhou* 戶後). The statute states:

> Should there be a widow who is pregnant, one must wait until the baby is born before the inheritance of the order of honor and the household (*jue, hu hou*) can be determined according to the statutes.[103]
>
> 死，其寡有遺腹者，須遺腹産，乃以律為置爵、戶後.

The terms "inheritor of the order of honor" (*juehou* 爵後) and "inheritor of the household register" (*hu hou* 户後) are both employed here.

100 *Mencius*, 7.26.

101 The scope may vary depending on the situations. I will discuss this aspect in detail later.

102 ZJS strip (*Zouyan shu*) no. 180, p. 108. My translation follows Michael Nylan, "Notes on A Case of Illicit Sex from Zhangjiashan: A Translation and Commentary," 27 (slightly modified).

103 ZJS strip (*Statutes*) no. 376, p. 60.

3.1.2 *Jue, hu hou* 爵、戶後

The term "inheritor of orders of honor" (*juehou* 爵後) appears in the *Shuidi Qin Bamboo strips*. The *Falü dawen* 法律答問 states:

> What is the meaning of the term "*houzi*"? His son, making him inheritor of the order of honor (*juehou*), as well as the heirs-apparent established by the princes or chiefs of states that are subjects [of Qin] are all *houzi*[104]
>
> 可（何）謂後子? 官其男為爵後及臣邦君長所置為後太子，皆為後子.

On the basis of these materials, Yun Jae-seug 尹在碩, Wang Yanhui 王彥輝, and other scholars have inferred that the notion of *hou* already existed during the Qin and that the Han inherited the Qin *houzi* system.[105] However, we must not overlook the fact that the we do not yet observe the usage of the term *huhou* in the Qin strips. The Qin strips contain only one example of the term *hou* as it relates to household registrations. The *Falü dawen* states:

> If a *shiwu* (士伍) does not have a son, his nephew is taken as his *hou* and lives with him.[106]
>
> 士伍無子，其弟子以為後，與同居.

Because a *shiwu* is without any orders of honor, the '*hou*' of a *shiwu* is only able to become an inheritor of household registration. The text however, does not contain the technical term *huhou* 戶後 (inheritor of the household [register]), which is rather thought provoking.[107] The first instance of the term *huhou*

---

104 *SHD* strip (*Falü dawen*) no. 72, p. 110; cf. *RCL*, 139. My translation follows Hulsewé (slightly modified).

105 Yun Jae-seug, "Shuihudi Qinjian he Zhangjiashan Hanjian fanying de Qin Han shiqi houzi zhi he jiaxi jicheng," 41–42. See also Wang Yanhui 王彥輝, *Zhangjiashan Han jian Ernian lüling yu Handai shehui yanjiu* 張家山漢簡二年律令與漢代社會研究 (Beijing: Zhonghua shuju, 2010), 81–84.

106 *SHD* strip (*Falü dawen*) no. 71, p. 110.

107 In two other occasions, the Qin strips also mention *hou*, but the *hou* both refers to *juehou* 爵后, not *huhou*. Specifically, (1) in the *Miscellaneous Excerpts from Qin Statutes*, it regulates: "When someone has died in battle for the service without surrendering, a decision is taken (to reward) his successor (*hou*). When again later it is shown that he did not die, the successor is divested of the orders of honor" (戰死事不出，論其後. 又後察不死，奪後爵). (2) In the *Statutes concerning Aristocratic Rank bestowed for Military Action*, it regulates: "When a person who had joined the army is warranted for a decision to award him orders of honor because of his meritorious service, if he dies before having been

appears in the *Ernian lüling*. Apart from the instance in strip 376, we have the following example:

> [If] a widow becomes the "inheritor of the household" (*huhou*), grant [her] the agricultural land and residence comparable to [that of] the son as one who inherits the orders of honor. [If] she is not fit to be the "inheritor of the household", and yet desires to be the householder so as to receive a reduced [amount] of agricultural land and residence, it is permitted to grant [her the same portion] of agricultural land and residence as a common person.[108]
>
> 寡為戶後，予田宅，比子為後者爵．其不當為戶後，而欲為戶以受殺田宅，許以庶人予田宅．

The use of the term *huhou* here indicates the inheritor of the position of head of household.

Under normal circumstances, the position of "inheritor of orders of honor" (*juehou*) and the "inheritor of household" (*huhou*) are borne by the same person. This is usually the eldest son of the primary wife, and if there is no eldest son of the primary wife, then this is borne by the eldest son born of a concubine. There are, however, some atypical instances which emerge in these two situations – the "inheritor of orders of honor" does not have an identical status with the inheritor of the head of household status:

1. The head of the household does not have a son. This situation is the reason for the division between the "inheritor of orders of honor" and the "inheritor of household". If the posthumous child is male, then he automatically becomes the *hou* (this regulation is identical for both "inheritor of orders of honor" and the "inheritor of household"); If the child is female, then they will be set up differently (see below for a detailed analysis of inheritance).[109]

---

invested, if his successor (*hou*) committed a crime that deserves the penalty of *nai* or banishment, or his successor is already punished with *nai* or banishment, the successor could not inherit the rank and award" (從軍賞以勞論及賜, 未拜而死, 有罪法耐遷其後及法耐遷者, 皆不得受其爵及賜). Translation follows Hulsewé with modification.

108 ZJS strip (*Statutes*) no. 387, p. 61.

109 Wang Yanhui believes that among those people who had orders of honor, the *juehou* (inheritor of orders of honor) and *huhou* (inheritor of household) are identical; see Wang Yanhui, *Zhangjiasha Hanjian Ernian lüling yu Handai shehui yanjiu*, 107. I disagree with Wang. I believe that due to the differences between the sequence of succession of orders of honor and household, the orders of honor and the household of the deceased could be separately passed down to different persons.

2. The eldest son of the primary wife has received punishment of shaving or amputation and above. Under these circumstances, the eldest son of the primary wife can still assume the role of "inheritor of household [register]", but other sons assume the role of "inheritor of orders of honor". This is because:

 Those who have had criminal punishments greater than shaving are not permitted to be a person's "inheritor of orders of honor".[110]

 嘗有罪耐以上，不得為人爵後.

3.2 Zi *Category* (zi, zinan, houzi, niezi, jiazi)

3.2.1 *Zi* 子

The term *zi* 子 in the *Ernian lüling* has three types of uses: sometimes it makes a general reference to children, yet sometimes it also specifically refers to a son or specifically to a daughter. General references to *zi* are most numerous in this text. For instance, strip 358 states:

> Where a commoner has more than five children (*zi*), if [his] son has registered in the household (*fu* 傅) and [his] daughter is twelve, then [the commoner's] father is exempt from [corvee labor] …[111]
>
> 民產子五人以上，男傅，女十二歲，以父為免 …

Because of the distinction between registered sons and daughters of twelve and older, we can infer that in the phrase "more than five children" the term *zi* is a general reference to sons and daughters.

> If someone pregnant with child (*zi*) dare dispute with another, even if the [other] person hits [her] changing her [pregnant state (i.e. she miscarries)], fine the miscarried woman four *liang* of gold.[112]
>
> 懷子而敢與人爭鬭，人. 雖毆變之，罰為人變者金四兩.

The use of *zi* here is a clear general reference to sons and daughters because ancient technology was unable to predict the gender of a child.

---

110 ZJS strip (*Statutes*) no. 390, p. 61.
111 ZJS strip (*Statutes*) no. 358, p. 58.
112 ZJS strip (*Statutes*) no. 31, p. 13.

> The guilty party, whose [punishment has rendered him] intact (*wang* 完), [has been sentenced to] wall building (*chengdan* 城旦) or grain pounding (*chong* 舂), [collecting] firewood for the spirits (*guixin* 鬼薪), or is liable for castration (*fu* 腐) on account of licentious acts, and will have their wife, children (*zi*), agricultural land, and residence taken away. If his children (*qi zi*) have a wife, husband, have formed a household, possess orders of honor, or if they are seventeen or above …[113]
>
> 罪人完城旦舂、鬼薪以上，及坐奸府（腐）者，皆收其妻、子、財、田宅. 其子有妻、夫，若為戶、有爵，及年十七以上 …

From the fact that "his children" (*qi zi*) can have either a husband or wife, the use of *zi* here refers generally to sons and daughters. However, in the *Ernian lüling*, the term *zi* also specifically refers to situations involving sons.

> If a man commits incest with the wife or slave girl of his elder brother, younger brother, youngest brothers, eldest uncle, father, or son (*zi*), then they should all be left intact and [sentenced to] wall building.[114]
>
> 復男弟兄子、孝（季）父、柏（伯）父子之妻、御婢，皆完為城旦.

From the phrase "son's wife" (*zi zhi qi*), we know that the *zi* here is male. In addition, there are also specific references to daughters:

> If a slave takes [his] mistress, [his] master's mother, or [his] master's wife and daughter (*zi*) as wife, then execute him in the market, shave his daughters, and make them slaves.[115]
>
> 奴取（娶）主、主之母及主妻、子以為妻，若與奸，棄市，而耐其女子以為隸妾.

It is clear from the use of the term *zi* here that it specifically refers to a daughter, otherwise it would not be possible to be "taken as a wife". However, when compared with the more general references, these examples of specific references are few, and can be determined by context. Therefore, under normal

113 *ZJS* strip (*Statutes*) no. 174, p. 32.
114 *ZJS* strip (*Statutes*) no. 195, p. 34.
115 *ZJS* strip (*Statutes*) no. 190, p. 34.

circumstances, the term *zi* generally refers to sons and daughters. This usage was also observed in the Juyan Han strips.

> Zhou Xian, a soldier of the Zhilu platoon …[had a] daughter (*zi*), a serving girl [named] Juanzhi who was eight years old … [and a] son (*zi*), a servant boy [named] Bing who was seven years old.[116]
>
> 制虜燧卒周賢 … 子，使女，捐之，年八 … 子，使男，並，年七 …

If we look at additional evidence contained in the received historical record, we find the usage of the term *zi* mirrored. For instance,

> You have taken my young ones (*zi*); Do not [also] destroy my nest.[117]
>
> 既取我子，無毀我室.
>
> A son/daughter (*zi*) is the heir of the parents.[118]
>
> 子也者，親之後也.

These two examples are general references to sons and daughters.

> This young lady (*zi*) is going to her future home, and will order well her chamber and house.[119]
>
> 之子於歸，宜其室家.

zi here refers to married-off daughters.

3.2.2 *Zinan* 子男

The flexible usage of the term *zi* brings several complications when deciphering these legal texts. How can we determine the gender of a *zi* if we lack context? Perhaps this complication was already an issue at that time, and it was solved by using *zinan* to refer specifically to a son and *nü* 女 to specify a daughter. For example:

116 *JY* strip no. 27.4, p. 41.
117 *The Book of Songs*, Mao no. 155. Translation follows Legge, vol. 4, 233.
118 *Liji*, 50.849b.
119 *The Book of Songs*, Mao no. 6. Translation follows Legge, vol. 4, 13.

> Other *zinan* (sons) wish to form [a new] household, so that their … agricultural lands and grant them.[120]
>
> 它子男欲為戶，以為其□田予之.
>
> The daughters (*nü*) of the regional lords and princes must not be called princesses.[121]
>
> 諸侯王女毋得稱公主.
>
> After the death [of a head of household], if there is no *zinan* (son) to inherit the household, let the father or mother inherit the household. If there is no father or mother, let the widow inherit it. If there is no widow, let the *nü* (daughter) inherit it.[122]
>
> 死毋子男代戶，令父若母，毋父母令寡，毋寡令女.

This distinction is also reflected in historical records. For example:

> Dingguo had intercourse with the concubine of his father, King of Kang, and [she] gave birth to a *zinan* (son).[123]
>
> 定國與父康王姬姦，生子男一人.
>
> As a result, Princess Pingyang, Princess Nangong, and Princess Linlü were summoned to come together to meet their elder sister, therefore, conferred her with the title Xiucheng Jun. She had a son and a daughter.[124]
>
> 於是召平陽主、南宮主、林慮主三人俱來謁見姊，因號曰脩成君. 有子男一人，女一人.

3.2.3 *Houzi* 後子

The words *zi* and *hou* are combined to produce the term *houzi* (heir-child). This term is not attested in the received historical records, however, in the

120 ZJS strip (*Statutes*) no. 313, p. 52.
121 ZJS strip (*Statutes*) no. 223, p. 39.
122 ZJS strip (*Statutes*) no. 379, p. 60.
123 *Hanshu*, 35.1903.
124 *Shiji*, 49.1982.

excavated materials it occurs predominantly in the context of the inheritance of orders of honor. In the excerpts taken from the *Shuihudi* to explain the term *houzi* in relation to Qin law, the term is defined as to refer to the "inheritor of orders of honor". Han law also had this tendency. For example:

> To establish heirs for those who died of illness, the heir-child (*houzi*) of a marquis becomes a marquis … The heir-child (*houzi*) of a lesser marquis becomes a lesser marquis.[125]
>
> 疾死置後者，徹侯後子為徹侯 … 關内侯後子為關内侯.

Does the term *houzi* require a gender? Yun Jae-seug puts forward the notion that *houzi* refers to a male being designated as "inheritor" *hou*, and that this definition does not include daughters. This view accords with the phrase "women are without orders of honor" (*furen wu jue* 婦人無爵) in the *Baihu tong*, and has therefore received the endorsement of numerous scholars. However, since the *Ernian lüling* clearly stipulates that daughters are entitled to inherit orders of honor ("the daughter of a deceased person" 死事者之女) with the term *zi* referring in general to sons and daughters, does the term *houzi* include daughters?[126] In addition, despite the fact that we already have materials where *houzi* is a specific reference to "inheritor of the orders of honor", we also need to ask logically whether or not this reference includes "inheritor of household [register]". In other words, are those without orders of honor also qualified to be established as a *houzi*? The materials we have at present are insufficient to answer this question, so it must remain in doubt.

3.2.4 *Niezi* 孽子

Owing to the ancient system of "one husband, one wife, many concubines", the technical term *niezi* 孽子 (son born of a concubine) arose. Today, this term is only considered an insult, yet during the Han, the term simply referred to a son born of a concubine. The *Shuowen jiezi* 說文解字 says: "*Nie*, is the son born of a concubine" (*nie, shuzi ye* 孽, 庶子也), and Duan Yucai 段玉裁 further explained:

125 ZJS strip (*Statutes*) no. 368, p. 59.

126 In the Qin law, the term seems to have specifically referred to heir-sons, but that was not necessarily the case in the Han law.

> Generally, a tree has a bud from the side of a branch, called *nie*. For the son born by a concubine called *nie*, the meaning is the same.[127]
>
> 凡木萌旁出皆曰櫱，人之支子曰孽，其義略同.

For instance, the *Shiji* says:

> The king had a son born of a concubine (*niezi*) [named] Buhai, [who was] the eldest among his sons. The king did not like him. The king, dowager queen, and heir-apparent all did not consider [him] as counted [among] the sons and brothers.[128]
>
> 王有孽子不害，最長，王弗愛，王、王后、太子皆不以為子兄數.

We also find the same usage in the *Ernian lüling*:

> All heirs who wish to divide the [agricultural land] of [their] father and mother, sons, siblings born of the same parents, principal mother(*zhumu*), step-mother as well as principal mother, step-mothers (*jiamu*) wishing to divide the agricultural land of a concubine's son (*niezi*) [or] step-son (*jiazi*), are all permitted to do so.[129]
>
> 諸（?）後欲分父母、子、同產、主母、叚（假）母、及主母、叚（假）母欲分孽子(叚）假子田以為戶者，皆許之.

This section of legal code illustrates that except for the general relationship between parents and children, there is still a special relationship between the principal mother, step-mothers, *niezi*, and step-sons. The principal mother (*zhumu*) clearly points to the principal wife; See the following from the *Shiji*:

> The wife sent a concubine to present the poisoned wine to give to him. The concubine wanted to say that there was poison in the wine but was afraid it [would result in] expelling the principal wife (*zhumu*). [She

127 Duan Yucai 段玉裁, *Shuowen jiezi zhu* 說文解字注 (Shanghai: Shanghai guji chubanshe, 1988 rpt.), 743a.

128 *Shiji*, 118.3088.

129 ZJS strip (*Statutes*) no. 340, p. 55.

> also] wanted to refrain from saying [anything], as she was afraid it will kill the master.[130]
>
> 妻使妾舉藥酒進之. 妾欲言酒之有藥, 則恐其逐主母也, 欲勿言乎, 則恐其殺主父也.

We can therefore infer that a *niezi* is a son born of a concubine with no blood relation to the primary wife. What then does "step-mother" (*jiamu* 假母) and "step-son" (*jiazi* 假子) refer to?

3.2.5 *Jiazi* 假子

In the received historical record, the term *jiezi* has two meanings. First, where a change in marital status has occurred, it refers to the son of the previous wife or husband. Second, it can also refer to an adopted son. See the following example from the *Shiji*:

> During the first month of spring, a woman from Meiyang accused [her] step-son (*jiazi*) of not being filial. She said: "The son always treated me as a wife and beat me severely."[131]
>
> 春正月，美陽女子告假子不孝，曰："兒常以我為妻，妒笞我".

The unfilial son here is clearly not of blood relation to the step-mother, and is also not a *niezi*. Therefore, as Wang Xianqian notes in his *Hanshu buzhu* 漢書補注 (Additional Notes to the Hanshu), quoting previous studies, this mode of speech refers to "the son of a previous wife."[132]

We find more specific examples in the *Gu lienü zhuan* 古列女傳(Biographies of Extraordinary Ancient Females, comp. 1st century BC). During the time of King Anli of Wei, there was a person known as "Kind Mother" Wei Mang who was very kind to the children of her husband's former wife. When the son of the former wife broke the law, the "Kind Mother" took pains to rescue him. When someone asked her why, she replied:

> Even though the son that I bore does not love me, I still saved him from disasters and eradicated what harmed him. So how can I act differently

130 *Shiji*, 69. 2265.
131 *Hanshu*, 76.3227.
132 Wang Xianqian 王先謙, *Hanshu buzhu* 漢書補注 (Beijing: Zhonghua shuju, 1975), 4970.

> concerning my step-son (*jiazi*)? His father made me his step-mother because he lost his mother ... Can it be called righteous if I only care about the son that I birthed yet ignore my step-son?[133]
>
> 如妾親子，雖不愛妾，猶救其禍而除其害，獨於假子而不為，何以異於凡母? 其父為其孤也，而使妾為其繼母 … 親其親而偏其假，可謂義乎?

Thus, here the term *jiazi* refers to the son of a former wife.

The commentary of the *Sanguo zhi* 三國志 draws out an example of a son from a former wife taken from the *Weishi chunqiu* 魏氏春秋 (Spring and Autumn of the Wei). It goes: Cao Cao 曹操 once took a concubine from the Du clan who already had a son. Cao Cao was very proud that he loved this boy, and he asked his guests: "In the world, who loves his *jiazi* as much as I do?"[134] (世有人愛假子如孤者乎?) The *jiazi* referred to here, who received the devotion of Cao Cao, is clearly the son of the concubine's former husband. The historical texts record that his name was Qin Liang, and that his surname was not changed to Cao.

The term *jiazi* also possibly refers to an adopted son. The commentary of the *Sanguo zhi* draws from the *Weilüe*:

> Taizu was in Hanzhou while Liu Bei dwelt on the mountain top and dispatched Liu Feng to challenge Taizu. Taizu scolded [Liu Bei]: "you, the shoe-selling peddler, dare to send your *jiazi* (adopted son) to resist your father?"[135]
>
> 太祖在漢中，而劉備栖於山頭，使劉封下挑戰. 太祖罵曰："賣履舍兒，長使假子拒汝公乎！"

In this case, Liu Feng, who was the adopted son of Liu Bei, was called a *jiazi*. However, this meaning as "adopted son" appears relatively late, with the earliest instance found in the *Sanguo zhi*, and is not seen in documents from the Han period. Furthermore, the term seems not to have been employed in the legal codes. Dong Zhongshu 董仲舒 notes in the *Chunqiu jueyu* 春秋決獄 (*Cases Tried on the Basis of the Spring and Autumn Annals*) that:

---

133 *Gu lienüzhuan* 古列女傳 (Beijing: Zhonghua shuju, 1985 rpt.), 27.

134 *Sanguo zhi* 三國志 (Beijing: Zhonghua shuju, 1959), 3.100, n. 1.

135 *Sanguo zhi*, 19.556, n. 2.

> A had no children. He picked up B, an abandoned child, from the street sidewalk and raised him up as his own son. When B grew up, he committed the crime of murder and confessed his crime to A. A hid B ...[136]
>
> 甲無子，拾道旁棄兒乙，養之以為子．及乙長，有罪殺人，以狀語甲，甲藏匿乙 …

This case involved a situation regarding an adopted child but did not use the term *jiazi*. Therefore, the term *jiazi* does not include the sense of "adopted child" in the *Ernian lüling*, and specifically refers to the son of a previous wife or husband.[137] Correspondingly, the term *jiamu* means only "step-mother".

3.3 Tongchan *Category* (tongchan, nan tongchan, nü tongchan)

3.3.1 *Tongchan* 同產

This term is often seen throughout the received historical record. The Tang commentator Li Xian 李賢 took it to mean "brothers who share the same mother."[138] However, the implied meaning of the term *tongchan* in the *Ernian lüling* is exactly the opposite. Here it simply makes a general reference to brothers and sisters but does not include situations where the mother is the same but the fathers are different. For example, strip 191 states:

> When one has illicit sex with one's sibling (*tongchan*), takes a sibling as wife, or marries a sibling, the offenders shall all be executed in the marketplace.[139]
>
> 同產相與奸，若取（娶）以為妻，及所取（娶）皆棄市．

From the fact that fornication or marriage is forbidden between *tongchan*, we know that this term includes both males and females and refers generally to brothers and sisters.

> When siblings (*tongchan*) become the heirs, the priority goes to those who share the same household. Only when no siblings share the same household, are the siblings who do not share the same household entitled.

136 Cheng Shude 程樹德, *Jiuchao lü kao* 九朝律考 (Beijing: Zhonghua shuju, 1963 rpt.), 164.

137 Zhangjiashan zhengli xiaozu 張家山整理小組 renders *jiazi* 假子 as the children of the ex-wife. This opinion is not accurate.

138 *Hou hanshu* 2.97, n. 6.

139 *ZJS* strip (*Statutes*) no. 191, p. 34.

> Under all situations, the priority goes to the senior siblings. If the sibling is not born by the same mother [of the deceased person], even if he or she is senior, the priority goes to those siblings born by the same mother.[140]
>
> 同產相為後，先以同居，毋同居乃以不同居，皆先以長者．其或異母，雖長，先以同母者．

This shows that those who have the same father but different mothers are categorized as *tongchan*. In the regulations of the legal code mentioned above, when inheritors are related, the regulations are only concerned with those who have the same father but different mothers, or the same father and same mother, but ignore situations involving those with the same mother but different fathers. From a semantic viewpoint, the phrase "first select one who has the same mother" (*xian yi tongmu zhe* 先以同母者) should refer to a situation involving the same father and same mother. The legal code tacitly agrees with the previous circumstances of those born to the same father and only differentiates the situation as to whether or not they have the same mother.

This finding seems to indicate the exact opposite of view held by Li Xian. In fact, *tongchan* in the legal code does not include siblings born from the same mother but different fathers. They are not able to make each other inheritors. Therefore, those qualified to inherit under the term *tongchan* only refers to brothers and sisters born from the same father.[141]

3.3.2 *Nan, nü tongchan* 男，女同產

The sequence of inheritance sometimes required division along gender lines. Therefore, *nan tongchan* 男同產 refers to brothers, and *nü tongchan* 女同產 refers to sisters.[142]

---

140 ZJS strip (*Statutes*) no. 378, p. 60.

141 Hsing I-tien holds a similar view; see Hsing, "Zhangjiashan Hanjian Ernian lüling duji er" 張家山漢簡二年律令讀記（二）, http://www.bsmorgcn/show_articlephp?id=175=. Professor Hsing argues that the annotation of Zhang Yan in the chapter of the biography of Yuanhou in the *Hanshu*, saying that the phrase "as long they have the same father, the sibling are called *tongchan*, not necessarily when born by the same mother" (*tong fu ze tong chan, bubi tong mu ye* 同父則為同產，不必同母也), was accurate in early Western Han. I believe we also need to distinguish different contexts, i.e., legal language vs. generic usages. The word *tongchan* has varying denotations in these difference contexts.

142 For a detailed study, see Ma Rui 馬瑞 and Li Jianping 李建平, "Tongchan ciyi kaoxi" 同產詞義考析, *Hanzi wenhua* 漢字文化 no. 2 (2011): 66–67. I disagree with Ma and Li in regard to the methodology and conclusion.

> If there is no son, let the daughter [inherit the order of honor], and if there is no daughter, let the father [inherit the order of honor], and if there is no father, let the mother [inherit the order of honor], and if there is no mother, let the brother (*nan tongchan*) [inherit the order of honor], and if there is no brother, let the sister (*nü tongchan*) [inherit the order of honor].[143]
>
> 毋子男以女，毋女以父，毋父以母，毋母以男同産，毋男同産以女同産.

There is a division here between *nan tongchan* and *nü tongchan*. The usage of these terms in the *Juyan Han* strips also reflects this division.

> Xu Zong is 50 years old. He has a wife, two sons, two daughters, two male siblings (*nan tongchan*), and two female siblings (*nü tongchan*).[144]
>
> 徐宗年五十. 妻一人，子男二人，子女二人，男同産二人，女同産二人.

3.4 Hu *Category* (weihu, shuhu, daihu)

3.4.1 *Weihu* 為戶

Hu (household) originally refers to a single door. It was used to indicate the basic social-economic unit in the Warring States period.[145] Members of the *hu* co-inhabited and shared property. They supported each other and bore legal responsibility, household taxes, and corvee. Under this historical background, the term *weihu* referred to establishing a new household; "*wei* means to make" (*wei, zaozuo*為, 造作).[146] This usage is quite common in the Statutes on Households. For instance, strip 318 says:

---

143 *ZJS* strip (*Statutes*) no. 369, p. 59.

144 *JY* strip no. 24.1a, p. 34.

145 There are three views regarding the origin of *hu* (household). (1) See Ikeda On 池田溫, *Zhongguo gudai jizhang zhidu de yanjiu* 中國古代籍帳制度的研究 (Beijing: Zhonghua shuju, 2007). On Ikeda directly links the emergence of *hu* to Shang Yang's reforms with 375 BC as the starting point. (2) See Du Zhengsheng 杜正勝, *Bianhu qimin: chuantong zhengzhi shehui jiegou zhi xingcheng* 編戶齊民: 傳統政治社會結構之形成 (Taipei: Lianjing chuben shiye gongsi, 1990). Du Zhengsheng attributes the rise of household to a series of military reforms and argues that the invention of the institute of household was to meet the needs of resource control and conscription of soldiers by the rulers. (3) See Toshikazu Hori 堀敏一, *Chūgoku kodai no ie to shūryaku* 中國古代の家と集落 (Tokyo: Kyūko sōsho, 1996). Contrary to the first two points, Toshikazu Hori points out that besides military causes, the development of a small peasant economy also contributed to the rise of households.

146 Wang Li 王力, *Wang Li gu Hanyu zidian* 王力古漢語字典 (Beijing: Zhonghua shuju, 2000), 676.

> For those who have not received farming land and dwelling sites, the district officials shall compile a list according to the dates when they established their households (*weihu*), putting the earlier ones on the right.[147]
>
> 未受田宅者，鄉部以其為戶先後次次編之，久為右.

Strip 316 says:

> Grant *gongzu*, *shiwu*, and *shuren* one dwelling site, and *sikou* and *yinguan* half of a dwelling site. If one wants to establish a household (*weihu*), it is permitted.[148]
>
> 公卒、士五（伍）、庶人一宅，司寇、隱官半宅. 欲為戶者，許之.

Strip 345 says:

> A wife cannot set up a separate household on her own (*weihu*) [when her husband is still alive].[149]
>
> 為人妻者不得為戶.

In these examples, the term *weihu* denotes the act of establishing a new household.

3.4.2 *Shuhu* 書戶

The term refers to register the household on official documents. Strip 335 says:

> As for the farming land and dwelling sites that are divided, the recipient can hold them without establishing a household until the 8th month comes to register the household (*shuhu*).[150]
>
> 所分田宅，不為戶，得有之，至八月書戶.

---

147 ZJS strip (*Statutes*) no. 318, p. 52.
148 ZJS strip (*Statutes*) no. 316, p. 52.
149 ZJS strip (*Statutes*) no. 345, p. 56. Here, *renqi* 人妻 (someone's wife) stands in stark contrast to *gua* (widow).
150 ZJS strip (*Statutes*) no. 335, p. 54.

The claimed farming land and dwelling sites would be recognized and protected by the state after completing the procedure of *shuhu* 書戶 (documenting household). This procedure seems to be alternatively called *dingji* 定籍.

Strip 322:

> As for replacing the head of household, or buying or selling farming land and dwelling site, if the officers of the district or farming land delay the process and fail to make a register (*dingji*) for them, the officers shall be fined with two *liang* of gold per day.[151]
>
> 代戶、貿賣田宅, 鄉部、田嗇夫、吏留弗為定籍, 盈一日, 罰金各二兩.

Strip 337:

> For cases among the ordinary people of [paternal] grandparents, parents, children, grandchildren, siblings, or children of siblings who wish to divide among themselves, or give to each other, male and female slaves, horses, cattle, sheep, or other valuable items: in every case, permit it. Immediately make a register (*dingji*) [of the exchange].[152]
>
> 民大父母、父母、子、孫、同產、同產子, 欲相分予奴婢、馬牛羊、它財物者, 皆許之, 輒為定籍.

Concerning household regulations, there existed many kinds of *ji* in the Han dynasty. Strip 331:

> As for the ordinary people's household registers of their dwelling sites and grounds, the detailed age registers, the land registers indicating neighboring fields, the unified registers of agricultural fields, and the registers of their agricultural field taxes, carefully make copies and forwarded these up to the County Court, and in every case, contain them in a bamboo chest or a wooden coffer bound shut with cords, and seal [the chest or coffer] using the seal of the Magistrate, the Assistant Magistrate, or the Bailiff of the Office.[153]

---

151 ZJS strip (*Statutes*) no. 322, p. 53; Anthony Barbieri-Low and Robin Yates, *Law, State, and Society in Early Imperial China: A Study with Critical Edition and Translation of the Legal Texts from Zhangjiashan Tomb no. 247* (Leiden: E.J. Brill, 2015) [hereafter, LSS], 797.

152 ZJS strip (*Statutes*) no. 337, p. 55; LSS, 801. Translation follows Barbieri-Low and Yates (slightly modified).

153 ZJS strip (*Statutes*) nos. 331–332, p. 54; LSS, 799. Translation follows Barbieri-Low and Yates.

民宅園戶籍、年細籍、田比地籍、田命籍、田租籍，謹副上縣廷，皆以篋若匣匱盛，緘閉，以令若丞、官嗇夫印封.

These five types of *ji* mentioned here must represent the details of the *shuhu* procedure, including registering the information regarding the dwelling and garden, ages, the boundaries of the property, tax, and so on. Therefore, we can tell that *shuhu* and *dingji* are the two sides of the same coin.[154]

3.4.3 *Daihu* "代戶"

According to the *Shuowen*, "*dai* means to replace" (*dai, geng ye* 代，更也). Duan Yucai 段玉裁 (1735–1815) annotates: "*dai* means to replace B with A" (*fan yi ci yi bi wei zhi dai* 凡以此易彼謂之代).[155] Therefore, literately, *daihu* refers to the inheritance of household, establishing a new head of household to replace the old one. Strips 378–379 say:

> After the death [of a head of household], if there is no son to inherit the household, let the father or mother inherit the household (*daihu*). If there is no father or mother, let the widow inherit it. If there is no widow, let the daughters inherit it. If there are no daughters, let the grandchildren inherit it. If there are no grandchildren, let the great-grandchildren inherit it. If there are no great-grandchildren, let the grandparents inherit it. If there are no grandparents, let the nephews inherit the household. When nephews inherit the household, they must have co-habited in the household [with the deceased household head]. The sons of divorced wives are not allowed to compete with the sons of the later legal wife. If the later legal wife does not have sons, let the sons of divorced wives inherit it.[156]
>
> 死毋子男代戶，令父若母，毋父母令寡 … 毋大父母令同產子代戶. 同產子代戶，必同居數. 棄妻子不得與後妻子爭後. 後妻毋子男為後，乃以棄妻子男.

Here, the term *daihu* refers to replacing the deceased head of household with a new one. However, one instance of *daiweihu* in the *Ernian lüling* is hard to interpret. It goes:

---

154 *Ji* in this context must refer to documents related to the household, but scholars are not sure what kind of documents they were. For the discussions, see Zhu Hongling 朱紅林, *Zhangjiashan Hanjian Ernian lüling yanjiu* 張家山漢簡二年律令研究 (Harbin: Heilongjiang renmin chubanshe, 2008), 244–260.

155 *Shuowen jiezi zhu*, 375a.

156 ZJS strip (*Statutes*) nos. 379–380, p. 60.

> When a grandson becomes the head of household and lives together with his grandparents, if the grandson fails to take good care of the grandparents, [the authorities] shall order the grandson to move out of the house and let his grandparents move into his house, be supported by his farming land, and utilize his slaves. The grandparents are not allowed to buy or sell [the farming land, houses, and slaves of the household]. If the grandson dies and his mother becomes the head of household (*daiweihu*), the mother is not permitted to expel her parents-in-law, take a new husband to the household, or illegally take away the belongings of her son.[157]
>
> 孫為戶，與大父母居，養之不善，令孫且外居，令大父母居其室，食其田，使其奴婢，勿貿賣．孫死，其母而代為戶，令毋敢遂（逐）夫父母及入贅及道外取其子財．

The langue of the sentences appears to be a bit vague. There seems to be two possible circumstances that the regulation is referring to: (1) When the grandson has no child, the mother of the grandson automatically becomes the new household head, or (2) the grandson has a child, but the child is too young to serve as the household head, so the mother of the grandson becomes the deputy head of the household on behalf of the young child.[158] Despite this ambiguity, it is clear that in both situations, *daiweihu* is an alternative term for *daihu*, and the regulation cited above means that when the grandson dies, the mother of the grandson inherits the status of household head.

4 Concluding Remarks

Written laws regarding civil matters, such as debt, compensation, and inheritance emerged in the Qin and Han periods. Among them, domestic statutes were very rich in content and inspired scholars to conduct research. These statutes contain four groups of important legal concepts, which could be divided into the *hou* category, *zi* category, *tongchan* category, and *hu* category. The terms included in each category have subtle differences. Some of them are identical to the usages in the received literature, while some are different. Some of them do not exist in the received literature. As a result, these terms often cause confusion. This chapter clarifies these terms to clear the path for scholars to better appreciate the sophistication of the domestic statutes.

157 *ZJS* strip (*Statutes*) no. 339, p. 55.

158 However, in the second situation, what is the role of the wife of the grandson, i.e. the mother of the young child? The new widow seems to be more legitimate to serve as the deputy head. Therefore, the first situation is perhaps more plausible.

CHAPTER 4

A Detailed Study on Three Civil Cases

1 Two Cases from the *Fengsu tongyi*[1]

A close study of two cases from the *Fengsu tongyi* offers an opportunity to enhance our understanding of inheritance issues in the Han.

Case 1 goes:

> A rich gentleman from Chen Liu was ninety years old, but he had no son. He took a girl from the Tian family as his concubine. Right after they copulated for the first time, he died. Later, a son was born from that union. The daughter of the gentleman accused the concubine of having had an illicit relationship [with another man] and of giving birth to his son: "When my father passed away, he was already aged. How could a son be born after only one night together?" The dispute over the property could not be resolved for several years. Chancellor Bing Ji came to the court to judge the case. He said: "I learned that a son born by an old man cannot bear cold [since the aged cannot bear it either]. In addition, he has no shadow." This was in the eighth month. Several children of the same age as the son were brought to court. All were stripped naked, but only the son of the concubine complained of the cold. When Bing Ji let them all walk out into the sun at midday, only the son had no shadow. The old and the young all exclaimed. [Bing Ji] thus took the property [of the father] and gave it to the son."[2]
>
> 陳留有富室翁, 年九十無子. 取田家女為妾. 一交接, 即氣絕. 後生得男, 其女誣其淫佚有兒, 曰: 我父死時年尊, 何一夕便有子? 爭財數年不能決. 丞相邴吉出殿上決獄[3]云: 吾聞老翁子不耐寒, 又無影, 可共試

1 The content of this section has been published in the article "Zhangjiashan *Ernian lüling* yu *Fengsu tongyi* zhong liangze anli de duidu 張家山<二年律令>與<風俗通義>中兩則案例的對讀, *Shilin* no. 4 (2009): 127–131, 191.

2 *Fengsu tongyi jiaozhu*, 587.

3 I think there may be a mistake here. The word "*jueyu*" 決獄 in the text should be "*duansong*" 斷訟, as the nature of the case is a dispute over property, and this scenario was called *song* (See Chapter 2 on *song*). The mistake could be the compiler's original mistake, or it could be a mistake that occurred during the transmission of the text. I think the latter is more likely

 | DOI:10.1163/9789004513907_006

之．時八月，取同歲小兒，俱解衣裸之，此兒獨言寒．復令並行日中，獨無影．大小歎息，因以財與兒．

Information newly acquired from the Statutes on Establishing Heirs helps to clarify the events described in this case report. On the surface, this was a clash between an elder daughter and her newborn half-brother (and, by proxy, the boy's concubine mother) over the disposition of the household's property. However, delving deeper, we find the story to be much more complicated.

The events described probably took place sometime between the 4th year of Yuankang 元康 (62 BC) and the 3rd year of Wufeng 五鳳 (55 BC), during the reign of Emperor Xuan 宣 (r. 73–49 BC), since Bing Ji was identified as the current chancellor and became chancellor during that time frame according to his biography in the *Hanshu*.[4] The Chenliu commandery (present-day Kaifeng, Henan province), the residence of the rich old man, was a prosperous commandery located approximately 500 km from the capital Chang'an. Let us review the facts of the case: the old rich gentlemen had no son; therefore, he took a concubine (*qie* 妾).[5] He died after a single act of intercourse. We can assume that he left no will with which to guide his heirs on how to dispose of his legacy. His sudden death, the presence of the concubine, and her unexpected pregnancy created an inheritance crisis. Everyone with a claim on the property had to wait to see if the concubine would give birth to a son. Such

because Ying Shao was a famous legal expert who would have known the difference between *song* and *yu*.

4 We need to consider the possibility that officials were often addressed by the highest positions they achieved in their lives. However, I think that should not be the case here. Ying Shao was very specific in mentioning official titles. In the second case, which we will discuss later, Ying Shao introduced the judge He Wu as follows: "The governor at that time was the Grand Minister over the Masses, He Wu." Thus, Ying Shao specified that He Wu, whose highest post was a Grand Minister over the Masses, was indeed a governor at the time when the second case took place. Assuming Ying Shao was consistent and Bing Ji was not a chancellor when the case was tried, we would expect Ying Shao to mention Bing Ji's real post in addition to his highest post "chancellor." As Bing Ji was only addressed as "chancellor," we believe that Bing Ji was indeed a chancellor when he tried the case. In addition, the biography of Bing Ji in the *Hanshu* does not indicate that he once served as the governor of the Chenliu commandery. If my understanding is correct, then this story suggests that a civil case could reach the highest authority in the system, i.e., the chancellor. However, this speculation cannot be cross-checked by other evidence. This story is the only instance in which a chancellor tried a property dispute.

5 *Qie* 妾, referring to concubines, was a very generic term. There were many different types of concubines, such as *ruren* 孺人, *xiaofu* 小婦, *pangqi* 旁妻, *pianqi* 偏妻, and *xiaqi* 下妻, as Wang Zijin argued. See Wang, "Pianqi xiaqi kao," 151–152.

prudence was actually enjoined in the provisions pertaining to the Statutes on Establishing Heirs, as stated in ZJS strip (*Statutes*) no. 376:

> Should there be a widow who is pregnant, one must wait until the baby is born before the inheritance of the order of honor and the household can be determined according to the statutes.[6]

In the absence of other male children, if a son were born, he would become the legal heir even if his mother was a concubine. ZJS strip (*Statutes*) nos. 367–368 states:

> To establish heir-sons for those who died of illness, the heir-son of a marquis becomes a marquis. If there are no sons born by the wife, let the sons born by *ruzi* and *liangren* become successors ... If there are no sons born by the wife, let the sons born by the *xiaqi* (concubine) and *pianqi* (concubine) become successors.[7]

This particular provision pertains to the inheritance of orders of honor, but it could also apply to the inheritance of household property. As we know, the highest tiers in both types of inheritance designated the sons. Since we know that the rules governing the inheritance of orders of honor were much stricter than those governing the inheritance of household property, if sons born of concubines were counted in the first tier when considering orders of honor, surely they would also be counted in the first tier when determining the disposition of household property.

In the case under examination, a healthy son was born. In keeping with the provisions regulating statutory inheritance, this newborn son became the heir to the legacy. The adult daughter was understandably upset. If this newborn son inherited the property of her rich father, she would be left little besides her dowry. Refusing to believe that a single union between her aged father and the concubine could conceive a child, she insisted that the son must be illegitimate, even though she had no way of proving it. We can imagine that the local authorities must have felt that even without conclusive evidence, the daughter had a reasonable claim, but following the procedures for handling doubtful cases, they must have reported this case to higher authorities.[8] The

6 ZJS strip (*Statutes*) no. 376, p. 60.

7 ZJS strip (*Statutes*) nos. 379–383, pp. 60–61.

8 See my previous study on the hierarchy of appeals. However, this case is unusual. It is the only evidence that shows a property dispute reaching the chancellor.

case eventually reached the highest authority in the system, the chancellor, Bing Ji. Bing Ji followed the common wisdom that a child from the loins of an aged father would be more susceptible to cold than other children of the same age, and that such a child would cast no shadow.[9] Despite the subjectivity and popular beliefs at play, Bing Ji determined, to his satisfaction, that the son had the characteristics appropriate to the child of an aged father, and therefore ruled that the son was a legitimate heir.[10]

An interesting hypothetical question to ask, in terms of household inheritance, is what if the "tests" had proven the son illegitimate? Would the daughter have inherited the household property? As seen earlier, *ZJS* strip (*Statutes*) nos. 379–383 regulate a long line of candidates for household inheritance,[11] of which only the topmost need concern us here: son-father-mother-*gua* (widow)-daughter. In cases where there were no sons, the parents became the first candidates for inheritance. The parents of the rich ninety year old man must have been long dead, making the legitimate widow or *gua* 寡 next in line. Scholars tend to interpret the word "gua" as "*gua qi*" 寡妻, or "widowed wife."[12] If the principal wife, who was the mother of the daughter, had still been alive, the whole matter of inheritance would have been easily resolved; the official wife, as widow, would have inherited the household property. When she died, again, in the absence of sons, the property would go to her daughter by statutory inheritance, or simply by the widow's will.[13] But in this case, the principal wife pre-deceased her rich husband, raising the question of whether the concubine could assume the status of legal widow (*gua*) and hence become the rightful heir. To answer this question, we first need to understand the status of concubines.

Scholars have generally agreed that in the Han period, it was proper for an elite husband to take a wife and multiple concubines, but the status of those concubines remains an issue of debate. Qu Tongzu 瞿同祖 for one, believed that prior to the twentieth century, concubines were not considered family

9 The belief that the son born by an aged father must be weak might have some sort of scientific basis, but the theory "no shadows under the sun" is unlikely. Thus, I suspect the test implied some sort of magic. We are not told of the whole process of the test, so I cannot judge how it worked. In addition, the meaning of *ying* (shadow) was perhaps not literal.

10 There is another possibility: both Bing Ji and the daughter were not aware of the logic I mentioned. Thus, they both believed that the test indeed "proved" the paternal relationship between the son and the old gentleman from Chenliu.

11 *ZJS* strip (*Statutes*) nos. 379–38, pp. 60–61.

12 For instance, Zhu Honglin annotates that this *gua* 寡 refers to the wife of the deceased. See Zhu, *Zhangjiashan Hanjian*, 231.

13 Widows made wills in the Han dynasty as we know from the "Xianling quanshu" from Yizheng, Jiangsu. See my previous discussions on this matter in Chapter 3.

members, and thus enjoyed no privileges whatsoever.[14] But Tao Yi 陶毅 argued the opposite by pointing to passages in the *Tanglü shuyi* that suggested that concubines enjoyed domestic privileges that were similar to, if somewhat less than, those of legal wives.[15] Since Tao's evidence was limited to Tang law, his argument may not apply to the Han period. Zhao Yupei 趙裕沛 touched upon this issue in his recent work, *Liang Han jiating neibu guanxi ji xianguan wenti yanjiu* 兩漢家庭內部關係及相關問題研究 (Research on Domestic Relationships and Relevant Issues in the Two Han Dynasties, 2006).[16] Zhao basically made two assertions. First, the relationship between the husband and concubines was loose, insofar as the husband could easily rid himself of concubines, and the concubines could also leave the husband and freely choose to discontinue the relationship. Second, the concubines had much lower status in a family than that of the wife.[17] Since Zhao provided no evidence, we cannot judge the accuracy of Zhao's assertions. However, contrary to Zhao's views, evidence from the Han laws shows that concubines sometimes enjoyed a certain status akin to that of the wife:

> Whoever beats the parents of the concubines ... will all be punished with *nai* (shaving off the beard and hair on the temples), just as if he were beating the parents of the principal wife. Those who scolded them [the parents] will be fined four *liang* of gold.[18]
>
> 毆父偏妻父母 … 若毆妻之父母，皆贖耐．其𦘦訽詈之，罰金四兩．

Since beating or scolding the parents of one's concubines incurred the same punishment as beating or scolding the parents of one's wife, these provisions attribute nearly equal status to concubines and wives. Moreover, if we read the provisions governing inheritance carefully, we find that the line of succession was very extensive, extending from eldest sons to "slaves." Nevertheless, concubines were not singled out as an independent category. If "slaves" had a place in the line of inheritance, it stands to reason that concubines must also have had a place. Therefore, the only reasonable supposition is that concubines

---

14 Qu Tongzu 瞿同祖, *Zhongguo falü yu Zhongguo shehui* 中國法律與中國社會 (Shanghai: Shangwu yinshuguan, 1947), 142–148.

15 Tao Yi 陶毅, *Zhongguo hunyin jiating zhidu shi* 中國婚姻家庭制度史 (Beijing: Dongfang chubanshe, 1994), 291–292.

16 Zhao Yupei 趙裕沛, *Liang Han jiating neibu guanxi ji xiangguan wenti yanjiu* 兩漢家庭內部關係及相關問題研究 (Wuhan: Hubei renmin chubanshe, 2006), 176–180.

17 Ibid., 175–184.

18 *ZJS* strip (*Statutes*) nos. 42–43, p. 14.

were included in the category of "widow" (*gua*). According to the Statutes on Establishing Heirs, the widow took precedence over daughters in statutory inheritance. Thus, if the principal wife were dead or absent, the concubine could probably inherit the property. In other words, in our case of the concubine's son, even if the daughter had won the case, proving that the son was not a legitimate heir, she still could not have inherited the property of the gentlemen. Curiously, the case report makes no reference to the relative positions of the concubine and eldest daughter in the line of succession, something that the chancellor and even the litigants must have known. The chancellor was arguably obliged to focus on the issue as presented to him, namely whether or not the child was legitimate. The daughter may have had additional reasons for pressing the issue for so long and at such enormous cost.

I speculate that if the daughter could demonstrate that the concubine had an illegitimate son, that meant that the concubine had illicit sex with someone other than the father, putting the concubine in extreme jeopardy. There are two possible consequences: (1) If the illicit sex took place when the rich old man was still alive, the concubine would be punished with the *nai* penalty (shaving off the beard and hair on the temples) and enslaved as a bond-servant, in accordance with ZJS strip (*Zouyan shu*) no. 182: "Those who commit illicit sex will be punished with the *nai* penalty (shaving off the beard and hair on the temples) and enslaved as bond-servants (male or female)" (奸者, 耐為隸臣妾).[19] Additionally, the concubine would lose her claim of inheritance, since those who received *nai* penalty (shaving off the beard and hair on the temples) were deprived of that privilege. (2) If the illicit sex took place after the old man's death, the act itself was not punishable.[20] However, if the concubine made false statements during the trial, she could be charged on that basis. When the suit was brought by the daughter, the son was still an infant, thus the concubine was obligated to respond to the suit on behalf of her son. Since her sexual activities were crucial factors in establishing the legitimacy of her son, she faced the inquiries of the authorities charged with establishing the facts. If she denied her illicit sex, and if that fraud were discovered, she perhaps would still be deprived of her privilege of inheritance and even jailed. In pressing the case, the daughter, at the very least, had the satisfaction of knowing that the concubine was forced to live with the anxiety of potentially grave punishments.

Case 2: A second case from the *Fengsu tongyi* is equally interesting:

19 ZJS strip (*Zouyan shu*) no. 182, p. 108.

20 See the illicit case.

There was a rich gentleman from the Pei commandery (present-day Xuzhou, Jiangsu province) who had more than twenty million cash in property. He had a son born by his concubine, who was only a few years old. The child's mother had died, and he had no close relatives. The daughter born by the principal wife was not particularly honorable. When the gentleman became very sick, he was concerned that the daughter and her husband would fight for the property, and his son would be [wrongly] deprived of a certain portion of the property. Therefore, he called together his clansmen and made a will, saying: "All the property I have is to be given to my daughter but for a sword left for my son. When he is fifteen years old, the sword should be given to him." Later, the son grew up, but the elder sister begrudged him the sword. The son then went to the commandery court to submit a complaint to ask for his sword.

My considered judgment: The governor at that time was the Grand Minister over the Masses, He Wu. When he received this complaint, he called the daughter and her husband. After examining the handwritten document, he looked at his assistants and said: "The daughter's personality is strong, and her husband is greedy, and mean. The father was worried that they might badly harm the son. The father also calculated that even if the son got the whole property, he would not be able to protect it. Therefore, the father temporarily gave the property to the daughter. In fact, he only wanted the daughter to safeguard it. Why didn't he give the daughter the sword? A sword is to 'cut off.' The fifteen years' time limitation was because he thought his son would be grown up after fifteen years, and he figured that the daughter and her husband would defy his wishes and would fail to give the sword to the son, and so the matter would be brought to the officials for adjudication. The officials might then be able to find the truth, and the real intention would be known and extended. How could an ordinary person so deeply and forwardly think like this?!" Therefore, He Wu confiscated all the property from the daughter and gave it to the son, saying, "It is fortunate enough that this mean daughter and her bad husband have been warmly clothed and well-fed for fifteen years." Thus, those who discussed the case were all convinced and said that He Wu had traced the origin of the circumstances and found the reason for them.[21]

21 *Fengsu tongyi jiaozhu*, 588.

沛郡有富家公，資二千餘萬，小婦子年裁數歲，[22] 頃失其母，又無親近，其大婦女甚不賢．公病困，思念惡聓爭其財，兒判不全，因呼族人為遺令云：悉以財屬女，但遺一劍與兒，年十五，以還付之．其後兒大，姊不肯與劍，男乃詣郡自言求劍．

謹案：時太守大司空何武也，得其辭，因錄女及聓，省其手書，顧謂掾史曰：女性強梁，聓復貪鄙，其父畏賊害其兒，又計小兒正得此財，不能全護，故且俾與女，內實寄之耳，不當以劍與之乎？夫劍者，亦所以決斷也．限年十五者，度其子智力足以自活，此女聓必不復還其劍，當聞縣官，縣官或能證察，得以見伸展也．凡庸何能思慮強遠如是哉！悉奪取財以與子，曰：弊女惡聓溫飽十五歲，亦以幸矣．於是論者乃服，謂武原情度事得其理．

This events described in this story must have taken place a few years before the first year of the Suihe 綏和period (8–7 BC), near the end of the reign of Emperor Cheng 成 (8 BC) since, according to his biography in the *Hanshu,* that was when He Wu served as governor of the Pei commandery.[23] Unlike the previous case in which the father died without leaving a will, this case centers on the issues surrounding a father's final will: the circumstances under which it was written, the testator's intent, the manner of its writing and execution, the subsequent actions of the beneficiaries, the legal challenges, and the judge's ruling. According to the rules for statutory inheritance, the eldest daughter by the man's principal wife should have inherited the household property only if her much younger half-brother, the son of the father's concubine, died. As the case report makes clear, the son was not only too young to establish his claim, he also no longer had a mother and did not even have close relatives to help him. The rich man was understandably anxious about his son's fate, given his assessment of his daughter's character. The report offers a valuable snapshot of how at that point in Han society, a last will and testament was made, providing such details as the gathering of witnesses, a declaration, and the fact that the final will was handwritten by the testator. The events described comport with provisions in the Statutes on Households, ZJS strip (*Statutes*) nos. 334–335:

22 "*Xiaofu*" 小婦, according to Yan Shigu 嚴師古 (581–645), means "concubines." In his commentary on the "Biography of Yuanhou" 元後 of the *Hanshu*, Yan explains, "*Xiaofu* means concubines" (*xiaofu qieye*小婦妾也). See *Hanshu*, 98.4021 n. 6; cf. Wang Zijin, "Pianqi xiaqi kao," 151–152.

23 *Hanshu*, 86.3484. The specific date cannot be inferred. However, from He Wu's biography in the *Hanshu*, we know that he served as the governor of Pei commandery a few years before the first year of the Suihe period (8–7 BC).

> If an ordinary person wants to make a *xianling* (pre-mortem will) to dispose of real estate, slaves, and property, the district bailiff should listen to his or her will in person. Everything needs to be written in three copies and submitted by following the same procedure for household registers.[24]

Since, in following the prescriptions set forth in this regulation, wills were to be submitted to the authorities "by following the same procedure for household registers," to understand the process of filing and keeping records of wills, we first need to know the procedure for household registration. ZJS strip (*Statutes*) no. 328 reads:

> Always order the district bailiff, officers, and the clerk of the magistrate to check the household registers in the eighth month. Make an extra copy (*fu*) of each document and keep it in the county court.[25]
>
> 恆以八月令鄉部嗇夫、吏、令史相襍案戶籍，副臧（藏）其廷.

Since there was cooperation between local district bailiff and the official from the county administration, and since the word *fu* ("extra") indicates that there were at least two copies made for a register, we can deduce that separate copies of the register were kept by the local district bailiff and the county court. We also know that the statute required three copies of a will. We can reasonably assume that this third copy was kept in the family. Such a system virtually eliminated the possibility of forging wills, since during a trial, the presiding judge could cross-check the three copies for inconsistencies.

The case includes one divergence from the procedure prescribed by the statute: only the clansmen were called in as witnesses to the father's final testament, but in this case, no officials had been summoned. Perhaps Ying Shao, who edited the case report, merely oversimplified the narrative, or the old gentleman was unfamiliar with the procedure for making a will.[26] The father's bequest of all his property to the daughter, and nothing but his sword to the son is very odd on the surface. Even stranger is the stipulation in the will that the daughter was to keep the sword in trust for fifteen years before releasing

---

24 ZJS strip (*Statutes*) nos. 334–335, p. 54.

25 ZJS strip (*Statutes*) no. 328, p. 54.

26 The statutes tell us what was supposed to be done, but not what was always done. Many people might not know the correct procedure.

it to the son. The terms of the will were binding since testimonial inheritance took precedence over statutory inheritance.[27]

As the case reveals, the father's true intention was to give his son all his property, but accurately assessing his daughter's character, he shrewdly constructed the ruse of the sword as a way of ultimately fulfilling his wishes. The gift of the sword was also, we gather, symbolic. In giving the sword to the son, the father was saying that fifteen years hence, the property should be cut off from his daughter. The vocabulary used in the report to describe the son's legal action to claim his testamentary inheritance, i.e., his father's sword, is very subtle: *ziyan* 自言 was indeed a legal term that refers to the action of submitting a complaint. This usage appears frequently in Han legal contexts, as demonstrated in the following passage:

> On *bingzi*, the leap month with *yisi* the first day, the fifth year of the Yongshi period (12 BC), the district bailiff of Beixiang dares to say that Cui Zidang submits a complaint saying that he went to the Juyan market to conduct personal business for his family.[28]
>
> 永始五年閏月己巳朔丙子，北鄉嗇夫忠敢言之. 義成里崔自當自言為家私市居延.
>
> The officials forwarded the document to Juyan, saying that Zhang Zijun from the Wansui ward submitted a complaint to demand the repayment of a debt from Xu, who is the officer in command of the Linzhi section ...[29]
>
> 官移居延書曰：萬歲里張子君自言責臨之隧長徐 …
>
> Inspector Li Feng submitted a complaint saying that he was previously the head of Gao pavilion at Juyan ... testified what he said.
>
> 尉吏李鳳自言故為居延高亭亭長 … 證所言.[30]

In addition, the word *ci* 辭 in the phrase *de qi ci* 得其辭 also has a specific meaning: it refers to testimony, as we see below:

27 Daughters inheriting a property through a will was not uncommon during the Han period. See the "Xianling quanshu" we studied earlier.

28 *JY* strip no.15.19, p. 24.

29 *JY* strip no. 132.36, p. 220.

30 *JY* strip no.178.30, p. 285.

> The testimony says: This *gongcheng* from the Yishou ward, Rile county is thirty years old, and his last name is Sun ...[31]
>
> 劾狀辭曰：公乘日勒益壽里，年卅歲，姓孫氏 …
>
> The testimony says: This *gongcheng* from the Linren ward, Juyan county is thirty-one years old, and his last name is Wu.[32]
>
> 劾狀辭曰：公乘居延臨仁里，年卅一歲，姓毋☐

In terms of procedure, the case also diverges from the statutory norm. Typically, a civil suit makes its way up the bureaucratic chain from district bailiff, to the county court, and finally to the commandery.[33] Perhaps because the case involved a very rich family, the son was allowed to bypass the lower courts and appeal directly to the highest authority in the commandery. Governor He Wu's examination of the will conforms to a provision set forth in *ZJS* strip (*Statutes*) no. 335:

> When a dispute occurs, carry out matters according to the written contract. If there is no written contract, do not listen to the dispute.[34]

While He Wu's deciphering of the riddle of the sword makes for a satisfying story, it raises questions about how much discretion a senior judge could have in making a judgment. If he strictly followed the statutes, the only issue before him was the matter of the sword. Had he ruled strictly, he would have simply ordered the daughter to deliver the sword to the son in keeping with the statutes governing testamentary inheritance.[35] But clearly, He Wu went much further. His goal, as a wise judge, was to see justice done and the true intention of the testator satisfied. Given his decision to supplant the literal terms of the will with his understanding of the testator's deeper intention, He Wu apparently felt he needed to explain the rationale for his decision (or the

---

31 *JY* strip no. 20.6, p. 33.
32 *JY* strip no. 45.12, p. 78.
33 See my previous discussion on this matter in Chapter 2.
34 *ZJS* strip (*Statutes*) no. 335, p. 54.
35 The statute from Zhangjiashan does not really fully discuss such imaginative readings. Of course, it does not prevent them either. This built-in ambiguity in the statutes gave He Wu much leeway in interpreting the document. As the statutes we currently have are incomplete, we do not have sufficient evidence to understand why He Wu could have this leeway in interpreting the will in such a manner.

chronicler or editor felt that the decision needed explanation). The *lunzhe* 論者 (discussants?)[36] were convinced that He Wu had "gotten at the principle by tracing back and deliberating upon the circumstances" (*yuan qing duo shi de qi li* 原情度事得其理). This emphasis on the "principle" (*li*) behind the resolution of civil disputes presaged Chen Shi's 陳寔 (104–187) concept of civil disputes, since he believed that resolving such disputes entailed a search for establishing facts through an appeal to legal principles (*li* 理).[37]

Opinions differ on the meaning of the case and its resolution. Wei Daoming, whom we encountered earlier, argued that the case history demonstrates that the inheritance rights of the son were inalienable, since, in the end, He Wu ordered the property to be given to the son.[38] In my opinion, Wei misread the story. The daughter did in fact get the property in conformity with the rules governing testamentary inheritance. In the absence of the father's will, the son would have been designated the heir according to the rules governing statutory inheritance. Since the father could freely dispose of his property through a will, the case history illustrates the fact that the rules for testamentary inheritance trumped those for statutory inheritance. He Wu ordered the daughter to give the property to the son, as stipulated in the will, because, as He Wu interpreted that will, he determined that the true intention of the testator was that the son should inherit the property. In other words, Hu Wu followed the order of precedence, acknowledging the greater authority of testament over statute. Significantly, He Wu never once questioned the validity of the will, nor did he argue that the will was invalid. He did not argue that the "rights" of the son were inalienable. Instead, He Wu based his decision on his understanding of the "true" meaning of the will. These two facts – that the daughter got the property through her father's will and that she lost the property through a reinterpretation of the will – demonstrate that the will was indeed the determining factor in disposal of the property in this dispute.

The two cases examined above were both disputes over property between a son born of a concubine and a daughter born of the principal wife, and both

36 I am not sure who the *lunzhe* (discussants?) were. In the story, it seems that their opinions carried some weight in confirming He Wu's judgment.

37 The result of the case was indeed strange. The father's will could be interpreted quite differently than what He Wu did: the father indeed wanted to give all the property to the daughter. Furthermore, he wanted his son to become a hero through his own efforts, and for that reason, he bequeathed the sword, a symbol of heroes, to his son. He Wu personally was irritated by the greediness of the daughter and sympathetic to the son, so he interpreted the will differently from its literal meaning to punish the daughter and help the son. The discussants might have felt the same, or they just might have agreed that He Wu affirmed the true meaning of the will.

38 Wei Daoming, "Zhongguo gudai yizhu jicheng," 163–164.

involved wealthy families. In some ways, these two cases remind us of the almost commonplace observation that then and now, legal battles over inheritances among the members of rich families are perhaps so intense because the stakes are so high. But these two cases also show something very important to life in the Han: that daughters were not necessarily disinherited in favor of sons. Seniority and the status of one's mother seems to have been an important factor in determining status within a household. In the first case, the elder sister, as daughter of the principle wife, probably presumed that she had higher status than her younger half-brother born of a concubine, and such a presumption of superiority may have motivated her to challenge her brother's inheritance. In the second case, the elder sister was so proud and greedy that she ignored the rightful claim of her younger brother to her father's sword.

A third example highlights many of the same issues surrounding the cases just examined. According the *Shiji*, the powerful Emperor Wu (r. 141–87 BC) learned that he had an elder sister living in Changling 長陵, a mausoleum town near Chang'an. He also discovered that his half-sister was the daughter of a commoner father and Empress Dowager Wang 王, the issue of the Empress Dowager's first marriage.[39] Upon learning of this, the emperor sent an inspector to investigate. The inspector found the elder sister still living at her home. The emperor went to the village accompanied by his cavalry. The sister was so frightened by the unexpected arrival of the imperial cavalry that she hid herself. She was eventually found and brought into the imperial presence.

> Emperor Wu descended from his carriage and cried: "Ah, elder sister, why did you hide yourself so well?" He then summoned a side carriage (*fuche*), to transport her back to Chang'an, where he had her sent straight through to the Changle Palace. While on the way back to capital, he ordered envoys to send ahead a message to notify the Empress Dowager that [his sister] would be paying her a visit.[40]
>
> 武帝下車泣曰: "嚄! 大姊, 何藏之深也!" 詔副車載之, 迴車馳還, 而直入長樂宮. 行詔門著引籍, 通到謁太后.

The emperor's actions reveal his great respect toward his elder sister. He cried and addressed the lady as "elder sister." He placed her in a side carriage right

39 Emperor Wu's mother had two marriages. She first married a commoner, then she divorced and married Emperor Wu's father, Emperor Jing 景 (r. 156–141 BC).

40 *Shiji*, 49.1982.

beside his own.[41] Without hesitation or delay, he brought his newly found sister to their mother. During the family reunion,

> Emperor Wu raised his wine cup to toast the Empress Dowager and his elder sister. He gave his sister ten million cash, three hundred slaves, one hundred *qing* of official land, and mansions … His sister had one son and one daughter. The son was enfeoffed as *xiucheng zizhong*,[42] and the daughter was married off to a king as a queen.[43]
>
> 武帝奉酒前為壽，奉錢千萬，奴婢三百人，公田百頃，甲第，以賜姊… 有子男一人，女一人．男號為脩成子仲，女為諸侯王王后．

If the Son of Heaven was regarded as a role model for the people, the extraordinary respect the emperor demonstrated toward his elder sister was surely meant to say something about family values in the Han dynasty. Whether the emperor was sincere in paying such respects to an elder sister whom he did not even know, or if he was just making a public statement, is not relevant. The story illustrates just how important elder sisters could be among siblings. In short, this story involving Emperor Wu and his elder sister reinforces a significant aspect of the two *Fengsu tongyi* cases: that elder sisters held generally and legally acknowledged status within their families.

While one can reasonably ask if the two *Fengsu tongyi* cases were real or fictional, both cases pointedly illustrate Han legal principles and procedures in action. Granted, both narratives have legendary elements. It is unlikely that a ninety-year old man could impregnate a woman so quickly or that a father could predict future events so well.[44] Still, as illustrations of Han legal principles and procedures, they remain invaluable, especially since Ying Shao, the

---

41 Regarding the status of the accompanying carriage (*fuche* 副車), the *Hanyi* 漢儀 says: "The imperial carriages of the Son of the Heaven are such: What the Son of Heaven took is called the carriage of Golden Root. He rides six dragons to manage all under Heaven. There is one five-colored sitting carriage (*anche* 安車) and one five-colored standing carriage (*liche* 立車), both being driven by four horses. That was the accompanying carriage for five seasons (Spring, Summer, the transitional period from Summer to Autumn, Autumn, and Winter)" (天子法駕, 所乘曰金根車, 駕六龍, 以禦天下也. 有五色安車, 有五色立車, 各一, 皆駕四馬. 是為五時副車). Thus, we know that the status of the accompanying carriages was very high, only next to the emperor's main carriage. See *Hanyi* 漢儀, in *Hanguan liuzhong* 漢官六種, ed., Zhou Tianyou 周天遊 (Beijing: Zhonghua shuju, 1990), 200.

42 *Xiucheng zizhong* 脩成子仲appears to be a noble title.

43 *Shiji*, 49.1982.

44 Or, He Wu deliberately reinterpreted the will of the father to punish the greedy daughter.

compiler of the *Fengsu tongyi*, was a famously recognized legal expert. Ying Shao's reputation is acknowledged in this passage from the *Hou Hanshu*:

> Previously, during the reign of Emperor An, Yin Ci from Hejian and Shi Yu from Yingchan both were sentenced to death for murder. Yin Chu, the elder brother of Yin Ci, and Jun, the mother of Shi Yu, both went to see the authorities with proposals to have themselves killed as substitutes for their relatives. They then committed suicide by hanging. Secretariat Chen Chong argued that Yin Ci and Shi Yu should be given more lenient punishments and be spared the death penalty. Ying Shao later corrected him in such a way as to correct the precedents and penal laws, so his judgment was worth preserving.[45]
>
> 初，安帝時河間人尹次、潁川人史玉皆坐殺人當死，次兄初及玉母軍並詣官曹求代其命，因縊而物故．尚書陳忠以罪疑從輕，議活次、玉．劭後追駮之，據正典刑，有可存者．

Indeed, Ying Shao had very comprehensive knowledge of Han laws.[46] Ying Shao submitted a book named *Hanyi* 漢儀 (Principles of the Han) to the throne, in which "he reconstructed and corrected the Han statutes and ordinances."[47] Ying Shao's legal expertise lends even greater authority to the accuracy of the two case reports from the *Fengsu tongyi* as descriptions of the legal practices of the time.

2 Litigation concerning Agricultural Land during the Eastern Han Dynasty in the Excavated Texts from Changsha

If we take a step back on account of the discomfort we feel at the fictitious composition of the stories contained in the *Fengsu tongyi*, we still possess actual records by which we can verify the implementation of Han dynasty

---

45 *Hou Hanshu*, 48.1610.

46 See Michael Nylan, "Ying Shao's *Feng su t'ung yi*" (Ph.D. diss., Princeton University, 1982), 52. As Nylan observes, based on this following account of Ying Shao in the *Hou Hanshu*: "When the Han court moved to the interim capital at Xuchang in AD 196, Ying Shao set about reconstructing and augmenting the ancient law codes and casebooks, which had been destroyed in the burning of Luoyang or lost in the court's subsequent moves. Two hundred and eighty rolls of legal writings ... were prepared for the edification of the Han court."

47 Ibid., 52.

domestic statutes. Because this record clearly shows the date, it can assist us to infer the time that these rules were implemented. Specifically, a text excavated at Dongpailou, Changsha records a case dated to the sixth year of the Guanghe era (AD 183), which "is until now, our nation's earliest property inheritance document related to an already married woman's property inheritance where the household is without a male heir."[48] The text is as follows:

> On the 10th day (*wuwu*), the 9th month with *yiyou* the first day, the 6th year of the Guanghe period, Li Yong, who serves as Jianlinxiang, and Yin He, who serves as the investigator on robbers and thieves (*li du daozei*), bow and dare to say:
>
> The office of the Investigator of Central Part (*zhongbu duyou*) forwarded a report saying commoner adult male Li Jian brings a lawsuit against adult male Jing Zhang and Jing Xi. Li Jian says: "My mother Zheng had 13 *shi* of land. We cultivated it for three years and the land tax was 102 *xiashi*. She managed to hold a funeral for my grandfather Zong and buried him. Zhang and Xi occupied 8 *shi* of her land. Even though I repeatedly asked them to return the land, they refused to comply. Therefore, I am bringing a lawsuit against them, and the facts are stated in my statement." Why did Zhang and Xi occupy Jian's land by force? After receiving the report, the officer who is in charge shall summon Zhang and Xi and investigate and check the land, shall punish the criminals according to the law, attach the clear evidence, and correctly report the findings.
>
> He bows as if suffering death penalty. Upon receiving the report, I immediately went to the Chouzhong pavilion to interrogate Zhang and Xi with torture and question Sheng, who is the father of Jian. They all say: Sheng is from Luo county, and Zhang and Ji are the residents of [Linxiang] county. Earlier on, Sheng married Zheng, whose father Zong was the brother of Zhang. Zheng gave birth to a daughter named Ti, Ti's younger brother is Jian, Jian's younger brother is Yan, and Yan's younger sister is Tiao. Xi is the younger brother of Zhang. Zong died of illness and his corpse was in the hallway. Later on, Zheng also died. Zong had no sons, but had property of 8 *shi*. Ti and Jian were very little, so Zhang, Sheng and Xi provided funds to bury Zong. Sheng returned to Luo. Zhang and Xi cultivated and lived upon Zong's land. I verify that Zhang is the brother of Zong while Jian is the son of Zheng. Zhang and Jian both have their portion of land. Grant 2 *shi* of land to Zhang, and the remaining 6 *shi* of land shall all be returned to Jian. The land tax of the 6 *shi* that

48 *Changsha dongpailou Donghan jiandu*, 73–74.

Zhang and Xi returns to Jian shall be shared by Zhang, Jian, and Xi. They willingly compromise and there is no more need to investigate. If issues occur later on, I will report again. He trembles, bows, and dares to die to report.

The Inspector of Linxiang (*jian Linxiang*) Li Yong, and Investigator on Robbers and Thieves Yin He state: We verify the reconciliation agreement between adult male Li Jian and Jing Zhang regarding their land dispute. Come to the office. 9th month, 26th day.

光和六年九月己酉朔十日戊午， 監臨湘李永、例督盜賊殷何叩頭死罪敢言之． 中部督郵掾治所檄曰： 民大男李建自言大男精張、精昔等．母姃有田十三石，前置三歲，田稅禾當為百二下石．持喪葬皇宗事以，張、昔今強奪取田八石；比曉，張、昔不還田．民自言，辭如牒．張、昔何緣強奪建田？檄到，監部吏役攝張、昔，實核田所，畀付彈處罪法，明附證驗，正處言．

何叩頭死罪死罪．奉桉檄輒徑到仇重亭部，考問張、昔，訊建父升，辭皆曰：升羅，張、昔縣民．前不處年中，升娉（?）取張同產兄宗女姃為妻，產女替，替弟建，建弟顏，顏女弟條．昔則張弟男．宗病物故，喪尸在堂．後姃復物故．宗無男，有餘財，田八石種．替、建皆尚幼小．張、升、昔供喪葬宗訖，升還羅，張、昔自墾食宗田．首核張為宗弟，建為姃嫡男，張、建自俱為口分田．以上廣二石種與張，下六石悉畀還建．張、昔今年所畀建田六石，當分稅張、建、昔等．自相和從，無復證調，盡力實核．辭有後情，續解復言．何誠惶誠恐，叩頭死罪死罪敢言之．

監臨湘李永、例督盜賊殷何言實核大男李建與精張諍田自相和從書詣在所．九月其廿六日若．

This is a document of agreement aimed at settling a long-held property dispute. We can see that the two parties involved (Li Jian 李建 vs. Jing Zhang 精張 and Jing Xi 精昔) are all commoners from the fact that are all known as "adult male" (*da nan*). The dispute concerns the property of Jing Zheng, who was the plaintiff Li Jian's mother. Jing Zheng was the heiress of her father Jing Zong 精宗 (Jing Zong was without a son). After Jing Zong passed away, Jing Zheng inherited eight *dan* of agricultural farmland. However, Jing Zheng also passed away soon after. Her daughters and sons were still young at this stage, and so her two uncles took the opportunity to seize the land. After Jing Zheng's son, Li Jian came of age, he went to the authorities to bring a lawsuit demanding the recovery of the bequest. The lawsuit finally reached an agreement: with Li Jian receiving back six *dan* fields and the remainder equally distributed between Jing Zhang and Jing Xi.

The odd thing about this case is that Jin Zheng's husband, Li Sheng did not have a say at all in the matter. He did not appear personally in the dispute when his wife's land was seized by her uncles; when his son Li Jian appeared in the dispute we do not see Li Sheng playing any role; and the official documents settled the name of the case as "the land dispute between Li Jian and Jing Zheng", which excludes Li Sheng entirely. These factors leave us rather bewildered as to the extent that Li Sheng was a *zhuixu* 贅婿 (son-in-law who lives in the home of his wife's parents) and suffered discrimination.[49] However, since Li Jian carried on the paternal surname, Li Sheng cannot have been a *zhuixu*.[50] Therefore, his lack of the right of speech was not based on any discrimination as to his identity. What then is the reason for this? Han domestic statutes provide us with an explanation as the following regulation shows:

> When a female becomes the head of a household, if when she marries, she has no heirs [to succeed her], let her husband take the land and houses of his wife up to his own quota. If the houses [she had] are not adjacent to her husband's, the husband cannot take them. When the husband divorces his wife, or when the husband dies, the wife can retrieve her property and become a household head again. When a husband divorces, he gives the wife her property back.[51]
>
> 女子為戶，毋後而出嫁者，令夫以妻田宅盈其田宅．宅不比，弗得．其棄妻，及夫死，妻得復取以為戶．棄妻，畀之其財．

The materials above have been analyzed previously where it stipulates how to deal with a situation when a woman marries after she has inherited agricultural farmland and residence from her parents: The agricultural farmland and residence is passed onto the heir, and only if there is no heir is it brought into the husband's household. However, after divorce or death of the husband, it can be retrieved again. This regulation illustrates how a woman can have absolute *mingfen* 名分 "title and portion"[52] in terms of the inheritance of property, and that marriage does not alter this situation. It is only on account of the stipulation that "one who is acting as a man's wife is not permitted to be the householder" that the husband held property in trust within married life.

---

49 Cao lüning believes that Li Sheng was a son-in-law who lived in the home of his wife's parents, and people of this category were prohibited from inheriting household property. See Cao lüning, "Ernian lüling yu Qin Han jichengfa," no. 1 (2008): 62–68.

50 See Ye Yuying, "Donghan Jiandu hecong shu," 100–105.

51 *ZJS* strip (*Statutes*) no. 384, p. 61.

52 I will discuss the notion of *mingfen* in detail later.

Even though the situation of the case is slightly different from what is stipulated by strip 384 in that when inheriting the land of her father, Jing Zheng was married, we do not find any regulations for this type of situation from the legal materials known to us. However, even though there are no relevant regulations, we are able to draw an analogy with the principles found in strip 384: property is still under the held in trust by the husband, yet the "*mingfen*" of the property still belongs to Jing Zheng. After Jing Zheng's death, the son Li Jian was the first heir according to the laws related to inheritance succession. Therefore, if we analyze this from the angle of "*mingfen*", Li Sheng is an outsider. The same is also true for Jing Zheng's daughter, who was also an outsider. She did not appear personally with her brother during the litigation and did not receive any portion of the inherited property. This is because, in accordance with the succession of inheritance, she came after her younger brother Li Jian, and therefore had no right to inherit any land or residence.

This case proves that Han dynasty domestic statutes were in effect until the late Eastern Han. We should keep in mind that that period (AD 183) was the eve of the Yellow Turban Rebellion (commenced AD 184), where "the firmament has already expired and the yellow heaven will soon hold sway" (*cangtian yi si, huangtian dang li* 蒼天已死, 黃天當立), that the rule of the Eastern Han was on the verge of collapse, and that the civil law of the Han was still upheld in the then-relatively-remote district of Linxiang in the Changsha commandery.

3 Concluding Remarks

The three cases above are from received literature and excavated materials. They took place respectively in 68 BC, 8 BC, and 183 AD, and they were related to different regions: Chenliu-Chang'an, Pei, and Changsha. They also involved three levels of administration: chancellor, governor, and magistrate. However, they all shared similar features and were consistent with the domestic statutes discussed in the previous chapter. They demonstrate the consistency and actual application of the early civil law.

CHAPTER 5

Fundamental Concepts: *Zhi*, *Mingfen* and *Min-si*

This chapter focuses on the terms *zhi* 直, *mingfen* 名分, and *min-si* 民-私. I will argue that even though *zhi* has different meanings in different situations, in the context of civil disputes, *zhi* refers to a simple, straight-forward, unadorned account of the facts of the case. Ideally, the party who provides the most accurate, and therefore most credible, account of the facts of the case will win the suit. The primary goal of civil litigation in early China was to establish facts, and thereby justify one's claim.

In legal contexts, the term *mingfen* denoted ownership of both movable and real property. Subjects of all ranks in early China had the "right" to own both movable and real property; and in civil disputes, disputants were supposed to be treated as equal parties. By contrast, the term *min-si* refers to the non-official private sphere of interests that were recognized and protected by the state. The significance, in legal practice, of these three notions, *zhi*, *mingfen*, and *min-si* reflect the emphasis on verification of fact, equality of standing, and the non-official sphere in early China's system of civil law.

1 The Concept of *Zhi* 直 ("A Straight Account of the Facts")[1]

This section will argue that the term *zhi* 直 refers to an unadorned, "straight" account of the facts in civil disputes. This particular meaning of *zhi* is not obvious, since *zhi* has various connotations and meanings depending on the context.

1.1 *Various Meanings of "*Zhi*" Not Related to Civil Disputes*

In its most common usage, "*zhi*" indicates "straightforwardness," as conveyed in the expression, "straight as an arrow." The Way of Zhou was praised as *zhi* in the "Great East" (Dadong 大東) ode of the *Book of Songs*.

> The Way of Zhou was like a whetstone. And straight as an arrow.[2]
>
> 周道如砥, 其直如矢.

1 The content of this section has been published in the article "The Legal Concept of Zhi: The Emphasis of Verification in Early China," *Monumenta Serica* 59 (2011).

2 The *Book of Songs*, Mao no. 203. Translation follows Legge, vol. 4, 353.

 | DOI:10.1163/9789004513907_007

This verse was interpreted by the commentator Zheng Xuan (AD 127–200) as follows:

> The analogy to the whetstone refers to taxation that is equally and fairly [applied], whereas the arrow metaphor refers to rewards and punishments that are [administered] without bias.[3]
>
> 如砥, 貢賦均平; 如矢, 賞罰不偏.

Thus, according to Zheng Xuan, in this context *zhi* refers to the quality of the impartial administration of rewards and punishments, and literally, to officials acting "as straight as arrows."

In the *Analects*, this sense of *zhi* as meaning "straight" (i.e., appropriate) treatment of others also occurs, and Confucius used it to praise the integrity of Scribe Yu 史魚 (fl. 5th century BC) of the Wei 衛 state:

> Truely *Zhi* [straight] was the Scribe Yu! When the Way prevailed in his state, he was like an arrow; when the Way ceased to prevail, he was like an arrow.[4]
>
> 直哉史魚！ 邦有道， 如矢； 邦無道， 如矢.

Confucius may even have been alluding to the "Great East" verse just cited above. This usage of *zhi* is subsequently elaborated in three additional early texts that provide concise definitions of *zhi*. The *Five Conducts* (*Wuxing pian* 五行篇) from Guodian 郭店, dated no later than 300 BC, says:

> To be able to be analytical in the heart and then act upon that analysis, as is appropriate, is *zhi*.[5]
>
> 中心辯然而正行之， 直也.

3 *Maoshi zhengyi* 毛詩正義 (Hongkong: Zhonghua shuju, 1964), 13.438.

4 *Analects*, 15.7. Translation follows Legge, vol. 1, 296 (slightly modified).

5 *Guodian Chumu zhujian* 郭店楚墓竹簡, ed., Jingmen shi bowuguan 荊門市博物館 (Beijing: Wenwu chubanshe, 1998), strip (*Wuxing*) no. 34, p. 150. The *Wuxing pian* 五行篇 (Five Conducts) was excavated from Shayang 沙洋, Hubei in 1993 along with other texts. For a detailed study of the *Wuxing*, see Ikeda Tomohisa 池田知久, "Kakuten Sokan 'Gogyō' no kenkyū" 郭店楚簡〈五行〉の研究, *Guodian Chujian guoji xueshu yantaohui lunwenji* 郭店楚簡國際學術研討會論文集 (Wuhan: Hubei renmin chubanshe, 2000), 210–239; cf. Mark Csikszentmihalyi, *Material Virtue: Ethics and the Body in Early China* (Leiden: Brill, 2004).

When used in this way, *zhi* refers to appropriate conduct.

Xunzi 荀子 (313–238 BC) provides a second definition of *zhi* in the "Self-cultivation" (Xiushen 修身) chapter:

> To recognize as right what is right and as wrong what is wrong is called "wisdom." To regard as wrong what is right and as right what is wrong is called "stupidity." Doing injury to honorable people is "slander." Doing harm to honorable people is "destructive behavior." "Straightforwardness" (*zhi*) is calling right what is right and wrong what is wrong.[6]
>
> 是是非非謂之知, 非是是非謂之愚, 傷良曰讒, 害良曰賊. 是謂是, 非謂非, 曰直.

In contrast to practical wisdom, which refers to the proper recognition of right and wrong in a given situation, we find that *zhi* is directed outward and refers to the action taken, specifically one's straightforwardness when speaking to others about right and wrong. Perhaps influenced by his teacher Xunzi, Han Fei, in the "Explaining Laozi" (Jielao 解老) chapter of the *Han Feizi*, defines *zhi* in a similar way when interpreting this line from the *Laozi*, "*Zhi* but not unbridled, bright but not shining" (直而不肆, 光而不耀):

> What we mean by *zhi* is to do one's duty impartially and honestly, with an unbiased heart always.[7]
>
> 所謂直者, 義必公正, 心不偏黨也.

Han Fei's definition of *zhi*, while maintaining the emphasis on straightness, inserts the notion of an unbiased heart, which may imply intentionality.

It is relevant that the notion of *zhi*, emphasizing honest conduct without biased intention, underlies the Qin and Han penal laws. Making biased, and therefore dishonest, judgments is defined as the crime of "not straight" (*buzhi*), in the Shuihudi manuscript entitled "Answers to Questions concerning Laws" (Falü dawen, strip no. 463), which poses the question: "In pronouncing judgments in criminal cases, what is meant by *buzhi*?" (*lun yu he wei buzhi* 論獄何謂不直) To which, the author of the text answers:

---

6 Wang Xianqian 王先謙, *Xunzi jijie* 荀子集解 (Beijing: Zhonghua shuju, 2011), 1.24. My translation follows John Knoblock from his work in *Xunzi: A Translation and Study of the Complete Works* (Stanford: Stanford University Press, 1988), vol. 2, 153.

7 *Han Feizi yizhu* 韓非子譯注, annot., Zhang Jue 張覺 (Shanghai: Shanghai guji, 2007), 6.200.

> When a crime warrants a heavy [punishment], but the judge purposely makes it lighter, or when it warrants a light [punishment], but the judge purposely makes it heavier, that is the meaning of *buzhi* ["not straight," meaning "biased" and "unfair"].[8]
>
> 罪當重而端輕之, 當輕而端重之, 是謂 "不直."

Buzhi was therefore defined as "purposely" (i.e., intentionally, *duan* 端) handing down judgments in which the punishment is not appropriate to the crime. It is important to note that the Qin laws clearly distinguish *buzhi* from "unintentionally making a mistake in judging or punishing a crime" (*shixing* 失刑).

Another Shuihudi strip in the same "Falü dawen" section (strip nos. 33–34) explains the difference between *buzhi* and *shixing* through a hypothetical case:

> Let us say that the *shiwu* A commits a theft. At the moment of capture, the criminal profit is to be evaluated ... What if the value of the illegal profit is more than 660 cash, and the officials do not evaluate it until the case is tried, or what if the value of the profit to the criminal is 110 cash, and [A] is then sentenced to having his beard shaved off? Question: "How are A, as well as the officials, to be sentenced?" "A warrants tattooing and enslavement as a wall-builder. As for the officials, it may be [a case of] making a mistake in punishing a crime. But if they did it on purpose, it is *buzhi*."[9]
>
> 士五 (伍) 甲盜, 以得時直 (值) 臧 (贓). 臧 (贓) 直 (值) 過六百六十, 吏弗直 (值), 其獄鞫乃直(值) 臧 (贓), 臧 (贓) 直 (值) 百一十, 以論耐, 問甲及吏可 (何) 論? 甲當黥為城旦; 吏為失刑罪, 或端為, 為不直.

Because the officials significantly undervalued the illegal profits, they gave the thief an overly lenient punishment. In this case, the issue is how to rectify an earlier error. In this hypothetical situation, the prescription is that the thief should be given the heavier punishment he deserves, and that the intentions of the presiding judges should be assessed by their superiors. If the superiors determine that the presiding officials intentionally underestimated the value

8 SHD strip (*Falü dawen*) no. 93, p. 115; cf. RCL, 144. My translation follows Hulsewé (slightly modified).

9 SHD strip (*Falü dawen*) nos. 33–34, p. 101; cf. RCL, 130. My translation follows Hulsewé (slightly modified).

of the stolen items, those officials were liable to be charged with the crime of *buzhi*. Alternatively, the superiors could determine that the presiding officials simply committed an unintentional mistake (*shixing* 失刑). The importance of intention, as attested by the legal distinction made between *buzhi* and *shixing*, makes it abundantly clear that *buzhi* describes intentionally unfair or biased judgments.

The Qin and Han states considered "not straight" acts committed by its bureaucrats to be serious crimes, and "not straight" judges were punished accordingly. For example, the *Shiji* says:

> In the 34th year [of the First Emperor of Qin, 213 BC], the emperor ordered the officials who had been *buzhi* when trying criminal cases to [be sent to] build the Great Wall or exiled to Nanyue.[10]
>
> 三十四年，適治獄吏不直者，築長城及南越地.

Similarly, the ZJS strip (*Statutes*) no. 93 states that "not straight" judgments are prohibited, and that those who commit such violations are to be seriously punished:

> In trying a penal case, [if the judges] deliberately release a criminal, if they are *buzhi*, and if they purposely do not make the facts clear when investigating, reporting, or hearing the case, when the case concerns a crime that merits the death penalty, [the corrupt officials] should be subjected to penalties of cutting off left toes and serving as *chengdan* (wall-builders). In other cases, [the corrupted officials] shall be subject to the penalty of those crimes.[11]
>
> 鞠（鞫）獄故縱、不直，及診、報、辟故弗窮審者，死罪，斬左止（趾）為城旦，它各以其罪論之.

In a related passage, the character *zhi* ("straight") is used when assessing the propriety of testifying against one's own father in a criminal proceeding. The *Analects* records a famous debate between Confucius and the Duke of She 葉.

> The Duke of She informed Confucius, saying, "Among us here, there are those who may be styled *zhi* in their conduct. If their fathers have stolen

10 *Shiji*, 6. 253.
11 ZJS strip (*Statutes*) no. 93, p. 22.

goats, these sons will bear witness to the fact." Confucius said, "Among us, in our part of the country, those who are *zhi* are different from this. The father conceals the misconduct of the son, and the son conceals the misconduct of the father. *Zhi* is to be found in this."[12]

葉公語孔子曰: "吾黨有直躬者, 其父攘羊, 而子證之." 孔子曰: "吾黨之直者異於是. 父爲子隱, 子爲父隱, 直在其中矣."

In this exchange, the Duke of She praised as *zhi* the conduct of his state's subjects, who were so principled that they were even willing to testify against their fathers who had committed theft. Confucius, however, disputed the alleged association between principled behavior and reporting one's parents to the authorities. He presented an alternative interpretation of *zhi*, in which fathers and sons would never report each other to the authorities, lest the all-important bond binding father and son be broken. At the root, the Duke of She and Confucius disagree over which relationship, ruler-subject or father-child, held greater authority in the sociopolitical order; their disagreement addressed the very definition of *zhi*.

Similar stories of stealing goats occur in the *Han Feizi* and the *Lüshi chunqiu*. The *Han Feizi* says:

In Chu, there was one whom we deem to be *zhi*. When his father stole a goat, he reported him to the officials. The magistrate said, "Execute him [the son]!" [The magistrate] thought the son was *zhi* to the ruler but *qu* [crooked] with respect to his father, so [the magistrate] reported his crime and charged the son. For this we observe that the *zhi* subject of a ruler may be a vicious son of his father.[13]

楚之有直躬, 其父竊羊, 而謁之吏. 令君曰: 殺之. 以為直於君而曲於父, 報而罪之. 以是觀之, 夫君之直臣, 父之暴子也.

In this story from the *Han Feizi*, the magistrate decided that it was so important to promote the father-son bond that he ordered the execution of the son who had reported his father. By contrast, a story from the *Lüshi chunqiu* portrays a son skillfully managing his conflicting loyalties, for which he earns a good reputation, even though Confucius scorns him as someone angling for fame. The *Lüshi chunqiu* says:

12 *Analects*, 13.18. My translation follows Legge, vol. 1, 270 (slightly modified).

13 *Han Feizi yizhu*, 19.685–686.

In Chu there was one whom we might call *zhi*. When his father stole a goat, he reported him to the authorities. The authorities arrested the thief and were about to execute him when his honest son requested that he be allowed to be executed in his father's place.

When the son was on the point of being executed, he announced to the officer: "When my father stole a goat, I reported him. Is this not the true meaning of being honest? When my father was about to be executed, I offered to take his place. Is this not the true meaning of being filial? If you execute one who is both honest and filial, then whom will the state not execute?"

When the King of Chu learned of this, he decided not to execute the man. But when Confucius heard of this incident, he said: "Remarkable indeed, is the person who regards his own *zhi* as honesty! It was merely at the expense of his father's [reputation] that he was able to gain a reputation. Therefore, it would be far better to lack honesty altogether than to practice the so-called 'honesty' of this type of *zhi*."[14]

楚有直躬者，其父竊羊而謁之上，上執而將誅之．直躬者請代之．

將誅矣，告吏曰：父竊羊而謁之，不亦信乎？父誅而代之，不亦孝乎？信且孝而誅之，國將有不誅者乎？

荊王聞之，乃不誅也．孔子聞之曰：異哉直躬之為信也，一父而載取名焉．故直躬之信，不若無信．

These stories from the *Han Feizi* and *Lüshi chunqiu* both reflect an ongoing tension between loyalty to one's ruler and the laws of the state versus loyalty to one's father as head of the household and family, the same tension displayed in the debate between Confucius and the Duke of She. Yet, despite some minor variations, the term *zhi* in both cases is used to address the issue of ideal conduct in the courts, and ultimately refers to a sense of being "straight as an arrow" in assessing the character of a person's conduct.

In a third sense, *zhi* refers to "due requital," the basis for a primitive sense of justice. When someone asked Confucius what he thought of the idea that one uses gracious acts or favor (*de* 德) to repay injury (*yuan* 怨), Confucius answered: "With what then will you recompense kindness? Recompense injury with justice (*zhi*), and recompense kindness with kindness" (何以報德?

14 *Lüshi chunqiu yizhu* 呂氏春秋譯注, ed., Zhang Shuangdi 張雙棣 (Beijing: Beijing daxue chubanshe, 2000), 11.298; cf. John Knoblock and Jeffrey Riegel, *The Annals of Lü Buwei* (Stanford: Stanford University Press, 2000), 251–252. My translation follows Knoblock and Riegel (slightly modified).

以直報怨, 以德報德).[15] Kong Anguo glossed this passage as, "This *de* 德 refers to the *de* of obligation and favor" (德, 恩惠之德), but he neglected to explain what *zhi* referred to, perhaps because he considered it obvious.[16] Zhu Xi 朱熹 (1130–1200) explained it this way:

> Concerning those people whom he holds a grudge against, in the matters of loving and hating, or choosing or rejecting, he shall treat them with perfect impartiality, with no selfishness – that we call *zhi*,[17]
>
> 與其所怨者，愛憎取捨，一以至公而無私，所謂直也.

This interpretation of *zhi* emphasizes fairness or unbiased attitude in the treatment of others. However, in the original *Analects* context, *zhi* refers to proper punishment or a demand for due compensation, not merely to conduct that which causes injury or reciprocates favor. Rendering the term *zhi* as "due requital" comes closest to its core meaning. This sense of *zhi* can also be found in a passage from the *Hanshu*:

> In addition, in Taiyuan and Shangdang there are many descendants of the Jin ruling line. They strive to outdo each other by deceit and force; they boast of their achievements and fame; they seek revenge in ways that exceed what due requital requires (*zhi*).[18]
>
> 太原、上黨又多晉公族子孫，以詐力相傾，矜誇功名，報仇過直.

Yan Shigu glossed this passage as: "*Zhi* 直is interchangeable with *dang* 當, meaning 'what is warranted'" (*zhi yi dang ye* 直亦當也). Hulsewé explained why he used the word "warranted" to translate *dang* when used as a verb:

> I have recently been told that my rendering of *tang* [*dang*] by "warranted; warranting," is contrary to correct English usage. However, I have not corrected this. Perhaps this unidiomatic expression will remind the reader that *tang* basically means "to be equivalent; to outweigh; to counterbalance," in the sense that the negative effect of the crime is neutralized

15 *Analects*, 14.36. My translation follows Legge, vol. 1, 288 (slightly modified).
16 *Lunyu jishi* 論語集釋, ed., Cheng Shude 程樹德 (Taipei: Yiwen yinshuguan, 1965), vol. 2, 30.884.
17 Ibid., 30.885.
18 *Hanshu*, 28B.1656.

> by the punishment. In theory, it is the crime which is *tang* and not the criminal; this meaning would not come out clearly if *tang* had been rendered as "to deserve; to merit," both words with moral overtones which are wholly absent in the Chinese term.[19]

Hulsewé's explanation of how he rendered *dang* can serve as a model for how to understand *zhi* when used in the sense of "due requital."

A fourth, related sense of *zhi* depends on its contrast with *qu*, in which *zhi* describes one's strength and *qu* describes one's weakness. The *Zuozhuan* 左傳 (Zuo Commentaries to the Spring and Autumn Annals) contains a story about the famous battle at Chengpu 城濮, fought between Jin and Chu in 632 BC; in that battle, the Jin general Zifan ordered his army to retreat when his army was attacked by the Chu general. When questioned by his aides about his decision, Zifan replied:

> When an army is *zhi*, it is strong; by contrast, if an army is *qu*, it is weak. [The strength of an army] certainly does not depend on the length of time [in the battlefield]. But for the kindness of Chu, we should not be in our present circumstances, and this retreat of a three days' march is to repay that kindness. Were our army to show ingratitude for that and eat its words, confronting Chu as its enemy in battle, we should be *qu* and Chu would be *zhi*. Its soldiers have high morale, and they cannot be pronounced old [and weary].[20]
>
> 師直為壯，曲為老，豈在久矣. 微楚之惠不及此，退三舍辟之所以報也. 背惠食言，以亢其讎，我曲楚直，其眾素飽，不可謂老.

The background for this story is that Chong'er 重耳, a noble scion of the Jin line who eventually became Duke Wen 文 of Jin (r. 636–628 BC), once took refuge in Chu to escape political strife in Jin. In Chu, he was well received by his host, King Cheng 成 of Chu (r. 674–626 BC). The future duke promised that if the armies of Jin and Chu were ever to meet on the battlefield, he would order his army to retreat by the distance of a three days' march (*sanshe* 三舍) in order to repay the king's kindness.[21] The passage cited above exemplifies

19 *RCL*, 5. Hulsewé used *tang* in the original text, following Wade-Giles Romanization.

20 *Zuozhuan zhushu* 左傳注疏, Lord Xi 28 僖, 16.272–273. All references to the *Zuozhuan* cite the *Shisanjing zhushu* 十三經注疏 (Ruan Yuan 阮元 1815 ed.; rpt., Taipei: Yiwen chubanshe, 1965). My translation follows Legge, vol. 5, 209 (slightly modified).

21 This story is in the *Zuozhuan*, Lord Xi 23, 15.252; cf. David Schaberg, *A Patterned Past: Form and Thought in Early Chinese Historiography* (Cambridge and London: Harvard University Press, 2001), 216–217.

the *Zuozhuan*'s typical emphasis on the value of due recompense (*bao* 報), as David Schaberg has noted.[22]

However, what makes this passage from the *Zuozhuan* stand out, is the pairing of the words *qu* and *zhi*, in the context of a confrontation between two parties. By this formulation, *qu* would cause a party's weakness (*lao* 老), which in turn leads to defeat in battle, and by contrast, *zhi* results in the second party's strength (*zhuang* 壯), promoting victory. Chu was deemed to be *zhi* because Duke Wen of Jin was willing to acknowledge a kindness received from Chu, even if this acknowledgment meant retreating by the distance required for a three days' march. This gloss for *zhi* allows for drawing analogies in the legal realm, with promises analogous to debts and expectations of satisfaction comparable to a creditor's claim.[23] While the arenas of commerce and war are clearly different, the marketplace is often characterized as a battlefield. As we have just seen, *zhi* can and has been used in both contexts.

1.2 Zhi *as a Straight Account of the Facts* (*True Facts*) *in Civil Disputes*

The *Yantielun* 鹽鐵論 (Discourses on Salt and Iron, comp. ca. 70 BC) contains a passage in which the counselor (*dafu* 大夫) and the Wise and Good (*xianliang* 賢良) debated the consequences of the elite's propensity to indulge in luxuries.[24] The counselor defended the elite's style of living while his opponent harshly criticized it. To demonstrate the extravagance and greed of the powerful elites, the latter referred to a well-known case:

> Therefore, Marquis Wu'an and the chancellor [Dou Ying 竇嬰] had a dispute over orchards and cultivated fields. They fought over the twisted and straight account of the facts (i.e., who was telling the truth) in front of the ruler.[25]
>
> 故武安丞相訟園田，爭曲直人主之前.

---

22 Schaberg, *A Patterned Past*, 191–221.

23 "Creditor's claim" is defined as "a claim that a creditor has against a debtor." See *Black's Law Dictionary*, 205.

24 *Yantielun jiaozhu* 鹽鐵論校注, annot., Wang Liqi 王利器 (Beijing: Zhonghua shuju, 1992), 6.405–410. The *Yantielun* compiled by Huan Kuan 桓寬 (81 BC–AD 9) dealt with debates on state policies, such as government monopoly, laissez faire, etc., between ministers (*dafu* 大夫), who were sometimes identified with Sang Hongyang 桑弘羊 and Sang's critics, who were described as the Literati (*wenxue* 文學) or Wise and Good (*xianliang* 賢良). See also Michael Loewe, *Crisis and Conflict in Han China* (London: George Allen and Unwin Limited, 1974).

25 *Yantielun jiaozhu*, 6.401.

This case refers to a real estate dispute brought before Emperor Wu between chancellor Tian Fen 田蚡 (d. 131 BC), Marquis of Wu'an 武安, and Dou Ying 竇嬰 (d. 131 BC), Marquis of Weiqi 魏其, who had served as a chancellor before Tian Fen.[26] In their dispute, each questioned the other's account of the facts (*qu* 曲 and *zhi* 直).

This particular usage of *qu* and *zhi* is consistent with its use in a passage from judge Lu Gong's 魯恭 (32–112 AD) biography in the *Dongguan Hanji* 東觀漢記 (Records of the Han Imperial Library, comp. ca. AD 196),

> When Lu Gong was the magistrate of Zhongmou, there was a long-standing civil dispute in which Xu Bo and some others were fighting over paddy fields. This case could not be resolved by the provincial or commandery [courts] for several years. [Lu] Gong was able to fairly discern the distorted account of the facts [*qu*] from the straight account of the facts [*zhi*], so the disputants all yielded, criticized themselves, and yielded in the dispute.[27]
>
> 魯恭為中牟令, 宿訟許伯等爭陂澤田, 積年州郡不決. 恭平理曲直, 各退自相責讓.

The key to resolving this difficult land dispute was in distinguishing between *qu* and *zhi*.

But why were *qu* and *zhi* so important? We find a possible answer in the works of the famous thinker Wang Chong 王充 (AD 27–ca. 100). In his *Lunheng* 論衡 (Doctrines Evaluated, comp. ca. AD 90), Wang Chong offered his view on the antonyms *qu* and *zhi*, as applied to lawsuits, by associating them with another pair of antonyms, right (*shi* 是) and wrong (*fei* 非).

> The district [officials] judge confusing *song* [disputes], while the *yu* [jailors] determine suspected crimes. If right and wrong cannot be determined, and the *qu* and *zhi* [distorted account of the facts and straight account of the facts] cannot be established, people of the time will

26 This case is recorded in the *Shiji*, 107.2849; cf. Wang Liqi's footnote 11 on p. 403 in the *Yantielun jiaozhu*.

27 *Dongguan Hanji jiaozhu* 東觀漢記校注, ed., Wu Shuping 吳樹平 (Beijing: Zhonghua shuju, 2008), 13.475; cf. *Hou Hanshu*, 25.874. The language of the same story in the *Hou Hanshu* is slightly different.

> definitely say that the abilities of the district officials and the abilities of the jail officials are not adequate to their duties.[28]
>
> 鄉決疑訟, 獄定嫌罪, 是非不決, 曲直不立, 世人必謂鄉獄之吏才不任職.

If we pay attention to the verbs that precede the respective pairs of antonyms, *zhi* and *qu,* and *shi* and *fei* (right and wrong), we find that the pair *zhi* and *qu* take the verb "to establish" (*li* 立), whereas *shi* and *fei* use the verb "to settle or judge" (*jue* 決). Therefore, in Wang Chong's view, judicial officials were responsible for establishing facts (*zhi* or *qu*) in a dispute, and rendering judgment based on the circumstances. By this construction, a "straight account of the facts" (*zhi*) and right (*shi*) are set in opposition to "distorted account of the facts" (*qu*) and wrong (*fei*).

In another passage, Wang Chong expressed a similar opinion with greater clarity.

> In a court, there are sure to be judges. Within [even] a single village, there are sure to be disputants. In any dispute, there are sure to be some distorted accounts of the facts (*qu*) and some straight accounts of the facts (*zhi*). In any judgment, there are sure to be some right and some wrong points. Those who are wrong and who provide a distorted account of the facts (*qu*) are the losing parties, and those who are right and provide a straight account of the facts (*zhi*) should win.[29]
>
> 一堂之上, 必有論[30]者; 一鄉之中, 必有訟者. 訟必有曲直, 論必有是非. 非而曲者為負, 是而直者為勝.

In analyzing this passage, we need to point out two additional matters. First, if Wang Chong strictly used *song* to refer to legal cases, as he seems to do in this passage, he was probably referring to civil disputes, since he referred to winners and losers in the case. But what if Wang Chong was referring to both civil and criminal cases? We know that *qu* and *zhi* are used in the context of the discussions of disputes ("In any dispute, there are sure to be some distorted

---

28 *Lunheng jijie*, 29.571. We previously encountered this passage in Chapter 2. As I argued in that chapter, jailers belonged to the county court. There were no jails (*yu*) at the district level.

29 *Lunheng jijie*, 3.153.

30 *Lun* 論, in a legal context, means "to judge, to decide, to sentence." See *RHL*, 80; cf. *RCL*, 186, n. 5.

accounts of the facts and some straight accounts of the facts [*qu* ... *zhi*].") Yet, as we shall see in the following example, these words are employed as adjectives to characterize the disputants who made statements before the court. The usage of "right" and "wrong," in parallel with "distorted account of the facts" and "straight account of the facts" seen in the earlier passage, also occurs here.

Elaborating on Wang Chong's generalization, we see that in any suit, there are two groups: the officers who draw up case summaries (*lunzhe* 論者) and the disputants (the defendant and the claimant). Drawing up the case requires sorting out *zhi* (a straight account of the facts) and *qu* (a distorted account of the facts), whereas a judgment involves a decision over right and wrong based on those facts. A dispute may be characterized as a conflict between *zhi* and *qu*, while a judgment begins with assessing the veracity of the disputants' presentation of the facts and ends with a decision on what is right and what is wrong based on that determination of fact. For Wang Chong, *zhi* was essential to winning a dispute since the purpose of all legal proceedings, civil and criminal, was to establish facts in order to pass down fair and impartial judgments. Ideally, a good judge recognizes the straight account of the facts (*zhi*) and rewards the party who provided that straight account with due restitution. Of course, in the real, less than ideal world, the first obligation of the judge is to determine which disputant's version of the facts was "straighter," i.e., "more *zhi*" than the other. Fair and impartial judgment is then, as it is now, a goal, not a given.

Like Wang Chong, Zheng Xuan stated that *zhi* referred to straight accounts of the facts, and Wei Zhao 韋昭 (204–273) stated that *qu* referred to distorted accounts of the facts; departing from Wang Chong, both Zheng Xuan and Wei Zhao limited the application of *qu* or *zhi* to the realm of civil disputes. Specifically, Zheng's commentary concerned the following line from the *Zhouli*:

> Use [the requirement that there be] two visits to court to restrict suits among the people. Before a suit is heard, the disputants should present arrow bundles to the court.[31]
>
> 以兩造禁人訟，入束矢於朝，然後聽之.

Zheng Xuan interpreted this line as follows:

> *Song* 訟 refers to "suing others over property." *Zao* 造 means "to come." [In a civil dispute], order the disputing parties to both come [to the court].

31 *Zhouli zhushu*, 34.517.

> After they have both come [to the court], order each of them to present a bundle of arrows, and then the judge will take their case. Failure either to appear in court or to present a bundle of arrows should be tantamount to admission that one lacks a straight account of the facts. The disputants must present their arrows to symbolize the straightness of their account of the facts. As the *Book of Songs* says, "It is to be as straight as an arrow."[32]
>
> 訟，謂以財貨相告者．造，至也．使訟者兩至，既兩至，使入束矢乃治之也．不至，不入束矢，則是自服不直也．必入矢者，取其直也．《詩》曰其直如矢．

Zheng Xuan commented on the *Zhouli*'s prescription to present a bundle of arrows prior to a hearing as part of the judicial ritual. Two features are worth noting in Zheng's interpretation. First, he clearly places the ritual of presenting arrows in the context of civil litigation, not merely because he pointed out that *song* refers to disputes over property, but also because he characterizes the parties as disputants and uses the language of "summoning" and "default judgment" for failure to appear – the language of civil law. In criminal cases, the accused would be arrested and brought to the court. In theory, at least, it should be impossible for him to avoid an appearance in court.[33] Second, Zheng Xuan asserts that failure to present a bundle of arrows constitutes, in effect, an admission of a lack of factual accuracy in one's account (*buzhi*), insofar as the arrows symbolized the straightness of one's account of the facts (*zhi*). Any party providing a distorted account of the facts should lose his civil suit, just as a straight account of the facts should result in a positive outcome for the claimant or defendant in a civil suit.

One may ask whether the compound *buzhi* here could simply mean "dishonest" or "deceitful." If so, one might argue that *buzhi* merely functions as an ordinary adjective, rather than a specialized legal term. In other words, are *zhi* and *buzhi* prescriptive terms, idealized goals, and therefore terms of jurisprudence? Or are they merely descriptive, acknowledgement of degrees of credibility in conflicting accounts? Two reasons suggest that *zhi* and *buzhi* can, and do, function in this context as legal terms. First, the legal ritual that Zheng Xuan described endows *zhi* and *buzhi* with strong legal overtones. Second, *buzhi* is the object of the verb *fu* 服 (admit or confess), which is also a strong legal term

32 Ibid.

33 See my previous summary of Momiyama's study on this issue.

that appears frequently in Qin and Han case reports.[34] Thus, by tradition and practice, the chief elements of all jurisprudence, *zhi* and *buzhi* are used prescriptively rather than descriptively.

Since the *Zhouli* is mostly a prescriptive text written about Western Zhou, we cannot know whether there was any ritual in Qin or Han in which arrows were presented. An alternative explanation concerning the presentation of arrow bundles was proposed by Chen Huan 陳奐 (1786–1863) and Wang Yuansun 汪遠孫 (1789–1834). Both scholars argued that the bundle of arrows represented a deposit made by the parties before asking for a judgment. The losing party would then be fined one bundle of arrows.[35] However, we have already seen that Zheng Xuan, at least, linked the presentation of arrows as integral to the core function of civil litigation, which was to reveal which party provided a straight account of the facts (*zhi*).

Wei Zhao expressed a comparable opinion in interpreting a similar account in the *Guoyu*, especially concerning this phrase:

> When the authorities agree to take the case, [the disputants] present arrow bundles [to the court].[36]
>
> 坐成以束矢.

Wei Zhao interpreted this phase as follows:

> *Zuocheng* 坐成 means that the authorities agree to take a case, criminal or civil. Twelve arrows make up a bundle. When the authorities agree to take a case, the disputants each present a bundle of arrows to the court, and then the court hears their case. When the two parties in the dispute engage in a civil dispute, if one disputant presents a bundle of arrows while the other person fails to do so, then the former party is deemed to be *qu*. The person who is deemed to be *qu* then has to admit his distorted

34 This term *fu* (admit or confess) occurs in both civil cases and criminal cases. Hulsewé discussed how *fu* was used in criminal cases: "In the statement made during trial, the accused had 'to submit,' *fu*, i.e., he had to admit the truth of the accusation." For detailed discussions, see *RHL*, 77.

35 This interpretation is found in Chen Huan's and Wang Yuansun's annotations to a similar prescription of presenting arrow bundles in the *Guoyu jijie*, 6.230.

36 *Guoyu jijie*, 6. 230. The date of the compilation of this text is controversial. According to the recent study of David Schaberg, the cores of the *Guoyu* and the *Zuozhuan* were compiled in the 4th century BC, although both texts contain many later interpolations. See Schaberg, *A Patterned Past*, 8.

account of the facts. If two [bundles] of arrow are presented, then the case will be heard. The "arrow" signifies "going but not returning" [i.e., that one will not retract his words]. As the *Zhouli* says, "Use two visits to court to restrict suits among the people. Before a suit is heard, the disputants should present arrow bundles to the court."[37]

一人入矢，一人不入則曲，曲則服，入兩矢乃坐成，獄訟之坐已成也．十二矢為束．訟者坐成，以束矢入於朝，乃聽其訟．兩人訟，治之．矢，取往而不反也．周禮“以兩造禁人訟，入束矢於朝，然後聽之”也．

In interpreting the term, *zuocheng* 坐成, Wei Zhao specified that the term was applicable in both *yu* and *song*, which shows his awareness of the distinction between *yu* and *song*.[38] Clearly, Wei Zhao was mindful of the line in the *Zhouli* annotated by Zheng Xuan, and his interpretation seems to adopt Zheng Xuan's interpretation in the *Zhouli*, with the difference that Wei Zhao also introduces the term *qu*. Wei Zhao stated that not presenting an arrow bundle was equivalent to admitting one's distorted account of the facts (*qu*). In any case, according to Zheng Xuan and Wei Zhao, *zhi* simply referred to the straight account of the facts in a civil dispute, while *qu* referred to a distorted account of the facts. The two commentators' understanding of *zhi* and *qu* confirms the observation we have already made concerning the use of these terms by Wang Chong.[39]

A slightly different way of looking at these terms is to ask whether the words *zhi* and *qu*, in the context of civil disputes, are ordinary words or technical terms. I think the latter is the case. First, as observed earlier, in the *Yantielun*, *qu* and *zhi* refer to accounts of facts only, without any moral connotations, strongly suggesting that they were legal terms. Second, in Zheng Xuan's description of arrow bundles, *buzhi* and *zhi* were clearly used as legal terms. Third, one more piece of evidence to support the idea that these are legal terms is provided by Wei Zhao's annotation on a land dispute case recounted in the *Guoyu*, even though the use of *buzhi* is very puzzling.

---

37 *Guoyu jijie*, 6.230.

38 This aspect suggests that *zuocheng* 坐成 as a legal term applied to both civil and criminal cases, whereas the ritual of presenting arrow bundles applied to civil cases (*song*) only. The ritual, in the depictions of Zheng Xuan and Wei Zhao, implied two equal parties contesting each other.

39 We should ask: is it possible that the arrow bundles were intended to demonstrate disputants' good faith? This is possible in theory. However, that was not how Zheng Xuan and Wei Zhao interpreted the ritual, and our overall analysis of civil litigation in this book shows that good faith was not a concern. We do not find good faith as a significant concern in any of the civil cases that we have studied.

> Marquis of Xing and Yongzi had a dispute over land. Yongzi presented his daughter to [the judge] Shuyu to seek *zhi*. On the day of trial, Shuyu put down [the evidence of?] Marquis Xing. Marquis Xing then killed Shuyu and Yongzi in court.[40]
>
> 邢侯與雍子爭田， 雍子納其女於叔魚以求直． 及斷獄[41]之日， 叔魚抑邢侯，邢侯殺叔魚與雍子於朝.

This dispute presumably occurred sometime in the mid-sixth century BC in Jin. Wei Zhao annotated this line, "Yongzi presented his daughter to [the judge] Shuyu to seek *zhi*," with the following phrase: "As he had no intention to give a straight account of the facts, [Yongzi] hence resorted to bribery to establish his [distorted] version of the facts as 'straight'" (不直, 故賄以求直). As all our evidence above implies, to achieve the ideal outcome of a fair and impartial judgment in a civil case, "to establish facts" was sufficient to establish one's claims and realize the goal of fairness and impartiality.

In reality, one can resort to bribery to "establish facts," but ideally, all facts should be established according to legal principles, those principles being *zhi* and *buzhi*, *zhi* and *qu*. This ideal is reflected in Chen Shi's stories, which drew us to this inquiry into *zhi* in the first place.

> There was a certain official who was worried about civil disputes. He reported to Chen Shi [his concerns] and wanted to prohibit them. Chen Shi replied: "Civil disputes are meant to establish facts. If I prohibit them, to what can *li* 理 be applied? Do not impose any restraints [on civil disputes]."[42]
>
> 吏慮有訟者, 白欲禁之. 寔曰: "訟以求直, 禁之理將何申?其勿所拘."

The *song* in the passage most likely refers to civil disputes, not only because *song*, as a legal term can mean "civil disputes", but also because elements of the story indicate that the topic was civil disputes. Since the lower-ranking officials

40 *Guoyu jijie*, 15.443. Chronologically, the *Guoyu* is earlier than the *Yantielun*. I discuss the *Guoyu* passage after the *Yantielun* passage, even though the *Guoyu* passage is earlier, because my focus in the *Guoyu* passage is on Wei Zhao's annotations, which date later than the *Yantielun* passage.

41 The passage uses the term *duanyu* 斷獄 to indicate the hearing of the land dispute. This aspect supports the claim that the terminological distinction between *song* (civil dispute) vs. *yu* (criminal dispute) might not have existed in pre-Han period as Momiyama argued.

42 *Hou Hanshu*, 62.2066.

suggested that Chen Shi prohibited *song*, *song* here could not have referred to criminal cases. Criminal cases involved actions that disturbed public order and threatened the stability of society. Officials were bound by duty to act against them. Hearing criminal cases was the primary duty of a county court, as prescribed in the statutes. ZJS strip (*Statutes*) no. 116:

> Those who ask for their cases to be reviewed should all report to [the officials] in the county or march where they reside. The county or march magistrate and deputy magistrates [shall] carefully listen to [what they say], note it down, and submit their statements to the official whose salary is 2,000 *shi* and has responsibilities over the criminal case. The official whose salary is 2,000 *shi* [shall] order his assistants to review these cases.[43]
>
> 气（乞）鞫者各辭在所縣道，縣道官令、長、丞謹聽，書其气（乞）鞫，上獄屬所二千石官，二千石官令都吏覆之.

While this passage deals with the procedural matter of how officials in the county courts or their jurisdictional equivalents are to handle appeals, the use of the term *yu* 獄 implies that these procedures apply to the management of criminal cases. As the passage cited above demonstrates, local officials were duty-bound to hear criminal cases; hearing such cases was not left to the official's discretion. By contrast, the subject of Chen Shi's story is being asked to decline to hear cases, and thus, those must be cases involving civil disputes.

The meaning of *li* 理 in the passage cited above is a bit obscure. A.C. Graham rendered *li* as "patterns" in discussing its usage in the *Laozi* 老子.[44] However, the legal expert Peerenboom preferred to render *li* as "principles," drawing on his studies of *li* in the excavated silk manuscripts from Mawangdui, observing that "*Li* are underlying patterns inherent in nature; they are the principles that structure the natural order."[45] In our context, we can perhaps render *li* as "legal principle."

Contrary to much mischaracterizations of jurisprudence in early China, the term "legal principle" was clearly used in early China. When annotating this phrase "one must investigate and must apply laws" (惟察惟法) from the "Lüxing" chapter of *The Book of Documents*, commentator Kong Anguo said:

43 ZJS strip (*Statutes*) no. 116, p. 24.

44 A.C. Graham, *Disputers of the Tao* (La Salle: Open Court, 1989), 286.

45 R.P. Peerenboom, *Law and Morality in Ancient China: The Silk Manuscripts of Huang-Lao* (Albany: State University of New York Press, 1993), 46–47.

> One must thoroughly investigate the statements of the culprits and attach [relevant] legal principles to them.[46]
>
> 惟當清察罪人之辭，附以法理.

The phrase *fali* (legal principles) also occurs in Zhang Yu's 張禹 (d. AD 113) biography in the *Dongguan Hanji* and Wang Huan's 王渙 (d. AD 105) biography in the *Hou Hanshu*. Zhang Yu was praised for understanding *fali* well, while Wang Huan was praised for being able to resolve difficult cases according to *fali* (legal principles).[47] Thus, we have reason to render *li* as "legal principle" in the passage from Chen Shi. As such, Chen Shi was describing an idealized civil procedure: given that establishing facts was the goal of civil disputes, the best way for a disputant to press his claims was to appeal to legal principles.

Chen Shi's assertion is consistent with this passage from the *Daofa* 道法 silk manuscript from Mawangdui,

> The Way gives birth to the laws. The laws are what draw the line between gain and loss and clarify distorted versus straight accounts of the facts. Therefore, the one who grasps the Way makes the laws but dares not break it. After the laws are established, he dares not abolish them.[48]
>
> 道生法. 法者，引得失以繩，而明曲直者. 故執道者，生法而弗敢犯也. 法立而弗敢廢也.

This passage, in addition to other passages in the *Daofa*, triggered a challenge from Peerenboom to Needham's widely accepted theory that China produced no theory of natural law and that Chinese laws were always contingent upon the emperors who were the law-givers.[49] Notably, the function of the laws here is said to be to distinguish distorted and straight accounts of the facts, those

---

46 *Shangshu zhushu*, 19. 302. *Fu* 附 is rendered as "to join, to add, to attach" by Hulsewé. See *RHL*, 389, n. 200.

47 *Dongguan Hanji jiaozhu*, 16.705; *Hou Hanshu*, 66.2469.

48 Chen Guying 陳鼓應, *Huangdi sijing jinzhu jinyi* 黃帝四經今注今譯 (Beijing: Shangwu yinshuguan, 2007); cf. Robin D.S. Rates, *Five Lost Classics: Tao, Huang-lao, and Yin-yang in Han China* (New York: Ballantine Books, 1997), 21–25. Yates translates *fa* 法 as "law."

49 Peerenboom, *Law and Morality*, 76–84. See also Haga Yoshinobu 芳賀良信, *Rei to hō no kangeki: Zenkan seiji shisō kenkyū* 禮と法の間隙: 前漢政治思想研究 (Tōkyō: Kyūko shoin, 2000), 218–235. Haga noted the passage quoted in this part and argued that the text was meant to guide and restrain the rulers. For Needham's theory, see Joseph Needham, "Human Laws and Laws of Nature in China and the West," *Journal of the History of Ideas* 12, no. 1 (1951): 3–30.

being two types of facts associated with loss and gain. While this passage may be about the laws in general, it is consistent with our observation that civil litigation was meant to establish facts, a process that ends in one litigant's defeat and the other's victory.

As we shall see, establishing facts was also a crucial element of criminal trials, but it appears that a different term was applied. The very beginning of "*Fengzhenshi*" 封診式 (Models for Sealing and Investigating) from Shuihudi states:

> If in trying criminal lawsuits it is possible by means of documents to track down a person's words, obtaining the facts about him without using the bastinado is the best; applying the bastinado is inferior, for when there is fear, everything is spoiled.[50]
>
> 治獄，能以書從迹其言，毋治（笞）諒（掠）而得人請（情）為上．治（笞）諒（掠）為下．有恐為敗．

Notably, the phrase "*de ren qing*" 得人情 denotes "to obtain the facts about the person." In the trial procedure, torture was allowed but regarded as an inferior method in obtaining facts. The text further explains,

> In all cases of interrogating suspects in a criminal lawsuit, one should first listen fully to his [or their] words and note these down, [letting] each [of the persons questioned] set out his statement. Although [the investigator] knows that he is lying, there is no need to inquire [on this] every time. When his statement has been completely noted down, and it cannot be understood, then insist on the points [which need] insisting. When, having insisted, one has again fully listened and noted down the explanatory statements, one looks again at other unexplained points and insists again on these. When one has insisted to the limit, but [the suspect] has repeatedly lied, changing his words and not submitting, then for those persons whom the statutes warrant to be bastinadoed, bastinado them. When bastinadoing him, be sure to note down: "Report – Because X repeatedly changed his words and made no explanatory statement, X has been interrogated with the bastinado."[51]

---

50 See, *SHD* strip (*Fengzhenshi*) no. 1, p.147. Translation follows Hulsewé, *RCL*, 183 (slightly modified).

51 *SHD* strip (*Fengzhenshi*) nos. 2–5, p. 148. Translation follows Hulsewé, *RCL*, 184 (slightly modified).

> 凡訊獄, 必先盡聽其言而書之, 各展其辭, 雖智 (知) 其訑, 勿庯輒詰. 其辭已盡書而毋（無）解，乃以詰[52]者詰之．詰之有（又）盡聽書其解辭，有（又）視其他毋（無）解者以復詰之．詰之極而數訑，更言不服，其律當治（笞）諒（掠）者，乃治（笞）諒（掠）．治（笞）諒（掠）之必書曰：爰書，以某數更言，毋（無）解辭，治（笞）訊某.

When a person repeatedly lied and refused to submit, torture could be applied, but a pre-condition governed that application, according to this provision: "For those persons, whom the statutes warrant to be bastinadoed, bastinado them." This provision is somewhat vague. There are two possibilities: (1) according to the statutes, some group of persons, regardless of the nature of the crimes, was subject to torture while other groups were not, or (2) some crimes, regardless of the status of the criminals, were subject to torture while other crimes were not. In either case, even if a culprit refused to submit, torture would not necessarily be applied to force him to admit his guilt. This seems to suggest that under certain circumstances, judges could pass judgment based solely on the facts they had found, without the need for culprits to admit guilt (服 *fu*).

The feature above is consistent with the emphasis on establishing facts in civil litigation, with the important reminder that torture had no place in civil disputes. Moreover, there are numerous cases in the Juyan strips where we find reports of authorities passing judgment after conducting hearings and establishing the facts, even when the party who was liable refused to admit his or her liability. For example, a fragment from 32 BC says:

> On the day *gengwu* of the 9th month, beginning with the day *xinyou*, in the first year of the Jianshi period (32 BC), [missing two characters] officials ordered the company commander of Jianbei to collect a debt. However, the debtor refused to admit owing the debt.[53]

> 建始元年九月辛酉朔庚午, □☒官令殲北候官收責. 不服負☒

Since the authorities ordered the commander of Jianbei to collect a debt, we know that they had already established that the here-unnamed person was liable, even though the debtor refused to admit his debt. Similarly, this fragment from AD 24 says:

---

52 Loewe rendered *jie* as "indictment," but Hulsewé rendered *jie* as "insist." In this passage, *jie* is used in the context of inquiring the suspect, so "insist" is a better rendition.

53 *JYX* strip no. E.P.T. 52.485, p. 260.

> On the day *xinchou* of the fourth month, beginning with the day *yihai*, in the second year of the Gengshi period (AD 24), two officials, who are the *zhangshouhou* (deputy garrison commander?) and the deputy commander of the Jiaqu company forwarded [a testimony?] to Chi. According to the statute, [missing seven characters] a certain official questioned [the defendant] and decided to collect the claimed debt from the defendant. The defendant was not willing to accept the judgment. Thus, the certain official reported the problem. [We] forward the testimony of the defendant according to the statutes and ordinances.[54]

We previously studied this fragment while discussing the appeal system. Here, I draw our attention to this fact: the authorities had clearly held hearings and decided liability, but the losing party refused to admit the debt and was determined to contest the judgment.

Taken together, these two fragments demonstrate that establishing facts was sufficient for the authorities to determine liability in civil litigation, with no need for a confession or admission of liability from the losing party. Yet, as we have seen, the losing party could still appeal to higher authorities to contest the judgment. Overall, we find that *zhi* (a straight account of the facts) was an important notion in civil litigation, reflecting the emphasis on verification in civil procedure. Furthermore, all available texts point to the rational orientation of civil law in early China, and the rationality demonstrated in that legal system's concern with evidence and evidentiary fact.

2 *Mingfen* 名分 as "Title and Portion"

This section will argue that the term *mingfen* refers to "title and portion." "Title" is defined in modern Western sources as:

> The union of all elements (as ownership, possession, and custody) constituting the legal right to control and dispose of property; the legal link between a person who owns property and the property itself.[55]

The "*Dingfen*" (定分) chapter of the *Shangjunshu* 商君書 (comp. ca. 3rd century BC) supplies an interesting story illustrating *mingfen*:

54 *JYX* strip no. E.P.C. 39, p. 548.

55 *Black's Law Dictionary*, 1243.

> One rabbit runs. A hundred people pursue it. This is not because the rabbit could be divided into a hundred pieces. It is because the title to the rabbit (*mingfen*) has not been determined. Now, as we all know, the market is crowded with people who sell rabbits, but thieves dare not steal them, because the *mingfen* there has been determined. Therefore, if the title is not yet determined, even [the sage-kings] Yao, Shun, Yu or Tang would [think it fair game] to approach the object and pursue it, but if the title is determined, even a poor thief would not steal it.[56]
>
> 一兔走，百人逐之，非以兔可分以為百，由名分之未定也. 夫賣兔者滿市，而盜不敢取，由名分已定也. 故名分未定，堯、舜、禹、湯且皆如物而逐之；名分已定，貧盜不取.

Similar stories occur in four other early texts: the *Yinwenzi*尹文子 (comp. ca. 3rd century BC), the *Lüshi chunqiu* 呂氏春秋 (comp. 239 BC), the *Shuoyuan* 說苑 (comp. ca. 20 BC), and the *Hou Hanshu* 後漢書 (comp. 445). The *Yinwenzi* says:

> When pheasants and rabbits are in the wild, everyone will chase after them, because the title (*fen*) to them has not been determined. However, when chicken and pigs fill the market, no one thinks of chasing after them [to catch them], because their titles have been determined.[57]
>
> 雉兔在野，眾人逐之，分未定也；雞豕滿市，莫有志者，分定故也.

The *Lüshi chunqiu* says:

> Now let us suppose that a rabbit is running, and a hundred people are chasing after it. This is not because there is enough rabbit meat to be shared by a hundred people, but because the title to it has not yet been

56 *Shangjunshu zhushi* 商君書注釋, ed., Gao Heng 高亨 (Beijing: Zhonghua shuju, 1974), 5.145. My translation follows J.J.L. Duyvendak, *The Book of Lord Shang* (London: A. Probsthain, 1928), 168 (slightly modified). The book was traditionally attributed to Shang Yang, who served as a minister of Duke Xiao of Qin (r. 361–337 BC). The date of compilation of the text is controversial. The received text cannot possibly originate entirely from Shang Yang. See the entry in *Early Chinese Texts: A Bibliographical Guide*, ed., Michael Loewe (Berkeley: Society for the Study of Early China, 1993), 368–376.

57 *Yinwenzi jiaozheng* 尹文子校正, ed., Wang Kailuan 王愷鑾 (Shanghai: Shangwu yinshuguan, 1935), 11–12.

determined. Because the title has not been determined, even [a sage like] Yao would exhaust every ounce of his strength [in the chase], not to mention the masses! Many rabbits fill the marketplace, but passersby do not give them a second look. This it is not because they do not want these rabbits, but because their title has been determined already. After their title has been determined, even dolts will not fight over them.[58]

今一兔走，百人逐之，非一兔足為百人分也，由分未定．由分未定，堯且屈力，而況眾人乎！ 積兔滿市， 行者不顧， 非不欲兔也， 分已定矣．分已定， 人雖鄙， 不爭．

The *Shuoyuan* says:

Now let us suppose that a single rabbit runs on the street, and ten thousand people pursue it. Once a single person captures it, the rest of the crowd will no longer run after it. When the title has not yet been determined, the rabbit on the run will cause ten thousand people to get all excited [at the prospect of owning it]. But once the title has been determined, even greedy people know to stop.[59]

夫一兔走於街， 萬人追之； 一人得之， 萬人不復走． 分未定， 則一兔走， 使萬人擾； 分已定， 則雖貪夫知止．

The *Hou Hanshu* says:

As the proverb goes, when ten thousand people chase after one rabbit, as soon as one person captures it, all the greedy people will stop [their pursuit], because the title has been determined.[60]

世稱萬人逐兔， 一人獲之， 貪者悉止， 分定故也．

---

58 *Lüshi chunqiu yizhu*, 17.532; cf. Knoblock and Riegel, *The Annals of Lü Buwei: A Complete Translation and Study*, 431–432. *Qu li* 屈力 is somewhat difficult to render. According to Gao You's 高誘 (fl. 205–212) annotation, *qu* means "to exhaust"; thus, *qu li* means to "exhaust every ounce of one's strength." See *Lüshi chunqiu* (*Gao You zhu*), 17.212.

59 *Shuoyuan jiaozheng* 說苑校正, ed., Xiang Zonglu 向宗魯 (Beijing: Zhonghua shuju, 1987), 3. 74.

60 *Hou Hanshu*, 74A. 2383. Ju Shou 沮授 (d. 201) was a strategist of warlord Yuan Shao 袁紹 (d. 202).

These five stories compel our attention, because they remind us of similar pronouncements by the famous Roman jurist Gaius (fl. AD 130–180) regarding the capture of wild animals, as preserved in the *Digest* (comp. 533). Gaius said:

> All animals that are captured on land, on sea, or in the air, that is to say, wild beasts and birds, as well as fish, become the property of those who take them … For what does not belong to anyone by natural law becomes the property of the person who first acquires it.[61]

Gaius justified the practice by asserting that people could obtain the ownership of certain properties by a law of nature that was universally observed in accordance with natural reason. The principle that Gaius was illustrating is identical to the principle illustrated by the Chinese stories about rabbits. Clearly, a concept resembling ownership did exist in early China, whereby "ownership" is defined as "the bundle of rights allowing one to use, manage, and enjoy property, including the right to convey it to others."[62]

We can classify these five rabbit stories into two different groups depending on whether they use the term *mingfen* or *fen*. Only the *Shangjunshu* story employs the binome *mingfen*, while the others employ *fen* 分 (portion, title). This difference may be because the *Shangjunshu* is the earliest text supplying the most complete account, or because a subtle difference distinguishes the *Shangjunshu* story from others (see below). We will first study the four stories using *fen* before turning to the *Shangjunshu* story to consider the binome *mingfen*.

2.1 *Rabbit Stories on* Fen *from the* Yinwenzi, Lüshi chunqiu, Shuoyuan, *and* Hou Hanshu

We can classify these four stories into two sub-groups based on their narrative structure: (1) The *Yinwenzi* and *Lüshi chunqiu* stories, and (2) the *Shuoyuan* and *Hou Hanshu* stories. The stories in the first sub-group share a basic narrative structure in which the chaotic situation of a horde chasing down free rabbits is contrasted with the orderly situation of a marketplace in which merchants

61 For the part before the ellipsis, see *The Digest of Justinian*, Book XLI, Title I, in *The Civil Law: Including the Twelve Tables, the Institutes of Gaius, the Rules of Ulpian, the Opinions of Paulus, the Enactments of Justinian, and the Constitutions*, ed., Samuel Parsons Scott (Clark: Lawbook Exchange, 2001), vol. 3, 154. For the part after the ellipsis, see Ibid., 156.

62 For the definition of ownership, see *Black's Law Dictionary*, 933. The stories were taken out of their contexts because I believe there is a legal concept embedded in the details of these stories. These stories are unintentional evidence for a concept resembling ownership in early China.

sell rabbits. The stories in the second sub-group share a slightly different narrative structure: the chaotic scene of people in pursuit of a free-running rabbit is contrasted with the orderly situation that occurs once the rabbit is captured by one person.[63]

In the two stories of sub-group 1, the animals are all free and in the wild. People try to capture them because they belong to no one. The *Yinwenzi* story neglects to identify who owns these animals; the *Lüshi chunqiu* story simply observes that a single rabbit is not big enough to be shared by all one hundred hunters. Ownership in the wild remains an open question, while in the marketplace, all the chickens, pigs, and rabbits belong to someone specific, with a title to these animals having already been determined. By the rules and practices of the marketplace, no one would ever try to acquire a chicken, pig, or rabbit without paying for it. The individual merchant holds title to the animal until transferred to the buyer through the implied contract of an exchange of money for meat. Title determines an object's legal and actual status.[64]

While both texts take as a given that, in the marketplace, shoppers acknowledge the individual merchants' titles to their goods, we all know that there were thieves in early China. In the idealized marketplace imagined in the two texts, thievery does not occur. Both texts, more importantly, imply a system in which either unwritten (i.e., customary) or written laws protect a person enjoying his possessions against theft, and ensure that he can seek redress for stolen possessions. Our inferences are corroborated by ZJS strip (*Statutes*) no. 59, which says:

> If a thief robs a person, [when the thief is caught], all the stolen objects that remain shall be given back to their [rightful] owner.[65]
>
> 盜盜人，臧（贓）見存者，皆以畀其主.

63 The analysis of the four stories ultimately requires that we put them in their original contexts. As we do so, we find that the stories all refer to notions of ownership, even if they do not explicitly speak about the laws.

64 A detail is worth noting: in the *Yinwenzi* story, there are a number of free objects (pheasants and rabbits) and only one free object (a single rabbit) in the *Lüshi chunqiu* story. This aspect shows that whether objects with no titles are many or few, people would strive to acquire them without paying for them if their title and status had not been determined. See also *Lüshi chunqiu* (*Gao You zhu*), 17.212. The famous commentator to the *Lüshi chunqiu*, Gao You 高誘 (fl. 205–212) glossed the phrase "*fen wei ding*" 分未定: "People will desire those objects whose [title] has not yet been determined" (未定者，人欲望之).

65 ZJS strip (*Statutes*) no. 59, p. 16.

Thus, when the title over an object has not yet been determined, the object is open to competing claims, but once the title has been determined, the object is legally possessed by its owner, whose interests are protected by the law.

If the two stories above both allude to the legal protection afforded by one's title to an object, then the two stories in the *Shuoyuan* and the *Hou Hanshu* emphasize the exclusivity attached to any title.

> Now let us suppose that a single rabbit runs on the street, and ten thousand people pursue it. Once a single person captures it, the rest of the crowd will no longer run after it. When the title has not yet been determined, the rabbit on the run will cause ten thousand people to get all excited [at the prospect of owning it]. But if the title has been determined, even greedy people know to stop.[66]
>
> As the proverb goes, when ten thousand people chase after one rabbit, as soon as one person captures it, all the greedy people will stop [their pursuit], because the title has been determined.[67]

Both passages feature a dramatic contrast between huge numbers of people trying to capture a rabbit on the run, and the sudden end of the pursuit once the rabbit is caught. That vivid contrast serves to highlight the exclusivity of the title conferred via the successful pursuit. In general, only one person or family may enjoy title to an object at a given time.

One more example reinforces these observations. A story in the *Shiji* features the newly established Emperor Gaozu 高祖 (r. 206–195 BC), who accused the strategist Kuai Tong 蒯通 (fl. 209–194 BC),[68] a follower of the powerful general Han Xin 韓信 (d. 196 BC), of urging Han Xin to turn against Gaozu. Kuai Tong defended himself by arguing:

> The Qin dynasty lost the deer [a metaphor for the throne] and all under Heaven joined in its pursuit. Thereupon, he with the tallest stature and the swiftest feet seized it first [and so ascended the throne] … At that time, I knew only Han Xin. I did not know your Majesty.[69]

66 *Shuoyuan jiaozheng*, 3.74.

67 *Hou Hanshu*, 74A. 2383.

68 According to Michael Loewe, Kuai Tong 蒯通 was a native of Qi, and "his activities are described in a manner that is reminiscent of the tales of the protagonists of pre-imperial days." See Michael Loewe, *A Biographical Dictionary of the Qin, Former Han and Xin Periods (221 B.C.–A.D. 24)* (Leiden and Boston: Brill, 2000), 212.

69 *Shiji*, 92.2629. My translation follows Watson, *Records of the Grand Historian*, 83.

> 秦失其鹿，天下共逐之，於是高材疾足者先得焉 … 當是時，臣唯獨知韓信，非知陛下也.

Kuai Tong was using the analogy of capturing a deer to describe the legitimacy of the Han house. Kuai Tong argued that before Liu Bang captured the throne, the throne was available to many competitors, and so it was legitimate for Kuai Tong to help anyone in such an open competition. Crucial to Kuai Tong's argument, is the prevailing assumption that the person who first captures the deer gains undisputed title to it, and thus, by analogy, Gaozu obtained the throne simply because he was the first to seize the "deer." Kuai Tong's argument convinced Gaozu, and he freed Kuai Tong without any further charges.[70] This example from the *Shiji*, taken with the other examples cited here and all the civil cases studied in previous chapters, further reinforces the conclusion that the concept of exclusive title, with its clear implication of individual ownership, was broadly accepted in early Western Han times.[71] To underscore this point, let me cite one final case.

> There was a certain person from Linhuai, who brought a piece of silk with him to sell at the market. On his way [to the market], it rained, so he covered himself with the silk [to protect himself against the rain]. Afterwards, a stranger asked to share the cover with him. The person gave the stranger a place for his head, but when the rain stopped and they were about to set off on their separate ways, they started to fight over [the ownership of the silk], with each claiming the silk as his own. So, they came to court to speak on their own behalf.
>
> When Governor Xue Xuan interrogated them, neither was willing to admit that his claim was false. Xue Xuan said: "This piece of silk is only worth a few hundred cash. It is not worth fighting over and bringing a case to court." He then ordered an officer in his cavalry to split the silk in half, giving one-half to each of the disputants. [After dismissing them from the court,] Xue ordered his men to follow and eavesdrop on them. The stranger said: "I got an unexpected favor!" and he went forward to grab the silk. The real owner of the silk could not stop complaining about the unfairness of the judgment. [Xue's subordinates went back and reported what they had heard to Xue Xuan.] Xue Xuan said: "Right, now I know what ought to be done." [He sent an officer to bring them back.]

70 Ibid.

71 We have not found an independent term indicating ownership, but that "ownership" was implied by the term "title" (*mingfen*).

> Then, he interrogated the stranger again. The stranger confessed every detail [of his dishonesty]. Xue Xuan ordered the stranger to return the silk to its original owner.[72]
>
> 臨淮有一人，持一匹縑到市賣之，道遇雨而披戴，後人求共庇蔭，因與一頭之地；雨霽，當別，因共爭鬬，各云：“我縑.” 詣府自言.
>
> 太守丞相[73]薛宣劾實，兩人莫肯首服. 宣曰：“縑直數百錢耳，何足紛紛，自致縣.”[74] 呼騎吏中斷縑，各與半；使追聽之. 後人曰：“受恩.” 前撮之. 縑主稱冤不已. 宣曰：“然，固知當爾也.” 因結責之，具服，俾悉還本主.

Admittedly, this story has a puzzling feature: we would not expect this kind of civil dispute to appear before the commandery court, since such a case would have had to have skipped two preliminary levels, the district and county. Despite this peculiar feature, the narrative matches what we know of the general procedures for Han civil litigation. The silk in dispute obviously had a rightful owner, the would-be seller. However, the would-be seller, en route to the market, had his ownership of the silk unexpectedly challenged.

The location is important. If the merchant had arrived in the market, there would have been witnesses who could reasonably assume that the merchant was the rightful owner of the silk. Moreover, the merchant's ownership would probably have been verified by two types of documents: inventories submitted to market officials, and contracts concerning transactions. According to the recent study by Zhang Jihai 張繼海, no later than Western Han times, marketplaces in China were well organized and overseen by designated officials.[75] According to the *Shiji*, both registered merchants[76] and unregistered peddlers and traders were required to report the estimated values of their goods to the officials.

---

72 *Fengsu tongyi jiaozhu*, 11. 589.

73 Xue Xuan should have been a Governor at the time, but the highest position he achieved in his lifetime was Chancellor. Therefore, he is given the title *Taishou Chengxiang* (Governor Chancellor) in this passage.

74 Readers are reminded that, according to Loewe, "In the majority of cases, *xianguan* 縣官 refers indiscriminately to organs of government, whether central or provincial, without any specification." See Loewe, "The Organs of Han Imperial Government" 71, no. 3 (2008): 510.

75 Zhang Jihai 張繼海, *Handai chengshi shehui* 漢代城市社會 (Beijing: Shehui kexue wenxian chubanshe, 2006), 220–263, especially 233–235.

76 Merchants were required to register themselves with the officials. See Ibid.

> Those traders who engage in secondary occupations [i.e., commercial activities] such as lending and loaning money on credit, or who live in the towns and have storehouses of various goods, and those merchants who sell goods to gain profits, even if there are no marketplace registers [because the town is too small?], should each self-assess the values of their goods and report them to the officials …[77]
>
> 諸賈人末作貰貸賣買，居邑稽諸物，及商以取利者，雖無市籍，各以其物自占 …

Guo Pu 郭璞 (276–324) and Sima Zhen 司馬貞 (679–732) glossed the word *zhan* 占 as follows:

> *Zhan* 占 refers to "self-assessment." It means that each seller by himself assesses the values of his goods, writes them down on a report, and submits the report to the officials. If the report is not complete, [those goods not included in the report] will all be confiscated by the proper officials.[78]
>
> 占，自隱度也．謂各自隱度其財物多少，為文簿送之官也．若不盡，皆沒入於官．

This requirement, on the one hand, was designed to facilitate tax-collection. On the other hand, it could also be viewed as a legal means to acknowledge and document the merchant's ownership of goods, since the reports were essentially inventories. Since all unreported goods would be confiscated, we know that "the officials" referred to in the passage above, were officials in charge of supervising the marketplaces, and that those officials were responsible for checking the accuracy of the inventories submitted to them. Such an inventory, once substantiated, could be used as proof of ownership in the event of a dispute over title. Zheng Xuan adds further information to this picture:

> When one buys goods in the market, each [of the two parties] should make copies of every contract. Each of the two parties keeps one copy of

77 *Shiji*, 30.1430. *Zuozhuan*, Lord Xuan 宣, Year 12, distinguishes *shang* 商 ("merchants" who operate over fairly long distances) from *gu* 賈 ("traders" who sell products in the marketplace). The term "traders" also includes "moneylenders," as is clear from this chapter. For further information, see Zeng Weihua 曾維華, "Shi *Shiji* Huozhi liezhuan zhong de yishi men" 釋史記貨殖列傳中的倚市門, *Xueshu yuekan* 學術月刊 no. 5 (2000): 88–89.

78 *Shiji*, 30.1430, n. 6.

> the contract. Should any disputes arise, [the authorities] will judge the case based on the contract.[79]
>
> 市買為券書以別之，各得其一，訟則案券以正之.

Thus, in a marketplace, legal ownership of goods was clearly established by at least two written documents, both of which would be available to the courts should disputes arise.

However, since the would-be seller in our current case had not yet arrived at the marketplace, there were no witnesses, no inventory submitted to the market officials, and no documentation of transactions. Lacking any of the customary and legally approved proofs of ownership, the merchant was vulnerable to the challenge of this opportunistic stranger. Once challenged, the burden of proof fell to the merchant, presumably the silk's rightful owner. With no way to prove that the silk was his, the merchant's only recourse was to submit his claim to the courts. Absent documentary evidence (inventories or transaction records) and witness testimony (marketplace merchants and shoppers), the judge needed to find some other way of ascertaining the silk's rightful owner. While feigning indifference, the judge, determined to find the "straight" facts, interrogated the stranger so deftly that the stranger ultimately confessed his malfeasance.

Our analysis of these examples demonstrates that there was a clear concept of property ownership in early China, and that the judicial authorities recognized their duty to protect rightful owners against dishonest claims. The principle of protecting ownership against theft and false claims incorporates other, non-legal social and moral attitudes, in particular, an attitude toward those who would steal or defraud legitimate owners. A passage from the *Yinwenzi's* rabbit illustrates this concern:

> Selfishness will not make a person successful, not because there are no selfish desires, but because when the title (*fen*) is clear, there is no place for one's selfish desires [to operate].[80]
>
> 私不行，非無欲，由分明，故無所措其欲.

79 Cheng Shude, *Hanlü kao*, 122. Cheng recovered this regulation based on Zheng Xuan's commentary in the "Qiuguan" 秋官 chapter of *Zhouli*.

80 *Yinwenzi jiaozheng*, 11.

If these selfish desires relate to property, the *fen* here must refer to title. But insofar as selfish desires also aim, through immoral possession of property, to raise a person's social status (also *fen*), the passage also points to larger social issues.

The use of *fen* in the rabbit story from the *Lüshi chunqiu* further illustrates this point:

> When feudal lords lose their proper places, all under Heaven falls into chaos; when counselors step out of their proper ranks, the court falls into chaos; when there are no distinctions between the wife and concubines, the household falls into chaos; and when there are no distinctions among sons born by the legal wife and sons born by concubines, the clan falls into chaos.[81]
>
> 諸侯失位則天下亂，大夫無等則朝廷亂，妻妾不分則家室亂，適孽無別則宗族亂.

Just as *fen* was applied to rabbits, here, by analogy, *fen* is applied to designated social roles and the norms attached to them.

In the *Shuoyuan* story, in a speech ascribed to the minister Qu Jian 屈建 (d. 545 BC), *fen* is employed in reference to claims on the throne, making explicit the analogy with claims of ownership of a rabbit pursued by many. We recall the story says: "When the title has not yet been determined, the rabbit on the run will cause ten thousand people to get all excited [at the prospect of owning it]. But once the title has been determined, even greedy people know to stop."[82] Then the story continues:

> Now since [the King of] Chu has many favorite sons but no heir-apparent, chaos will arise from there. As for the heir-apparent, he is the basis of the state and the hope of the people. [Without him], the state has no basis, and the people lose their hope for the future. [Not to appoint an heir] is to cut off the root of the state. When the root is cut off, [the state will descend into] chaos, just as in the story of the rabbit on the run.[83]

81 *Lüshi chunqiu yizhu*, 17.532. My translation follows Knoblock and Riegel, *The Annals of Lü Buwei*, 431 (slightly modified).

82 *Shouyuan jiaozheng*, 3.74.

83 Ibid.

今楚多寵子而嫡位無主，亂自是生矣．夫世子者，國之基也，而百姓之望也；國既無基，又使百姓失望，絕其本矣．本絕則撓亂，猶兔走也．

Not appointing an heir-apparent is equated with a free-running, unclaimed rabbit, an analogy that is even more clearly articulated in the statement, "When the title (*fen*) has not yet been determined, the rabbit on the run will cause ten thousand people to get all excited [at the prospect of owning it]." In this construction, *fen* corresponds to the legitimate claim on the title of heir-apparent (*zhu*主), a convergence of social role and ownership. The *Hou Hanshu* rabbit story seems to allude to a similar sense of *fen*.[84]

Even though *fen* appears in early texts in contexts that deal with prescribed social roles and the apportioned share of goods that accrue to those playing those roles, these four rabbit stories all attest to the fact that in early China, *fen* referred to "title" with the implication of ownership. While the stories cited above deal only with movable property (animals or goods), not land (i.e., real property), when we turn to the earliest known story concerning title, the *Shangjunshu* rabbit story on *mingfen*, we will find that ownership in early China covered both movable and real property.

2.2 *The* Shangjunshu *Rabbit Story and the Practice of* Mingtianzhai 名田宅 (*Title to Farmland and Dwelling Sites*)

Traditionally, *mingfen* has been understood to mean social roles and the normative behavior prescribed for those roles. However, the binome *mingfen* in the *Shangjunshu* rabbit story clearly means "title," implying ownership. More importantly, in the overall context of the book, *mingfen* underlines the practice of *mingtianzhai*, actual ownership of real property.[85]

In both narrative structure and detail, the *Shangjunshu* story closely resembles the rabbit stories of the *Yinwenzi* and *Lüshi chunqiu*. In all three, we are presented with an initially chaotic situation, with people running after a rabbit whose ownership has not yet been determined, that gives way to an orderly situation once ownership has been determined. Given these parallels, the term *mingfen* in the *Shangjunshu* rabbit story must also refer to ownership or "title," with "title" here denoted by the binome *mingfen*: a title and the portion (or due

84 In the *Hou Hanshu*, 74A. 2383, the story is followed by these words ascribed to the minister Ju Shou 沮授 (d. 201): "[Yuan] Tan is the eldest son and should become the heir-apparent. However, [you, Yuan Shao 袁紹] rejected him and ordered him to live outside [of the capital]. The calamities began from there, certainly" (譚長子, 當爲嗣, 而斥使居外, 禍其始此).

85 I suggest that the relationship between *mingtianzhai* and *mingfen* is as follows: *ming* is the same, while *tianzhai* (land and dwelling sites) corresponds to *fen* (portion).

share) entailed. This point is not obvious at first glance since the explanation that follows the rabbit story appears to give *mingfen* a rather different meaning than it carries in the story itself.

When taken in context, the subject of this story is the function of properly decreed laws and edicts. The postscript to the story includes the following:

> Now if the laws and edicts are not clear, nor the names and title determined, the subjects under Heaven will be able to debate them, and those who debate them will disagree and nothing will be determined. If the ruler of men makes laws above, but below his subjects debate them, this means that the laws and edicts have not been determined and subjects have become superiors. This we call "*mingfen* not yet determined." Now, as we all know, when *mingfen* is not yet determined, even Yao and Shun would both be tempted to do wrong, not to mention ordinary people.[86]
>
> 今法令不明，其名不定，天下之人得議之，其議人異而無定．人主為法於上，下民議之於下，是法令不定，以下為上也．此所謂名分之不定也．夫名分不定，堯舜猶將皆折而姦之，而況眾人乎?

Here, the phrase "*qi ming bu ding*" 其名不定 is quite difficult to contextualize. In the sentence, the *ming* seems to refer to the names of laws and ordinances. But what are the names of laws and ordinances? Why would those names be of such concern to all subjects under Heaven that they would want to debate those names? Moreover, where is *fen* in the greater context? With these questions in mind, we find that the text concludes:

> Therefore, the sages set up offices and appointed officials for the sake of the laws and edicts, who would act as models of authority for the entire realm, so as to determine everyone's title and proper share (*mingfen*). Once these were determined, the very crafty would become sincere and trustworthy, and the subjects all honest and guileless, with each one restraining himself or herself.[87]
>
> 故聖人必為法令置官也，置吏也，為天下師，所以定名分也．名分定，則大軸貞信，民皆願慤，而各自治也．

86 *Shangjunshu zhushi*, 5.145. My translation follows Duyvendak, *The Book of Lord Shang*, 168.

87 *Shangjunshu zhushi*, 5.146. My translation follows Duyvendak, *The Book of Lord Shang*, 169 (slightly modified).

Unfortunately, these passages provide little guidance in resolving our questions about the usage of *mingfen*. Perhaps, because the "Dingfen" chapter was compiled by different hands in a different time period, the difficulties that we are encountering may be due to inconsistencies among the various compilers. However, if we view *mingfen* in the larger context of the *Shangjunshu*, we find that *mingfen* is associated with a particular type of decree, the orders of honor, which links it with the practice of *mingtianzhai* credited to minister Shang Yang 商鞅 (ca. 390–338 BC), to whom authorship of the *Shangjunshu* was attributed.

An earlier chapter of the *Shangjunshu*, "Within Borders" (Jingnei 境内), opens with this line:

> Within the four borders, adult males and females are known by name to their superiors. When they are born, their names are registered, and when they die, their names are expunged from the records.[88]
>
> 四境之內，丈夫女子皆有名於上，生者著，死者削.

The remainder of the chapter deals with military and civilian orders of honor:

> The military orders of honor from the highest order down to the lowest order of *xiaofu* 小夫 are called *xiaotu* 校徒 and *caoshi* 操士. The official [civilian] orders of honor from the second degree upwards to the degree of *bugeng* 不更 are called *zu* 卒.[89]
>
> 軍爵，自一級已下至小夫，命曰校徒操士．公爵，自二級已上至不更，命曰卒.

According to historian Koga Noboru 古賀登, the ranking system was described here in order to explain an historical event: Shang Yang, who served as a minister of Duke Xiao of Qin (r. 361–337 BC), established orders of military honor and civilian honor during his reforms. These orders of honor, both civil and military, were bestowed upon individuals according to their military merits.

88 Ibid.

89 Ibid., 4.122. My translation follows Duyvendak, *The Book of Lord Shang*, 143 (slightly modified). This passage is somewhat confusing as it mentions *xiaotu* 校徒 and *caoshi* 操士. According to Koga, *xiaotu* and *caoshi* were the lowest military ranks, which were equivalent to *xiaofu* 小夫 and *gongshi* 公士 in civilian ranks. See Koga Noboru 古賀登, "Shin Shō Ō no gunsei gunkō hōshō to mibunsei" 秦商鞅の軍制軍功褒賞制と身分制, *Shakai keizai rekishi* 社會經濟歷史 40, no. 4 (1974): 339.

The state would then grant them farmland, dwelling sites, and servants according to their rank in the orders of honor. For instance, a person with the lowest military honor was granted one *qing* (頃) of cultivated land, five *mu* (畝) for a dwelling site, and one servant who, in peacetime, was to serve the person six days a month, and in wartime, was to accompany him as a military aide.[90]

Thus, in the larger context of the arguments in the *Shangjunshu*, *mingfen* is associated with the orders of honor (*ming*) and the portion (*fen*) of farmland, dwelling sites, and servants attached to them. To determine the *ming* was to determine the appropriate distribution of land and servants. Ownership of real property derives from this practice. As the *Shiji* says:

> [Shang Yang in 359 BC ordered the state's officers] to distinguish the high-ranking from the low-ranking, and to clarify the hierarchy of the orders of honor and salaries, so that each person could claim farmland and dwelling sites according to his position in the hierarchy.[91]
>
> 明尊卑爵秩等級，各以差次名田宅.

Admittedly, given the paucity of evidence, we cannot prove that this reform, attributed to Shang Yang, was carried out in Shang Yang's time (ca. 350 BC). If subjects only had the privilege of using the land but could not transfer their titles to it, then the argument that *mingfen* in the *Shangjunshu* refers to the distribution of lands becomes doubtful, since the word "title" implies ownership, not temporary allotment. However, we can be confident that the practice attributed to Shang Yang was certainly in place in Han times since the practice was reflected in provisions concerning *mingtianzhai* from Zhangjiashan.[92]

What does *mingtianzhai* mean? Literally, *ming* means "name" or "title," *tian* means "cultivated field," and *zhai* typically means "dwelling," though in this particular case, it refers to a "dwelling site."[93] Historians have long puzzled over the term *mingtianzhai*. Faced with a paucity of source material, no one could explain the term in detail or with any certainty until the discovery of the

---

90 Koga, "Shin Shō Ō no gunsei gunkō," 335–360. Koga Noboru argued that the "Jingnei" 境内 chapter describes the situation of the Qin state in the late Warring States period, as the system described by the chapter is consistent with how the "Dingfa" 定法 chapter of the *Han Feizi* describes Shang Yang's reforms. Ibid., 335–336.

91 *Shiji*, 68.2230.

92 ZJS strip (*Statutes*) nos. 305–345, pp. 51–56.

93 Zhu Shaohou 朱紹侯, "Lun Handai de mingtian (shoutian) jiqi pohuai" 論漢代的名田（授田）及其破壞, *Henan daxue xuebao* (*Shehui kexue ban*) 河南大學學報(社會科學版) no. 1 (2004): 36.

"Statutes of Households" from Zhangjiashan. The *ZJS* strip (*Statutes*) nos. 313–316 stipulate, with notable precision, the parameters of individual claims to farmland and dwelling sites determined by rank.

1. Regarding farmland:

> Lesser marquis [can claim] ninety-five *qing* [of cultivated field], *dashuzhang* 大庶長 ninety *qing*, *sicheshuzhang* 駟車庶長 eighty-eight *qing*, *dashangzao* 大上造 eighty-six *qing*, *shaoshangzao* 少上造 eighty-four *qing*, *yougeng* 右更 eighty-two *qing*, *zhonggeng* 中更 eighty *qing*, *zuogeng* 左更 seventy-eight *qing*, *youshuzhang* 右庶長 seventy-six *qing*, *zuoshuzhang* 左庶長 seventy-four *qing*, *wudafu* 五大夫 twenty-five *qing*, *gongcheng* 公乘 twenty *qing*, *gongdafu* 公大夫 nine *qing*, *guandafu* 官大夫 seven *qing*, *dafu* 大夫 five *qing*, *bugeng* 不更 four *qing*, *zanniao* 簪褭 three *qing*, *shangzhao* 上造 two *qing*, *gongshi* 公士 one and a half *qing*, *gongzu* 公卒, *shiwu* 士伍, and *shuren* 庶人 one *qing*, and *sikou* 司寇 and *yinguan* 隱官 fifty *mu* [i.e., one-half *qing*].[94]
>
> 關內侯九十五頃. 大庶長九十頃. 駟車庶長八十八頃. 大上造八十六頃. 少上造八十四頃. 右更八十二頃. 中更八十頃. 左更七十八頃. 右庶長七十六頃. 左庶長七十四頃. 五大夫廿五頃. 公乘廿頃. 公大夫九頃. 官大夫七頃. 大夫五頃. 不更四頃. 簪褭三頃. 上造二頃. 公士一頃半頃. 公卒、士五（伍）、庶人各一頃. 司寇、隱官各五十畝.

2. Regarding dwelling sites:

> The area of one *zhai* is thirty square feet [in Han measure]. A marquis [shall receive] one hundred and five *zhai* [of dwelling site]; a lesser marquis ninety-five *zhai*; a *dashuzhang* 大庶長 ninety *zhai*; a *sicheshuzhang* 駟車庶長 eighty-eight *zhai*; a *dashangzao* 大上造 eighty-six *zhai*; a *shaoshangzao* 少上造 eighty-four *zhai*; a *yougeng* 右更 eighty-two *zhai*; a *zhonggeng* 中更 eighty *zhai*; a *zuogeng* 左更 seventy-eight *zhai*; a *youshuzhang* 右庶長 seventy-six *zhai*; a *zuoshuzhang* 左庶長 seventy-four *zhai*; a *wudafu* 五大夫 twenty-five *zhai*; a *gongcheng* twenty *zhai*; a *gongdafu* nine *zhai*; a *guandafu* 公乘 seven *zhai*; a *dafu* 大夫 five *zhai*; a *bugeng* 不更 four *zhai*; a *zanniao* 簪褭 three *zhai*; a *shangzhao* 上造 two *zhai*; a *gongshi* 公士 one and a half *zhai*; a *gongzu* 公卒, *shiwu* 士伍, or *shuren* 庶人 one *zhai*; and a *sikou* 司寇 or *yinguan* 隱官, one-half *zhai*. If a person

94 *ZJS* strip (*Statutes*) nos. 310–313, p. 52. One *qing* 傾 is approximately 4.6 hectares. See Hulsewé, "Ch'in-Han Weights and Measures," in *RCL*, 19.

who [has newly received his portion of farmland and dwelling sites] wants to establish an [independent] household [, instead of merging them into his old household], that is permitted.[95]

宅之大方卅步. 徹侯受百五宅. 關內侯九十五宅. 大庶長九十宅. 駟車庶長八十八宅. 大上造八十六宅. 少上造八十四宅. 右更八十二宅. 中更八十宅. 左更七十八宅. 右庶長七十六宅. 左庶長七十四宅. 五大夫廿五宅. 公乘廿宅, 公大夫九宅. 官大夫七宅. 大夫五宅. 不更四宅. 簪裹三宅. 上造二宅. 公士一宅半宅. 公卒、士五(伍) 、庶人一宅. 司寇、隱官半宅. 欲爲戶者, 許之.

Based on this information, we have constructed Figure 4.[96] The horizontal axis of the chart represents the orders of honor, *jue* 爵. During the Han dynasty, there were twenty orders of honors: from the highest, marquis, to the lowest, *gongshi* 公士. Each order of honor was associated with a clearly defined claim to farmland and dwelling sites, ranging from 105 *qing* + 105 *zhai*[97] to 1.5 *qing* + 1.5 *zhai*. In addition, commoners, such as *gongzu* 公卒, *shiwu* 士伍 and *shuren* 庶人, and even those who were socially discriminated against (e.g., the *sikou* 司寇 and *yinguan* 隱官) were also granted shares in the land distribution system.[98] Notably, from the highest rank, marquis, to the eleventh, *zuoshuzhang* 左庶長, the amounts of land which one was entitled to claim declined gradually. However, there is a very steep decline in lands granted to those below the eighth rank (*zuoshuzhang* 左庶長). Evidently, rank nine (*wudafu* 五大夫) marks a sharp break, since the holders of rank eight (*zuoshuzhang*) can claim almost three times the amount of land as the holders of rank nine (*wudafu*). From the rank *wudafu* down to the *sikou* and *yinguan*, the land each holder can claim once more declines very gradually. Clearly, the system was designed to create a sharply defined social gap between those holding the rank of *wudafu*

95 ZJS strip (*Statutes*) nos. 314–316, p. 52.

96 This chart reverses the order of the ranks during the Han dynasty, taking rank 1 as the highest (named as rank 20 in the sources) and rank 2 as the second highest (rank 19 in Han sources), etc. In the Han dynasty, the higher the number, the higher the rank.

97 The highest rank, marquis, does not occur in the regulations concerning granting farming land. Since a marquis was entitled to claim 105 *zhai* of dwelling site as ZJS strip (*Statutes*) no. 314 stipulates, it is plausible that he could also claim 105 *qing* of farming land.

98 The precise meaning of *yinguan* is a matter of debate. See Michael Loewe, "On the Terms *baozi*, *yinggong*, *yinguan*, and *shou*: Was Zhao Gao a Eunuch?" *Toung P'ao* 91 (2005): 314. Loewe argued that *yinguan* refers to "persons who were 'concealed in the offices' or were kept 'in the concealed offices'." He further pointed out that "[It is] a category which is seen principally in the legal material from Shuihudi and (more frequently) in that from Zhangjiashan."

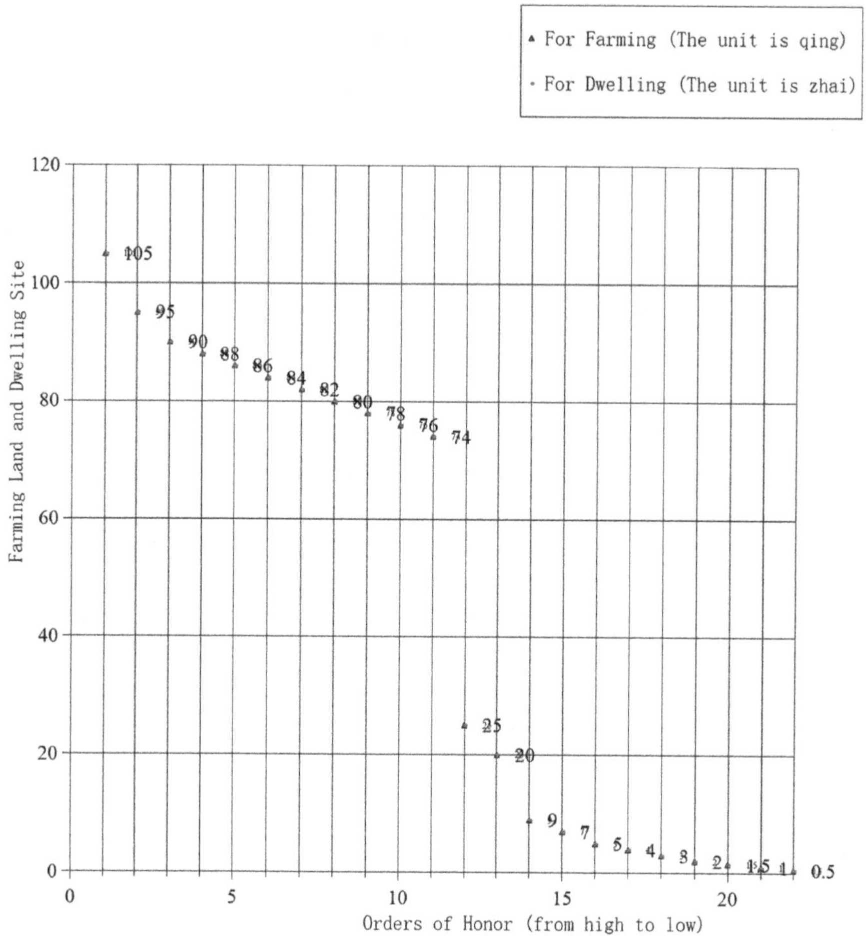

FIGURE 4 Orders of honor

rank or higher and those below *wudafu*. Even with these disparities, it is worth noting that the system granted all eligible adults a share in land.[99] In short, the system was hierarchical, but inclusive, intended to serve a very broad range of the population across different social strata.

On what basis, then, do we call the practice described above *mingtianzhai*? ZJS strip (*Statutes*) nos. 323–324 state:

99 This pattern is consistent with Nishijima's classification of ranks for officials and ranks for ordinary people. In Nishijima's classification, the dividing line is also *wudafu*.

> For those people who do not establish their own households, but attach their farmland and dwelling sites to other people's names on the registers, or those people who claim title to farmland and dwelling sites (*mingtianzhai*) on behalf of others, let them all [be punished by being sent to] guard the frontiers for two years, and let their farmland and dwelling sites be confiscated by the local officials who represent the central government. For those people who claim title to farmland and dwelling sites (*mingtianzhai*) on behalf of other people, if they report their own fraudulent claims before they are discovered, their crimes will be forgiven and they will be granted the land that they have claimed. All other affairs should be handled according to the statutes and ordinances.[100]
>
> 諸不為戶, 有田宅附令人名, 及為人名田宅者, 皆令以卒戍邊二歲, 沒入田宅縣官. 為人名田宅, 能先告, 除其罪, 有（又）畀之所名田宅, 它如律令.

This regulation clearly shows that at the time, the practice of claiming title to lands was called *mingtianzhai*. In this system, based upon one's rank in the orders of honor, a person was entitled to claim a certain amount of land and register that property with the local authorities, thereby establishing a registered household.[101]

The duly registered head of household owned the cultivated field and dwelling site, not only the privilege of using them. The principle of ownership is underscored in two crucial ways: First, one could give or sell one's land to others. ZJS strip (*Statutes*) no. 321 states:

> After one receives farmland and dwelling sites, if he or she gives or sells the land to others, he or she is not allowed to receive new land.[102]
>
> 受田宅, 予人若賣田宅, 不得更受.

The purpose of this provision was to prohibit those who give or sell their land to others from claiming new land from the state. This provision clearly implies

100 ZJS strip (*Statutes*) nos. 323–324, p. 53.

101 The following statement is puzzling: "If they report their own fraudulent claims before they are discovered, their crimes will be forgiven, and they will be granted the land that they have claimed." In this case, it seems that those individuals who committed fraud by claiming land for others still received benefits and rewards at others' expense if they made timely confessions.

102 ZJS strip (*Statutes*) no. 321, p. 53.

that giving or selling land to others was legal. Second, the cultivated field and dwelling site to which a person held title could be inherited by that person's heirs.[103] Yet in the process of inheritance, title to the rank (*ming*) – but not title to the farmland – was automatically reduced by two degrees, before being passed on to the heirs, with the notable exception of the nobility (ranks nineteen and twenty). Prior to Emperor Wu's reign, title to farmland and dwelling sites was to be divided more or less equally among all the sons, again, with an exception for the nobility (ranks nineteen and twenty). So, we see that title to rank (*ming*) could be separated from the portion (*fen*) in inheritance laws. In this regard, even though a subject's title and portion of land was not absolutely inalienable, it was substantially integrated.

All land transactions had to be reported to the officials and documented. If the officials failed to process the documentation on time, they would be fined. *ZJS* strip (*Statutes*) no. 322 says:

> As for replacing the head of household, or buying or selling farming land and dwelling sites, if the officers of the district or farming land delay the process and fail to make a register (*dingji*) for them, the officers shall be fined with two *liang* of gold per day.[104]

This provision further confirms the subjects' ownership over their farmland and dwelling sites.

In the following story from the *Shuoyuan* that deals with the distribution of land, the verb used is *fen* 分 (participate, divide), which reinforces our understanding that *mingtianzhai* corresponds to *mingfen* in that *ming* remains the same, while land (*tianzhai*) corresponds to the portion (*fen*):

> Duke Wen of Jin asked Jiu Fan on governance, and he answered: To divide and grant cooked [meat] is not as good as to divide and grant raw [meat]. To divide and grant raw [meat] is not as good as to divide and grant land. Divide [it] into pieces and grant them to the people and add to their orders of honor and salaries. Therefore, when the ruler acquires land, then the people know they are enriched. When the ruler loses land, the people know they have become poor …[105]

103 See my analysis of this subject in Chapter 3.
104 *ZJS* strip (*Statutes*) no. 322, p. 53.
105 *Shuoyuan jiaozheng*, 7.168.

晉文公問政於咎犯，對曰：分熟不如分腥，分腥不如分地，割以分民而益其爵祿，是以上得地而民知富，上失地而民知貧 …

The key message of this passage is that by dividing land into pieces and granting them to the people according to their orders of honor and salaries, the subjects will have a common interest with the ruler. The "people" here perhaps refers to those in the officialdom since "salary" is mentioned in the passage. There is no evidence in the *Zuozhuan*, the *Guoyu*, or other pre-Han texts to indicate that Jin ministers in the reign of Duke Wen (r. 636–628 BC) invented such a practice. Very likely, the author Liu Xiang 劉向 (77–6 BC), was projecting the *mingtianzhai* practice of his own time back to the pre-Qin time of Duke Wen of Jin, even though Liu Xiang seems to limit the beneficiaries to officials. But, as we have seen, Han provisions concerning *mingtianzhai* included commoners in the prescribed distribution of land. Those provisions requiring land conferrals seem to have had an unforeseen consequence, as witnessed by the lament of minister Gong Yu 貢禹 (ca. 129–47 BC) to Emperor Yuan (r. 49–33 BC):

> Therefore, people abandon their primary occupation [farming] in order to pursue secondary occupations [i.e., commercial activities]. Now, farmers are less than a half of our population. Even though we grant farmland to the poor, they still sell them cheaply in order to do business.[106]

> 故民棄本逐末，耕者不能半．貧民雖賜之田，猶賤賣以賈．

The important point here is that Han laws concerning land ownership applied to all imperial subjects, with those subjects classified according to twenty hierarchical orders of honor, with the high-ranking elite enjoying special legal privileges.[107] This feature of all-inclusiveness clearly parallels the provisions concerning inheritance that we studied before. Even household slaves had a place in the sequence of household inheritance whereby they could inherit their masters' households when there was no other rightful heir.

Consistent with this all-inclusive feature is the empire-wide ("All under Heaven") implementation of Han laws as a whole. This was the case for most of the Western Han and Eastern Han. We are not sure about the situation in the

106 *Hanshu*, 72.3075. There is an alternative interpretation of the story. The practice could be a charity that involves the granting of land to the poor. However, this alternative interpretation does not contradict our interpretation; the crucial point is that the state did grant land to the lower strata of the society, not just officials.

107 Loewe, *The Government of the Qin and Han Empires*, 119–150; cf. *RHL*, 4–11.

very early period of the Western Han (206–174 BC). When Liu Bang established himself as the emperor, he enfeoffed various kings who were not from the Liu clan to assist him in ruling the empire. Those kings had nearly autonomous power. They may have been able to make their own laws. But over time, their independence was whittled down. By 174 BC, nearly all the formerly autonomous kingdoms were in the hands of the Liu family, except for the small state of Changsha. Once members of the Liu clan were in charge, the head of the Liu clan, the emperor, expected them to obey Han laws.[108] For example, in 174 BC the King of Huainan 淮南, Liu Zhang 劉長 (r. 196–174 BC), was charged with unauthorized law-making: "He made his own laws and ordinances without authorization, and did not use Han laws" (擅為法令, 不用漢法).[109]

For most of Western Han and Eastern Han, imperial subjects throughout the empire, from all social strata, enjoyed legally defined ownership of real property in accord with the *mingtianzhai* provisions. They also surely enjoyed ownership of personal property, as demonstrated by the "rabbit" stories. This universality of ownership rights and inclusion in an integrated hierarchical system of social ranking comports with our earlier observation that both elites and commoners resorted to the civil justice system to seek protection of their interests, and that in civil litigation, the disputants were mostly treated as equal parties regardless of their ranks.[110]

As historian Yu Zhenbo 于振波 recently argued, it may be that, beginning with the reign of Emperor Wu, the practice of *mingtianzhai* gradually declined because the state had less free land to grant to its subjects.[111] But Gong Yu's words show that the practice of granting land and dwelling sites still occurred during the reign of Emperor Yuan. Moreover, the gradual collapse of the *mingtianzhai* practice had little to do with the imperial subjects' "rights" to own real property.[112] All the land and inheritance disputes that we have reviewed support this claim. As a reminder that ownership was society-wide, we have the following land transfer document, dated AD 169:

108 For details of the political changes in 206–174 BC, see *CHC*, 110–127.

109 *Hanshu*, 44.2141.

110 One's order of honor entailed certain legal privileges in criminal litigation, but not in civil litigation.

111 Yu Zhenbo 于振波, "Zhangjiashan Hanjian zhong de mingtianzhi jiqi zai Handai de shishi" 張家山漢簡中的名田制及其在漢代的實施, *Zhongguo shi yanjiu* 中國史研究 no. 1 (2004): 29–40.

112 Legally speaking, in the worst case, even if the state stopped granting land to imperial subjects, those subjects still could retain their "*mingfen*" to own and dispose of real property.

> On the 5th day of the 8th month, beginning with the day *gengwu*, in the 2nd year of the Jianning period (AD 169), a male from Henei named Wang Weiqing buys from a male named Yuan Shuwei, three *mu* of his land to the west of the border of the 13th station of the Gaomen pavilion (*tingbu* 亭部). Each *mu* is worth 3,100 cash. In total, the value is 9,300 cash. Payment of the money is completed on the same day. Yuan Shuwei is present when the agreement is made. Buying wine, each party drinks half of it [to bind the transaction]. On the same day, an iron contract in red ink is made to record the agreement.[113]
>
> 建宁二年八月庚午朔五日，河內懷男子王未卿，從河南街郵部男袁叔威，買皐門亭部十三陌西袁田三畝．畝賈價三千一百，並直九千三百．錢即日畢．時約者袁叔威．沽酒各半，即日丹書鐵券爲約．

Since the two parties, Wang Weiqing 王未卿 and Yuan Shuwei 袁叔威, are simply referred to as "male," they must have been commoners without any orders of honor. This document, which concerns land transfer among commoners, further demonstrates that the notion of land ownership existed at the lowest level of society.

The following is a land transfer document, dated AD 184:

> On the 6th day, which is the day *wuyin*, the 9th month beginning with the day *kuiyou*, in the 7th year of the Guanghe period (AD 178–184), Fan Lijia from Pingyin purchased five *mu* of land from Du Gezi and his younger brother X. The east limit of the land is in conjunction with the north border of the Shimo village, Shiliang pavilion. One *mu* is worth 3,000 cash. In total, the price is 15,000 cash. The payment is fully made the same day.
>
> The middle root of the land is in the soil. From the Heaven above down to the Yellow Springs, all [missing two characters] the south limit of the land reaches to the end of the boundary road the north and east of the land is next to that of Du Gezi, and the west limit of the land is next to Yulin Meng [missing one character]. If the land is entitled to others, Du Gezi shall automatically dissolve his title over the land. At the time, the

113 Luo Zhenyu 羅振玉, *Zhensong tang ji gu yiwen* 貞松堂集古遺文 (Beijing: Beijing tushuguan chubanshe, 2003), 347–348; cf. Niida Noboru 仁井田陞, *Chūgoku hōseishi kenkyū* 中國法制史研究 (Tōkyō: Tōkyō daigaku shuppankai, 1980), vol. 2, 403–422, especially 418–419. Niida already surmised that private land ownership existed in early China. He noticed the term *mingtian* 名田 in the *Hanshu* and several excavated land transfer documents dated in the Eastern Han period. Given the paucity of evidence at the time of his study, he could not pursue his point further.

witnesses are Du Ziling and Li Jisheng. The parties purchase wine and each drink half of it. The price of the wine is 950 cash.[114]

光和七年九月癸酉朔六日戊寅, 平陰男子樊利家從雒陽男子杜謌子、子弟□買石梁亭部桓千東比是陌北田五畝, 畝三千, 並直萬五千, 錢即日畢.

田中根土著, 上至天, 下至黃, 皆□□並. 田南盡陌, 北, 東自比謌子. 西比羽林孟□. 若一旦田爲吏民秦胡所名有, 謌子自當解之. 時旁人杜子陵, 李季盛. 沽酒各半, 錢千無五十.

Lu Xiqi 魯西奇 recently argued that this document might not reflect an actual land transfer, since the land described very likely refers to a piece of imagined land in the underworld, making this a religious land transfer.[115] Regardless of whether this transaction involves real or imagined land, the document clearly reflects commonly accepted notions of the legal process of transferring a land title. Taking special note of the construction, *wei … suomingyou* 為 … 所名有, we find that the core verb phrase is *mingyou* (literally, "to claim the title to and possess the object"), further confirming our understanding of ownership of land, especially the way in which *ming* is used as referring to title.

---

114 Luo, *Zhensongtang*, 349–351; cf. Niida, *Chūgoku hōseishi*, 429–430.

115 Lu Xiqi 魯西奇, "Handai maidiquan de shizhi yuanyuan yu yiyi" 漢代買地券的實質淵源與意義, *Zhongguo shi yanjiu* no. 1 (2006): 47–68, especially 52–53; Tomiya Itaru 富谷至, "Yomi no kuni no tochi baibai: Kan Gi Rikuchō baichiken kō" 黄泉の国の土地売買—漢魏六朝買地券考, *Ōsaka daigaku kyōyōbu kenkyū shūroku* (*Jinbun shakai kagaku*) 大阪大學教養部研究集録 (人文社會科學) 36 (1987): 1–32; Ikeda On 池田溫, "Chūgoku rekidai boken ryakukō" 中國歷代墓券略考, *Tōkyō teikoku daigaku tōyō bunka kenkyūjo* 東洋文化研究所紀要 86 (1981): 193–278, especially 193–202. In addition, my translation consulted Yang Shuda 楊樹達, "Han Fan Lijia mai di qianquan ba" 漢樊利家買地鉛券跋, *Jiweiju jinwen shuo* 積微居金文說 (Beijing: Zhonghua shuju, 1997), 234.

In his article, Lu argued that all the land transfer documents excavated from Eastern Han tombs were not about real land transfers in this world but, reflecting popular beliefs, were instead transfers of imagined land in the underworld. Therefore, according to Lu, the AD 169 document also concerned the buying of land in the underworld. I disagree with Lu's overgeneralization. Unlike in the other documents, the language of this material does not include indications of the underworld or similar ideas. There is simply no evidence to support an assertion that the document concerns imagined land transfer in the underworld. By contrast, Niida treated all the excavated land transfer documents as documentations of real land transfers, not imagined ones (Niida, *Chūgoku hōseishi*, 429–430). There is actually a third interpretation. According to Anna Seidel, there were land contracts for the dead. Seidel, "Buying One's Way to Heaven: The Celestial Treasury in Chinese Religions," *History of Religions* 17, no. 3 (1978): 423–424.

Thus, neither Niida nor Lu may be entirely right. As a general principle, we need to examine the details of a particular land contract to determine its nature.

The following Juyan fragment is undisputedly a contract concerning a real land transfer. There are no mentions of the underworld, and the document specifies that the seller must make good the deficit if the amount of the land transferred proves not to be as large as what had been agreed upon.

> … to purchase 35 *fan* of land from Le Nu of Changle district [Juyan county]. The buying price is 900 cash. The payment is already made. We will measure the land. If the area is not as large as it is specified, Le Nu shall return the money by calculating the deficit. The witnesses are Chunyu Ciru, Wang Chong, and Zheng Shaoqing. Buying two *dou* of wine, the two parties and the witnesses all will drink it.[116]
>
> ☒置長樂里樂奴田卅五仮.[117] 賈錢九百錢，畢已. 丈田即不足計仮數環錢. 旁人淳于次孺，王充，鄭少卿，古酒旁二斗，皆飲之.

Based on the "rabbit" stories and these examples of land transfer, we can confidently conclude that the Han authorities had a universal and complete commitment to the concept of imperial subjects' ownership of both movable and real property. Imperial subjects were also clearly aware of their property "rights," going so far as to apply those "rights" to the underworld. This universal "right" of ownership, especially when it involved real property, was anything but trivial in world legal history. By contrast, in the Principate period of the Roman Empire (27 BC–AD 284), just as Roman law was taking its final shape, only Roman citizens (who comprised less than 15% of the population prior to the grand enfranchise in AD 212) had real property rights, while the majority of the free inhabitants, provincial subjects, had no real property rights at all.[118] As George Mousourakis, an expert on Roman law, pointed out:

---

116 *JY* strip 557.4, p. 653, cf. Zhang, *Zhongguo minfa*, 170–171.

117 This aspect appears to be a unit of measurement, but I am not sure what it is.

118 This involves the sharp division between citizens and provincial subjects and the sharp division between free inhabitants and slaves in Roman society. The numbers of citizens varied throughout the Principate period, due to the changes in citizenship policies and natural population growth. According to the AD 14 census, the Roman Principate had 4,937,000 citizens, including women and children. Modern historians estimate the entire population at 45.5 million. Claudius (r. AD 41–54) opened more channels for provincial subjects to acquire citizenship. Under Flavian (r. AD 69–96), efforts to expand the franchise intensified. By AD 164, the population reached approximately 61.4 million, although it remains difficult to accurately assess the number of citizens. Nonetheless, according to Professor Carlos Norena, until the late 2nd century AD, citizens comprised only approximately 15% of the whole population (private communication). See also

> With the exception of those territories belonging to communities which had been granted the *ius italicum*, provincial lands could not be subject to private ownership according to the rules of the Roman *ius civile* (dominium ex iure Quiritium). Land belonging to a community as a whole, on the other hand, was usually seized by the Romans and was disposed of in various ways: a part was sold and the proceeds were deposited into the Roman public treasury (aerarium); a part was left to tenants who were required to pay a fixed rent to the Roman state; and a part was left in the hands of the community to which it originally belonged, although it became subject to taxation.[119]

If the prominence of the notion of *zhi* (a straight account of the facts) in civil litigation points to the importance of verification in civil procedures and the emphasis on evidence in general, then universally accepted concept of *mingfen* (*fen*) shows that, at least in Han times, imperial subjects of all ranks enjoyed ownership throughout the empire, both for movable property and real property. This finding is consistent with the fact that civil disputants were treated as equal parties, regardless of their ranks. This finding also suggests that the early civil laws were grounded on and unified by quite rational notions, not only a conglomeration of pragmatic regulations.

3 *Min-Si* 民-私 (people-private)

In Chapter 1, this book argues that civil lawsuits in the Han period had such a feature: the lawsuits were brought by "individuals". Even though, there was no equivalent term of "individual" in Early China, the connotation of the word, i.e., a non-state actor, is denoted by *min* 民 (people, civilian) or *si* 私 (private) on the basis of context. *Min* and *si* are the antonyms of *gong* 公 (state, public) and *guan* 官 (official), roughly delineating the boundary of non-state, non-official spheres of interests.

3.1 Si *and the Attitude of the Law towards the Interests of* Si

In the 1930's, Nishijima Taichiro 西島太一郎 had already payed attention to the notions of *gong* 公 and *si* 私. He argued that *gong* originally referred to the ruler, and to serve the ruler was considered to engage in the affairs of *gong*. Thus,

---

A.N. Sherwin-White, *Roman Citizenship* (Oxford: Clarendon Press, 1973), 225–236; cf. *The Cambridge Ancient History* (Cambridge: Cambridge University press, 2006), 812.

119 George Mousourakis, *A Legal History of Rome* (New York: Routledge, 2007), 120.

gong also referred to government offices and official property. By contrast, *si* was the antonym of *gong*. Originally referring to serving the ministers, the word *si* acquired the meaning of "secretive" and "private" by an extension.[120] Nishijima's observation is indeed insightful. It can be attested by plenty of evidence in early Chinese texts. For instance, Xunzi says:

> Not following the way of the state and general principles, but making partisan group to surround the ruler for private gains, this is called a transgressing minister.[121]
>
> 不卹公道通義，朋黨比周以環主圖私為務，是篡臣也.

Jia Yi 賈誼 says:

> The Han has been established for forty years. However, the savings of the state (*gong*) and the private (*si*) are pitifully scarce.[122]
>
> 漢之為漢，凡四十年矣，公私之積，猶可哀痛.

Indeed, in early Chinese texts, *si*, representing non-official or private matters, and *gong*, representing the state or official matters, are often used in contrast.

How did early China view *si* vis-a-vis *gong*? There existed a well-observed tendency in early Chinese thought that *gong* was stressed at the expense of *si*. Early thinkers often dreamed for an ideal situation where *gong* completely triumphed over *si*. Except for the Yangzhu 楊朱 School, all the other major schools held negative attitudes towards *si*. Among them, the Legalists were very sharp in their criticisms. For example, Han Fei believed,

> To establish law is to abolish *si*. When the law and order proceed, the way of *si* is abolished. *Si* is to disturb the law.[123]
>
> 夫立法者，以廢私也. 法令行而私道廢矣. 私者，所以亂法也.

The *Weiliaozi* 尉繚子 says:

---

120 Nishijima Taichiro 西島太一郎, Koshi kannen no tankai to burai beeto no yimi 公私観念の展開と私人的意義, *Shina gaku* 支那学 no. 9 (1931): 87–106.

121 *Xunzi jijie*, 9. 247.

122 *Hanshu*, 24A. 1128.

123 *Han Feizi*, 17. 414.

> What is called governance is to eradicate *si* (private interests) from the people. When the people have no *si*, all under the heaven becomes one family. Without private farming and weaving, all the people share the same coldness and same hunger.[124]
>
> 夫謂治者，使民無私也．民無私則天下為一家，而無私耕私織，共寒其寒，共饑其饑．

This negative view of *si* also permeates official histories. Historians often praised the deeds of "one's household having no private property" (*jia wu si cai* 家無私財). For instance, general Ji Zun 祭遵 of the Eastern Han was praised as such:

> His unimpeachable reputation is known throughout the country, and his integrity is outstanding in the world. He shares all what he is awarded with his subordinates. He has no extra cloth, and his household has no private property.[125]
>
> 清名聞於海內，廉白著於當世．所得賞賜，輒盡與吏士，身無奇衣，家無私財．

The tendency of stressing *gong* at the expense of *si* is apparently undeniable, however, we shall ask: If, according to Han Fei, the aim of law was to eliminate *si*, how could early civil law, which was aimed to define and protect private interests, exist? This paradox suggests what was prescribed and advocated by the early thinkers was contrary to the social reality; perhaps because of the fever of over-selfish pursue of personal interests in reality, the early thinkers wanted to counter it by vehemently criticizing and denying it.

Therefore, this is perhaps close to what happened: the early law was not moral teachings, and neither were the ideals of the Legalists, who dreamed for an absolute control by the state. For the law to function, it must face the reality that individuals had private interests, and it needs to properly balance state and private interests. The early law was cautious: while it was suspicious about matters of *si*, it also recognized reasonable private interests.

We shall now explore the Statutes and Ordinances of the Second Year to explore the attitude of the law towards *si*. On one hand, the word *si* often contains negative connotations. For instance,

---

124 Liu Yin 刘寅, *Weiliaozi zhijie* 尉缭子直解 (Nanjing: Jiangsu guji, 1988), 3.122.

125 *Hou Hanshu*, 20. 742.

(1) For all cases of [authorized] borrowing (e.g., of objects, tools, or commodities) from the offices of a county or march, when the affair has been completed, the borrowed [item] matches being returned. When [a person] does not return it for a full twenty days, sentence [the person] according to the statutes concerning private (*si*) and unauthorized borrowing.[126]

諸有叚（假）於縣道官，事已，叚（假）當歸．弗歸，盈廿日，以私自叚（假）律論.

(2) When it is a case of being at a location that does not match issuing conveyances, do not dare to issue conveyances or food rations to him. For one who makes conveyances for more than [the stipulated] personnel, as well as for one who employs persons in a private (*si*) capacity and dares to have rations given to them at conveyance stations: in every case, hold him liable for the illicit profit of what has been eaten and consider him to be a robber.[127]

非當發傳所也, 毋敢發傳食焉. 為傳過員, 及私使人而敢為食傳者, 皆坐食臧（贓）為盜.

Si in these two cases, refers to unauthorized behavior that shall be punished. However, not all the interests of *si* are prohibited by the law. For instance,

The Chancellor of State submitted a document from [the Director of] the Grand Masters of the Imperial Palace, petitioning: "Receptionists of [the Director of] the Grand Masters of the [Han] Palace and the Shield Bearers and Halberdiers [subordinate to the Director of] the Gentlemen of the Imperial Palace Interior whose families are located outside the passes may privately (*si*) purchase horses in the Land within the Passes.[128]

□相國上: 中大夫書請, 中大夫謁者、郎中執盾執戟家在關外者, 買私買馬關中.

126 *ZJS* strip (*Statutes*) no. 78, p. 19; *LSS*, 473. Translation follows Barbieri-Low and Yates.
127 *ZJS* strip (*Statutes*) no. 230, p. 40; *LSS*, 683. Translation follows Barbieri-Low and Yates.
128 *ZJS* strip (*Statutes*) no. 504, p. 85; *LSS*, 1143. Translation follows Barbieri-Low and Yates (slightly modified).

Here, "*si mai ma* 私買馬" (privately purchase horses) clearly refers to buying horses for private uses. In early Western Han, horses were regarded as a strategical resource and were tightly controlled by the state. How could the private purchase be allowed? As long as it was reasonable: the officials who were granted the permit all worked in the imperial palace, but their families were far away, outside the Hangu 函谷 pass, so they needed horses to commute. This means that even though horses were tightly controlled, the law also took reasonable private uses into account.

Similarly, private operations in the salt industry and mining are also permitted by the law, as long as the merchants pay tax. For instance,

> (1) For all cases of privately (*si*) producing salt from saline ponds and soils or [natural rock] salt, boiling [seawater at the mouth of the] Ji River [or water from saline ponds along the course of the] Han River, as well as boiling brine from privately (*si*) owned wells: tax it [in cash payments]. The government is to take one portion (16.67%), while the owner/operator is to retain five portions (83.33%).[129]
>
> 諸私為鹵(鹵)鹽, 煮濟、漢及有私鹽井煮者, 稅之, 縣官取一, 主取五.
>
> (2) For a case of ordinary people privately (*si*) mining cinnabar: tax it in kind; for each man-month [of labor], six *jīn* and nine *liǎng* (approx. 1.63 kg) [of cinnabar]; for each woman[-month of labor], four *jīn* and six *liǎng* (approx. 1.09 kg) [of cinnabar].[130]
>
> 民私采丹者租之, 男子月六斤九兩, 女子四斤六兩.

In the first case, people are allowed to set up a private business of producing salt, if they contribute 16.67% of their product to the state as tax. In the second case, ordinary persons are allowed to engage in private mining, if they pay tax in kind. The law even distinguishes female miners from male miners in demanding less tax from the females, supposedly due to them having less physical strength. These two cases demonstrate that reasonable private interests are allowed and protected by the law, even in the very crucial businesses for state revenue; we do not know much of the role of cinnabar in the state's finances, but we surely know that salt was crucial as later discussions on salt and iron proved.

---

129 *ZJS* strip (*Statutes*) no. 436, p. 68; *LSS*, 927. Translation follows Barbieri-Low and Yates.
130 *ZJS* strip (*Statutes*) no. 438, p. 68; *LSS*, 929.Translation follows Barbieri-Low and Yates.

3.2 *Min and the Attitude of the Law towards the Interests of* Min

Similar to the word *si*, which denotes private interests, the word *min*, which is often translated as "people", "ordinary person", or "civilian" in English scholarship, also denotes interests that do not belong to the "official" or "state". If the early law has a mixed attitude towards *si*, then the law definitely holds a more positive attitude towards the interests of *min*. For instance, it regulates:

> If an ordinary person (*min*) wants to make a pre-mortem will to dispose of real estate, slaves, and property, the district bailiff should listen to his or her will in person. Everything needs to be written in three copies and submitted by following the same procedure for household registers. When a dispute occurs, carry out matters according to the written contract. If there is no written contract, do not listen to the dispute. As for the farming land and houses that are divided, the recipient can hold them without establishing a household until the 8th month comes to register the household. If the officials obstruct the pre-mortem will or do not make a written document for it, the fine is one *liang* of gold.[131]
>
> 民欲先令相分田宅、奴婢、財物，鄉部嗇夫身聽其令，皆三辨券書之，輒上如戶籍. 有爭者，以券書從事；毋券書，勿聽. 所分田宅，不為戶，得有之，至八月書戶. 留難先令、弗為券書，罰金一兩.
>
> For cases among the ordinary people (*min*) of [paternal] grandparents, parents, children, grandchildren, siblings, or children of siblings who wish to divide among themselves or give to each other male and female slaves, horses, cattle, sheep, or other valuable items: in every case, permit it. Immediately make a register [of the exchange].[132]
>
> 民大父母、父母、子、孫、同產、同產子，欲相分予奴婢、馬牛羊、它財物者，皆許之，輒為定籍.
>
> For an ordinary person (*min*) who desires to separate [from his or her current household] and form [a new] household: in every case, [carry this out] during the time of the household[-register examination], in the

131 *ZJS* strip (*Statutes*) nos. 334–336, p. 54.

132 *ZJS* strip (*Statutes*) no. 337, p. 55; *LSS*, 801. Translation follows Barbieri-Low and Yates (slightly modified).

> eighth month. When it is not the time of the household[-register examination], do not permit it.[133]
>
> 民欲別為戶者，皆以八月戶時，非戶時勿許.

These regulations above are all concerned with the interests of *min*. They grant the legal capacity of making a will, dividing household, and establishing a new household to the *min*. In all these contexts, the word *min* could be understood as implying an individual who possesses an independent will and the capacity of action, and his will and action are respected and protected by the law.

For instance, the phrases "If an ordinary person wants to make a *xianling* ..." (*min yu xian ling* 民欲先令), "who wish to divide among themselves" (*yu xiang fen* 欲相分), and "for an ordinary person who desires to separate [from his or her current household] and form [a new] household ..." (*yu bie wei hu* 欲別為戶) reflect the respect of the state towards the will of individuals: if one has the desire to do a certain thing, it is allowed. Among this evidence, "when an ordinary person wishes to make a will ..." stated in strip 334 is most revealing. In this case, officials have no power to intervene, and they only "listen personally to his directives" (*shen ting qi ling* 身聽其令), faithfully recording what the *min* desires. However, if officials delay or make trouble during the process, they will be punished. This shows that to make a will belongs to the sphere of *min*, and *min* has the autonomy in this respect. *Min* could dispose his property according to his will, and the state shall not intervene.

The respect towards the will of the *min* is consistent with what the "Xingfazhi" Chapter of the *Hanshu* says:

> Xiao and Cao served as the chancellors. They governed by little intervention. They followed the will of the people (*min*) and never disturbed them. Therefore, clothes and food were abundant, and punishments were seldom used.[134]
>
> 蕭、曹為相, 鎮以無為, 從民之欲, 而不擾亂, 是以衣食滋殖, 刑罰用稀.

In this idealized account, the desires and wills of *min* were respected by the state in the early Western Han. The state did not bother to intervene, and everyone was pleased.

---

133 *ZJS* strip (*Statutes*) no. 345, p. 56; *LSS*, 803. Translation follows Barbieri-Low and Yates.

134 *Hanshu* 23.1097.

More importantly, the regulations that recognize the interests and desires of *min* are consistent with the idea of benefiting the *min* in early Chinese thought; the interests of *min* are regarded as legitimate in general. For instance, Confucius says:

> Is not this to deliver bounties with ease: to benefit the people (*min*) by following what they held as their interests?[135]
>
> 因民之所利而利之，斯不亦惠而不費乎.

This shows that Confucius believes that *min* have their private interests, and it is reasonable for them to pursue their interests. The state shall follow the interests of *min*, instead of preventing them.

Confucius is not alone. In 81 BC, during the famous debate regarding the state monopoly of salt and iron, the critics criticized the state monopoly as "competing with the *min* for profits" (*yu min zheng li* 與民爭利). It goes:

> In the commanderies and kingdoms, the state set up monopoly on salt, iron, wine, and requisition and transportation to compete with the people (*min*) for profits. This practice disrupts the simple and plain custom and encourages the spread of greed.[136]
>
> 今郡國有鹽、鐵、酒榷、均輸, 與民爭利. 散敦厚之樸, 成貪鄙之化.

This criticism shows that in the eyes of the critics, there exists a clear division between the interests of the state and that of *min*. The industries of salt, iron, and wine belong to the sphere of the interests of the *min*, therefore the state shall not intervene. If the state intervenes, bad results will occur.

In this overall historical background, the regulations in early law that recognize and protect the interests of *min* are not a surprise. Thus, reasonable actions of *si* and rightful interests of *min* constitute a private sphere of interest, and private properties were recognized and respected by the state. For instance, when the Han state enlisted private horses to serve in the posts on the frontiers, the official records always indicate those horses as private property (*si cai wu* 私財物).

---

135 *Analects*, 20.2.

136 *Yantielun*, 1. 1.

(1) Private property (*si caiwu*): one mare, black color, with a mark on the left side, nine years old, white back, 6 *chi* and 1 *cun* tall. This horse is enlisted to fill a vacancy in the Xuanquan post.[137]

私財物馬一匹,騩,牡,左剽,齒九歲,白背,高六尺一寸小.補懸泉置驛馬缺.

(2) Private property (*si caiwu*): one mare, cyan color, with a mark on the left side, white back, 5 *chi* and 9 *cun* tall. This horse is enlisted to fill a vacancy in the Xuanquan post.[138]

私財物馬一匹,駹,牡,左剽,齒七歲,白背,高五尺九寸.補懸泉置驛馬缺.

This evidence shows that the state was not allowed to misappropriate private property, even in the name of national defense; they could borrow horses from ordinary people but needed to recognize and indicate their private ownership.

In conclusion, in early China, *min-si* (people, private) denoted the sphere of private interests of the people, which were recognized by the state. The early civil law was applied to the *min-si* sphere, which included private matters regarding debt disputes, compensation, house division, inheritance, and so on, as our previous study demonstrates.

4 Concluding Remarks

Through the analysis above, it is reasonable to conclude that early Chinese civil laws were based on three fundamental concepts: *mingfen*, *zhi* and *min-si*. *Mingfen* referred to the legitimacy of possessing a certain portion of resources, *zhi* referred to a straightforward account of facts, and *min-si* denoted a non-official, non-state sphere of interests. They constituted the cornerstones of early Chinese civil law; all the civil statutes/regulations revolved around these three concepts. Civil laws of early China were applicable to the disputes in the *min-si* sphere, and these disputes were understood as a fight over *mingfen*. As long as the *mingfen* was not determined, the disputes would not be solved, and vice versa. The means to protect one's *mingfen* was a lawsuit, which was understood as a process to seek *zhi* on the basis of legal principles. Whoever possessed *zhi* won. In short, these three concepts demonstrate the rationales of the existence of early civil laws in China.

137 "Fuma mingji" 傅马名籍, in *Dunhang Xuanquan Hanjian shicui*, 81.

138 Ibid.

CHAPTER 6

Beyond Civil Laws

This chapter will explore three issues that lie beyond the boundaries established in previous chapters: the legal ideal of reforming people's morals to reduce lawsuits, the influence of ethical principles on laws, and the relationship between the laws and the Classics. I will argue three points: first, even though civil laws were quite sophisticated in early China, especially during the Han, with clear evidence of parties settling disputes through lawsuits, the prevailing legal ideal was to reform people's morals to reduce lawsuits; second, ethical principles, such as filial piety and revenge, deeply influenced Qin and Han laws; and third, the Classics were often cited by judges in ways that suggest that they held equal authority with statutes in legal matters.

I believe putting early civil laws in their larger context is essential to obtain a fuller picture of the justice system. This chapter will illuminate the distinctive characteristics of early civil laws as they relate to social harmony, their collaboration with ethical principles, and the overlapping authority of statutory laws and the Classics in actual legal practice.

1 The Legal Ideal of Reforming People's Morals to Reduce Lawsuits

The existence and importance of civil laws in early China are now beyond doubt. In summary, our sources show that civil statutes and civil legal notions emerged in the fourth century BC, with a system of civil statutes developing during the Qin and Han periods. This early civil justice system had five features that demonstrate its accessibility and sophistication: (1) civil disputes were common, even among family members who regularly sued one another over property issues; (2) the authorities considered resolving civil disputes their responsibility; (3) civil disputes were mostly resolved by district bailiffs, but disputants had the right to appeal to the county court, and then to the commandery court; (4) specific statutes were devoted to civil disputes involving compensation, debt, contract, and inheritance; and (5) civil laws were based on notions such as *zhi*, *mingfen* and *min-si*, which reveal the role of verification of facts, ownership of property and private sphere of interests in legal thinking.

Paradoxically, despite the sophistication of the civil justice system and the frequency of civil cases, the presumably prevailing legal ideal was to reform people's morals, especially by promoting ritual yielding to reduce lawsuits,

 | DOI:10.1163/9789004513907_008

instead of refining and perfecting the laws.[1] Many Han judges whom our sources portray as benevolent and fair held that in an ideal world, there should be no civil suits. Their ultimate goal in hearing civil cases was to achieve greater social harmony above and beyond simply granting each party his or her due. This goal is reflected in the Han dynasty accounts of an antique paragon of justice, the Earl of Shao, otherwise known as Shao Bo 邵伯.

Shao Bo was one of the two famous ministers credited with putting the Zhou on a firm footing in the early 11th century BC. The earliest story about him appears in the poem "Sweet Pear" (Gantang 甘棠) in the *Book of Songs*,[2] a reference that was then was elaborated in the *Hanshi waizhuan* 韓詩外傳 (compiled ca. 160 BC):

> In the old days, when the way of the Zhou was magnificent, the Earl of Shao was at court. Some officials asked to build a palace at Shao for him to live in. The Earl of Shao said: "No! To make the commoners toil for my own sake is certainly not what my ancestor, the King of Wen, intended." Whereupon the duke went out to reach the commoners between the paths and dikes in the field and to hear disputes and give out judgments there. The Earl of Shao exposed himself in the far-off fields and dwelt under a [sweet pear] tree. The people greatly rejoiced. The tillers of the fields and tenders of the silkworms doubled their labors because he had encouraged them.[3]
>
> 昔者周道之盛, 邵伯在朝, 有司請營邵以居. 邵伯曰: 嗟! 以吾一身而勞百姓, 此非吾先君文王之志也. 於是出而就蒸庶於阡陌隴畝之間而聽斷焉. 邵伯暴處遠野, 廬於樹下, 百姓大悅, 耕桑者倍力以勸.

It appears that Shao Bo, who was famous for his impartial judgments, became the paragon of benevolence and justice in the Han period, if not earlier. His image reflected in the Han account is that of a benevolent local lord who went out into the remote areas of the countryside to guide and help the commoners, bringing his wisdom to bear on their problems and to deliver relief and happiness. It is worth noting that our passage specifies that Shao Bo heard disputes

1 This ideal appears to be applicable to both civil and criminal cases. However, I will argue that this ideal is mostly tied to civil disputes.

2 *The Book of Songs*, Mao no. 16.

3 *Hanshi waizhuan jishi* 韓詩外傳集釋, ed., Xu Weichi 許維遹 (Beijing: Zhonghua shuju, 1980), 1.28; cf. James Robert Hightower, *Han shih wai chuan: Han Ying's Illustrations of the Didactic Application of the Classic of Songs* (Cambridge: Harvard University Press, 1952), 36–37. Translation follows Hightower.

and passed judgments (*tingduan* 聽斷), suggesting the importance of bringing justice to the commoners. Underscoring this image is Shao Bo's devotion to King Wen, his father and ruler, and to the way of the Zhou. Readers will recall that King Wen was a byword for benevolence, and that the way of Zhou was deemed to be straight (*zhi* 直), i.e., fair and impartial. The "Great East" (Dadong) poem in the *Book of Songs* says: "The way of Zhou was like a whetstone, and straight (*zhi*) as an arrow."[4]

This Han interpretation of the story of Shao Bo perhaps simply projected features of Han legal ideals back onto his biography. We know that Shao Bo was revered as a paragon of mercy and justice by members of the Han governing elite, insofar as he was frequently invoked in passages appraising the achievements of famous Han judges.[5] Moreover, as K.E. Brashier in 2005 observed:

> When alluding to the Sweet Pear tree poem, Han sources depict the Earl of Shao 'holding court' (*shuzhi* 述職), 'passing judgments' (*tingduan* 聽斷), or 'carrying out justice and governance' (*jueyue zhengshi* 決獄政事). The Eastern Han commentator Zheng Xuan explains that 'the Earl of Shao listened to the litigations of men and women.'[6]

In sum, the central theme in the lore of Shao Bo is how a fair judge can bring about great social harmony, i.e. transform the people.[7]

In the extant sources, we find seven judges who were deemed to resemble Shao Bo in transforming their jurisdictions. The cases they reportedly handled were all typically civil in nature: Han Yanshou 韓延壽 (d. 57 BC) and Xu Jin 許荊 (fl. AD 90), appear in the sources as judges adjudicating difficult disputes

4 The *Book of Songs*, Mao no. 203. Translation follows Legge, vol. 4, 353.

5 We know of four occasions: (1) the biography of Wang Ji 王吉 (d. 84 BC) in *Hanshu* 72.3058, and the biography of Feng Yan 馮衍 (d. AD 30) in *Hou Hanshu* 28a.968; and (2) the two commemorative stele entitled "Xianyu Huang bei" 鮮于璜碑 (AD 165) and "Han gu guchengzhang Tangyin ling Zhang jun biaosong" 漢故穀城長蕩陰令張君表頌 (AD 186). See *Han bei jishi*, 285, 490.

6 K.E. Brashier, "Symbolic Discourse in Eastern Han Memorial Art: The Case of the Birchleaf Pear," *Harvard Journal of Asiatic Studies* no. 2 (2005): 299. In his article, Brashier translated "*gantang*" 甘棠 as "birchleaf pear," which I have amended to "sweet pear tree" following the standard translation similar to that in Legge, vol. 4, 26.

7 We can further deduce that there would be no lawsuits in the transformed jurisprudence because people would be living together in harmony. The fundamental assumption underlying this ideal is that justice and social harmony are inseparable. Of course, in reality, justice often disrupted social harmony. For example, family members sued each other over property issues during household division or inheritance. The focus of this discussion is the belief that justice can bring forth social harmony, and that social harmony, as the ultimate goal, justifies the moral approach that a judge should adopt in handing disputes.

between brothers over land;[8] Lu Gong 魯恭 (AD 38–119), appears as a judge presiding over a case that involved a borrowed ox;[9] three judges, Wu You 吳祐 (fl. 2nd century), Cai Yan 蔡衍 (d. 167) and Liu Ju 劉矩 (d. 168) were all credited with the successful handling of numerous civil disputes;[10] and finally, Chen Gang 陳綱 (fl. 2nd century) reportedly handled a dispute of an unspecified nature between brothers.[11] The accounts of these judges are so highly idealized that their stories appear to be normative depictions of morally idealized jurisprudence. Nevertheless, such hagiographical accounts are invaluable if we wish to understand prevailing Han ideals as opposed to actual legal practices. What made these model judges exemplars was the way in which they supposedly transformed the behavior of the subjects who lived within their jurisdictions.

We first encountered Han Yanshou's story from the *Hanshu* in Chapter Two of this study. It involved a dispute between two brothers over the ownership of land. Han Yanshou, governor at the time, traced the origin of the dispute to his own personal failure to educate his people by moral suasion. Han Yanshou retired to his own rooms to reflect upon his errors while his subordinates bound themselves as if they were criminals. The narrative continues:

> The two brothers deeply repented. They both shaved their hair, undressed themselves [a ritual to demonstrate one's sincere repentance], and apologized, and they were each willing to yield the land to the other. [Moreover, they vowed] down to their deaths, never to dare to dispute anything else. Han Yanshou was greatly delighted [by this]. He opened the gates to invite them in for a meeting, for which he provided wine and meat, and ate and drank with them. He forcefully urged them to report their intentions to the districts, so that they might make an example of those who repented their faults and followed the good. Han Yanshou, only at that point, started to hear cases [again] … Han Yanshou's generous favors and reliability benefited the twenty-four counties [in his jurisdiction], so much so that the people no longer had disputes over property for adjudication. [Han Yanshou] exhibited the deepest integrity (誠), so neither his officials nor the ordinary people could bear to cheat him.[12]

8 For Han Yanshou, see *Hanshu*, 76.3213. For Xu Jing, see *Hou Hanshu*, 76.2472.

9 *Hou Hanshu*, 25.874.

10 *Hou Hanshu*, 64.2101; *Hou Hanshu*, 67.2208; *Hou Hanshu*, 76.2476.

11 Chang Ju 常璩, *Huayang guozhi* 華陽國志 (Beijing: Zhonghua shuju, 1985), 10B.160.

12 *Hanshu*, 76.3213.

此兩昆弟深自悔，皆自髡肉袒謝，願以田相移，終死不敢復爭．延壽大喜，開閤延見，內酒肉與相對飲食，厲勉以意告鄉部，有以表勸悔過從善之民．延壽乃起聽事 … 延壽恩信周徧二十四縣，莫復以辭訟自言者，推其至誠，吏民不忍欺紿．

The message embedded in this passage is that Han Yanshou's self-critical approach not only successfully resolved this particular case, but it also eventually transformed the twenty-four counties of the entire commandery.

A similar story is told in the *Hou Hanshu* about Wu You:

> Whenever the people brought disputes and litigation, he (Wu You) always closed the doors and reflected upon his own faults. Then he would hear the cases and instruct the [disputing] parties in the Way.[13]
>
> 民有相爭訴者，輒閉閤自責，然後斷其訟，以道譬之．

Xu Jing's story employs the same tropes:

> During the reign of Emperor He (r. AD 89–105), he (Xu Jing) was gradually promoted until he became governor of Guiyang.... He once, in spring, inspected Leiyang county, where there was a certain person named Jiang Jun, who had been involved in a property dispute with his brothers, in which each accused the other of wrongdoing in a civil suit. Xu Jing responded to it with a sigh, saying, "I bear an important responsibility for the state, and if its moral teachings do not prevail, the blame lies with me, as governor." Therefore, he turned back and had his scribe submit a report to explain the situation and ask that it be referred to the superintendent of justice. Jiang Jun and his brothers repented, and each requested to receive punishment [rather than having the governor be punished]. He (Xu Jing) served in his post for twelve years and the local elders praised him in songs.[14]

13 *Hou Hanshu*, 64.2101. Readers are reminded that the similar story we encountered in Chapter 2 (p. 73) of this study is from Xie Cheng's 謝承 work, in which the story is slightly different from what is given in the *Hou Hanshu* by Fan Ye. According to Xie Cheng's account, when a civil dispute arose, Wu You first sent the *sanlao* to instruct the parties in the virtues of filial piety and fraternal love as the first step in his attempt to resolve a dispute. No mention is made of Wu's self-criticism. However, the two details of the hagiography are not in contradiction.

14 *Hou Hanshu*, 76.2472.

和帝時，稍遷桂陽太守 … 嘗行春到耒陽縣，人有蔣均者，兄弟爭財，互相言訟．荊對之歎曰："吾荷國重任，而教化不行，咎在太守．" 乃顧使吏上書陳狀，乞詣廷尉．均兄弟感悔，各求受罪．在事十二年，父老稱歌．

Lu Gong handled two difficult cases, a dispute over land and a dispute concerning a borrowed ox:

> The litigants Xun Bo and others engaged in a dispute over farmland. A succession of previous magistrates could not determine the [rights and wrongs of] the case. Lu Gong made the principles fair and just and distinguished straight accounts of the facts and distorted accounts of the facts. Thus, the parties all retired and criticized themselves. They [even] laid down their plough so as to yield to one another.[15]
>
> 訟人許伯等爭田，累守令不能決，恭為平理曲直，皆退而自責，輟耕相讓．
>
> The head of a certain village borrowed an ox from someone and then refused to return it to its owner. Lu Gong summoned the head of the village and repeatedly ordered him to return the ox. Still, he did not comply. Lu Gong sighed: "This shows that [the court's] moral teachings do not prevail." So, he wanted to take off his seals of office and quit his job. The members of his staff all wept and asked him to stay. The head of the village then regretted his action. He returned the ox and went [on his own initiative] to the jail to receive his punishment. Gong pardoned him and did not formally interrogate him, whereupon the officials and ordinary people all sincerely submitted [in their hearts to his decisions].[16]
>
> 亭長從人借牛而不肯還之，牛主訟於恭．恭召亭長，勑令歸牛者再三，猶不從．恭歎曰："是教化不行也．" 欲解印綬去．掾史泣涕共留之，亭長乃慙悔，還牛，詣獄受罪，恭貰不問．於是吏人信服．

Chen Gang, we are told, resolved a civil dispute among at least two brothers over a non-specified problem:

15 *Hou Hanshu*, 25.874. Readers are reminded that I discussed this case in Chapter 5 of my work while studying *zhi* (a straight account of the facts).

16 *Hou Hanshu*, 25. 874.

> Chen Gang's styled name is Zhong Qing; he was a native of Chenggu ... The bureau of the Three Lords all recommended him as "Flourishing Talent" (*maocai*). Later on, he was appointed governor of Hongnong. When he first arrived [in that post], there were [two?] brothers who brought suits against each other. [Chen Gang] blamed himself [for their obstinacy] and retreated [from the public view], after which [there] were no more civil disputes.[17]

> 陳綱字仲卿，成固人也 … 三府並辟舉茂才，拜弘農太守．初至，有兄弟相爭，自相責引退，是後無訟者．

The four stories above all mention moral teachings (*jiaohua* 教化) without specifying precisely what kinds of moral teachings were being undermined by litigation. These teachings can probably be traced to the same principles that informed the ritual canon *Liji* (comp. ca. 2nd century BC),

> Therefore, brothers should not divide [the household] in principle. However, when there is such a division, it then acknowledges the sons' selfishness ... [Brothers] may live separately but still regard the family wealth as common. And when they have surpluses, they should be sent back to the clan [common fund]. And when someone is in need, then the clan will subsidize that person [and his family].[18]

> 故昆弟之義無分，然而有分者，則辟子之私也 … 異居而同財，有餘則歸之宗，不足則資之宗．

Given the abundant examples of divisions of inherited wealth, land, and property, and the clear evidence of frequent disputes over the fairness of those apportionments, we know that this ideal was seldom followed by the people. First, as Lai Mingchun's dissertation on household morphology in early China shows, simple households (parents and their children) and household divisions were the norm in Qin and Han times. The sources mention extended households (three-generations) and joint households (in which adult siblings

17 *Huayang guozhi*, 10B.160. The original passage provides no clues about when Chen Gang served in the post, and Chen Gang does not appear in any extant sources, such as the *Hanshu* or the *Hou Hanshu*. However, we know that Chen Gang must have been active before the 4th century since the author Chang Ju (291–361), who cited his case, was active at that time. Therefore, Chen Gang very possibly lived in the Han period or the Three Kingdoms period (AD 220–280).

18 *Liji*, 30.356.

lived together) as exceptional.[19] Second, the received and excavated sources supply abundant evidence that disputes over property among brothers were frequent. A passage from the *Huainaizi* 淮南子 (comp. 139 BC) offers a caustic view of such household divisions:

> In today's world, whoever does something ugly surely pretends to be kind to make excuses for himself, and whoever is evil surely pretends to be righteous to get away with his or her evildoing.... When it comes to dividing up the household and disputes over property, close kin [including] brothers have grievances against each other, while flesh and blood relatives harm one another. And this they call the principles of the Duke of Zhou.[20]
>
> 當今之世，醜必托善以自為解，邪必蒙正以自為辟 … 分別爭財，親戚兄弟構怨，骨肉相賊，曰周公之義也.

19 Makino Tatsumi 牧野巽 (1905–1975) argued that a nuclear family of four or five members prevailed in the Han dynasty. See Makino, "Kandai ni okeru kazoku no ōkisa" 漢代における家族の大きさ, *Kangakkai zasshi* 漢學會雜誌 3, no. 1 (1934): 32–42. Beginning with Makino's study in 1934, scholars have debated the issue of family size in early China. For example, Shimizu Morimitsu 清水盛光 argued that there were two typical types: big families were typical for rich elite families, whereas small families were typical for ordinary peasant families. However, Moriya Mitsuo 守屋美都雄 disagreed with both Makino and Shimizu by arguing that the typical family in the Han period was the "three generation big family" (*sanzokushi* 三族制) that included an old couple, their sons and daughters-in-law, and the grandchildren. See Shimizu, *Shina kazoku no shokōzō* 支那家族の諸構造 (Tōkyō: Iwanami Shoten, 1942), 127–136, and Moriya, "Kandai kazoku no keitai ni kansuru shiron" 漢代家族の型体に関する試論, *Shigaku zasshi* 史學雜誌 52, no. 6 (1941): 35–43. For a detailed review on this topic, see Iio Hideyuki 飯尾秀幸, "Chūgoku kodai ni okeru kazoku kenkyu o megutte" 中國古代における家族を研究めぐって, *Rekishi hyōron* 歴史評論 12 (1985): 69–70.

This book adopts Lai Mingchun's estimation in "Family Morphology in Han China" (Ph.D. diss., University of Toronto, 1995), 1–30, 220–225. Lai's work is the most comprehensive study to date on this topic. His estimation is consistent with the household registration records excavated from Yinwan 尹灣. The "Jibu" 集簿 (Register, 15 BC) excavated from Yinwan shows that the Donghai 東海 commandery had 266,290 households, consisting of 1,397,343 individuals. Thus, the average size of each household was 5.2 individuals, confirming the estimation that a typical Han household consisted of one couple with three children. See *Yinwan Hanmu jiandu* 尹灣漢墓簡牘, ed., Lianyungang shi bowuguan 連雲港市博物館 (Beijing: Zhonghua shuju, 1997), 77; cf. Michael Loewe, *The Men Who Governed Han China: Companion to A Biographical Dictionary of the Qin, Former Han and Xin Periods* (Leiden and Boston: Brill, 2004), 60.

20 *Huainanzi* 淮南子 (Shanghai: Shanghai guji, 1989), 20.225b.

The phrase "today's world" (*dangjin zhi shi* 當今之世) draws attention to how widespread the phenomena was, at least in the opinion of the text's author or compiler. The foregoing cases of land disputes among brothers reinforce this view. If an exemplary judge regarded such land disputes among brothers as a sign of moral collapse and a prompt for self-criticism, why do we not see Lu Gong blaming himself for the dispute between Xu Gong and the counter-claimants? We can assume that if the disputants were not close kin, the offense against morality was probably deemed to be correspondingly less severe, and as such, Lu did not feel morally obligated to criticize himself for failing to inculcate moral teachings on behalf of the throne. But if the disputants were not close kin, which by inference meant that their dispute did not rise to the level of a moral offense, why would the parties to the dispute criticize themselves after the case was resolved?

A likely answer may be supplied by Liu Ju's 劉矩 (d. 168) account, which points to the significance of ritual yielding (*lirang* 禮讓):[21]

> [Liu Ju] gradually was promoted to the magistracy of Yongqiu, where he transformed [the local customs] through the ritual of yielding. Those who [until then] had had no filial piety and sense of duty were all moved [by his model] and awakened to the need to reform themselves. When the local people had quarrels or civil disputes, Liu Ju always brought them into his presence, lent them an ear, and closely admonished them. By these means, he let them know that they could have managed their anger and spats themselves, and they should not get officials involved. Then he had them go home and think it over. The litigants were moved, and each thereupon quit [trying to gain property].[22]
>
> 稍遷雍丘令，以禮讓化之．其無孝義者，皆感悟自革．民有爭訟，矩常引之於前，提耳訓告，以為忿恚可忍，縣官不可入，使歸更尋思．訟者感之，輒各罷去．

21 *Lirang* 禮讓 is difficult to render. There are two possibilities: (1) ritual yielding, meaning the specific rituals that express the ideal of yielding and (2) ritual and yielding. I think the first choice is preferable. I rule out the second one because this phrase on "ritual and yielding" seems to suggest that yielding itself is parallel to ritual in significance, endowing too strong of a meaning to yielding alone. I choose "ritual yielding" because on the one hand, *li* 禮 clearly refers to ritual; however, in our stories, the emphasis is always on yielding.

In addition, we may consider yielding a moral value. As we know, rituals and morals in pre-modern China were often intertwined.

22 *Hou Hanshu*, 76.2476.

Here we find Liu Ju, in his capacity as a local judge, encourages, even commands ritual yielding. The theory driving his actions appears to be that if the people learn to yield to one another, disputes will be privately resolved and eliminate the need for civil litigation, thus achieving the greater goal of creating social harmony.

We find a similar pattern in all five stories: when disputes are brought to the attention of the judges, they are reluctant to take formal legal action to resolve those disputes. Instead, they typically criticize themselves for a personal lack of virtue and for their failure to set a good example, at which point the litigants are moved to repent and criticize themselves, yielding to one another, peaceably resolving their own disputes, thereby bringing great social harmony to the whole territory within the judge's jurisdiction. This scenario is highly moralistic in that the key to resolving the disputes was ritual yielding, which was considered a moral teaching. In addition, the judges' self-criticism was undoubtedly a moral stance.[23] Clearly, local officials in their capacity as judges felt that their position required them to try to reform people's morals in the hopes of creating a healthier social environment that would be conducive to the reduction or, ideally, the elimination of lawsuits.

Inspired by the judges' self-criticism, this ideal of reforming people's morals to reduce lawsuits, especially by promoting ritual yielding, seems to be applicable to both civil and criminal cases. However, the extant sources only show that judges applied this practice of self-criticism to promote ritual yielding in civil cases. By contrast, in criminal cases, if a crime was brought to the attention of the judges, they typically applied the statutes to the best of their abilities in determining guilt and assigning punishment.[24] As an edict by Emperor Jing dated to 156 BC says: "The bastinado is the means to teach them [the people]; let there be established ordinances [fixing the size and heft of] the stick" (笞者, 所以教之也, 其定箠令).[25] Ban Gu's treatise also urges authorities to deter crime by making potential criminals fear the consequences of criminal actions.

23 Self-criticism was a quite common practice in Han China. Even Han emperors sometimes practiced self-criticism. This scenario is reflected in the edicts preserved in the standard histories.

24 There are stories in which a moral exemplar moved thieves to quit their criminal activities. For instance, Chen Shi's 陳寔 biography in *Hou Hanshu* (62.2067) tells a story of a thief who was attempting to sneak into Chen's house to steal from him, but was moved by his moral power. Those stories are of a different nature compared with the stories of ritual yielding that we have studied. The former are not lawsuits in nature. By contrast, the latter are cases that have been officially brought to the attention of the authorities to seek their judgment.

25 See, *Hanshu*, 23.1100.

> When the crimes are extremely grave, but the punishments are extremely light, the people have nothing to fear. There is no greater disorder than this. In all cases, the basic issue in regulating punishments is to prohibit violence and wrongdoing and to deter crimes before they happen. Not to have those who kill people die, and not to have those who wound people punished, is to be kind to the violent and lenient to the evil.[26]
>
> 罪至重而刑至輕, 民無所畏, 亂莫大焉. 凡制刑之本, 將以禁暴惡, 且懲其未也. 殺人者不死, 傷人者不刑, 是惠暴而寬惡也.

Perhaps because civil suits were considered less destructive of the public order, the judges had more leeway to resort to moral suasion. While many factors surely contributed to the inclination among the Han governing elite to nurture social harmony to reduce civil lawsuits through the promotion of ritual yielding, this ideal has deep philosophical roots. One of the earliest expressions of this ideal is a precept put forward by Confucius:

> When hearing cases, I am as [capable as] all the other judges. But I must cause there to be no cases of litigation![27]
>
> 聽訟, 吾猶人也. 必也使無訟乎!

This precept was further associated with Confucius's general view on laws and rituals.

> The Master said: If the people be led by laws, and uniformity sought to be given them by punishments, they will try to avoid the punishment, but have no sense of shame. If they be led by virtue, and uniformity sought to be given them by established ritual principles, they will have the sense of shame, and moreover will become good.[28]
>
> 子曰: 導之以政, 齊之以刑, 民免而無恥. 導之以德, 齊之以禮, 有恥且格.

---

26 *Hanshu*, 23.1111. My translation follows Hulsewé, *RHL*, 347. In a sense, this scenario can explain why penal laws were so complicated in early China, and indeed, pre-modern China.

27 *Liji*, 60.986.

28 *Analects*, 2.3. My translation here follows Legge, vol. 1, 146 (slightly modified).

While Confucius was not discussing civil laws, per se, but rather expressing his preference for ritual principles in guiding society, evidence shows that Confucius's sayings were quoted during court debates, demonstrating his influence on the Han legal system.[29] We know that Confucius's emphasis on moral force was reiterated and developed by many Han thinkers. For example, the famous classicist Dong Zhongshu 董仲舒 (179–93 BC) once urged Emperor Wu,

> In ancient times, [the state] cultivated and trained the officials to surely use virtues and benevolence to transform the people. After they were transformed, no one went to jail all under Heaven, always! In today's world, we abandoned [those moral teachings] and do not cultivate them. We have no means to transform the people. Thus, they have abandoned virtues and died for wealth and profits. Therefore, lawbreakers and criminals are abundant. Criminal cases number thousands each year.[30]
>
> 古者修教訓之官，務以德善化民．民已大化之後，天下常亡一人之獄矣．今世廢而不脩，亡以化民，民以故棄行誼而死財利，是以犯法而罪多，一歲之獄以萬千數.

Another master, Yang Xiong 楊雄 (53 BC–AD 18) held:

> We can let the people see virtues, but cannot let them see penal laws. If they see virtues, they are pure, but if they see penal laws, they are disordered.[31]
>
> 民可使見德, 不可使見刑. 見德則純, 見刑則亂.

The famous thinker Wang Fu (ca. AD 76–157) made it plain by quoting Confucius in his "*dehua*" 德化 chapter ("Moral transformation") of *Qianfu lun*:

> Therefore, a supreme sage surely does not administer people's business, but surely administers people's heart. Thus, [Confucius] says: "When hearing cases, I am as [capable as] all the other judges. But I must cause there to be no cases of litigation!"[32]

29 We will soon encounter a case in which Confucius's sayings were quoted during the court debate.

30 *Hanshu*, 56.2515. Dong referred to criminal cases, but his argument could also be easily applied to civil cases.

31 Yang Xiong 楊雄, *Fayan zhu* 法言注, ed., Han Jing 韓敬 (Beijing: Zhonghua shuju, 1992), 9.212.

32 *Qianfu lun jian jiaozheng*, 8.376.

> 是故上聖不務治民事，而務治民心．故曰：聽訟，吾猶人也．必也使無訟乎！

This recurring emphasis on reforming people's morals can be nicely summarized by Peerenboom's theory of the "Politics of Harmony." He argued that Confucius offered "an ethic of virtues of qualitative excellence in interpersonal relations (*ren* 仁) and harmony among social beings."[33] And,

> Confucius's jurisprudence, in making the sage responsible for engineering and ensuring the smooth operation of a harmonious social order, constitutes 'a rule of man.' There are, of course, still laws. Hence, Confucianism remains a rule of law broadly construed to entail the existence of the legal and enforcement mechanisms necessary to ensure the ability of society to function.[34]

This ideal of reforming people's morals, especially by promoting ritual yielding, to reduce lawsuits, had a significant impact on the legal development of imperial China. On the one hand, realization of this ideal, together with many other factors, restrained Han China from developing its system of civil laws more fully, beyond the quite substantial and rational levels it achieved.[35] On the other hand, this ideal inspired later dynasties to develop a unique mechanism for resolving civil disputes that stressed reconciliation. We find the echo of this tendency as late as the Qing (1644–1911), during the so-called "the third realm of justice," where we find a comparable emphasis on peace-making compromises, described by Philip Huang in his *Civil Justice in China: Representation and Practice in the Qing* (1996).[36]

---

33 Peerenboom, *Law and Morality*, 128.

34 Ibid., 132. This statement touches upon the issue of "rule of law" vs. "rule of man." Obviously, it is difficult to put the legal system of early China in either of these categories.

35 Besides this ideal, I can think of two other factors: the inability of the dynasty to have enough officials in local administration, and the rise of the big clans in the Eastern Han, in which negotiations between members and between clans tended to be conducted by the parties themselves.

36 Huang, *Civil Justice in China*, 110–137, especially, 135–137. Huang distinguished the third realm of justice from strictly informal justice and strictly formal justice. The former referred to customary practices, whereas the latter referred to magisterial adjudication. The third realm designates a system in which formal and informal justice operated on relatively equal terms. "The magistrate's opinion, to be sure, carried all the weight of the official legal system. But that opinion was expressed within an ideology that differed to informal justice, so long as that justice worked within the boundaries set by the law. Thus, magistrates routinely accepted peacemaking compromise settlements worked out by community and kin mediators in preference to continuing on to court adjudication" (p. 136).

Having noted that the key to achieving this ideal was to reform the morals of the people, our attention is drawn to the influence of ethics on the justice system. Actually, Joseph Needham already observed that in the Han, laws were firmly embedded in ethics.[37] The influence of ethical thinking was not limited to civil laws. Thus, in the following section, I will expand my inquiry from civil laws into the realm of criminal laws as well.

2 Ethical Principles and Laws

I maintain that two ethical principles, filial piety and revenge, deeply influenced the Qin and Han laws. What precisely was filial piety? In its earliest formulation in Shang and Western Zhou, the term referred to offering sacrifice to one's dead ancestors, but very early on, duties to living parents also became part of the definition.[38] During the pre-Han period, the term filial piety underwent a series of subtle changes in meaning, as Keith Knapp argued:

> By contrasting the meaning of *xiao* in the Western Zhou and the Spring and Autumn period sources with its meaning in *ru* philosophical texts of the early and late Warring States period, one may see that the *ru* masters fundamentally reinterpreted *xiao*. Namely, they de-emphasized one of *xiao's* earliest meanings, feeding one's elders, and instead accentuated a derivative meaning of obeying one's parents, and by further extension, obeying one's lord. This reinterpretation adapted the concept of *xiao* to the emerging dominance of the household and bureaucratic state in place of lineage and kingdom.[39]

---

37 Joseph Needham, *Science and Civilization in China* (Cambridge: Cambridge University Press, 1956), vol. 2, p. 214.

38 The most extensive research on this topic is Harry Hsin-i Hsiao, "Filial Piety in Ancient China: A Study of the Hsiao-ching" (Ph.D. diss., Harvard University, 1978). Hsiao, by studying the *Documents*, the *Book of Songs*, and the Zhou bronze vessel inscriptions, argues that in the Western Zhou period (ca. 1046–771 BC), the concept of filial piety referred to offering sacrifices to the ancestors and to commemorating them in the heart (pp. 79–80). In "Saishu Shunjū jidai no kō to sosen saishi ni tsuite" 西周春秋時代の孝と祖先祭祀に就いて, *Tsukuba daigaku chiiki kenkyū* 築波大學地域研究 10 (1992): 57–119, Ikezawa Masaru 池澤優, by studying the usage of the word *xiao* in bronze inscriptions, traces the origin of the notion to ancestor worship in the Western Zhou period. In "The Ru Interpretation of Xiao," *Early China* 20 (1995): 199, Keith Knapp suggests that the original meaning of *xiao* was to provide food offerings to one's ancestors. In "Confucian Piety and Individualism in Han China," *Journal of the American Oriental Society* 116, no. 1 (1996): 2–3, Michael Nylan argues that filial piety was originally associated with ancestral worship but was later expanded to mean duties to living parents.

39 Knapp, "The *Ru* Reinterpretation of *Xiao*," 197.

According to Knapp, from the late Warring States period onwards, filial piety referred not only to the care and feeding of one's elders, but, more importantly, to obeying one's parents.[40] However, we need to remain aware that filial piety was a very complicated notion. Filial piety had a hierarchy that mirrored social status. The Han-era *Classic of Filial Piety* (*Xiaojing* 孝經) delineates five levels of filial piety corresponding to five different social strata, from the Son of Heaven (*tianzi* 天子), feudal lords (*zhuhou* 諸侯), ministers (*qing daifu* 卿大夫), men in service (*shi* 士), to commoners (*shuren* 庶人).[41] Among these five levels, caring for one's parents is prescribed for commoners.

> Use the way of the heaven, share the benefits of the earth, and be cautious about one's own person and be frugal in order to take care of one's parents. This is the filial piety of commoners.[42]
>
> 用天之道，分地之利，謹身節用，以養父母，此庶人之孝也.

With this notion of filial piety in mind, we now examine how the values of filial piety influenced criminal and civil laws.[43]

With respect to criminal laws, "lack of filial piety" was a crime in Qin and Han laws. Perhaps we should not expect filial piety to have become a legal principle in early China since the Legalists, who were traditionally believed to be the masterminds behind the promulgation of laws in early China, held very negative views toward filial piety.[44] For example, The *Book of the Lord Shang*

---

40 Knapp regards obeying one's lord (*zhong* 忠) as a further extension of filial piety by analogy to obeying one's parents (p. 217). In any case, in this book, my treatment of filial piety is restricted to domestic settings. In addition, Knapp argues that feeding one's parents was de-emphasized by the *ru* masters (pp. 218–219). I disagree with this analysis. I believe that the notion of filial piety acquired a broader meaning through the re-interpretation of the *ru* masters.

41 Nylan's dissertation argues that the scope of *xiao* in the *Classics of Filial Piety* was expanded from the conventional definition of *xiao* alluded to by Mencius. See Nylan, "Ying Shao," 186–190.

42 *Xiaojing zhushu*, 3.6, in the *Shisanjing zhushu* 十三經注疏 (Ruan Yuan 阮元 1815 edition, rpt., Taipei: Yiwen chubanshe, 1965).

43 *Xiao* was also very important in criminal laws, as the lack of filial piety (*buxiao* 不孝) was considered a serious crime in Qin and Han laws. See Nylan, "Ying Shao," 177–178; Wakae Kenzo 若江賢三, "Shin Kan ritsu ni okeru fukyōzai" 秦漢律における不孝罪, *Tōyōshi kenkyū* 東洋史研究 55, no. 2 (1996): 249–282; and Liu Min 劉敏, "Cong Ernian lüling lun Handai xiaoqin de falühua" 從二年律令論漢代孝親的法律化, *Nankai xuebao* (*Zhexue shehui kexu ban*) 南開學報 (哲學社會科學版) no. 2 (2006): 91–98.

44 Martin Kern has argued that the Qin was not simply "Legalist" and anti-traditional. He points out that the First Emperor's stele celebrated *xiao*. See Kern, *The Stele Inscriptions of Ch'in Shih-huang: Text and Ritual in early Chinese Imperial Representation* (New Haven:

attacks filial piety along with other *ru* values as not only useless, but even harmful to the state.

> If in a country there are the following ten evils: rites, music, odes, history, virtue, moral culture, filial piety, brotherly duty, integrity, and sophistry, the ruler cannot make the people fight and dismemberment is inevitable; and this brings extinction in its train. If the country has not these ten things and the ruler can make the people fight, he will be so prosperous that he will attain supremacy.[45]
>
> 國有禮有樂，有《詩》有《書》，有善有修，有孝有悌，有廉有辯．國有十者，上無使戰，必削至亡；國無十者，上有使戰，必興至王．

The *Han Feizi* 韓非子 specifically attacks Confucius's idea of filial piety as something deadly harmful to the state:

> There was a man of Lu, who followed the ruler to war. He fought three battles and ran away thrice. When Confucius asked him his reason, he replied: "I have an old father. Should I die, nobody would take care of him." So Zhongni (Confucius) regarded him as a man of filial piety, praised him, and exalted him. From this, it can be seen that the dutiful son of the father was a rebellious subject of the ruler.[46]
>
> 魯人從君戰，三戰三北．仲尼問其故，對曰：吾有老父，身死莫之養也．仲尼以為孝，舉而上之．以是觀之，夫父之孝子，君之背臣也．

Despite such attacks, we find references to filial piety in the earliest known legal documents in China, the Shuihudi Qin legal documents. Qin laws treated acts deemed lacking in filial piety as a serious crime, namely the crime of "lack of filial piety" (*buxiao zui*不孝罪), as Wakae Kenzo 若江賢三 pointed out in 1996.[47] Unfortunately, even though the term *buxiao zui* occurs twice in the Shuihudi Qin legal documents, these references provide no explanation of what constituted a lack of filial piety. Wakae, however, suggested that scolding

---

American Oriental Society, 2000). His study agrees with my observation here: Qin laws also emphasized *xiao*, and hence, not simply "Legalist."

45 *Shangjunshu zhuizhi*, 1.29–30. My translation follows Duyvendak, *The Book of Lord Shang*, 107.

46 *Han Feizi yizhu*, 19.680.

47 Wakae, "Shinkanritsu ni okeru fukyōzai," 249–282, especially, 280–280.

and blaming one's parents were considered *buxiao*.[48] Wakae based his conclusion on the following evidence: in order to eliminate the prince-apparent Fusu 扶蘇 (d. 210 BC), an edict forged by Zhao Gao 趙高 (d. 207 BC) in 209 BC charged Fusu with *buxiao*, and, in the name of the First Emperor of the Qin, ordered him to commit suicide. The basis for the charge was that Fusu held a grudge against his father, the First Emperor of the Qin.

> However, on the contrary to [express his gratitude], [Fusu] frequently submitted letters to me to blame me directly for what I did for him [which he should have appreciated]. Fusu felt hatred all the days and nights, because he was not able to withdraw [from the frontier] and go home to become the prince apparent.[49]
>
> [扶蘇] 乃反數上書直言誹謗我所為, 以不得罷歸為太子, 日夜怨望.

Wakae also found that Han laws from Zhangjiashan also punished the crime of "lack of filial piety." ZJS strip (*Statutes*) nos. 35–37 state:

> If a son murders his parent, beats or scolds his grand-parents, his [natural] parents, his parents [who adopt him], the principal mother [the principal wife of the father], and the later mother [the later wife of the father], or the parents accuse the son as lacking filial piety, under all these circumstances, the son shall be executed in the marketplace ... If a person teaches others to act in an unfilial manner, that person will be tattooed and enslaved as a wall-builder [for males] or grain-pounder [for females].[50]
>
> 子牧殺父母, 毆詈泰父母、父母、叚 (假) 大母、主母、後母, 及父母告子不孝, 皆棄市 … 教人不孝, 黥為城旦舂.

ZJS strip (*Zouyan shu*) nos. 181–182 restate the statute quoted above:

> If a person teaches others to act unfilially, his crime is to be punished one degree less than that of lacking filial piety. Those who commit the crime of lack of filial piety shall be executed in the market. One degree less than

48 Ibid., 256.
49 *Shiji*, 87.2551.
50 ZJS strip (*Zouyan shu*) nos. 35–37, p. 13.

> executing in the market is to be tattooed and enslaved as a wall-builder [for males] or grain-pounder [for females].[51]
>
> 教人不孝，次不孝之律．不孝者棄市，棄市之次，黥為城旦舂．

On the basis of this evidence,[52] Wakae concluded that Qin and Han laws defined *buxiao zui* as including the offenses of scolding or blaming one's parents and beating one's parents or grandparents. The penalty for the crime was execution in the marketplace.

Actually, we have more information regarding the crime called "lack of filial piety." Case no. 21 in the *Zouyan shu* from Zhangjiashan indirectly refers to filial piety. According to the text, sometime around 190 BC, a mother-in-law accused her daughter-in-law of having consensual sex with a male near the coffin of the daughter-in-law's recently deceased husband. For unspecified reasons, the case eventually came before the superintendent of trials for his review. He and his junior staff initially considered the widow guilty and sentenced her to hard labor. However, a court scribe challenged the sentence. After serious debate, the case was ultimately dismissed on the recommendation of the court scribe.[53] What makes this account relevant to our examination of filial piety is that during the debate, the court scribe questioned his judicial colleagues:

> According to the statutes, "A person who is unfilial deserves execution in the marketplace. If a living father had a [son] who failed to feed him for three days, how should an officer of the court sentence the son?" He should be executed in the marketplace," said the *tingwei* Xiao and others. "Let us suppose that the father has died, and his son does not offer cult in his house for three days. What sentence does the son deserve?" "He ought not to be sentenced." "And suppose there is a son who ignored his father's injunctions while his father alive? Who is reckoned to have committed the more serious crime: a son who disobeyed his dead father's injunctions or a son who ignored the injunctions of his father while alive?" "We

51 ZJS strip (*Zouyan shu*) nos. 181–182, p. 108.

52 Readers are reminded that the complete strips from Zhangjiashan were not published until 2001. Wakae had to combine his evidence from various articles that published excerpts of the strips.

53 ZJS strip (*Zouyan shu*) nos. 180–196, p. 108. For a detailed study on this case, see Michael Nylan, "Notes on a Case of Illicit Sex from Zhangjiashan: A Translation and Commentary," *Early China* 30 (2005–6): 25–45.

should not hear a case involving a dead father's injunctions; [the son] would have committed no crimes."[54]

律曰：不孝棄市．有生父而弗食三日，吏且何以論子？廷尉穀等曰：當棄市．有（又）曰：有死父，不祠其家三日，子當何論？廷尉穀等曰：不當論．有子不聽生父教，誰與不聽死父教罪重？穀等曰：不聽死父教毋罪．

The authorities agreed that: (1) a son's failure to feed his living father would constitute a criminal lack of filial piety, but failure to offer cult to his dead father would not; and (2) a son ignoring the injunctions of his living father would constitute a criminal lack of filial piety, but disobeying his dead father's injunctions would not. To put it another way, while offering sacrifice to one's ancestors was an important aspect of filial piety, failure to do so did not rise to the level of a criminal offense, nor did disobeying the teachings of one's dead father. These distinctions point to a pragmatic pre-occupation of the state: acts of filial piety involving living parents had a much more immediate impact on social order.

Turning to the question of civil laws, Han civil laws that reflected concerns with filial piety emphasized the feeding of one's parents or grandparents and, by extension, taking care of one's elders. To that end, the civil laws stipulated civil penalties for those who neglected their elders, and stipulated privileges for the elderly. A provision from the Statutes on Households directs:

> When a grandson becomes the head of household and lives together with his grandparents, if the grandson fails to take good care of the grandparents, [the authorities] shall order the grandson to move out of the house and let his grandparents move into his house, be supported by his farming land, and utilize his slaves. The grandparents are not allowed to buy or sell [the farming land, houses, and slaves of the household]. If the grandson dies and his mother becomes the head of household (*daiweihu*), the mother is not permitted to expel her parents-in-law, take a new husband to the household, or illegally take away the belongings of her son.[55]

54 ZJS strip (*Zouyan shu*) nos. 189–191, p. 108; cf. Nylan, "Notes on a Case," 32. My translation follows Nylan.

55 ZJS strip (*Statutes*) nos. 337–339, p. 55. We notice that, in this particular situation, the widow could not freely remarry if she served as head of household and assumed responsibility of taking care of the elders.

Above and beyond the pragmatic social need to take care of the elders in a household, absent any other formalized social welfare system, the notion of filial piety gives these legal guidelines a moral or ritual underpinning. Since the subject here is grandchildren rather than children, the prescriptions contained in the passage quoted above clearly imply that the obligations of filial piety are inherited along with the title of head of household and the household's land and property. The death of a father or his incapacitation raises questions of filial obligations as they affect the well-being of all the surviving members of the household. Of particular concern are the filial obligations of the grandson when the grandparents are still members of the household (and at least seventy years old or unable to be self-supporting) and when other adult sons are dead or otherwise absent. This concern for the well-being of aged grandparents underscores the prescription contained in ZJS strip (*Statutes*) no. 342:

> If the husband and wife are both sick and they cannot work, or they are over seventy years old, do not allow the [main] son to live separately.[56]
>
> 及夫妻皆癃病，及老年七十以上，毋異其子.

ZJS strip (*Statutes*) nos. 337–339, cited above, all deal with such three-generational households. In such a household, if the father is alive, he is obliged to care for his own father. If the father dies, his (eldest) son becomes the head of household and is obliged to accept his father's filial duties to his grandparents in addition to satisfying his on-going filial duty to his mother. If the grandson fails to care for his grandparents, he risks being deprived of his privileges as head of household. If the grandson dies, his mother becomes head of household, and must accept the filial duty of taking care of her parents-in-law.[57] Principles of filial piety govern the restructuring and redefining of household relationships in all of these possible situations.

Filial piety is also the implied principle that governs the situation described in ZJS strip (*Statutes*) no. 408:

---

56 ZJS strip (*Statutes*) no. 342, p. 55.

57 The reader should note that the mother could become the head of household if the son had no sons, according to ZJS strip (*Statutes*) no. 379, p. 60.

> For those who ought to transport grains [for the state], the sons are all exempted from the duty if they live alone with their parents who are aged, or if the parents are very old and/or disabled.[58]
>
> 諸當行粟,獨與若父母居老如睆老,若其父母罷癃者,皆勿行.

The labor service exemption referred to here incorporates an implied obligation to care for one's elders. The state is willing to forego the corvée duty owed by these sons and grandsons in exchange for the sons and grandsons fulfilling their filial duties. In a sense, given the requirement of sons and grandsons to care for their elders, this labor service exemption can be understood as an implicit reward for those who fulfill their filial duties.

As we have just seen, the obligations of filial piety go beyond service to one's own parents. In a broader sense, respecting one's elders is also an aspect of filial piety or an extension of filial piety. According to the *Kongzi jiayu*, in a conversation between Zengzi 曾子 (505–435 BC)[59] and Confucius concerning the Way of the Enlightened Former Kings (*mingwang* 明王), Confucius said: "If superiors respect the elders, then their subordinates will become more filial" (*shang jing lao, ze xia yi xiao* 上敬老,則下益孝).[60] This idea of filial piety extended to elders in general can be observed in ZJS strip (*Statutes*) nos. 354–357, which stipulate the welfare privileges granted to the very elderly. For instance, ZJS strip (*Statutes*) no. 355 states:

> [All these people shall be granted staffs]: *daifu* above seventy years old, *bugeng* above seventy-one years old, *zanniao* above seventy-two years old, *shangzao* above seventy-three years old, *gongshi* above seventy-four years old, and *gongzu* or *shiwu* above seventy-five years old.[61]
>
> 大夫以上年七十,不更七十一,簪褭七十二,上造七十三,公士七十四,公卒、士五(伍)七十五,皆受仗(杖).

In other words, elders above a certain age (70–75), should be granted staffs appropriate to their status. From the so-called "Ten Jade Staff Documents"

58 ZJS strip (*Statutes*) no. 408, p. 64.

59 Tradition made Zengzi 曾子 a disciple of Confucius and a filial exemplar. Traditionally, Zengzi was believed to be the compiler of the *Classic of Filial Piety*.

60 *Kongzi jiayu shuzheng* 孔子家語疏証, ed., Chen Shike 陳士珂 (Beijing: Zhonghua shuju, 1985), 1.11.

61 ZJS strip (*Statutes*) no. 355, p. 57.

(Yuzhang shi jian" 王杖十簡), dated to 10 BC and excavated from Wuwei 武威, Gansu 甘肅 in 1959, we know that these staffs were symbols of royal respect. The "Ten Jade Staff Documents" have been carefully studied by many accomplished historians.[62] According to these studies, these documents granted various privileges to those who were at least seventy years old. For example, one decree from the "Ten Jade Staff Documents" states:

> Decree: An edict is hereby proclaimed to the imperial counsellor: those men of 70 years of age on whom a jade-staff has been bestowed shall have status comparable with that of officials of 600 *shi* 石 grade. They are permitted to enter offices and official courtyards without hurrying ... Any person who ventures to summon them for attendance or to treat them with insult or contumely shall be subject to treatment as if he were guilty of gross moral turpitude. Promulgated on the day *jiazhen*, of the ninth month of the second year of Jianshi (7th November, 31 BC).[63]
>
> 制:詔御史:年七十以上杖王杖,比六百石入官府不趨吏 ... 民有敢毆辱者達不道棄市. 建始二年九月甲辰下.

Given that filial piety was so fundamental to the Han political and social orders, it should come as no surprise that its influence pervaded the Han legal world. As Nylan recently argued:

> The *Classic of Filial Duty* (*Xiao jing* 孝經) provided the most systematic exposition of the idea that filial duty undergirds political loyalty. Elsewhere, analogies constructed between families (*jia* 家) "below" and

62 Chen Zhi 陳直, "Gansu Wuwei Mozuizi Hanmu chutu Yuzhang shi jian tong kao" 甘肅武威磨阻子漢墓出土王杖十簡通考 *Kaogu* no. 3 (1961): 160–162,165; Guo Moruo 郭沫若, "Wuwei Yuzhang shi jian shangmian" 武威王杖十簡商免, *Kaogu xuebao* 考古学報 no. 5 (1965): 1–6; Ōba Osamu, "Kandai no ketsugotohi: Tamatsue jū kan hairetsu no ichian" 漢代の決事比 – 王杖十簡配列の一案, *Kense daigaku bungaku ronshū* 関西大学文学論集 25 (1975): 271–287; Tomiya Itaru 冨谷至, "Tamatsue jū kan" 王杖十簡, *Tōhō gakuhō* 東方學報 64 (1992): 61–113; Michael Loewe, "The Wooden and Bamboo Strips Found at Mo-Chü-Tzu (Kansu)," *Journal of the Royal Asiatic Society of Great Britain and Ireland* no. 1 (1965): 13–26.

63 My translation follows Loewe, "The Wooden and Bamboo Strips," 19–20 (slightly modified). This decree differs slightly from ZJS strip (*Statutes*) no. 355. Strip 355 contains two criteria for its eligible grantees, orders of honor and age, whereas the "Ten Jade Staff Document" contains only one criterion, age. Furthermore, while the "Ten Jade Staff" edict is consistent with the strip 355 in spirit, it appears to be more generous to its beneficiaries in terms of expanding and equalizing privileges for elders.

> the ruling house (*guo jia* 國家) "above" likened the ruler's position vis-à-vis his people to that of parents to children or husbands to wives.[64]

Filial piety was a notion that inextricably linked public order and private interests. By incorporating principles of filial piety, civil laws could anticipate the simplest and most complicated situations involving households and inheritance, the kind of situations that often provoked the most divisive conflicts, the kind most likely to prompt lawsuits.

Just as filial piety influenced the legal system, the ethical principle mandating revenge exerted an influence on the articulation and interpretation of both civil and criminal laws. In a way, revenge and filial piety are related concepts. As Anne Cheng has argued, the duty of vengeance appeared to be "the absolutizing of filial piety."[65] Violent attacks motivated by filial revenge were never treated as simple murder or battery since avenging an injury to one's parents brought maintaining public order and the rendering of familial obligation into direct conflict. For example, in 7 BC, Xue Kuang 薛況 (d. AD 3), son of the famous judge Xue Xuan 薛宣 (fl. 20–15 BC),[66] hired a third party to attack the academician Shen Xian 申咸 near the palace, to take revenge on Shen Xian for Shen Xian's supposedly false accusation against Xue Xuan. Xue Kuang's action triggered a heated debate among the central authorities at the court of Emperor Ai 哀 (r. 7–1 BC), who personally presided over the case. Officials were divided into two camps. The assistant to the imperial counselor and others argued that the offense was heinous and that Xue Kuang should be executed at the marketplace.

> [Xue] Kuang was a minister of the court. His father [Xuan] was a former grand councilor who was twice enfeoffed as an adjunct marquis, but who failed to instruct his son so that he would receive the transformative influence [of the emperor]. Suspicion also existed between the close relatives, as [Xue Kuang] suspected that Shen Xian had received instructions from [his uncle, Xue] Xiu to slander [his father] Xuan. All that [Shen]

64 *China's Early Empires*, eds., Michael Nylan and Michael Loewe (Cambridge: Cambridge University Press, 2010).

65 Anne Cheng, "Filial Piety with a Vengeance: The Tension between Rites and Law in the Han," in *Filial Piety in Chinese Thought and History*, ed., Alan K.L. Chan (London: Rutledge Curzon, 2004), 36–39. However, filial piety is not the entirety of revenge, as men also sought revenge for the deaths of brothers.

66 According to the *Fengsu tongyi*, the same Xue Xuan 薛宣 once resolved a dispute over the ownership of a piece of cloth. See Chapter 5 for a detailed analysis of the case.

Xian said of Xuan's doings, however, was recorded, and was witnessed by numerous people, so the authorities should have known about them.

[Xue] Kuang knew that [Shen] Xian was a palace steward and he feared that [Shen] Xian would write a memorial against Xuan on behalf of the metropolitan commandant. So, he openly commanded [Yang] Ming and others to wait near the palace watchtowers to intercept Shen Xian. [Yang Ming] wounded a close underling of the emperor along the main route to the palace in the midst of a crowd, desiring to impair his hearing and sight to impede and sever the source of these discussions and deliberations. He was cruel and crafty, lacking any sense of awe or fear. The noisy swell of the multitudes has spread rumors of the incident to the four corners of the empire. [Yang Ming's actions] are not commensurate with [the statute dictating punishment for] 'ordinary people who become angry and incensed and consequently quarrel and fight.'

We, your subjects, have heard that one shows respect for members of the imperial coterie because they are close to the ruler. The rites dictate that one dismounts at the palace gates and one bows to the horses of the ruler's carriage. That one shows respect even to the ruler's animals is a precept of the *Spring and Autumn Annals*. Thus, when the intent was evil, one is not pardoned from punishment, even if meritorious results follow. The spring floods that overflowed above cannot be allowed to persist. [Xue] Kuang initiated the crime, and [Yang] Ming wounded [Xian] with his own hands. When both the act and the intent were evil, this corresponds to [the crime] 'great disrespect.' It is appropriate to apply the most severe punishment to [Yang] Ming. He and [Xue] Kuang should both be executed in the marketplace.[67]

況朝臣，父故宰相，再封列侯，不相敕丞化，而骨肉相疑，疑咸受修言以謗毀宣．咸所言皆宣行跡，眾人所共見，公家所宜聞．

況知給事中，恐為司隸舉奏宣，而公令明等迫切宮闕，要遮創戮近臣於大道人眾中，欲以鬲塞聰明，杜絕論議之端．桀黠無所畏忌，萬眾讙譁，流聞四方，不與凡民忿怒爭鬭者同．

臣聞敬近臣，為近主也．禮，下公門，式路馬，君畜產且猶敬之．春秋之義，意惡功遂，不免於誅，上浸之源不可長也．況首為惡，明手傷，功意俱惡，皆大不敬．明當以重論，及況皆棄市．

In rebuttal, the superintendent of trials argued for mitigation of the punishment:

67 *Hanshu*, 83.3395. My translation follows Queen, *From Chronicle to Canon*, 165–166.

The statute states: "When a person wounds another with a sharp object during a brawl, [condemn the accused] to hard labor while [allow the accused] to remain physically intact. When there is premeditated murder, increase the punishment by one degree, so that the punishment is commensurate with one who has plotted murder." An imperial edict states: "Do not rely on slanderous lies to construe a crime." The *Commentary* states: "When a person treats someone unrighteously, and thereby precipitates a physical assault, it is equivalent to the crime of assaulting another; that person is guilty of an injustice"…

Confucius said: "What is necessary is to rectify names." If names are not correct, then penalties and punishments will not hit the mark, and if penalties and punishments do not hit the mark, then the common people will not know where to put their hands and feet. Now to maintain that since [Xue] Kuang initiated the crime and [Yang] Ming wounded [Shen Xian] with his own hands, both are [guilty of] 'great disrespect', is to cause the public and the private realms to lack any distinction. According to a righteous principle of the *Spring and Autumn Annals*, one must probe to the original intentions to determine the crime. When you probe to the source of Kuang's intentions, you will find that he was angered by the slander against his father. He did not commit any other more serious crime. If you rely on slanderous lies and knit together small transgressions to construe a serious crime, and thereby entrap [Xue Kuang] in the death penalty, you will defy the enlightened edict [of the emperor concerning slander]. I fear this verdict runs contrary to the intent of the law and should not be put into effect. The sage kings did not increase punishments on account of their anger. [Yang] Ming is not warranted to be punished as committing the crime of "intentionally injuring people." [Xuan] Kuang and the accessory criminal [Yang Ming] should be demoted in rank and sentenced to serve hard labor while remaining physically intact.[68]

律曰: 鬭以刃傷人, 完為城旦, 其賊加罪一等, 與謀者同罪. 詔書無以詆欺成罪. 傳曰: 遇人不以義而見疻者, 與痏人之罪鈞, 惡不直也…

孔子曰: 必也正名. 名不正, 則至於刑罰不中; 刑罰不中, 而民無所錯手足. 今以況為首惡, 明手傷為大不敬, 公私無差. 春秋之義, 原心定罪. 原況以父見謗發忿怒, 無它大惡. 加詆欺, 輯小過成大辟, 陷死刑, 違明詔, 恐非法意, 不可施行. 聖王不以怒增刑. 明當以賊傷人不直, 況與謀者皆爵減完為城旦.

68 *Hanshu*, 83.3395–3396. My translation follows Queen, *From Chronicle to Canon*, 166–167.

The emperor invited other officials to express their opinions. Chancellor Kong Guang 孔光 (64 BC–AD 5) and imperial counsellor (*dasikong* 大司空) Shi Dan 師丹 (d. AD 3) agreed with the assistant to the imperial counselor, but the general, the academicians (*boshi* 博士), and the court gentlemen (*yilang* 議郎) all agreed with the superintendent of trials. The superintendent's argument prevailed, thus, Xue Kuang received a reduced sentence.[69]

It is important to note that, during the debate, the assistant to the imperial counselor never referred to any statutes. He cited a ritual principle to illustrate the culprit's transgression of ritual propriety and a "principle from the *Spring and Autumn Annals*" (*Chunqiu zhiyi* 春秋之義) to justify his advocacy for harsh punishment, as noted by Sarah Queen, an expert on Dong Zhongshu.[70] By contrast, the superintendent of trials cited one statute and one imperial edict, offering a legal basis for his argument. To enhance his argument, he also referred to Confucius's idea of the "rectification of names" (*zhengming* 正名), as well as a line from the *Spring and Autumn Annals* and an unknown tradition. As Sarah Queen analyzed the case in 1996:

> The spokesmen for both sides of the legal argument cited the identical principle from the *Spring and Autumn Annals* to establish the importance of intent when considering the proper punishment for Xuan Kuang. However, their evaluations of Xuan Kuang's intent differed.[71]

I would add that the key issue in Xue Kuang's case was his motivation: was revenge prompted by a desire to defend his father's reputation sufficient justification for his actions? The superintendent of trials believed that Shen Xian had in fact defamed the character of Xue Xuan. Therefore his son, Xue Kuang, was obligated, as a matter of filial piety, to defend his father's reputation and deserved a reduced sentence. This case reveals a certain uneasiness when dealing with revenge and slander. On the one hand, as Queen pointed out, the superintendent of trials considered the case "a private and unofficial matter," suggesting that it should be designated a case of family revenge.[72]

---

69 This aspect particularly shows that the emperor relied on the opinion of the majority to make the final judgment.

70 Sarah Queen, *From Chronicle to Canon, the Hermeneutics of the Spring and Autumn, According to Tung Chung-shu* (Cambridge: Cambridge University Press, 1996), 165. Consistent with Dong Zhongshu's dicta, we see the *Spring and Autumn Annals* being treated as a source of legal principles. We will discuss this matter in detail later.

71 Ibid., 167–168. Queen argues that this case indicates that motive was a factor in judging cases.

72 Ibid., 167.

Nevertheless, the real question is if a slander against one's father deserved a revenge of murder from the filial son. This question reminds us of a line in the *Hanshu* that we encountered in Chapter Five of this study, "They seek revenge in ways that exceed what due requital requires."[73] The superintendent of trials argued that since a man had been killed, the authorities were obliged to take action against the offender. The disagreement among the officials centered on the degree of the punishment. This ambivalence about revenge, arising from the conflicting obligations of filial piety and maintaining social order, implicitly reveals the influence of ethical principles on the laws.

The ritual canons and other Classics sanction revenge by a son for his father's death.[74] For instance, the "Quli" 曲禮 says:

> One should not live under the same Heaven with the murderer of one's father. One should never turn aside one's weapon if one encounters the murderer of a brother. One should not dwell in the same state with the murderer of a friend.[75]
>
> 父之仇弗與共戴天, 兄弟之仇不反兵, 交遊之仇不同國.

The famous classicist Kong Yingda annotated the passage in this way:

> One should not together uphold the same Heaven as the murderer of one's father … This phrase "not together upholding the same Heaven" means that the heart of a filial son does not allow him to together uphold the same Heaven as the enemy [who murdered his father]. The son must not stop until he has killed the enemy.[76]
>
> 父之仇, 弗於共戴天者 … 此不共戴天者, 謂孝子之心, 不許共仇人戴天, 必殺之乃止.

Certainly, among the *ru* masters there were disagreements over the question of how and when to carry out acts of vengeance. For instance, Xu Shen in his

73 *Hanshu*, 28B.1656.

74 According to Makino Tatsumi 牧野巽, the "Quli" 曲禮 and "Tangong" 檀弓 chapters of the *Liji*, the *Baihutong* 白虎通, the *Gongyang zhuan* 公羊傳, and the *Zhouli* 周禮, all encourage sons to exact vengeance for their fathers' deaths. See Makino, "Kandai ni okeru fukushu" 漢代における復讐, in *Makino Tatsumi chosakushū* 牧野巽著作集 (Tōkyō: Ochanomizu shobo, 1980), vol. 2, 3–20.

75 *Liji*, 3.57.

76 *Liji*, 3.57.

Disputes concerning the Five Classics (*Wujing yiyi* 五經異議, comp. ca. AD 100) disagreed with the *Gongyang* traditions about revenge:

> The *Gongyang* traditions encourage vengeance for one hundred generations. The ancient *Zhouli* encourages revenge within five generations only … Carefully note: The Duke Huan of Lu was killed by Duke Xiang of Qi. The son of Duke Huan participated in the meeting between Duke Zhuang of Lu and Duke Huan of Qi, yet the *Spring and Autumn Annals* does not criticize the son. In addition, Duke Ding of Lu was the ninth-generation grandson of Duke Huan of Lu. Confucius assisted Duke Ding to meet the Qi ruler at Jiagu. These facts suggest that one should not take vengeance even for one hundred generations. I follow the saying of the *Zhouli*.[77]
>
> 公羊說，復百世之讎．古周禮說復讎可盡五世之內 … 謹案，魯桓公為襄公所殺，其子在莊公與齊桓公會，春秋不譏．又定公是魯桓公九世孫，孔子相定公與齊會與夾谷，是不復百世之讎也．從周禮說．

Generally speaking, however, the sanction, if not the encouragement of vengeance, seems to have had a huge impact during the Han, given its widespread practice.[78] Makino collected from the received texts, ninety-eight passages concerning vengeance in the Han dynasty.[79] The motivating factors included the murder or humiliation of one's parents or siblings. For instance, one passage in the *Hou Hanshu* says:

> Also, Wuqiu Zhang, a male from Anqiu, went to the market with his mother. On their way, they ran into a drunken person who insulted Wuqiu Zhang's mother. Wuqiu Zhang killed the drunken person and ran away.[80]
>
> 又安丘男子毋丘長,與母俱行市,道遇醉客辱其母,長殺之而亡.

---

77 This passage from Xu Shen's *Wuying yiyi* 五經異議 is preserved in Zheng Xuan 鄭玄, *Bo Wujing yiyi* 駁五經異議 (*Sikuquanshu* 四庫全書 edition, Taipei: Taiwan Shangwu yinshuguan, 1983), vol. 182, 318. Zheng, on this particular issue, agreed with Xu.

78 Alternatively, if the popularity of taking revenge was not due to any encouragement from the Classics, it might be that the people customarily exacted vengeance and that the Classics simply acknowledges that fact.

79 Makino, "Kandai ni okeru fukushu," 3–20; cf. Li Longxian 李隆獻, "Handai yijiang fuchouguan de xingcha yu quanshi" 漢代以降復仇觀的省察與詮釋, *Taiwan daxue wenshi xuebao* 臺灣大學文史學報 68 (2008): 39–78; Qiu Libo 邱立波, "Handai fuchou suojian zhi jing lü guanxi wenti" 漢代復仇所見之經律關系問題, *Shilin* 史林 no. 3 (2005): 80–110.

80 *Hou Hanshu*, 64.2101.

Official attitudes towards vengeance were mixed. On one hand, according to Makino's study, in eight cases, the avenger was forgiven or even praised. For example, in Yang Qiu's 陽球 case:

> One or more commandery officials insulted the mother of Yang Qiu. Yang Qiu made a pact with dozens of youths, who killed the official(s) and exterminated their family or families. Therefore, Yang Qiu became famous. First, he was recommended as Filially Pious and Incorrupt (*xiaolian* 孝廉), and later he filled the vacancy of the attendant secretariat (*shangshu shilang* 尚書侍郎).[81]
>
> 郡吏有辱其［陽球］母者，球結少年數十人，殺吏，滅其家，由是知名．初舉孝廉，補尚書侍郎．

On the other hand, a great deal of evidence shows that the laws forbade vengeance. Makino found seventeen cases in which the avengers evaded the authorities after carrying out their acts of revenge. For example, in Wang Chang's 王常 case (ca. AD 9):

> Near the end of Wang Mang's reign, [Wang Chang] avenged his younger brother's death and ran away to Jiangxia [far from home].[82]
>
> 王莽末，為弟報仇，亡命江夏．

Makino interpreted this inconsistency among the cases as a conflict between laws and their execution: laws treated vengeance as a crime of murder, but the prevailing mores did not approve of punishments in cases involving "justifiable" revenge. Indeed, this ambivalent attitude concerning revenge is best reflected in an incident from ca. AD 80, in which an imperial precedent for forgiving an act of vengeance was established.

> During the Jianchu period (AD 76–84), someone insulted another person's father, and so the son killed the man. Suzong (i.e., Emperor Zhang 章帝) commuted the death penalty and forgave the son. Thereafter, he

81 *Hou Hanshu*, 77.2498.

82 *Hou Hanshu*, 15.578. Wang Chang later became one of the leaders of the anti-Wang Mang 王莽 (r. AD 8–23) rebellion.

> required that the case be followed as a precedent. This even then settled the deliberations, and the case became the law concerning humiliation.[83]
>
> 建初中有人侮辱人父者，而其子殺之，肅宗貰其死刑而降宥之，自後因以為比．是時遂定其議，以為輕侮法.

However, this law was soon repealed during the reign of Emperor He 和 (r. AD 89–105), following the memorial of minister Zhang Min 張敏 (d. AD 112), who argued that this law encouraged murder. Despite the uneasiness, "vengeance was perceived as a duty as well as a, if not legal, at least legitimate sanction" throughout the Han.[84]

Filial piety and attitudes toward revenge clearly influenced how laws were applied in early China. This influence relates to the influence of the Classics on the laws in general. We should recall that in the debate over Xue Kuang's revenge case, both camps referred to the *Spring and Autumn Annals* to enhance their arguments. In addition to underscoring the relationship between the laws and the Classics, we find the Classics are frequently cited as a source of legal authority.

3 Laws and the Classics

Both Michael Nylan (1982) and Sarah Queen (1996) have extensively studied the relationship between the laws and the Classics.[85] Queen pointed out:

> Dong's legal interpretations of the *Spring and Autumn Annals* influenced Chinese jurisprudence in significant ways. During the Han dynasty, a wide variety of officials adopted his mode of citing the *Spring and Autumn Annals* as both a code of ethical principles and book of legal precedents. Therefore, it became standard practice to cite the *Spring and Autumn Annals* as a source of legal authority. In this respect, Dong's new readings liberalized the legal corpus. Administrators often employed precedents from the *Spring and Autumn Annals* established by Dong Zhongshu and

83 Suzong was Emperor Zhang's temple name. The word *shi* 貰 means "to spare someone." See *Gudai Hanyu cidian*, 1438. This piece of case law was repealed during the reign of Emperor He (r. AD 89–105).

84 Cheng, "Filial Piety with a Vengeance," 39.

85 Nylan, "Ying Shao;" Queen, *From Chronicle to Canon*; cf. Nylan's review of Queen's work, in *Harvard Journal of Asiatic Studies*, 57, no. 2 (1997): 629–638.

his disciples as a model for leniency rather than harshness, and as means to humanize the cruel and impersonal laws inherited from the Qin.[86]

Dong Zhongshu's efforts were probably not intended to humanize the early laws. As this book demonstrates, imputing cruelty to the laws in the era before and during Dong's career was a rhetorical trope. There were civil statutes in the early Western Han that were anything but cruel. Indeed, Dong's efforts seem to have been devoted to addressing issues that were difficult to adjudicate by means of existing statutes, as we find in his *Chunqiu jueyu*. According to Ying Shao, as recorded in the *Hou Hanshu*:

> When the former chancellor of the Jiaoxi kingdom Dong Zhongshu was old and sick, he tendered his resignation. But whenever the court had a discussion of governmental matters, they repeatedly sent Zhang Tang, the Superintendent of Trials, personally to the mean alley [where Dong lived] to ask about the merits and mistakes [of the matters under discussion]. Thereupon Dong wrote the *Chunqiu jueyu*, comprising 232 cases by always using the Classics to respond and explain in detail.[87]
>
> 故膠西相董仲舒老病致仕, 朝廷每有政議, 數遣廷尉張湯親至陋巷, 問其得失. 於是作春秋決獄二百三十二 事, 動以經對, 言之詳矣.

Only six fragments of this work have survived. Several were studied by Nylan in 1982 and five were translated and studied by Queen in 1996. I believe the extant fragments are likely to be summaries of the precedents given in the *Chunqiu jueyu*, rather than original case records.[88] Still, it is worth noting that except for Case 4 ("A was an attendant in an armory"), the other cases all concern family relationships. Cases 1 and 2 ("A had no son" and "A had a son ...") are about adoption. Case 3 ("A lord was hunting") also concerns the parent-child relationship, even though it is ostensibly about animals. Case 5 ("A' s father, B, was arguing with C") also concerns family ties. Case 6 ("A's husband, B, was taking a boat") concerns a widow's remarriage. A closer look at Case 1 will give us a sense of the style of the argument:

86 Queen, *From Chronicle to Canon*, 228.

87 *Hou Hanshu*, 48.1612.

88 We will soon find that two cases in the *Chunqiu jueyu* were cited as authoritative principles in an appeal.

> At the time a doubtful criminal case went like this: A had no son. By the side of the road, he came upon an abandoned baby boy, B, which he raised as his own. When B reached adulthood, he committed the crime of murder. After he related the circumstances to his father A, A hid him. How should A be judged?
>
> Dong Zhongshu's decision said: A had no son, and so he rescued and raised B. Although A did not sire B, for whom would he have exchanged B? The *Book of Songs* says, "The moth has its young, but the wasp sustains them." It is a righteous principle of the *Spring and Autumn Annals* that the father conceals his son [from the legal authorities]. It was right for A to hide B and A does not warrant adjudication.[89]
>
> 時有疑獄曰: 甲無子, 拾道旁棄兒乙養之, 以為子. 及乙長, 有罪殺人, 以狀語甲, 甲藏匿乙. 甲當何論?
>
> 仲舒斷曰: 甲無子, 振活養乙, 雖非所生, 誰與易之? 詩云: 螟蛉有子, 蜾蠃負之. 春秋之義: 父為子隱. 甲宜匿乙而不當坐.

Even though there was some hesitation about identifying this case as a criminal case, it dealt with the relationship between father and son, a relationship considered crucial to the public order, and therefore a subject of concern to officials. Moreover, the case involved an adopted son's legal status: whether the adopted son enjoyed the same legal protections as a natural son. Dong was guided by passages from the *Book of Songs* and the *Spring and Autumn Annals* in reaching his conclusion that adopted sons did enjoy the same legal status as natural sons. By pronouncing this judgment, he implicitly argued that the father-son bond (even the father-adoptive son bond), in which the "natural feelings" of the parent would compel him to shield the child, should take precedence over one's loyalty to the ruler in extreme cases.

This Case and Case 2 ("A has a Son …"), both from the *Chunqiu jueyu*,[90] were classified as criminal cases, but both also involved the civil matter of an adopted son's status. Both cases became influential precedents in civil

---

89 Cheng Shude, *Jiuchao lü kao*, 164. My translation follows Queen, *From Chronicle to Canon*, 144.

90 Case 2 is preserved as follows: "A had a son B who was entrusted to C. B was raised to adulthood by C. On one occasion, his face flushed with intoxication. A confessed to B: 'You are my son.' B was angered and beat A with a staff twenty times. Since B was originally his son, A could not overcome his anger and reported him to the prefecture officials. Dong Zhongshu judged the case stating: 'A sired B. He was unable to raise him and entrusted him to C. A had already severed the obligations binding father and son. Although B beat A, B does not warrant adjudication'." See Queen, *From Chronicle to Canon*, 143–144. The judicial opinion concerning adoption expressed in Case 2 is consistent with that in Case 1: the father-son bond was cultivated through nurture, not simply by blood.

litigations concerning adoptions and inheritance. In AD 330, both cases were cited by an elite lady in her memorial to the emperor concerning the status of her adopted son and his inheritance rights.[91]

Lady Yu, the principal wife of minister He Qiao 賀喬 (d. AD 330), adopted her brother-in-law's son. Subsequently, a concubine of He Qiao gave birth to a son. One year before He Qiao died, the adopted son was sent back to his biological parents, lest he inherit the household. When He Qiao died, lady Yu sought to have her adopted son returned so that he might inherit the household. In her argument, she quoted the two cases judged by Dong, saying:

> Dong Zhongshu has been famous for generations as a pure *ru* 儒 (Confucian, classicist). When the Han court had doubtful cases, [the authorities] always sent messengers to visit Dong. He fairly settled those cases with simple words. At the time, a doubtful criminal case went like this: A had no son. By the side of the road, he came upon an abandoned baby boy B, which he raised as his own ...
>
> Another case went like this: A had a son, B, who was given to C. [Hence] B grew up due to C's nurturance ...[92]
>
> 董仲舒命代[93]純儒，漢朝每有疑議，未嘗不遣使者訪問，以片言而折中焉．時有疑獄曰：甲無子，拾道旁棄兒乙養之以為子 … 又一事曰：甲有子乙以乞丙，乙後長大而丙所成育 …

We know that the authorities differed in their opinions on the merits of Lady Yu's argument, even though our documents do not indicate how the case was eventually decided. What is clear, however, is that after four centuries, Dong's Classics-based legal reasoning was still considered to be authoritative.

Dong was not alone in citing the Classics when trying cases in the Han. Cheng Shude collected twenty-one Han cases that were judged by referring to principles drawn from the *Spring and Autumn Annals*.[94] Evidently, Dong and others promoted the Classics, especially the *Spring and Autumn Annals*, as a

91 Du You 杜佑, *Tongdian* 通典 (Shanghai: Shanghai renmin chubanshe, 1988), vol. 3, 69.431–432.

92 *Tongdian*, vol. 3, 69.431–432.

93 This phrase "*mingdai*" 命代 is difficult to render. My translation in this book is tentative. I suggest that *ming* 命 is a loan word for *ming* 名 (fame), whereas *dai*, as a noun, refers to generations. Thus, *mingdai* means "being famous for generations." There is another possibility that we shall seriously consider. The phrase may have been an editorial mistake during the transmission of the text.

94 Among them, five cases were related to family relationships even though they were all deemed criminal cases. This feature may be explained by the sources made available to Cheng Shude being predominantly standard histories.

source of legal precedents on a par with the statutes and edicts. In an extreme case, even an attempt appeared that tried to apply classical principles to revise the entire body of statutory laws. Chen Chong 陳寵 (d. AD 106) in AD 94 argued that the statutes and ordinances of his time were too complicated and that their interpretations were too diverse. Chen Chong urged the emperor to amend and emend the statutes according to classical principles:

> [The throne] should order the Three Lords (*sangong* 三公) and the Superintendent of Trials to make more impartial and fix the statutes and ordinances. If those statutes and ordinances are to be in accord with the Classics, we should cause there to be 200 crimes with the death penalty and 2,800 crimes that receive the *nai* or *shu* (redemption) penalty. Together, [those categories of crimes] would total 3,000. We should excise the remaining ordinances, so that [the number] would be in accord with the rituals.[95]
>
> 宜令三公, 廷尉平定律令, 應經合義者, 可使大辟二百, 而耐罪, 贖罪二千八百, 并為三千. 奚刪除其餘令, 與禮相應.

As a vivid instantiation of the quasi-legal status of the Classics as a whole, both the statutes and the Classics were presumably written on strips that were 2.4 Han feet long.[96] The *Yantielun* says: "The statutes are 2.4 feet long. [This rule] has been observed from the ancient time to today" (*er chi si cun zhi lü, gu jin yi ye* 二尺四寸之律, 古今一也).[97] The *Lunheng* says: "The patterned words of the sages were written on strips of 2.4 feet long. We teach and study them day and night" (*er chi si cun, shengren wenyu, zhao xi jiang xi* 二尺四寸, 聖人文語, 朝夕講習).[98]

This conflation of the Classics and laws implies a deep familiarity with both the Classics and the statutes among judges. It also says something about their training. The topic of legal training has been studied by Cheng Shude 程樹德 (1877–1944) in his *Hanlü kao* 漢律考 (Studies on Han Laws, 1926),[99] and more recently, in 1983, by Hsing I-tien 邢義田, in his study of the Qin and

95 *Hou Hanshu*, 46.1554. Here, Chen Chong seems to make no distinction between classical principles and ritual principles. While Chen explicitly refers to the rituals as the model for revising statutes and ordinances, he also alludes to the Classics in general.

96 What I am discussing here are the regulations. In actual practice, the situation was much more complicated. See Hu Pingsheng 胡平生, "Jiandu zhidu xin tan" 簡牘制度新探 *Wenwu* no. 3 (2000): 66–73.

97 *Yantielun jiaozhu*, 10.595.

98 *Lunheng jijie*, 12.258.

99 Chapter 8 of *Hanlü kao* is devoted to this topic. See Cheng Shude, *Jiuchao lü kao*, 178–196.

Han periods.[100] On a careful reading of the *Shangjunshu* and Shuihudi Qin strips, Hsing argued that during the Qin dynasty, judicial officials were also teachers, passing on their legal knowledge to the next generation of judges. According to Hsing, this manner of transmitting legal knowledge began in the late Warring States period in various states, before being consolidated and promoted by chancellor Li Si 李斯 (280–208 BC) following the Qin unification in 221 BC.[101] Hsing further argued that after the fall of the Qin, such legal knowledge was highly valued, even though Han officials were reluctant to acknowledge the legal legacy inherited from its predecessor. For example, according to the *Hanshu*, Dong Zhongshu believed that the relationship between laws and classical teachings was similar to the relationship between *yin* and *yang*, with each mutually assisting the other.[102] Legal knowledge was valued in the Han because mastery of that knowledge was considered an important skill for those who would enter the civil service. For instance, in 117 BC, Emperor Wu identified four broad categories that officials should master; the third category concerned laws:

> The third subject is called "understanding the laws and ordinances," [which means] having enough legal knowledge to resolve confusing cases and to be able to interrogate the suspects according to the [appropriate] sections of the laws, and to have one's writings suit a royal counsellor.[103]
>
> 三科曰明曉法令, 足以決疑, 能案章覆問, 文中御史.

By the time of the Eastern Han, there were seven positions in the central government reserved for legal experts.[104] Moreover, a common criterion for assessing officials' capabilities was their acquaintance with statutes and ordinances. As a testament to the importance of legal knowledge for officials, in the excavated

---

100 Hsing I-tien 邢義田, "Qin Han de lüling xue: jianlun Cao Wei lüboshi de chuxian" 秦漢的律令學: 兼論曹魏律博士的出現, *Zhongyang yanjiuyuan lishi yuyan yanjiusuo jikan* 中央研究院歷史語言研究所集刊 54, no. 4 (1983): 51–101.

101 Ibid., 61–67. The regulations concerning disciples were general regulations and not limited to students who were pursuing legal knowledge.

102 Ibid., 71–72; cf. *Hanshu*, 56. 2502.

103 Wei Hong 衛宏, *Hanjiuyi* 漢舊儀 (Beijing: Zhonghua shuju, 1985), 6a.

104 Hsing I-tien, "Qin Han de lüling xue," 75–76. These posts included the following: Attending Secretary in Charge of Documents (*zhishu shiyushi* 治書侍御史), Assistant to the Superintendent of Trials (*tingwei zheng* 廷尉正), Inspector to the Superintendent of Trials (*tingwei jian* 廷尉監), Judicial Referee (*tingwei ping* 廷尉平), Gentleman of the Palace in Charge of the Seals (*shangfuxi langzhong* 尚符璽郎中), the Head of Luoyang Market (*Luoyang shizhang* 洛陽市長), and the Vice Head of Luoyang Market (*Luoyng shicheng* 洛陽市丞).

Han strips, the phrase "being fairly knowledgeable about the statutes and ordinances" (*pozhi lüling* 頗知律令) frequently appears in reports concerning the merits of officials.[105] Given the value ascribed to legal expertise, it comes as no surprise that legal training flourished during the Han dynasty. This training had, as Hsing amply demonstrates in his essay, three main characteristics: (1) judicial officials were the teachers of legal knowledge, (2) legal study became a "family business," so that it eventually evolved into different interpretative traditions, and (3) experts tended to be versatile in both the Classics and the laws.[106]

In 2005, Hsing's work was greatly developed by Long Daxuan, who systematically studied the lineages of jurists sketched by Hsing. Identifying fifteen influential jurists who were active in annotating statutes and ordinances, Long Daxuan classified these jurists according to three periods.[107] He demonstrated that legal training and classical learning often overlapped, with many legal experts learning the Classics and many classicists learning the laws.[108] Long Daxuan enumerated nine pairs of experts. Among them was the jurist Huang Ba 黃霸 (d. 51 BC):

> [Huang Ba] studied statutes and ordinances when he was young. He was delighted to serve as an official ... Xiahou Sheng committed a crime of great disrespect by criticizing an imperial edict. Huang Ba agreed and followed him without indicting him. Their cases were both sent to the superintendent of trials, who had them bound and put into jail, where they awaited execution. Hence, Huang Ba received [the teaching of] the *Book of Documents* from Xiahou Sheng in the jail.[109]
>
> [黃霸] 少學律令, 喜為吏 ... 夏侯勝[110] 非議詔書大不敬, 霸阿從不舉劾, 皆下廷尉, 繫獄當死. 霸因從勝受尚書獄中.

105 Hsing I-tien, "Qin Han de lüling xue," 74–75.

106 Ibid., 85–91.

107 According to Long, the early stage includes Du Yannian 杜延年 (d. 52 BC), Yu Dingguo 于定國 (111–40 BC), and Chen Xian 陳咸 (d. 15 BC). The period of development includes Du Lin 杜林 (fl. AD 8–47), Guo Gong 郭躬 (AD 1–94), and Chen Chong 陳寵 (d. AD 106). The flourishing period includes Xu Shen 許慎 (AD 58–147), Ma Rong 馬融 (AD 79–166), Zheng Xuan 鄭玄 (AD 127–200), He Xiu 何休 (AD 129–180), Ying Shao 應劭 (AD 153–196), Fu Qian 苻潛 (fl. 2nd–3rd century), Wen Ying 文穎 (fl. 2nd–3rd century), Wu Xiong 吳雄 (fl. AD 143–153), and Zhong Hao 鍾皓 (AD 121–189). See Long, *Handai lüzhangjuxue*, 8–11.

108 Long Daxuan, *Handai lüzhangjuxue*, 126–127. In total, Long gives nine pairs of examples.

109 *Hanshu*, 89.3627.

110 Xiahou Sheng 夏侯勝 (fl. 86–70 BC) was a famous classicist of the time. His specialty was the *Book of Documents*.

Regarding Yu Dingguo 于定國 (111–40 BC), the standard history tells us,

> When [Yu] was young, he learned the laws from his father. After his father died, Yu Dingguo, on his part, became a jail officer ... Yu Dingguo only then met a teacher with whom he studied the *Spring and Autumn Annals*. Holding the Classics in person, he faced north [in the position of a subject] and performed the full ritual of a disciple.[111]
>
> 少學法於父. 父死, 後定國亦為獄吏 ... 定國乃迎師學春秋, 身執經, 北面備弟子禮.

Classicists also studied the laws. One example given by Long Daxuan is He Bigan 何比干 (fl. 126–73 BC):

> [He Bigan], whose style name was Shaoqing, clearly understood the Classics and built up his virtues. He also was fully conversant with the laws.[112]
>
> [何比干], 字少卿, 經明行[113]修, 兼通法律.

Another is Feng Kun 馮緄 (d. 167):

> The gentleman's respectable name was Kun, and his style name was Huangqing. He was the eldest son of a gentleman from Youzhou. When he was young, [Feng Kun] was addicted to learning. He practiced his father's business, studying the *Spring and Autumn Annals* and the *Book of Songs of Han Tradition* together with the statutes of the Elder Du tradition.[114]
>
> 君諱緄, 字皇卿, 幽州君之元子也. 少耽學問, 習父業, 治《春秋》, 《韓詩》倉氏, 兼律大杜.

Textual evidence also shows that famous classicists in the Han sometimes used the Han statutes to annotate the Classics. For example, in explaining the phrase, "Debase him in his debasedness" (*jian ye qi jian* 賤也其賤), from

111 *Hanshu*, 71.3042.

112 *Hou Hanshu*, 43.1480, n. 1.

113 In this context, *Xing* 行 means virtue (*dexing* 德行). See *Gudai Hanyu cidian*, 1746.

114 See "Cheji jiangjun Feng Kun bei" 車騎將軍馮緄碑, in *Lishi, Lixu* 隸釋, 隸續, ed., Hong Gua 洪適 (Beijing: Zhonghua shuju, 1986), 7.13–15. Elder Du 大杜 should refer to the jurist Du Yannian 杜延年.

the *Gongyang Commentaries* to the *Spring and Autumn Annals*, He Xiu 何休 (AD 129–182) said:

> A person is debased, hence [the state] strips away the person's rank to make visible that person's low and debased status. This is similar to the [Han] statute saying that if an adopted son has sex with his mother, whoever catches them in the act may kill him.[115]
>
> 賤而去其爵者起見其卑賤. 猶律文立子奸母, 見乃得殺之也.

In his annotation to the phrase "the officials in charge set out the vessels and sacrifices" (*yousi guan chen qimin* 有司官陳器皿) in the *Liji*, Zheng Xuan said:

> Those vessels for sacrifices were the objects originally bestowed. The statute says: when someone divorces his wife, he shall give back what she was bestowed [in her dowry].[116]
>
> 器皿，其本所賫物也．律：棄妻，畀所賫．

With such a strong emphasis on both legal training and study of the Classics, it is not surprising that many famous classically trained judges emerged during the Han dynasties. This phenomenon invites us to rethink the term *ru* in early China.[117] As in the case of Zheng Xuan and many others, they were capable of both annotating the Classics and the statutes, of engaging in scholarly pursuits, and adjudicating cases. This interplay between Classics and laws also leads us to rethink how people in early China thought about laws. Evidently, men concerned with the laws in early China did not accord law with the exalted status in enjoyed in Western tradition.

4 Concluding Remarks

All the issues addressed in this chapter, namely the legal ideal of reforming people's morals, especially by promoting ritual yielding to reduce lawsuits, the

115 *Gongyang zhuan*, 4.54.

116 *Liji*, 43.755. Zheng' s quotation here seems to refer to *ZJS* strip (*Statutes*) no. 384, p. 61.

117 There are several studies on this topic. Michael Nylan, *Five "Confucian" Classics* (New Haven: Yale University Press, 2001); cf. Nicolas Zufferey, *To the Origins of Confucianism: The 'Ru' in Pre-Qin Times and during the Early Han Dynasty* (New York: Peter Lang, 2003).

influence of ethical principles on the shaping and interpretation of statutes and ordinances, and the conflation of laws and the Classics, point to one fact: laws were not regarded as the singular supreme force guiding human society in early China (actually, in all of pre-modern China).

Actually, in the same manner, rituals were as important as laws.[118] As Ban Gu stated:

> Since the sages possessed enlightened and wise natures, they fully understood the wishes of Heaven and Earth as their model and example. In making ritual rules, in providing instruction, in establishing laws, and in instituting punishments, [the sages] always conformed to the feelings of the people and took Heaven and Earth as their model and examples. Hence, it is said that the former kings, in establishing ritual rules, "took the brightness of Heaven as their model and conformed to the nature of the Earth. [They made] punishments and penalties and [they had] awe-inspiring lawsuits, by means of which they emulated the killing and destruction of Heaven's thunder and lightning. They were kind and gentle, benevolent and harmonious, by means of which they imitated the productive and fostering action of Heaven." *The Book of Documents* says: "Heaven advances those who possess rituals," "Heaven punishes those who commit crimes." Therefore, the sages, according to Heaven's advancing, instituted the Five Rituals, and according the Heaven's punishing, they made the Five Punishments.[119]
>
> 聖人既躬明哲之性，必通天地之心，制禮作教，立法設刑，動緣民情，而則天象地．故曰：先王立禮，則天之明，因地之性也．刑罰威獄，以類天之震曜殺戮也；溫慈惠和，以效天之生殖長育也．《書》云天秩有禮，天討有罪．故聖人因天秩而制五禮，因天討而作五刑．

Even though Ban Gu was discussing penal laws, his discussion also captures his view of the relationship between laws and rituals in general. They were characterized as the two hands of the sage-kings in maintaining and sustaining human society.

The relationship between rituals and laws is worth a further study. Such a study would shed light on a fundamental question that this book cannot

118 The relationship between ritual and Classics is very tricky because ritual canons are Classics. But still there was a difference. In legal practices, the Classics (*jing* 經) usually referred to the *Spring and Autumn Annals* and sometimes also referred to the *Book of Songs*.

119 *Hanshu*, 23.1080. My translation follows Hulsewé, *RHL*, 321–322.

possibly answer: on what theoretical basis, did the laws protect one's property in early China (or in pre-modern China in general)? I suggest that scholars who pursue this issue pay particular attention to the work of Xunzi. Xunzi regarded the rituals as nurturance.

> Thus, the meaning of ritual is to nurture. The meat of pastured and grain-fed animals, rice and millet, and blends and combinations of the five flavors are what nurture the mouth. The fragrances of peppercorns and orchids, aromas, and bouquets, are what nurture the nose. Carved and polished [jade], incised and inlaid [metals], and [fabrics] embroidered with the white and black axe emblem, the azure and black notched-stripe, the azure and crimson stripe, and the white and crimson blazon are what nurture the eye. Bells and drums, flutes and chime-stone, lutes and zithers, and reed pipes and organs are what nurture the ear. Spacious rooms, secluded chambers, mats of plaited rushes, couches and bed mats, and armrests and cushions are what nurture the body. Thus, rituals are what nurtures.[120]
>
> 故禮者養也. 芻豢稻粱, 五味調香, 所以養口也; 椒蘭芬苾, 所以養鼻也; 雕琢刻鏤, 黼黻文章, 所以養目也; 鍾鼓管磬, 琴瑟竽笙, 所以養耳也; 疏房檖貌, 越席床笫幾筵, 所以養體也. 故禮者養也.

For Xunzi, this nurturance entails hierarchical differentiations (*bie* 別).

> When the gentleman has been nurtured by these things, he will also be fond of ritual distinctions. What is meant by "distinctions"? I say that these refer to the gradations of rank according to nobility or baseness, disparities between the privileges of old and young, and modes of identification to match these with poverty or wealth, and insignificance or importance.[121]
>
> 君子既得其養, 又好其別. 曷謂別? 曰: 貴賤有等, 長幼有差, 貧富輕重皆有稱者也.

This hierarchy is based on the nobility or baseness of one's contribution to the well-being of the community, not blood. Such a hierarchy encourages social mobility: a commoner could become a prime minister through ritual

120 *Xunzi jijie*, 13.346–347. My translation follows Knoblock, vol. 3, 55.
121 Ibid.

cultivation, and a prince could be demoted to a commoner if he fails to observe rituals. This idea is most clearly expressed in the "Wangzhi 王制" chapter (Kingly Regulation) of the *Xunzi*:

> Although they are the descendants of kings and dukes or knights and grand officers, if they are incapable of devotedly observing the requirements of ritual and moral principles, they should be relegated to the position of commoner. Although they are the descendants of commoners, if they accumulate culture and learning, rectify their character and conduct, and are capable of devotedly observing the requirements of ritual principles and justice, they should be brought to the ranks of a prime minister, knight or grand officer.[122]
>
> 雖王公士大夫之子孫也，不能屬於禮義，則歸之庶人．雖庶人之子孫也，積文學，正身行，能屬於禮義，則歸之卿相士大夫．

Thus, if we combine this sense of ritual as nurturance and ritual as a reflection of social hierarchy based on merits, and if we further associate these aspects of ritual with the distribution of resources,[123] we arrive at what feels very much like a meritocracy:

> When the people go about their daily lives, trusting (correctly) to the justice of a system that allocates resources according to societal contributions, each person feels confident that he will receive his due share of the goods that have long been accounted 'good' by ordinary men, as well as by the wise: long life, wealth, rank, a good name, social standing, beauty, honor, and freedom.[124]

Interestingly, the provisions of *mingtianzhai* in the Statutes on Households from Zhangjiashan also assumed the hierarchical organization of society and the existence of sumptuous regulations. The Han society was arranged hierarchically according to orders of honor, with twenty (or twenty-one) degrees, and land was distributed to imperial subjects according to their ranks. With certain limitations, ranks could be inherited, but one also could accumulate

122 Ibid., 5.148–149. My translation follows Knoblock, vol. 2, 94 (slightly modified).

123 "Nurturance" implies some sort of resource distribution. The passage in the *Xunzi*, "Thus, the meaning of ritual is to nurture. The meat of pastured and grain-fed animals, rice and millet," refers to sumptuous regulations.

124 Michael Nylan, "On the Politics of Pleasure," *Asia Major* 14 (2001): 114.

rank by merit, and thereby move up in the hierarchy. One's place in this hierarchy, based on a combination of blood inheritance and meritorious action, defined the "due-ness" of each person's share in the fundamental resources and land.[125] Underlining this principle, we seem to discern a notion that each person should own what was due to him/her and not be dependent on a ruler's arbitrarily granted favors and rewards.

Therefore, as hinted above, I believe that a further study of the relationship between laws and rituals might resolve the fundamental issue of determining the principles on which the laws in early China that protected a person's property were based. Such a study would need to address this question without invoking or borrowing from doctrines of natural law that sanction rights in Western legal traditions. Thus, such a study would not only contribute to a deeper understanding of both laws and rituals in pre-modern China, but also invite us to appreciate the subtle yet fundamental differences in the world's different legal cultures.

125 If we believe Sima Qian, *mingtianzhai* was credited to Shang Yang's reform in 359 BC, prior to Xunzi. In the *mingtianzhai* practice, blood was still an important factor on determining one's rank in two aspects: (1) the top two ranks would be transmitted to their heirs intact; and (2) other ranks would be demoted two degrees before being transmitted to their heirs. Perhaps Xunzi was reflecting upon the practices in his time and was attempting to improve them. He argued for completely excluding the concern of blood relations from the hierarchy and transforming it into a pure meritocracy. Xunzi argued that the descendants of a prince could be demoted to the ranks of commoners if they failed to cultivate themselves, and that commoners could become princes. We should recall that there was no emperor in Xunzi's time, and thus, strictly speaking, prince was the highest rank in the nobility.

CONCLUSION

The Civil Law of Early China

Our evidence and analysis show that laws and practices dealing with civil matters in a civil manner, that is civil law, which existed in early China. Their seeds were seen in as early as the Western Zhou period and they truly emerged during the Qin and Han dynasties. Sharing many common features with its Western counterpart, the early Chinese civil law possessed significantly distinctive characteristics.

Stretching over a long duration of almost six centuries, the formation of the early civil law could be divided into two stages: (1) Its innate stage could be traced back to as early as the Western Zhou-Warring States periods, as far as our sources demonstrated. Bronze vessels cast during 8th to 7th century BC started to record sporadic lawsuits between nobles regarding land disputes, and in the 4th century BC, various types of civil disputes between commoners occurred in the legal documents excavated by archaeologists. At this innate stage, civil suits were perhaps extremely rare and the rules followed by the judges to resolve the cases were unclear, because no statutes or regulations were ever mentioned during the litigation; (2) In the following Qin and Han dynasties, civil law was truly developed and acquired a certain degree of sophistication: quite well-designed regulations and rules concerning civil matters, such as debt, compensation, household inheritance, and so on were promulgated by the state to deal with economic and personal relationships between the individuals. Civil disputes were frequently recorded both in the legal documents excavated and extant sources, and there were clear examples that statutes and legal stipulations were cited by the judges when adjudicating the cases, indicating that civil cases were heard on a regular basis and were part of the formal justice system.

In terms of its characteristics, on the one hand, the civil law of early China exhibited features that were common to civil laws elsewhere in two aspects: (1) Civil statutes and regulations were promulgated by the state to adjust the economic and personal relationships among individuals, including compensation, debt, inheritance, and household divisions; (2) In civil litigation, the authorities did not apprehend the parties, apply tortures to try the disputes, and regard the responsible as criminals who offended public order. The state held no interest with, and did not inflict penal punishments to the liable party, and parties involved in civil disputes over property were usually treated as equals by the authorities.

 | DOI:10.1163/9789004513907_009

On the other hand, the civil law of early China possessed three distinctive characteristics that shall be emphasized: (1) the law was not based on the concept of individual property rights. It was based on ancient Chinese notions such as *mingfen*, *zhi*, and *min-si*. *Mingfen* referred to the legitimacy of possessing a certain portion of resources, *zhi* referred to a straightforward account of facts, and *min-si* denoted a non-official, non-state sphere of interests. All civil statutes/regulations revolved around these three concepts; Civil laws in early China were applicable to the disputes in the *min-si* sphere, wherein these disputes were understood as a fight over *mingfen*, and litigation was understood as a process to seek *zhi* on the basis of legal principles.

(2) The known civil statutes have placed great emphasis on handling domestic matters, although debt and compensation were also touched upon. They delineated strikingly detailed rules for household establishment and division, inheritance, testament, the disperse of property during divorce, widow's status, the care of seniors, and so on, while their treatment of debt and compensation were quite scanty, although they constituted the majority of the known civil suits as our survey of cases discovered from Juyan demonstrated.[1] Admittedly, this feature could be due to the bias of our evidence because only a small portion of the Han law has survived and been discovered, but it reflected the general trend of the early civil law and the crucial importance of family/household in the eyes of the legislators.

(3) Although civil law was relatively sophisticated in early China, especially during the Han dynasty with clear evidence of parties settling disputes through lawsuits, the prevailing legal ideal was not to refine and perfect the legal regime to give each one one's due; rather, it was to reform people's morals to reduce lawsuits. The ultimate purpose of hearing civil cases was to eradicate the sources of disputes to achieve social harmony. Furthermore, Confucian Classics also carried the force of legal authority and were often referred to by judges during litigation.[2]

Lastly, the author feels compelled to ask a lingering question in his mind when concluding this work: was the civil law significant in early China? The author believes that we should think from the perspective of a commoner to appreciate the crucial changes brought about by the civil law. We determined that the law enabled commoners to enjoy ownership of land, establish heirs, and dispose their property through their will. The civil law cemented the radical change of land tenure in early China. From the legal reforms of Shang Yang to the Statutes and Ordinances of the Second Year of Early Western Han, state

1 See Chapter 1 and Appendix 1 for the survey.
2 This feature is not limited to civil litigation.

ownership over land was abandoned, the early civil law legalized the participation of land by small households, and the commoners acquired the *mingfen* of their allotments, which was protected by the law. Since then, the commoners acquired the legal capacity to participate in the business of buying, selling, and renting land, and could resort to legal means to solve their problems when disputes arose.

This change was tied to another significant change: the entitlement of establishing heirs to the commoners. Establishing heirs was initially a noble privilege: when a noble died, his order of honor and the privilege of offering sacrifice to the ancestors within his clan were passed down to an heir. However, the early civil law empowered commoners to establish heirs to pass down their household property and orders of honor. They were also entitled to divide their property through their will. These entitlements encouraged commoners to accumulate wealth and find their daily works meaningful. Therefore, the emergence of early civil law was an extremely significant change, which improved the social status of the commoners and enabled them some control over their life. The early civil law forced us to pay attention to the other side of pre-modern Chinese law in addition to punishment and social control.

APPENDIX 1

Table of Legal Cases from Juyan

Note: *JX* stands for *Juyan Hanjian shiwen hejiao* 居延漢簡釋文合校, eds. Xie Guihua 謝桂華, Li Junming 李均明 and Zhu Guozhao 朱國炤 (Beijing: Wenwu chubanshe, 1987). *JXY* stands for *Juyan xinjian* 居延新簡, ed. Gansu sheng wenwu kaogu yanjiusuo 甘肅省文物考古研究所 (Beijing: Wenwu chubanshe, 1990).

Number	Causes	Date	Strip nos.	Nature
1	Murder	77 BC	*JY* strip no. 88.5	Criminal
2	Armed fight	67 BC	*JY* strip no. 118.18	Criminal
3	Misconduct in performing duties	61 BC	*JYX* strip no. E.P.T. 5 6.255	Criminal
4	Misadministration by a military officer	1 BC	*JYX* strip nos. E.P.T. 59.548a–b	Criminal
5	Battery	AD 29	*JYX* strip nos. E.P.T. 68.179–195	Criminal
6	Misoperation in performing duties	AD 29	*JYX* strip nos. E.P.T. 68.81–68.107	Criminal
7	Misoperation in performing duties	AD 30	*JYX* strip nos. E.P.T. 68.134–68.161	Criminal
8	Steal public property and run away	AD 30	*JYX* strip nos. E.P.T. 68.54–68.80	Criminal
9	Armed fight	n/v	*JY* strip no. 148.45	Criminal
10	Armed fight and battery	n/v	*JY strip no. 13.6*	Criminal
11	Arson	n/v	*JYX* strip no. E.P.T. 52.207	Criminal
12	Banditry	n/v	*JYX* strip nos. E.P.T. 5.15–16	Criminal
13	Battery	n/v	*JY* strip no. 133.15	Criminal
14	Battery	n/v	*JY* strip no. 135.1	Criminal
15	Battery	n/v	*JY* strip no. 27.1a	Criminal
16	Battery	n/v	*JY* strip nos. 143.27, 143.32–33	Criminal
17	Battery	n/v	*JYX* strip no. E.P.T. 65.414	Criminal
18	Battery	n/v	*JYX* strip nos. E.P.T. 68.13–26.b	Criminal

 | DOI:10.1163/9789004513907_010

(*cont.*)

Number	Causes	Date	Strip nos.	Nature
19	Battery against one's parents	n/v	*JY* strip no. 122.7	Criminal
20	Battery or murder	n/v	*JY* strip no. 3.35	Criminal
21	Crossing the pass	n/v	*JYX* strip no. E.P.T. 51.411	Criminal
22	Crossing the pass	n/v	*JYX* strip nos. E.P.T. 68.34–40	Criminal
23	Illicit profit	n/v	*JY* strip no. 4.1	Criminal
24	Leaving one's post without permission	n/v	*JYX* strip no. E.P.F. 22.527	Criminal
25	Lost *fu* 符 (tablet)	n/v	*JYX* strip nos. E.P.F. 22.169–172	Criminal
26	Misconduct (using state-owned arms to hunt)	n/v	*JY* strip no. 12.1b	Criminal
27	Misconduct in performing duties	n/v	*JYX* strip nos. E.P.T. 44.30a–c	Criminal
28	Misconduct of police	n/v	*JY* strip no. 395.11	Criminal
29	Misconduct of soldiers in performing non-combat duties	n/v	*JY* strip no. 33.19	Criminal
30	Murder	n/v	*JY* strip no. 562.15	Criminal
31	Murder	n/v	*JYX* strip no. E.P.T. 51.275	Criminal
32	Murder	n/v	*JYX* strip no. E.P.T. 58.99	Criminal
33	Unclear (chasing the suspect)	n/v	*JYX strip nos. E.P.T. 56.127–128*	Criminal
34	Unclear (criminal sentence)	n/v	*JYX* strip no. E.P.T. 53.181	Criminal
35	Unclear (criminal sentence)	n/v	*JYX* strip no. E.P.T. 56.344	Criminal
36	Upheavals	n/v	*JY* strip no. 27.21a	Criminal
37	Murder?	n/v	*JYX* strip nos. E.P.T. 5.299–300	Criminal?
38	Debt	62 BC	*JYX* strip no. E.P.T.59.8	"Civil"
39	Last will	60 BC	*JY* strip nos. 202.9–15	"Civil"
40	Debt	51 BC	*JYX* strip no. E.P.T. 53.186	"Civil"
41	Debt	45 BC	*JY* strip nos. 282.9a–b	"Civil"

(cont.)

Number	Causes	Date	Strip nos.	Nature
42	Debt	32 BC	*JYX strip no. E.P.T. 52.485*	"Civil"
43	Transaction	32 BC	*JYX* strip no. E.P.T. 51.248	"Civil"
44	Debt	24 BC	*JY* strip nos. 157.5a–b	"Civil"
45	Debt	24 BC	*JY* strip nos. 213.41a–b	"Civil"
46	Debt	24 BC	*JYX* strip no. E.P.C. 39	"Civil"
47	Debt	24 BC	*JYX* strip nos. E.P.T. 52.88a–b	"Civil"
48	Debt	14 BC	*JY* strip nos. 229.1–2	"Civil"
49	Debt	13 BC	*JYX* strip nos. E.P.T. 50.22–23	"Civil"
50	Debt	12 BC	*JY* strip nos. 506.9a–b	"Civil"
51	Debt	AD 28	*JYX strip nos. E.P.F. 22.1–36*	"Civil"
52	Transaction (buying land)	2 BC	*JY* strip nos. 505.37a–b	"Civil"
53	Compensation (concerning a dead horse)	n/v	*JY* strip no. 46.34	"Civil"
54	Compensation (concerning a dead horse)	n/v	*JYX* strip nos. E.P.F. 2 2.186–201	"Civil"
55	Compensation? (losing state-owned livestock)	n/v	*JYX* strip no. E.P.T. 57.85	"Civil"
56	Debt	n/v	*JY* strip no. 3.2	"Civil"
57	Debt	n/v	*JY* strip no. 3.4	"Civil"
58	Debt	n/v	*JY* strip no. 132.36	"Civil"
59	Debt	n/v	*JY* strip no. 145.1	"Civil"
60	Debt	n/v	*JY* strip no. 157.12	"Civil"
61	Debt	n/v	*JY* strip no. 158.3	"Civil"
62	Debt	n/v	*JY* strip no. 178.8	"Civil"
63	Debt	n/v	*JY* strip no. 190.34	"Civil"
64	Debt	n/v	*JY* strip no. 193.30	"Civil"
65	Debt	n/v	*JY* strip no. 201.7	"Civil"
66	Debt	n/v	*JY* strip no. 214.34	"Civil"
67	Debt	n/v	*JY strip no. 259.1*	"Civil"
68	Debt	n/v	*JY* strip no. 26.9a	"Civil"

(*cont.*)

Number	Causes	Date	Strip nos.	Nature
69	Debt	n/v	*JY* strip no. 27.23	"Civil"
70	Debt	n/v	*JY* strip no. 3.6	"Civil"
71	Debt	n/v	*JY* strip no. 30.7	"Civil"
72	Debt	n/v	*JY* strip no. 35.4	"Civil"
73	Debt	n/v	*JY* strip no. *35.6*	"Civil"
74	Debt	n/v	*JY* strip no. 483.3	"Civil"
75	Debt	n/v	*JY* strip no. 507.14	"Civil"
76	Debt	n/v	*JY* strip no. 6.16	"Civil"
77	Debt	n/v	*JY* strip no. 6.17	"Civil"
78	Debt	n/v	*JY* strip nos. 145.36, 145.24, 317.4	"Civil"
79	Debt	n/v	*JY* strip nos. 185.27a–b	"Civil"
80	Debt	n/v	*JY* strip nos. 217.15, 19	"Civil"
81	Debt	n/v	*JY* strip nos. 35.12, 135.21	"Civil"
82	Debt	n/v	*JY* strip nos. 56.31–32	"Civil"
83	Debt	n/v	*JY strip no. 6.16*	"Civil"
84	Debt	n/v	*JYX strip no. E.P.T. 59.13*	"Civil"
85	Debt	n/v	*JYX strip no. E.P.T. 59.7*	"Civil"
86	Debt	n/v	*JYX strip no. E.P.T. 61.1*	"Civil"
87	Debt	n/v	*JYX strip no. E.P.T. 61.2*	"Civil"
88	Debt	n/v	*JYX strip no. E.P.T. 5.7*	"Civil"
89	Debt	n/v	*JYX* strip no. E.P.T. 51.194	"Civil"
90	Debt	n/v	*JYX* strip no. E.P.T. 51.255	"Civil"
91	Debt	n/v	*JYX* strip no. E.P.T. 51.519	"Civil"
92	Debt	n/v	*JYX strip no. E.P.T. 51.8*	"Civil"
93	Debt	n/v	*JYX* strip no. E.P.T. 52.110	"Civil"
94	Debt	n/v	*JYX* strip no. E.P.T. 52.21	"Civil"
95	Debt	n/v	*JYX strip no. E.P.T. 52.201*	"Civil"
96	Debt	n/v	*JYX* strip no. E.P.T. 52.247	"Civil"
97	Debt	n/v	*JYX* strip no. E.P.T. 52.319	"Civil"
98	Debt	n/v	*JYX* strip no. E.P.T. 52.487	"Civil"
99	Debt	n/v	*JYX* strip no. E.P.T. 52.506	"Civil"
100	Debt	n/v	*JYX strip no. E.P.T. 4.92*	"Civil"
101	Debt	n/v	*JYX* strip no. E.P.T. 5 9.13	"Civil"
102	Debt	n/v	*JYX* strip no. E.P.T. 51.8	"Civil"
103	Debt	n/v	*JYX* strip no. E.P.T. 61.1	"Civil"

(*cont.*)

Number	Causes	Date	Strip nos.	Nature
104	Debt	n/v	*JYX* strip nos. E.P.T. 52.496a–b	"Civil"
105	Debt	n/v	*JYX* strip nos. E.P.T. 58.45a–b	"Civil"
106	Debt (a female initiated the suit)	n/v	*JYX* strip no. E.P.T. 52.201	"Civil"
107	Land and houses dispute	n/v	*JYX* strip no. E.P.T. 40.47	"Civil"
108	Salary	n/v	*JY* strip no. 178.2	"Civil"
109	Transaction	n/v	*JYX* strip no. E.P.T. 59.923	"Civil"
110	Transaction	n/v	*JYX* strip no. E.P.T. 51.314	"Civil"
111	Transaction (not being able to make a payment)	n/v	*JYX* strip no. E.P.T. 51.199	"Civil"
112	Asking back public property	28 BC	*JYX* strip nos. E.P.T. 59.1–2	Unclear
113	Unclear	15 BC	*JYX* strip nos. E.P.T. 59.57–58	Unclear
114	Taking away a drum	AD 28	*JYX* strip nos. E.P.F. 22.329–332	Unclear
115	Chasing wild camels	n/v	*JYX* strip no. E.P.T. 5.97	Unclear
116	Unclear	n/v	*JYX strip no. E.P.T. 53.173*	Unclear
117	Unclear	n/v	*JYX* strip no. E.P.T. 56.183	Unclear
118	Unclear	n/v	*JYX* strip no. E.P.T. 4.40	Unclear
119	Unclear	n/v	*JYX* strip no. E.P.T. 52.417	Unclear
120	Unclear	n/v	*JYX* strip nos. E.P.T. 25.25a–b	Unclear
121	Unclear	n/v	*JYX* strip nos. E.P.T. 51.264–51.272	Unclear
122	Unclear	n/v	*JYX* strip nos. E.P.T. 52.280a–b	Unclear
123	Unclear (appeal)	n/v	*JY* strip no. 206.31	Unclear
124	Unclear (appeal)	n/v	*JYX strip no. E.P.T. 7.40*	Unclear
125	Unclear (explaining pertinent statutes by the judge)	n/v	*JY* strip no. 38.27	Unclear

(*cont.*)

Number	Causes	Date	Strip nos.	Nature
126	Unclear (explaining pertinent statutes by the judge)	n/v	*JYX* strip no. E.P.T. 51.290	Unclear
127	Unclear (explaining pertinent statutes by the judge)	n/v	*JYX* strip no. E.P.T. 51.509	Unclear
128	Unclear (explaining pertinent statutes by the judge)	n/v	*JYX* strip no. E.P.T. 54.9	Unclear

APPENDIX 2

Usages of *Song* in the *Shiji* and the *Hanshu* (Full Text)

Shiji	*Hanshu*
1. Disputes over Property	
詩人道西伯，蓋受命之年稱王而斷虞芮之訟. The poet recounted that the Western Lord (King Wen of Zhou) settled the dispute between Yu and Rui [over land] when he received the mandate and made himself the king (4.119).	其赦天下，與民更始. 諸逋貸及辭訟在孝景後三年以前，皆勿聽治. Grant amnesty to all under the heaven in order to let the subjects have a new start. Do not hear these cases: failing to return state-owned properties or disputes occurred prior to 141 BC (6.169).
周西伯政平，及斷虞芮之訟，而詩人稱西伯受命曰文王. The Western Lord from Zhou was fair in administration. When he settled the dispute between Yu and Rui, the poet said that the Western Lord received the mandate and became King Wen (32.1479).	辭訟在後二年前，皆勿聽治. Do not hear those property disputes that occurred prior to 87 BC (7.221).
及文王為西伯，斷虞芮之訟，始受命，呂望、伯夷自海濱來歸之. When King Wen was still the Western Lord, he settled the dispute between Yu and Rui and firstly received the mandate. Lüwang and Boyi joined him from the seashore (99.2715–2716).	嗇夫職聽訟，收賦稅. The bailiff's duties include hearing cases and collecting taxes (19A.742).

 | DOI:10.1163/9789004513907_011

(*cont.*)

Shiji	***Hanshu***
魯相初到， 民自言相， 訟王取其財物百餘人. When the Chancellor of Lu first arrived, more than one hundred people spoke uninvited to the Prime Minister and accused their king of taking away their property (104.2777).	衣食足而知榮辱，廉讓生而爭訟息，故三載考績. When the clothes and foods are sufficient, people would know honor and shame, and when rectitude and yielding occur, disputes cease (24A.1123).
	好文法，民以貪遴爭訟生分為失. The residents are fond of literature and law. They regard greed, disputes, and household division while parents are alive as wrongs (28B.1654).
	潁川好爭訟分異，黃韓化以篤厚. The residents of the Yingchuan commandery were litigious and inclined to divide their households. Governor Huang and Governor Han transformed them with the virtues of honesty and sincerity (28B.1654).
	崇推讓之風，以銷分爭之訟. To encourage the virtue of yielding in order to reduce the disputes regarding property and household division (36.1933).
	其卿大夫緩於誼而急於利， 亡推讓之風而有爭田之訟. Their ministers are very apathetic to righteousness but rush to profits. They do not have the virtue of yielding but engage in land disputes (56.2521).

(*cont.*)

Shiji	***Hanshu***
	延壽不得已, 行縣至高陵, 民有昆弟相與訟田自言, 延壽大傷之, 曰: "幸得備位, 為郡表率, 不能宣明教化, 至令民有骨肉爭訟" ... 延壽恩信周徧二十四縣, 莫復以辭訟自言者. [Han Yanshou] inspected the counties and arrived in Gaoling. Among the people, there were brothers who spoke uninvited to Han Yanshou to dispute over land. Han Yanshou was very upset and said: "I am fortunate to hold a position where I am to be the role model for the commandery. I have failed to exemplify moral teachings and transform the people, and so blood relatives have disputes [over land] in civil litigation" ... Han Yanshou's generous favors and reliability benefited the twenty-four counties [in his jurisdiction], so much so that the people no longer had disputes over property for adjudication (76.3213).
	交讓之禮興, 則虞芮之訟息. When the rites of yielding prevail, the dispute between Yu and Rui will cease (77.3265).
	辭訟者歷年不至丞相府 ... 宣為相, 府辭訟例不滿萬錢不為移書, 後皆遵用薛侯故事. Disputes over property were not brought to the office of the chancellor for years ... When Xuan became the chancellor, he made a rule that if the value of the dispute

(*cont.*)

Shiji	*Hanshu*
	over property was less than ten thousand cash, he would not take up the case. Later on this became the precedence that was observed by all (83.3391–3393). 其民為吏所冤及言盜賊辭訟事，各使屬其部從事. Whenever civilians were misjudged by the officials or complained about robberies or thieves, or disputes over property, he always assigned them to be handled by the corresponding divisions (83.3399). 蜀郡男子路建等輟訟慙怍而退，雖文王卻虞芮何以加! Lu Jian and others from the Shu commandery felt shameful and withdrew their disputes. This was not different from King Wen solving the dispute between Yu and Rui (99A.4068)!
2. General Litigation	
儉化俗民, 則尊卑之序得, 而骨肉之恩親, 爭訟之原息. 斯乃家給人足，刑錯之本也歟? If frugality [is employed] to educate the common people, then the arrangement of high and low will be obtained, the kindness [between] one's flesh and blood will be intimate, and the source of disputes and litigation will be extinguished (112.2963).	孔子曰:“聽訟，吾猶人也，必也使毋訟乎”. Confucius says: “When hearing disputes, I am the same as others. But the crucial thing is to eliminate disputes” (48.2253).

(*cont.*)

Shiji	*Hanshu*
故曰“聽訟, 吾猶人也, 必也使無訟乎”. Therefore, it is said: “When I hear disputes, I am the same as others. But the crucial thing is to eliminate disputes” (122.3131).	丞相司直郭欽奏“宣舉錯煩苛, 代二千石署吏聽訟, 所察過昭條...” The Rectifier to the Prime Minister, Guo Qin, presented a memorial saying, “Xuan's initiatives were confusing and convoluted. When he replaced a Petty Official [working under an administrator with an income of] two thousand bushels to hear ‘litigations’ (*song*), what [he] was investigating exceeded the clause of the imperial order ...” (72.3086).
	庶民所以安其田里而亡歎息愁恨之心者, 政平訟理也. The reason that commoners feel secure in their land and have no sorrows and grieves is because governance is fair and their disputes are justly solved (89.3624).

3. To Appeal/Defend

鄭悼公來訟. 鄭悼公費元年公如楚訟. Duke Dao of Zheng came to appeal. During the first year, Fei, Duke Dao of Zheng, went to Chu to appeal (14.623).	明年, 京兆尹王章訟商忠直, 言鳳顓權, 鳳誣章以大逆辠 ... The following year, Wang Zhang, the mayor of the capital, defended Zhang for his honesty and righteousness. He said that Feng arrogated all power to himself. Feng on the other hand, falsely accused Zhang of the crime of grand treason ... (27A.1334).
悼公元年, 鄦公惡鄭於楚. 悼公使弟睔於楚自訟. 訟不直, 楚囚睔. During the first year of Duke Dao, Duke Xu slandered Zheng in the Chu court.	德上書訟罪. 會薨, 大鴻臚奏德訟子罪, 失大臣體, 不宜賜謚置嗣. De submitted a petition to defend his son against criminal charges. He died soon

(*cont.*)

Shiji	*Hanshu*
Duke Dao [of Zheng] dispatched his younger brother Lun to Chu to defend Zheng. The appeal was not successful, and Chu put Lun into jail (42.1770).	afterward. The Grand Herald reported that De argued against the crime of his son and lost the demeanor of a grand minister, hence he was not suitable for a posthumous title and establishing an heir (36.1928).
趙國以冶鑄為業, 王數訟鐵官事, 湯常排趙王. The State of Zhao relied on the smelting and casting industry. The King of Zhao appealed several times regarding the affairs of the Iron Officials [from the central court]. [Zhang] Tang always dismissed those petitions from the King of Zhao (122.3142).	向自見得信於上, 故常顯訟宗室, 譏刺王氏及在位大臣, 其言多痛切, 發於至誠. Since Xiang believed that the emperor trusted him, he often openly defended the imperial clan and criticized the Wang clan and the ministers in power. His words were often critical and sharp with a sincere heart (36.1966).
	趙王彭祖, 帝異母兄也, 上書訟太子皋, 言充逋逃小臣, 苟為奸偽 ... Peng Zu, King of Zhao, was the half elder brother of the emperor. He submitted a petition to argue against the crimes of the crown prince, saying that Chong was a fugitive petite minister and perfunctory and treacherous ... (45.2175).
	是時, 上春秋高, 疑左右皆為蠱祝詛, 有與亡, 莫敢訟其冤者. At that time, the emperor was of an advanced age and suspected his close assistants of placing a curse [on him] and there were some who fled. There were none who dared defend themselves (*song*) in regard to this grievance (45.2179).

(*cont.*)

Shiji	*Hanshu*
	又訟淮南王無大罪, 宜急令反國. He defended the King of Huainan, claiming that the king did not commit any serious crime, therefore, the emperor should order the king to return to his own domain immediately (51.2337).
	彭祖上書冤訟丹,願從國中勇敢擊匈奴 ... Pengzu submitted a petition to defend Dan in regard to his grievance. Pengzu was willing to recruit brave warriors to fight the Xiongnu ... (53.2421).
	大司空師丹等劾宏誤朝不道, 坐免為庶人, 業復上書訟宏. Grand Minister of Works Shi Dan and others impeached Hong for missing attendance at the court, so Hong was demoted to be a commoner. Ye submitted a petition to defend Hong again (60.2682).
	上知太子惶恐無他意, 而車千秋復訟太子冤, 上遂擢千秋為丞相, 而族滅江充家. The emperor realized that the crown prince was just panicking with no other intentions, and Che Qianqiu defended the crown prince in regard to his grievance. The emperor then promoted Che Qianqiu to be chancellor, while exterminating the whole clan of Jiang Chong (63.2747).

(*cont.*)

Shiji	***Hanshu***
	會衛太子為江充所譖敗，久之，千秋上急變訟太子冤. It happened that the crown prince Wei was falsely charged by Jiang Chong and destroyed. After a while, Qianqiu submitted a petition to argue against the injustice suffered by the crown prince (66.2883).
	左馮翊韓延壽有罪下獄， 惲上書訟延壽. 郎中丘常謂惲曰: "聞君侯訟韓馮翊, 當得活乎?" Han Yanshou, Governor of Zuopingyi, was put in jail for his crimes. Yun submitted a petition to defend Yanshou. Gentlemen of the Palace Qiu Chang told Yun: "I heard that you defend Han Yanshou against the criminal charges. Can you save him?" (66.2891).
	咸素善雲, 雲從刺候, 教令上書自訟. Xian was a good friend of Yun. Yun approached Xian to acquire information. Xian told Yun to submit a petition to defend himself (66.2900).
	雲上書自訟, 咸為定奏草, 求下御史中丞. Yun submitted a petition to defend himself. Xian composed the memorial for Yun to request that the case be forwarded to the Assistant to the Imperial Counsellor (67.2914).

(*cont.*)

Shiji	*Hanshu*
	太中大夫谷永上疏訟湯曰: "臣聞楚有子玉得臣, 文公為之仄席而坐 ..." Grand Palace Grandee Gu Yong submitted a petition to defend Chen Tang, saying: "I heard that the Chu state had Ziyu, also known as Deche. Duke Wen of Jin respected him and sat with his knees to the side" (70.3020).
	恐下獄, 使人報湯. 湯為訟罪, 得逾冬月, 許謝錢二百萬. He (Zhang Kuang) was afraid of being jailed, so he sent his man to inform Tang that if Tang defended him against the criminal charges to let him survive the winter, he would gratefully give Tang two million cash (70.3025).
	議郎耿育上書言便宜, 因冤訟湯曰: "延壽, 湯為聖漢揚鉤深致遠之威 ..." Gentleman Consultant Geng Yu submitted a report to discuss what benefits the state, hence he argued against the injustices suffered by Tang, saying: "Yanshou and Tang greatly expanded the glory of sagely Han ..." (70.3027).
	賢父上書訟罪, 告廣漢, 事下有司覆治. The father of Xian submitted a petition to defend Xian against the criminal charges and accuse Guanghan. The case was sent down to the authorities for re-investigation (76.3204).

(*cont.*)

Shiji	***Hanshu***
	湖三老公乘興等上書訟尊治京兆功效日著. The *sanlao* of Hu and *gongcheng* Xing submitted a petition to defend Zun, saying that he successively governed the capital (76.3234).
	顯、恭恐望之自訟, 下於它吏 ... Xian and Gong were afraid that Wangzhi would defend himself, so they sent him down to other officials ... (78.3286).
	會望之子散騎中郎伋上書訟望之前事 ... The Attendant and Gentlemen of the Palace Ji, who was the son of Wangzhi, submitted a petition to defend Wangzhi against what he suffered previously ... (78.3287).
	於是杜欽上疏, 追訟奉世前功. Therefore, Du Qin submitted a petition to defend Fengshi for his previous contributions (79.3300).
	直臣京兆尹王章上封事召見, 訟商忠直無罪, 言鳳專權蔽主. The honest minister Wang Zhang, who served as the mayor of the capital, submitted a report and was summoned by the emperor. Wang Zhang defended Zhang for his honesty, righteousness, and innocence and said that Feng manipulated his power to cheat the emperor (82.3375).

(*cont.*)

Shiji	***Hanshu***
	大司農自訟不干屬車. The Superintendent of Agriculture defended himself saying that he did not offend the imperial carriage (90.3667). 賢良對策多訟新都侯莽者， 上於是征莽及平阿侯仁還京師侍太后. Many memorials of the Wise and Good defended the Marquise of Xindu, Mang. Therefore, the emperor summoned Mang and Marquis of Ping'a, Ren, to return to the capital to serve the empress dowager (98.4029). 在國三歲, 吏上書冤訟莽者以百數. Wang Mang stayed in his domain for three years, and hundreds of officials submitted petitions to defend Wang Mang in regard to his grievances (99A.4043).

4. To Argue/Debate

曆家曰小凶, 天人家曰小吉, 太一家曰大吉. 辯訟不決, 以狀聞. The Calendrical School declared it slightly in-auspicious. The School of Heaven and Man declared it slightly auspicious. The School of Supreme Unity declared it greatly auspicious. [They] debated and argued (*song*) and could not come to an agreement, and so [they] informed the [emperor of the divinatory] markings (127.3222).	不崇禮義, 而居公門下相非恨, 疾言辯訟, 媠謾亡狀. [They] did not esteem ritual and propriety, yet remained in the public sphere, reproaching and despising each other. [They] spoke irresponsibly, debated, argued (*song*), and were indolent. [Full of] slander, they lost [all proper] composure [as officials] (72.3082).

(*cont.*)

Shiji	*Hanshu*
5. To Declare Publicly	
歲時存問茂材, 賞賜閭里. 佗郡國吏欲來捕亡人者, 訟共禁弗予. [Liu Bi] expressed regards and concerns over talented people and granted awards to the residents and villagers in all seasons. He openly declared (*song*) that he forbade his subjects from handing over the fugitives from other kingdoms and commanderies to their officials who wanted to come to [Wu] to arrest them (106.2823).	
6. *Yu* and *Song* Combined	
夫豢豕為酒, 非以為禍也, 而獄訟益煩, 則酒之流生禍也. To raise pigs and make wine is not meant to incur disasters. However, when criminal and civil disputes grow day by day, disasters related to wine occur (24.1199).	宜定制度, 興禮樂, 然後諸侯軌道, 百姓素樸, 獄訟衰息. The state should set up institutions and rules and promote rites and music so that the lords would follow the right path, the commoners become simple minded, and criminal and civil disputes diminish and cease (22.1030).
	上自公侯, 下至小吏, 皆不得奉祿, 而私賦斂, 貨賂上流, 獄訟不決. From the dukes and marquises all the way down to clerks, all the officials could not receive their salaries. However, illegal taxes and bribes were everywhere, and criminal and civil disputes were not solved (24B.1185).

(*cont.*)

Shiji	*Hanshu*
	百姓素朴，獄訟衰息，大數既得，則天下順治 ... When the subjects are simple, criminal and civil disputes diminish, and the crucial points are gained, All under Heaven will become well-ordered ... (48.2231).
	寬既治民, 勸農業, 緩刑罰, 理獄訟, 卑體下士, 務在於得人心. Kuan governed his people in this way: encouraging them to practice farming, relaxing punishments, properly handling criminal and civil disputes, and humbling himself to extol talented people. The crucial thing was to win over the hearts of the people (58.2630).
	其務在於期會簿書, 斷獄聽訟而已, 此非太平之基也. Their important assignments were only meetings, writing up reports, adjudicating criminal cases, and hearing civil disputes, and that was not the foundation of grand peace (72.3063).
	吏民皆富實. 獄訟止息. The officers and civilians were all rich and satisfied. Criminal and civil cases ceased (89.3640).
	郡中莫不耕稼力田, 百姓歸之, 戶口增倍, 盜賊獄訟衰止. Residents of the commandery all diligently cultivated their fields, people

(*cont.*)

Shiji	*Hanshu*
	migrated to the commandery, the number of the households doubled, and robberies, thieves, and criminal and civil disputes all diminished (89.3642).
	官無獄訟, 邑無盜賊, 野無饑民. The officials were free from criminal and civil cases, the cities had no robbers and thieves, and the countryside had no hungry people (99A.4076).
	公卿旦入暮出, 議論連年不決, 不暇省獄訟冤結民之急務. Minsters arrived at the court in the morning and left during the night, and they discussed for years without making any decisions. They did not have time to adjudicate criminal and civil disputes and solve the crucial concerns of the people (99B.4140).

Bibliography

Astin, A.E. et al., ed. *The Cambridge Ancient History*. Cambridge: Cambridge University Press, 2006.

Ban Gu 班固. *Hanshu* 漢書. Beijing: Zhonghua shuju, 1982.

Barbieri-Low, Anthony and Robin Yates. *Law, State, and Society in Early Imperial China: A Study with Critical Edition and Translation of the Legal Texts from Zhangjiashan Tomb no. 247*. Leiden: E.J. Brill, 2015.

Black's Law Dictionary. 9th ed. St. Paul: West Publishing Company, 2009.

Bodde, Derk. *Festivals in Classical China: New Year and Other Annual Observances during the Han Dynasty 206 B.C.–A.D. 220*. Princeton: Princeton University Press, 1975.

Brashier, K.E. "Symbolic Discourse in Eastern Han Memorial Art: The Case of the Birchleaf Pear." *Harvard Journal of Asiatic Studies* 65, no. 2 (2005): 281–310.

Brown, Miranda and Rafe de Crespigny. "Adoption in Han China." *Journal of the Economic and Social History of the Orient* 52 (2009): 239–242.

Bu Xianqun 卜憲群. "Qin Han zhiji xiangli liyuan zakao: Yi Liye Qin jian wei zhongxin de Taolun" 秦漢之際鄉里吏員雜考 – 以里耶秦簡為中心的討論. *Nan du xue tan (Renwen shehui hexue ban)* 南都學壇 (人文社會科學版) no. 1 (2006): 1–6.

Cao Lüning 曹旅寧. "Ernian lüling yu Qin Han jicheng fa" 二年律令與秦漢繼承法. *Shaanxi shifan daxue xuebao (Zhexue shehui kexue ban)* 陝西師範大學學報 (哲學社會科學版) no. 1 (2008): 62–68.

Cao Lüning 曹旅寧. *Qinlü qintan* 秦律新探. Beijing: Zhongguo shehui kexu chubanshe, 2002.

Cao Lüning 曹旅寧. *Zhangjiashan Hanlü Yanjiu* 張家山漢律研究. Beijing: Zhonghua shuju, 2005.

Chang Qu 常璩. *Huayang guozhi* 華陽國志. Beijing: Zhonghua shuju, 1985.

Changsha shi wenwu kaogu yanjiu suo 長沙市文物考古研究所 and *Zhongguo wenwu yanjiusuo* 中國文物研究所, eds. *Changsha Dongpailou Donghan jiandu* 長沙東牌樓東漢簡牘. Beijing: Wenwu chubanshe, 2006.

Chang Wei-Ren 張偉仁. *Zhongguo fazhi shi shumu* 中國法制史書目. Taipei: Academia Sinica Press, 1975.

Chen Guying 陳鼓應. *Huangdi sijing jinzhu jinyi* 黃帝四經今注今譯. Beijing: Shangwu yinshuguan, 2007.

Chen Ping 陳平 and Wang Qinjin 王勤金. "Yizheng Xupu 101 hao Xihan mu Xianling quanshu chu kao" 儀征胥浦 101 號西漢墓先令券書初考. *Wenwu* 文物 no. 1 (1987): 20.

Chen Wei 陳偉. *Baoshan Chu jian chu tan* 包山楚簡初探. Wuhan: Wuhan daxue chubanshe, 1996.

Chen Wei 陳偉 et al., ed. *Chudi chutu Zhanguo jiance (shisizhong)* 楚地出土戰國簡冊 [十四種]. Beijing: Jingji kexue chubanshe, 2009.

Chen Zhi 陳直. "Gansu Wuwei Mozuizi Hanmu chutu Yuzhang shi jian tong kao" 甘肅武威磨咀子漢墓出土王杖十簡通考. *Kaogu* 3 (1961): 160–162, 165.

Cheng, Anne. "Filial Piety with a Vengeance: The Tension between Rites and Law in the Han." In *Filial Piety in Chinese Thought and History*, Alan K.L. Chan, ed.: 29–43. London: Routledge Curzon, 2004.

Cheng Shude 程樹德. *Jiuchao lü kao* 九朝律考. Beijing: Zhonghua shuju, 1963.

Cheng Shude 程樹德, ed. *Lunyu jishi* 論語集釋. Taipei: Yiwen yinshuguan, 1965.

Csikszentmihalyi, Mark. *Material Virtue: Ethics and the Body in Early China*. Leiden: E.J. Brill, 2004.

Du You 杜佑. *Tongdian* 通典. Shanghai: Shanghai renmin chubanshe, 1988.

Du Zhengsheng 杜正勝. *Bianhu qimin: chuantong zhengzhi shehui jiegou zhi xingcheng* 編戶齊民: 傳統政治社會結構之形成. Taipei: Lianjing chuben shiye gongsi, 1990.

Duyvendak, J.J.L., trans. *The Book of Lord Shang*. London: A. Probsthain, 1928.

Fan Ye 范曄. *Houhanshu* 後漢書. Beijing: ZhonghuZa shuju, 1965.

Fang Xinjun 方新軍. "Quanli gainian de lishi" 權利概念的歷史. *Faxue yanjiu* 法學研究 no. 4 (2007): 69–95.

Fang Xuanling 房玄齡, ed. *Jinshu* 晉書. Beijing: Zhonghua shuju, 1974.

Fang Xuanling 房玄齡. *Tanglü shuyi* 唐律疏議, ed. Liu Junming 劉俊明. Beijing: Zhonghua shuju, 1983.

Feng Zhuohui 馮卓慧. "Cong Chuanshi de he xin chutu de Shaanxi jinwen ji xian Qin wenxian kan Xizhou de minshi susong zhidu" 從傳世的和新出土的陜西金文及先秦文獻看西周的民事訴訟制度. *Xibei zhengfa daxue xuebao* 西北政法大學學報 no. 4 (2009): 159–168.

Forke, Alfred, trans. *Lun-heng*. New York: Paragon Book Gallery, 1962.

Gansu sheng wenwu kaogu yanjiusuo 甘肅省文物考古研究所, ed. *Juyan xinjian* 居延新簡. Beijing: Wenwu chubanshe, 1990.

Gao Heng 高恆. "Han dai shangji zhidu kao" 漢代上計制度考. In *Qin Han jiandu zhong fazhi wenshu jikao* 秦漢簡牘中法制文書輯考: 320–340. Beijing: Shehui kexue wenxian chubanshe, 2003.

Gao Kai 高凱. "Cong Juyan Han jian kan Han dai de nühu wenti" 從居延漢簡看漢代的女戶問題. *Shixue yuekan* 史学月刊 no. 9 (2008): 82–92.

Gao Wen 高文, ed. *Han bei jishi* 漢碑集釋. Kaifeng: Henan daxue chubanshe, 1997.

Ge Yinghui 葛英會. "Baoshan Chu jian zhi yu wenshu yanjiu" 包山楚簡治獄文書研究. *Nanfang wenwu* 南方文物 no. 2 (1996): 85–91.

Graham, A.C. *Disputers of the Tao*. La Salle: Open Court, 1989.

Guo Moruo 郭沫若. "Wuwei Yuzhang shi jian shangmian" 武威王杖十簡商免. *Kaogu xuebao* 考古学報 no. 2 (1965): 1–6.

Gu Jiegang 顧頡剛. "Zhougong zhili de chuanshuo he zhouguan yi shu de chuxian" 周公制禮的傳說和周官一書的出現. *Wenshi* 文史 no. 6 (1979): 172–242.

Gu Jiuxing 顧久幸. "'Zhigui' za kao: jianlun Chuguo juezhi" '執圭'雜考: 兼論楚國爵制. *Jianghan lun tan* 江漢論壇 no. 5 (1992): 79–81.

Haga Yoshinobu 芳賀良信. *Rei to hō no kangeki: Zenkan seiji shisō kenkyū* 礼と法の間隙-前漢政治思想研究. Tōkyō: Kyūko shoin, 2000.

Han Fei 韩非. *Han Feizi* 韩非子. References are to Zhang Jue 張覺. *Han Feizi yizhu* 韓非子譯注. Shanghai: Shanghai guji, 2007.

Han Ying 韓嬰. *Hanshi waizhuan* 韓詩外傳. References are to Xu Weichi 许维遅. *Hanshi waizhuan jishi* 韓詩外傳集釋. Beijing: Zhonghua shuju, 1980.

Hightower, James Robert. *Han shih wai chuan: Han Ying's Illustrations of the Didactic Application of the Classic of Songs*. Cambridge: Harvard University Press, 1952.

Hinsch, Bret. "Women, Kinship, and Property as Seen in a Han Dynasty Will." *T'oung Pao* 84 (1998): 1–20.

Hong Gua 洪適, ed. *Lishi, Lixu* 隸釋, 隸續. Beijing: Zhonghua shuju, 1986.

Hsiao, Harry Hsin-i. "Filial Piety in Ancient China: A Study of the Hsiao-ching." Ph.D. diss., Harvard University, 1978.

Hsing I-tien 邢義田. "Handai shuzuo, wenshu yongyu 'ta ru mou mou' ji 'Jianwu san nian Hou Su Jun zhai Kou En shi' jiance dang'an de goucheng" 漢代書佐、文書用語'它如某某'及'建武三年候粟君責寇恩事'簡冊檔案的構成. *Lishi yuyan yanjiusuo jikan* 歷史語言研究所集刊 70, no. 3 (1999): 559–588.

Hsing I-tien 邢義田. "Longshan Liye Qin Qianling xiancheng yizhi chutu mou xiang Nanyang li shi tan" 龍山里耶秦遷陵縣城遺址出土某鄉南陽里試探. http://www.bsm.org.cn/show_article.php?id=744.

Hsing I-tien 邢義田. "Qin Han de lüling xue: Jianlun Cao Wei lüboshi de chuxian" 秦漢的律令學: 兼論曹魏律博士的出現. *Zhongyang yanjiuyuan lishi yuyan yanjiusuo jikan* 中央研究院歷史語言研究所集刊 54, no. 4 (1983): 51–101.

Hsing I-tien 邢義田. "Zhangjiashan Hanjian Ernian lüling duji (er)" 張家山漢簡二年律令讀記（二）. http://www.bsmorgcn/show_articlephp?id=175=.

Hu Liuyuan 胡留元 and Feng Zhuohui 馮卓慧. *Xizhou fazhi shi* 西周法制史. Xi'an: Shaanxi renmin chubanshe, 1988.

Hu Pingsheng 胡平生. "Jiandu zhidu xin tan" 簡牘制度新探. *Wenwu* no. 3 (2000): 66–73.

Hu Pingsheng 胡平生 and Zhang Defang 張德芳, eds. *Xuanquan Hanjian shicui* 懸泉漢簡釋粹. Shanghai: Shanghai guji, 2001.

Huan Kuan 桓宽, ed. *Yantielun* 鹽鐵論. References are to Wang Liqi 王利器. *Yantielun jiaozhu* 鹽鐵論校注. Beijing: Zhonghua shuju, 1992.

Huang, Philip. *Civil Justice in China: Representation and Practice in the Qing*. Stanford: Stanford University Press, 1996.

Huang Sheng 黄生. *Zigu yifu he'an* 字詁義府合按. Beijing: Zhonghuashuju, 1984.

Huang Shengzhang 黃盛璋. "Jiangling Gaotai Han mu xin chutu gaodice, qiance yu xiangguan zhidu fafu" 江陵高臺漢墓新出土告地策,遣冊與相關制度發復. *Jianghan kaogu* 江漢考古 no. 2 (1994): 41–44.

Hubei Jingsha tielu kaogu dui 湖北荊沙鐵路考古隊, ed. *Baoshan Chujian* 包山楚簡. Beijing: Wenwu chubanshe, 1991.

Hubei Jingsha tielu kaogu dui 湖北荊沙鐵路考古隊. "Baosha erhaomu zhujian gaishu" 包山二號墓竹簡概述. *Wenwu* 文物 no. 5 (1988): 25–29.

Hulsewé, A.P.F. "Fragments of Han Law." *T'oung Pao* 76, nos. 4–5 (1990): 208–233.

Hulsewé, A.P.F. *Remnants of Han Law*. Leiden: E.J. Brill, 1955.

Hulsewé, A.P.F. *Remnants of Ch'in Law*. Leiden: E.J. Brill, 1985.

Hulsewé, A.P.F. "A lawsuit of A.D. 28." *Studia Sino-Mongolica*, Herausgegeben Von Wolfgang Bauer, ed., 23–34. Wiesbanden: Franz Steiner Verlag, 1979.

Hunan sheng wenwu kaogu yanjiusuo 湖南省文物考古研究所. "Xiangxi Liye Qindai jiandu xuanshi" 湘西里耶秦代簡牘選釋. *Zhongguo lishi wenwu* 中國歷史文物 no. 1 (2003): 8–25.

Iio Hideyuki 飯尾秀幸. "Chūgoku kodai ni okeru kazoku kenkyu o megutte" 中國古代における家族を研究めぐって. *Rekishi hyōron* 歴史評論 12 (1985): 69–70.

Ikeda Tomohisa 池田知久. "Kakuten Sokan 'Gogyō' no kenkyū" 郭店楚简〈五行〉の研究. *Guodian Chujian guoji xueshu yantaohui lunwenji* 郭店楚簡國際學術研討會論文集, 210–239. Wuhan: Hubei renmin chubanshe, 2000.

Ikeda On 池田温. "Chūgoku rekidai boken ryakukō" 中国歴代墓券略考. *Tōkyō teikoku daigaku tōyō bunka kenkyūjo* 東洋文化研究所紀要 86 (1981): 193–278.

Ikezawa Masaru 池澤優. "Saishu Shunjū jidai no kō to sosen saishi ni tsuite" 西周春秋時代の孝と祖先祭祀に就いて. *Tsukuba daigaku chiiki kenkyū* 筑波大學地域研究 10 (1992): 57–119.

Jia Liying 賈麗英. "Cong Changsha Dongpailou jiandu kan Handai chujia nu de caichan jicheng" 從長沙東牌樓簡牘看漢代出嫁女的財產繼承. *Guangming ribao* 光明日報, July 13, 2007.

Jingmen shi bowuguan 荊門市博物館, ed. *Guodian Chumu zhujian* 郭店楚墓竹簡. Beijing: Wenwu chubanshe, 1998.

Jingzhou bowuguan 荊州博物館, ed. *Jingzhou Gaotai Qin Han mu* 荊州高臺秦漢墓. Beijing: Kexue chubanshe, 2000.

Johnson, Wallace. *The T'ang Code: Vol. I, General Principles*. Princeton: Princeton University Press, 1979.

Johnson, Wallace. *The T'ang Code: Vol. II, Specific Articles*. Princeton: Princeton University Press, 1997.

Jones, William. "Studying the Ch'ing Code – The Ta Ch'ing Lü li." *The American Journal of Comparative Law* 22, no. 2 (1974): 356–357.

Jones, William. *The Great Qing Code*. Oxford: Oxford University Press, 1994.

Kern, Martin. *The Stele Inscriptions of Ch'in Shih-huang: Text and Ritual in Early Chinese Imperial Representation*. New Haven: American Oriental Society, 2000.

Knapp, Keith. "The *Ru* Reinterpretation of *Xiao*." *Early China* 20 (1995): 195–222.

Knoblock, John and Jeffrey Riegel, trans. and annot. *Xunzi: A Translation and Study of the Complete Works*. Stanford: Stanford University Press, 1988.

Knoblock, John and Jeffrey Riegel, trans. and annot. *The Annals of Lü Buwei*. Stanford: Stanford University Press, 2000.

Koga Noboru 古賀登. "Shin Shō Ō no gunsei gunkō hōshō to mibunsei" 秦商鞅の軍制功褒賞制と身分制. *Shakai keizai rekishi* 社會經濟歷史 40, no. 4 (1974): 335–360.

Kong Qingming 孔慶明. *Qin Han falüshi* 秦漢法律史. Xi'an: San Qin renmin chubanshe, 1992.

Lai Mingchun. "Family Morphology in Han China." Ph.D. diss., University of Toronto, 1995.

Lao Gan 勞榦, ed. *Juyan Hanjian* 居延漢簡. Taipei: The Institute of History and Philology Special Publication, 1960.

Lao Gan 勞榦. "Cong Han jian zhong de sefu lingshi houshi he shili lun Handai junxiang li de zhiwu he diwei" 從漢簡中的嗇夫令史侯史和史吏論漢代郡縣吏的職務和地位. *Zhongyang yan jiuyuan lishi yuyan yanjiusuo jikan* 中央研究院歷史語言研究所集刊 55, no. 1 (1983): 9–22.

Legge, James. *The Chinese Classics*. Hong Kong: Hong Kong University Press, 1960.

Li Fang 李昉, ed. *Taiping yulan* 太平御覽. *Sibu congkan xubian* 四部叢刊續編 edition, vol. 11. Shanghai: Shangwu yinshuguan, 1934.

Li Feng. *Bureaucracy and the State in Early China: Governing the Western Zhou*. Cambridge: Cambridge University Press, 2008.

Li Jiannong 李劍農. *Xian Qin liang Han jingji shi gao* 先秦兩漢經濟史稿. Beijing: Sanlian shudian, 1957.

Li Junming 李均明. *Qin Han jiandu wenshu fenlei jijie* 秦漢簡牘文書分類輯解. Beijing: Wenwu chubanshe, 2009.

Li Junming 李均明. "Zhangjiashan Hanjian suojian guifan jicheng guanxi de falü" 張家山漢簡所見規範繼承關係的法律. *Zhongguo lishi wenwu* 中國歷史文物 no. 2 (2002): 26–32.

Li Ling 李零. "Xizhou jinwen zhong de tudi zhidu" 西周金文中的土地制度. *Xueren* 學人 2 (1992): 224–256.

Li Longxian 李隆獻. "Handai yijiang fuchouguan de xingcha yu quanshi" 漢代以降復仇觀的省察與诠釋. *Taiwan daxue wenshi xuebao* 臺灣大學文史學報 68 (2008): 39–78.

Li Xueqin 李學勤. "Xizhou jinwen zhong de tudi zhuanrang" 西周金文中的土地轉讓. *Guangming ribao* 光明日報, Nov. 30, 1983.

Li Xueqin 李學勤. "Baoshan Chu jian zhong de tudi maimai" 包山楚簡中的土地買賣. *Zhongguo wenwu bao* 中國文物報, March 22, 1992.

Lian Shaoming 連邵名. "Hanjian zhong de zhaiwu wenshu ji shimai mingji" 漢簡中的債務文書及貰賣名籍. *Kaogu yu wenwu* 考古與文物 no. 3 (1987): 77–83.

Lianyungang shi bowuguan 連雲港市博物館, ed. *Yinwan Hanmu jiandu* 尹灣漢墓簡牘. Beijing: Zhonghua shuju, 1997.

Liang Qichao 梁啟超. *Yinbingshi heji* 飲冰室合集. Beijing: Zhonghua shuju, 1989.

Liang Zhiping 梁治平. *Xunqiu ziran zhixu zhong de hexie* 尋求自然秩序中的和諧. Beijing: Zhongguo zhengfa daxue chubanshe, 2002.

Lin Duan 林端. *Weibo lun Zhongguo falü chuantong: Weibo bijiao shehuixue de pipan* 韋伯論中國法律傳統: 韋伯比較社會學的批判. Taipei: San min shuju, 2003.

Liu An 劉安. *Huainanzi* 淮南子. Shanghai: Shanghai guji, 1989.

Liu Guang'an 劉廣安. "Ling zai Zhongguo gudai de zuoyong" 令在中國古代的作用. *Zhong wai faxue* 中外法學 no. 2 (2012): 369–37.

Liu Hainian 劉海年 et al. *Jiagu jinwen jiandu falü wenxian* 甲骨金文簡牘法律文獻. Beijing: Kexue chubanshe, 1994.

Liu Jinhua 劉金華. "Cong Baoshan Chu jian kan Chu guo de minshi falü guanxi" 從包山楚簡看楚國的民事法律關係. *Jianghan kaogu* 江漢考古 no. 2 (2001): 46–50.

Liu Min 劉敏. "Cong Ernian lüling lun Han dai xiaoqin de falühua" 從二年律令論漢代孝親的法律化. *Nankai xuebao (Zhexue shehui kexu ban)* 南開學報 (哲學社會科學版) no. 2 (2006): 91–98.

Liu Xiang 劉向. *Shuoyuan* 說苑. References are to Xiang Zonglu 向宗魯. *Shuoyuan jiaozheng* 說苑校正. Beijing: Zhonghua shuju, 1987.

Liu Xiang 劉向. *Gu lienüzhuan* 古列女傳. Beijing: Zhonghua shuju, 1985 rpt.

Liu Xinning 劉欣寧. *You Zhangjiashan Hanjian Ernian lüling lun Han chu de jicheng zhidu* 由張家山漢簡二年律令論漢初的繼承制度. Taipei: Guoli Taiwan daxue chuban weiyuanhui, 2007.

Liu Zhen 劉珍. *Dongguan Hanji* 東觀漢記. References are to Wu Shuping 吳樹平. *Dongguan Hanji jiaozhu* 東觀漢記校注. Beijing: Zhonghua shuju, 2008.

Loewe, Michael. "The Wooden and Bamboo Strips Found at Mo-Chü-Tzu (Kansu)." *Journal of the Royal Asiatic Society of Great Britain and Ireland* no. 1 (1965): 13–26.

Loewe, Michael. *Records of Han administration*. Cambridge: Cambridge University Press, 1967.

Loewe, Michael. *Crisis and Conflict in Han China*. London: George Allen and Unwin Limited, 1974.

Loewe, Michael, ed. *Early Chinese Texts: A Bibliographical Guide*. Berkeley: Society for the Study of Early China, 1993.

Loewe, Michael. *A Biographical Dictionary of the Qin, Former Han and Xin Periods (221 B.C.–A.D. 24)*. Leiden: E.J. Brill, 2000.

Loewe, Michael. *The Men Who Governed Han China: Companion to A Biographical Dictionary of the Qin, Former Han and Xin Periods*. Leiden: E.J. Brill, 2004.

Loewe, Michael. "On the Terms *Baozi*, *Yinggong*, *Yinguan*, and *Shou*: Was Zhao Gao a Eunuch?" *T'oung Pao* 91(2005): 301–319.

Loewe, Michael. *The Government of the Qin and Han Empires*. Cambridge: Hackett Publishing Company, 2006.

Loewe, Michael. "The Organs of Han Imperial Government: Zhongdu guan, duguan, xianguan and xiandao guan." *Bulletin of the School of Oriental and African Studies* 71, no. 3 (2008): 509–528.

Loewe, Michael and Denis Twitchett, eds. *The Cambridge History of China*, Vol. 1: *The Ch'in and Han Empires, 221 B.C.–A.D. 220*. Cambridge: Cambridge University Press, 1986.

Long Daxuan 龍大軒. "Han dai lü zhangju xue kaolun" 漢代律章句學考論. Ph.D. diss., Xinan zhengfa daxue 西南政法大學, 2006.

Lu Xiqi 魯西奇. "Han dai maidiquan de shizhi, yuanyuan, yu yiyi" 漢代買地券的實質、淵源、與意義. *Zhongguoshi yanjiu* 中國史研究 no. 1 (2006): 47–68.

Luo Zhenyu 羅振玉. *Zhensong tang ji gu yiwen* 貞松堂集古遺文. Beijing: Beijing tushuguan chubanshe, 2003.

Lü Buwei 呂不韋. *Lüshi chunqiu* 呂氏春秋. References are to Gao You 高誘. *Lüshi chunqiu (Gao You zhu)* 呂氏春秋(高誘注). Shanghai: Shanghai shudian, 1982 rpt.; Zhang Shuangdi 張雙棣. *Lüshi chunqiu yizhu* 呂氏春秋譯注. Beijing: Beijing daxue chubanshe, 2000.

Ma Rui 馬瑞 and Li Jianping 李建平. "Tongchan ciyi kaobian" 同産詞義考辨. *Hanzi wenhua* 漢字文化 no. 2 (2011): 66–67.

Makino Tatsumi 牧野巽. "Kandai ni okeru kazoku no ōkisa" 漢代における家族の大きさ. *Kangakkai zasshi* 漢學會雜誌 3, no. 1 (1934): 32–42.

Makino Tatsumi 牧野巽. "Kandai ni okeru fukushu" 漢代における復讐. In *Makino Tatsumi chosakushū* 牧野巽著作集. Tōkyō: Ochanomizu shobo, 1980.

Merryman, John Henry and Rogelio Perez-perdomo. *The Civil Law Tradition*. Stanford: Stanford University Press, 2007.

Miyake Kiyoshi 宮宅潔. "Kandai seigen kō" 漢代請讞考. *Tōyō shi kenkyū* 55, no. 1 (1996): 1–34.

Momiyama Akira 籾山明. *Chūgoku kodai soshō seido no kenkyū* 中國古代訴訟制度の研究. Kyōto: Kyōto daigaku gakujutsu shuppankai, 2006.

Moriya Mitsuo 守屋美都雄. "Kandai kazoku no keitai ni kansuru shiron" 漢代家族の型体に関する試論. *Shigaku zasshi* 史學雜誌 52, no. 6 (1941): 35–43.

Mousourakis, George. *A Legal History of Rome*. New York: Routledge, 2007.

Needham, Joseph. "Human Laws and Laws of Nature in China and the West." *Journal of the History of Ideas* 12, no. 1 (1951): 3–30.

Needham, Joseph, ed. *Science and Civilization in China*, Vol. 2. Cambridge: Cambridge University Press, 1956.

Niida Noboru 仁井田陞. *Chūgoku hōseishi kenkyū* 中國法制史研究. Tōkyō: Tōkyō daigaku shuppankai, 1980.

Ning Quanhong 寧全紅. *Chunqiu fazhi shi yanjiu* 春秋法制史研究. Chengdu: Sichuan daxue chubanshe, 2009.

Nishijima Taichiro 西島太一郎. "Koshi kannen no tankai to burai beeto no yimi" 公私観念の展開と私人的意義. *Shina gaku* 支那学 9 (1931): 87–106.

Nishijima Sadao 西嶋定生. *Chūgoku kodai teikoku no keisei to kōzō: Nijittō shakusei no kenkyū* 中国古代帝国の形成と構造: 二十等爵制の研究. Tōkyō: Tōkyō daigaku shuppankai, 1961.

Nylan, Michael. "Ying Shao's *Feng su t'ung yi*." Ph.D. diss., Princeton University, 1982.

Nylan, Michael. "Confucian Piety and Individualism in Han China." *Journal of the American Oriental Society* 116, no. 1 (1996): 1–27.

Nylan, Michael. "Review Article on *From Chronicle to Canon*." *Harvard Journal of Asiatic Studies* 57, no. 2 (1997): 629–638.

Nylan, Michael. *Five "Confucian" Classics*. New Haven: Yale University Press, 2001.

Nylan, Michael. "On the Politics of Pleasure." *Asia Major* 14 (2001): 73–114.

Nylan, Michael. "Notes on a Case of Illicit Sex from Zhangjiashan: A Translation and Commentary." *Early China* 30 (2005–6): 25–45.

Nylan, Michael and Michael Loewe, eds. *China's Early Empires*. Cambridge: Cambridge University Press, 2010.

Ochiai Hiroki 落合悠紀. "Kan 'Ninen ritsu ryō' ni okeru shaku to ko no keishō: Keishō yoteisha ni tsuite no ichi kōsatsu" 漢'二年律令'における爵と戸の継承 – 継承予定者についての一考察. *Hō shigaku Kenkyū kai kaihō* 漢史學研究會會報 12 (2007): 81–87.

Ōba Osamu. "Kandai no ketsugotohi: Tamatsue jū kan hairetsu no ichian" 漢代の決事比 – 王杖十簡配列の一案. *Kense daigaku bungaku ronshū* 関西大学文学論集 25 (1975): 271–287.

Ōba Osamu. *Shin Kan hōseishi no kenkyū* 秦漢法制史の研究. Tōkyō: Sōbunsha, 1982.

Ōba Osamu. "The Ordinances on Fords and Passes Excavated from Han Tomb Number 247, Zhangjiashan." trans. David Spafford, et al. *Asia Major* 14 (2001): 119–141.

On Ikeda 池田溫. *Zhongguo gudai jizhang zhidu de yanjiu* 中國古代籍帳制度的研究. Beijing: Zhonghua shuju, 2007.

Peerenboom, R.P. *Law and Morality in Ancient China: The Silk Manuscripts of Huang-Lao*. Albany: State University of New York Press, 1993.

Qian Mu 錢穆. "Zhouguan zhizuo shidai kao" 周官制作時代考. *Yanjing xuebao* 燕京學報 no. (1932): 1–109.

Qiu Libo 邱立波. "Handai fuchou suojian zhi jing lü guanxi wenti" 漢代復仇所見之經律關系問題. *Shilin* 史林 no. 3 (2005): 80–110.

Qiu Xigui 裘錫圭. "Lunheng zhaji" 論衡札記. *Wenshi* 文史 5 (1978): 229–233.

Qu Tongzu 瞿同祖. *Zhongguo falü yu Zhongguo shehui* 中國法律與中國社會. Shanghai: Shangwu yinshuguan, 1947.

Queen, A. Sarah. *From Chronicle to Canon: The Hermeneutics of the Spring and Autumn, according to Tung Chung-shu*. Cambridge: Cambridge University Press, 1996.

Rates, Robin D.S. *Five Lost Classics: Tao, Huang-lao, and Yin-yang in Han China*. New York: Ballantine Books, 1997.

Ruan Yuan 阮元, ed. *Shisanjing zhushu* 十三經注疏. Reprint of 1815 edition. Taipei: Yiwen chubanshe, 1965.

Samuel, Parsons Scott, ed. *The Civil Law: Including the Twelve Tables, the Institutes of Gaius, the Rules of Ulpian, the Opinions of Paulus, the Enactments of Justinian, and the Constitutions*. Clark: Lawbook Exchange, 2001.

Santangelo Paolo. *Individual Autonomy and responsibility in Late Imperial China*. Amherst: Cambria Press, 2021.

Schaberg, David. *A Patterned Past: Form and Thought in Early Chinese Historiography*. Cambridge and London: Harvard University Press, 2001.

Scogin, Huge T. "Between Heaven and Man: Contract and the State in Han Dynasty China." *Southern California Law Review* 63 (1990): 1326–1351.

Seidel, Anna. "Buying One's Way to Heaven: The Celestial Treasury in Chinese Religions." *History of Religions* 17, no. 3 (1978): 423–424.

Shang Yang 商鞅. *Shangjunshu* 商君書. References are to Gao Heng 高亨. *Shangjunshu zhushi* 商君書注釋. Beijing: Zhonghua shuju, 1974.

Shen Gang 沈剛. *Juyan Han jian cihui huishi* 居延漢簡語詞彙編. Beijing: Kexue chubanshe, 2008.

Shen Jiaben 沈家本. *Hanlü zhiyi* 漢律摭遺. Taipei: Shangwu yinshu, 1976.

Sherwin-White, A.N. *Roman Citizenship*. Oxford: Clarendon Press, 1973.

Shiga Shuzo 滋賀秀三. "Zhongguo fa wenhua de kaocha: yi susong de xingtai wei sucai" 中國法文化的考察: 以訴訟的形態為素材. *Bijiaofa yanjiu* 比較法研究 no. 3 (1988): 18–26.

Shimizu Morimitsu 清水盛光. *Shina kazoku no shokōzō* 支那家族の諸構造. Tōkyō: Iwanami Shoten, 1942.

Shuihudi Qinmu zhujian zhengli xiaozu 睡虎地秦墓竹簡整理小組 *Shuihudi Qinmu zhujian* 睡虎地秦墓竹簡. Beijing: Wenwu chubanshe, 1990.

Sima Qian 司馬遷. *Shiji* 史記. Beijing: Zhonghua shuju, 1977.

Skosey, Laura. *The Legal System and Legal Tradition of the Western Zhou CA 1045–771 B.C.* Chicago: University of Chicago Press, 1996.

Song Jie 宋傑. "Han dai jianyu jianzhi sheshi cong kao" 漢代監獄建置設施叢考. *Shoudu shifan daxue xuebao* (*Shehui kexue ban*) 首都師範大學學報 (社會科學版) no. 3 (2009): 1–9.

Sun Yirang 孫怡讓, ed. *Zhouli zhengyi* 周禮正義. Shanghai: Shangwu yinshuguan, 1934.

Tao Yi 陶毅. *Zhongguo hunyin jiating zhidu shi* 中國婚姻家庭制度史. Beijing: Dongfang chubanshe, 1994.

Tomiya Itaru 富谷至. "Ninen ritsu ryō ni mieru horitsu yōko" 二年律令に見える法律用語. *Tōhō gakuho* 東方學報 76 (2003): 240–250.

Tomiya Itaru 富谷至. "Tamatsue jū kan" 王杖十簡. *Tōhō gakuhō* 東方學報 64 (1992): 61–113.

Tomiya Itaru 富谷至. "Yomi no kuni no tochi baibai: Kan Gi Rikuchō baichiken kō" 黄泉の国の土地売買 – 漢魏六朝買地券考. *Ōsaka daigaku kyōyōbu kenkyū shūroku (Jinbun shakai kagaku)* 大阪大学教養部研究集録 (人文社会科学) 36 (1987): 1–32.

Torao Asai 淺虎武夫. *Shina hoseshi* 支那法制史. Tokyo: Hirobumi Kan, 1904.

Wakae Kenzo 若江賢三. "Shin Kan ritsu ni okeru fukyōzai" 秦漢律における不孝罪. *Tōyōshi kenkyū* 東洋史研究 55, no. 2 (1996): 249–282.

Wang Chong 王充. *Lunheng* 論衡. References are to Liu Pansui 劉盼遂. *Lunheng jijie* 論衡集解. Shanghai: Shanghai guji chubanshe, 1957.

Wang Fu 王符. *Qianfulun* 潛夫論. References are to Peng Duo 彭鐸. *Qianfulun jian jiaozheng* 潛夫論箋校正. Beijing: Zhonghua shuju, 1985.

Wang Jie 王捷. "Jiuti xinzheng: Xianqin 'yu' 'song' de falü yuyong yanbian" 舊題新證: 先秦'獄''訟'的法律語用演變. *Beifang faxue* 北方法學 no. 4 (2013): 133–138.

Wang Kailuan 王愷鑾, ed. *Yinwenzi jiaozheng* 尹文子校正. Shanghai: Shangwu yinshuguan, 1935.

Wang Li 王力. *Wang Li gu Hanyu zidian* 王力古漢語字典. Beijing: Zhonghua shuju, 2000.

Wang Liqi 王利器. *Zheng Kangcheng nianpu* 鄭康成年譜. Jinan: Qi Lu shushe, 1983.

Wang Pei 王沛. "Xizhou jinwen falü ziliao jikao" 西周金文法律資料輯考. *Zhongguo gudai falü wenxian yanjiu* 中國古代法律文獻研究 7 (2012): 16–65.

Wang Su 王素. "Changsha Dongpailou Donghan jiandu xuanshi" 長沙東牌樓東漢簡牘選釋. *Wenwu* 文物 no. 12 (2005): 69–75.

Wang Su 王肅, ed. *Kongzi jiayug* 孔子家語. References are to Chen Shike 陳士珂. *Kongzi jiayu shuzheng* 孔子家語疏証. Beijing: Zhonghua shuju, 1985.

Wang Xianqian 王先謙. *Hanshu buzhu* 漢書補注. Beijing: Zhonghua shuju, 1975.

Wang Yanhui 王彥輝. *Zhangjiashan Han jian Ernian lüling yu Handai shehui yanjiu* 張家山漢簡二年律令與漢代社會研究. Beijing: Zhonghua shuju, 2010.

Wang Zijin 王子今. "Pianqi xiaqi kao" 偏妻下妻考. *Huaxue* 华學 6 (2003): 151–152.

Wasik, Martin. "Compensation Orders and Civil Liability." *The Modern Law Review* 48, no. 6 (1985): 707–711.

Watson, Burton. *Records of the Grand Historian*. New York: Renditions-Columbia University Press, 1993.

Watson, Burton, trans. *Mozi: Basic Writings*. New York: Columbia University Press, 2002.

Wei Daoming 魏道明. "Zhongguo gudai yizhu jicheng zhidu zhiyi" 中國古代遺囑繼承制度質疑. *Lishi yanjiu* 歷史研究 no. 6 (2000): 156–165.

Wei Hong 衛宏. *Hanjiuyi* 漢舊儀. Beijing: Zhonghua shuju, 1985.

Wei Liao 尉繚. *Weiliaozi* 尉繚子. References are to Liu Yin 刘寅. *Weiliaozi zhijie* 尉繚子直解. Nanjing: Jiangsu guji, 1988.

Wei Sen 韋森. *Shichang, falü yu minzhu: yige jingji xuejia de richang sikao* 市場、法律與民主: 一個經濟學家的日常思考. Shanghai: Shanghai renmin chubanshe, 2008.

Weld, Susan. "Chu Law in Action: Legal Documents from Tomb 2 at Baoshan." In *Defining Chu: Image and Reality in Ancient China*, eds. Constance A. Cook and John S. Major. Honolulu: University of Hawaii Press, 1999.

Wu Rengxiang 吳礽驤, Li Yongliang 李永良, and Ma Jianhua 馬建華, eds. *Dunhuang Hanjian shiwen* 敦煌漢簡釋文. Lanzhou: Gansu renmin chubanshe, 1991.

Wu Wenling 鄔文玲. "Changsha Dongpailou Donghan jiandu Guanghe liunian zi xiang hecongshu yanjiu" 長沙東牌樓東漢簡牘光和六年自相和從書研究. *Nandu xuetan* 南都學壇 no. 3 (2010): 10–18.

Xie Cheng 谢承. *Hou Hanshu*. In *Bajia Hou Hanshu jizhu* 八家后漢書輯注, Zhou Tianyou 周天游, ed. Tianjin: Tianjin guji chubanshe, 1987.

Xie Guihua 謝桂華, Li Junming 李均明 and Zhu Guozhao 朱國炤, eds. *Juyan Hanjian shiwen hejiao* 居延漢簡釋文合校. Beijing: Wenwu chubanshe, 1987.

Xu Shen 許慎. *Shuowen jiezi*. References are to Duan Yucai 段玉裁. *Shuowen jizi zhu* 說文解字注. Shanghai: Shanghai guji chubanshe, 1988 rpt.

Xu Shihong 徐世虹. "Juyan Han jian zhong de 'wuzhuang' yu 'zhuangci'" 居延漢簡中的'毋狀'與'狀辭.' *Chutu wenxian yanjiu* 出土文獻研究 4 (1998): 52–56.

Xu Shihong 徐世虹. "Han dai minshi susong chengxu kaoshu" 漢代民事訴訟程序考述. *Zheng fa luntan* 政法論壇 no. 6 (2001): 122–130.

Xu Yuanhao 徐元浩, ed. *Guoyu jijie* 國語集解. Beijing: Zhonghua shuju, 2002.

Xu Zhongming 徐忠明. "Zhongguo falüshi yanjiu de keneng qian jing: Chaoyue xifang, huigui bentu" 中國法律史研究的可能前景: 超越西方回歸本土. *Zhengfa luntan* 政法論壇 no. 1 (2006): 3–15.

Xun Kuang 荀況. *Xunzi* 荀子. References are to Wang Xianqian 王先謙. *Xunzi jijie* 荀子集解. Beijing: Zhonghua shuju, 2011.

Xun Yue 荀悅. *Hanji* 漢紀. Beijing: Zhonghua shuju, 2002.

Yan Gengwang 嚴耕望. *Zhongguo gudai difang xingzheng zhidushi shangbian* 中國古代地方行政制度史上编. Nangang: Zhongyang yanjiuyuan lishi yu yanyanjiusuo, 1961.

Yang Shuda 楊樹達. "Han Fan Lijia mai di qianquan ba" 漢樊利家買地鉛券跋. In *Jiweiju jinwen shuo* 積微居金文說. Beijing: Zhonghua shuju, 1997.

Yang Xiangkui 楊向奎. "Zhouli de neirong fenxi jiqi chengshu niandai" 周禮的內容分析及其成書年代. In *Yishi zhai wenji* 繹史齋文集. Shanghai: Shanghai renmin chubanshe, 1980.

Yang Xiong 楊雄. *Fayan* 法言. References are to Han Jing 韓敬. *Fayan zhu* 法言注. Beijing: Zhonghua shuju, 1992.

Yang Yifan 楊一凡. "Zhonghua faxi yanjiu zhong de yige zhongda wuqu: 'zhufa heti, minxing bufen' shuo zhiyi" 中華法系研究中的一個重大誤區: '諸法合體、民刑不分'說質疑. *Zhongguo shehui kexue* 中國社會科學 no. 6 (2002): 78–94, 206.

Ye Yuying 葉玉英. "Donghan Jiandu hecong shu suojian Donghan ruogan zhidu tansuo" 東漢簡牘和從書所見若干制度探索. *Xiamen daxue xuebao* 廈門大學學報 no. 6 (2009): 100–105, 112.

Ying Shao 应劭. *Fengsu tongyi* 風俗通義. References are to Wang Liqi 王利器. *Fengsu tongyi jiaozhu* 風俗通義校注. Beijing: Zhonghua shuju, 1981.

Yu Jiang 俞江. "Guanyu gudai Zhongguo you wu minfa wenti de zai sikao" 關於古代中國有無民法問題的再思考. *Xiandai faxue* 現代法學 no. 1 (2001): 35–45.

Yu Zhenbo 于振波. "Zhangjiashan Hanjian zhong de mingtianzhi jiqi zai Handai de shishi" 張家山漢簡中的名田制及其在漢代的實施. *Zhongguo shi yanjiu* 中國史研究 no. 1 (2004): 29–40.

Yun Jae-seug 尹在碩. "Shuihudi Qinjian he Zhangjiashan Hanjian fanying de Qin Han shiqi houzi zhi he jiaxi jicheng" 睡虎地秦簡和張家山漢簡反映的秦漢時期後子制和家系繼 承. *Zhongguo lishi wenwu* 中國歷史文物 no. 1 (2003): 31–43.

Yun Jae-seug 尹在碩. "Qin Han funü de jichan chenghu" 秦漢婦女的繼產承戶. *Shixue yuekan* 史學月刊 no. 12 (2009): 115–125.

Zeng Weihua 曾維華. "Shi *Shiji* Huozhi liezhuan zhong de yishi men" 釋史記貨殖列傳中的倚市門. *Xueshu yuekan* 學術月刊 no. 5 (2000): 88–89.

Zhang Boyuan 張伯元. "*Hanlü zhiyi* yu *Ernian lüling* bikan ji" 漢律摭遺与二年律令比勘 記. In *Chutu falü wenxian yanjiu* 出土法律文獻研究. Beijing: Shangwu yinshuguan, 2005.

Zhangjiashan er si qi hao Hanmu zhujian zhengli xiaozu 張家山二四七號漢墓竹簡整理小組. "Jiangling Zhangjiashan Hanjian gaishu" 江陵張家山漢簡概述. *Wenwu* 文物 no. 1 (1985): 9–15.

Zhangjiashan er si qi hao Hanmu zhujian zhengli xiaozu 張家山二四七號漢墓竹簡整理小組, ed. *Zhangjiashan Han mu zhujian* (*er si qi hao mu*) 張家山漢墓竹簡 (二四七號墓). Beijing: Wenwu chubanshe, 2006 rev. edition.

Zhang Jihai 張繼海. *Handai chengshi shehui* 漢代城市社會. Beijing: Shehui kexue wenxian chubanshe, 2006.

Zhang Jianguo 張建國. "Junyan xin Hanjian 'Su Jun zhai Kou En' minshi susong ge'an yanjiu" 居延新漢簡 '粟君債寇恩' 民事訴訟個案研究. *Zhongwai faxue* 中外法學 no. 5 (1996): 15–21.

Zhang Jinfan 張晉藩, ed. *Zhongguo minfa tong shi* 中國民法通史. Fuzhou: Fujian renmin chubanshe, 2003.

Zhang Zhaoyang. "A Note on Civil Cases in Early China." *Journal of American Oriental Society* 128, no. 1 (2008): 121–131.

Zhang Zhaoyang. "Zhangjiashan Ernian lüling yu *Fengsu tongyi* zhong liang ze gushi de duidu" 張家山二年律令與風俗通義中兩則案例的對讀. *Shilin* 史林 no. 4 (2009): 127–131, 191.

Zhao Yupei 趙裕沛. *Liang Han jiating neibu guanxi ji xiangguan wenti yanjiu* 兩漢家庭內部關係及相關問題研究. Wuhan: Hubei renmin chubanshe, 2006.

Zheng Xuan 鄭玄. *Bo Wujing yiyi* 駁五經異議. In *Sikuquanshu* 四庫全書. Taipei: Taiwan Shangwu yinshuguan, 1983.

Zhongguo shehui kexueyuan kaogu yanjiusuo 中國社會科學院考古研究所, ed. *Yinzhou jinwen jicheng shiwen* 殷周金文集成釋文. Hong Kong: Xianggang zhongwen daxue zhongguo wenhua yanjiusuo, 2014.

Zhongguo wenwu yanjiusuo 中國文物研究所 and Hubei sheng wenwu kaogu yanjiusuo 湖北省文物考古研究所, eds. *Longgang Qin jian* 龍崗秦簡. Beijing: Zhonghua shuju, 2001.

Zhou Tianyou 周天遊, ed. *Hanguan liuzhong* 漢官六種. Beijing: Zhonghua shuju, 1990.

Zhu Shaohou 朱紹侯. "Lun Handai de mingtian (shoutian) jiqi pohuai" 論漢代的名田（授田）及其破壞. *Henan daxue xuebao (Shehui kexue ban)* 河南大學學報 (社會科學版) no. 1 (2004): 35–40.

Zhu Honglin 朱紅林. *Zhangjiashan Hanjian Ernian lüling jishi* 張家山漢簡二年律令集釋. Beijing: Shehui kexue wenxian chubanshe, 2005.

Zhu Honglin 朱紅林. *Zhangjiashan Hanjian Ernian lüling yanjiu* 張家山漢簡二年律令研究. Harbin: Heilongjiang renmin chubanshe, 2008.

Zufferey, Nicolas. *To the Origins of Confucianism: The 'Ru' in Pre-Qin Times and during the Early Han Dynasty*. New York: Peter Lang, 2003.

Index

www.ingramcontent.com/pod-product-compliance
Lightning Source LLC
Chambersburg PA
CBHW071249180926
51613CB00002B/180
* 9 7 8 9 0 0 4 3 9 3 7 3 8 *